The Sepoy Mutiny: 1857

The Sepoy Mutiny: 1857

An Annotated Checklist
of English Language Books

Richard Sorsky

A Craven Street Book

THE SEPOY MUTINY: 1857
An Annotated Checklist of English Language Books

by
Richard Sorsky

© 2007 Richard Sorsky

135798642

ISBN 13: 978-1-933502-014

In memory of S. Linden, Bookseller, 33 Craven Street, Strand, London

Library of Congress Cataloging-in-Publication Data

Sorsky, Richard, 1946-
    The Sepoy Mutiny, 1857 : an annotated checklist of English language books
    / Richard Sorsky.
        p. cm.
    "A Craven Street Book."
    Includes index.
    ISBN 978-1-933502-01-4 (hardcover : alk. paper)
    1. India--History--Sepoy Rebellion, 1857-1858--Indexes. I. Title.
    Z3208.A4S67 2007
    [DS478]
    016.95403'17--dc22
                                                                    2006103397

A Craven Street Book

Linden Publishing Inc.
2006 S. Mary
Fresno CA 93721
800-345-4447

Contents

Acknowledgments   vi

Introduction   ix

An Annotated Checklist   1

Index   228

Acknowledgments

Any project that takes nearly 40 years to complete must necessarily be a labor of love, or the author may be something of a procrastinator. In this case it was a bit of both. The extended research period reflects only geographical boundaries. The Mutiny of course was a British-Indian affair and the relevant research materials are predominantly located in the UK or India. Unfortunately the author lives in California. Our research began long before the Internet was a reality and an aid to research. This necessitated repeated travel to London.

When I began research for this book most of the libraries had no restrictions on the quantity of titles that could be requested from, and consulted in, the library itself. Thus it was relatively easy to spend my days requesting titles, annotating the contents, and returning them to the reference desk to exchange them for the next batch. That process came to a halt when I began to work in the British Library, first on Great Russell Street and then in their new quarters on Euston Road. I found there was a policy, sometimes rigidly enforced, regarding exactly how many titles can be requested in a given amount of time. Once the reading room was computerized there was no way to get around the imposed limit and because the British Library had titles that could be found nowhere else, I had no choice but to bide my time. My research finally was completed and hopefully I have produced a reference work that will be of value to scholars and collectors in the field.

A work of this nature is rarely a solitary undertaking. There are always helping hands extended along the way. Victor Sutcliffe of London was an invaluable aid. For more than 30 years he offered his advice and time, as well as his knack for locating numerous Mutiny titles. The breath and depth of his knowledge was instrumental in the production of this work.

An author contemplating a work on British India must consult the India Office Library now located within the British Library on Euston Road in London. When I began the research for this book the IO was still on Blackfriars Road and the British Library was at the circular reading room within the British Museum on Great Russell Street, Bloomsbury. The staff at both institutions were very helpful, as was the staff at the National Army Museum.

I would like to extend my thanks to Andy Ward, author of *Our Bones are Scattered*; the folks at South Asian Books in Columbia, Missouri; G. Sutton, Librarian, the Royal Artillery Institution, Woolwich, and Major A.G. Harfield, Royal Signals Museum, Dorset.

With the help of Jonathan Katz, formerly of the Indian Institute Library, Oxford, I was able to enjoy many hours of research at the Indian Institute as well as the Bodleian Library in Oxford.

Don Johnson of the Ames Library at the University of Minnesota was a great help and Jim Hartman of askSam Systems was instrumental in turning a mass of information into a useful document.

A Note on Methodology

The literature of the Mutiny consists of a vast array of material in various languages and states. This checklist is concerned with the entire field of non-fiction Mutiny literature that has been published in book form, in the English language. Approximately 1,100 titles are covered, from the earliest pamphlets and books published shortly after the commencement of the Mutiny, to the turn of the 21st century. There is occasional coverage of fiction and non-published works but only as they came to notice during collateral research; otherwise, these types of materials were not listed. I have, however, included a number of titles that upon inspection have revealed little of interest to the Mutiny student. These entries have been included for the benefit of collectors and researchers who, no doubt, will be the primary audience for this checklist. By consulting the checklist they can save time and limit their investigations to relevant titles.

Approximately 90% of the titles in the checklist were physically examined. This work is not presented as a bibliography nor should it be considered as such. If we accept the term bibliography in its strictest definition then there have been, to my knowledge, no published bibliographies of the Mutiny. This work does not include information on format, collational formula, issue, or variants. A true bibliography would indeed include this type of information.

Introduction

Background to the Mutiny

The Honorable East India Company, formed by a group of merchants in London, was granted the exclusive right of trade with the East Indies by the British Crown on December 31, 1600. By 1615 Jahangir, the Mughal Emperor of India, allowed them to establish a trading post at Surat. As time passed more trading posts were established and the Company became a political force to be reckoned with on the Indian subcontinent. The Mughals exempted the Company from paying customs duties in Bengal and later granted them the power to collect revenues on behalf of the Mughal empire. The turning point came in 1757 at the battle of Plassey. Robert Clive defeated a vastly superior army led by Siraj-ud-daulah and gained control of all of Bengal.

Slowly, but inexorably, the Company extended its grasp until it became the paramount power in India. It wasn't long before the Company found it was not only a mercantile power but a political power as well. To enforce its will, and to protect its revenue, the company soon found that an army was required. Native troops, called sepoys, were recruited and served under British officers. This was a corporate army, raised and supported by the Honorable East India Company. The stakes were high and many of those in charge were corrupt. Huge fortunes were made and entire kingdoms won.

In time, royal troops were used to augment the Company army. Although the proportion of European troops to native troops always remained about 1:6, it was recognized early on that the sepoys posed an internal threat that was not to be ignored. As the actual number of troops steadily increased, more than one Governor General requested more European troops and fewer sepoys.

The causes of the 1857 Mutiny were many and varied. Discontent had been building for years, partly because many company officers were unqualified to serve, and many that were qualified were on detached duty and had lost contact with their regiments. Other officers were so far past their prime that they were useless in an emergency.

For decades, the East India Company provided an avenue for many young officers to improve their social and economic standing. The pay was superior to that of the Royal Army, advancement was easier, and there was always the possibility of moving into a position of civil authority. A civil appointment could be extraordinarily lucrative and was much sought by young officers.

However, by the 1850's the lot of the regimental officer was not to be envied. Promotion was by seniority, not ability. Life consisted of long stretches of intense boredom, heat and disease, an almost universal disdain of everything Indian including the sepoys, and little or no English female companionship. The relations between the English officers and the sepoys slowly deteriorated to the point that there was little contact between them. Fewer officers spoke the native languages; they kept to their own society, and waited for the seniority system to take effect.

On May 10, 1857, the native troops of the Bengal army mutinied. The first actions of the mutiny took place in Meerut, a military station about 30 miles north of Delhi. There the troops rose up, murdered every European they could find, and rode off for Delhi where they hoped to resurrect the old Mughal Empire. The city was essentially defenseless and the scene at Meerut repeated itself in Delhi. From there the unrest spread rapidly and within a few weeks much of north India was in flames. The massacres and brutality on both sides were undeniable, as were the heroic actions found among both British and Indian participants. Mutiny literature abounds with horrific incidents, many biased and false, others quite accurate.

In 1857 India was organized into three military divisions (known as presidencies)—Bombay, Madras, and Bengal—each with its own military commander. The commander of the Bengal presidency was supreme military commander of India, and served at the pleasure of the Governor General, who resided at the British seat of government in Calcutta. The British had located in Calcutta through deference to the Mughal Emperor, located in Delhi, who was still the nominal ruler of much of India.

On the eve of the Mutiny there were approximately 40,000 European troops, both East India Company and Royal, stationed in India. They were faced by close to 300,000 native troops. The Bengal Army was composed of 24,000 European troops and 135,000 Indian troops. However, it must be remembered that not all of the native troops mutinied, and that only the Bengal Army broke into open mutiny. Still, the British were vastly outnumbered and it was not until the close of 1858 that peace was finally restored to Bengal.

The Mutiny shook the very foundations of the British Empire. In the years following the Mutiny, the Indian Army was reorganized, the East India Company was dissolved, India became a Crown Colony, the Governor General was replaced by a Viceroy, and thoughts of independence began to form in the minds of Indian intellectuals.

Literature of the Mutiny

The mutiny of the Bengal army in 1857 is no doubt one of the most written about events in British colonial history. The literature is quite astounding, not only because of the sheer volume but also the variety. We find personal diaries, eyewitness narratives, military analysis, official documentation, parliamentary publications, religious tracts, and scholarly analysis. The entire field of literature is quite fertile in this respect. When compared with other Victorian colonial wars, the breath and depth of Mutiny literature is remarkable.

The majority of the works written during the first hundred years after the Mutiny were narrative. They explained what happened but not why. Those authors that did strive for some explanation rarely produced work of penetrating insight. It was not until the centenary of the event that any substantial amount of analytical work was published. That period saw the publication of Majumdar's *The Sepoy Mutiny and Revolt of 1857,* Sen's *Eighteen Fifty Seven,* Chattopadhyaya's *The Sepoy Mutiny, 1857: A Social Study and Analysis,* Chaudhuri's *Civil Rebellion in the Indian Mutinies,* Joshi's *Rebellion, 1857: A Symposium,* and what has been called the most important collection of all, *Freedom Struggle in Uttar Pradesh, Source Material* edited by S.A.A. Rizvi and M.L. Bhargava. Until the centenary, new work by western writers with a clearly western point of view dominated the field. This all changed in 1957.

One of the pivotal questions found in many centenary writings was if the Mutiny was a war of national independence, a mutiny of the Bengal army, or a general revolt of the populace, both civil and military. Prior to this period most British historians held the view that the Mutiny was a military affair with little or no civil participation, except for Oudh.

In 1909 Vinayak Damodar Savarkar published *The Indian War of Independence 1857.* Savarkar condemned the British and espoused the view that the Mutiny was conducted by great Indian patriots fighting for a free India. This was a milestone in Mutiny literature and was promptly banned by the British from its first appearance until 1944. Savarkar arguably wrote the most famous work on the Mutiny by an Indian. His influence is touched upon in all of the later prominent Indian works on the Mutiny.

The question of revolution or rebellion faded after Savarkar and did not dominate the literature until the centenary publications. In the years following 1957 there were major scholarly additions to the existing literature. Embree published *1857 in India: Mutiny or War of Independence* in 1963, Metcalf's *The Aftermath of Revolt, India, 1857-1870*, was published in 1964, Chaudhuri, *Theories of the Indian Mutiny, 1965* and Jagdish Raj published *The Mutiny and British Land Policy in North India 1856-1868*. Raj wrote one of the earliest books that discussed land policy in any depth.

In 1961 the Information Department of Uttar Pradesh published *Nana Saheb Peshwa and the Fight for Freedom* by Anand Swarup Misra. This work must be in contention for the prize as the largest single volume work on the Mutiny. At over 650 pages it is a hefty book. Misra was not an historian but rather a civil servant in the Uttar Pradesh government. It seems that while in official discussions with the Memorial Well Garden Society at Cawnpore he developed the idea to produce a book on the Nana. Misra offers a great quantity of useful information and in the process attempts to rehabilitate the reputation of the Nana.

One other major work of the period must be mentioned: Richard Collier's *The Sound of Fury*, London 1963 and published in New York in 1964 under the title *The Great Indian Mutiny, a Dramatic Account of the Sepoy Rebellion*. This work is universally praised by scholars as a well-written and well-researched book. Collier concentrated on Delhi and Lucknow and produced a highly readable and valuable work. To quote the author, "My purpose in writing this book was solely to present an evocative portrait of the time through the eyes of a handful of people—what it looked like to them, how it felt, how it sounded and how it smelt."

A wealth of Mutiny literature was published in the succeeding decades. What follows is a brief survey of some of the more noteworthy books, up to the turn of the century. Many of the works that were published were of a scholarly nature but it is interesting to note that even at this late date there were still new eye-witness accounts being published. Witness the journal of Arthur Lang, the

Brydon diary, *From Minnie with Love* by Jane Vansittart, Harriet Tytler's journal by Sattin, and Esther Anne Bett's publication of *Reminiscences of the Indian Mutiny.*

Cambridge University Press published, in 1966, *The Mutiny Outbreak at Meerut in 1857* by J.A.B. Palmer. This is unquestionably the premier book on the outbreak at Meerut. Palmer studied the entire episode in minute detail and produced an excellent work that added substantially to the body of knowledge concerning Meerut and the individuals involved with events there on May 10th.

In 1973 Michael Edwardes published two excellent books, *A Season in Hell: The Defence of the Lucknow Residency* and *Red Year: The Indian Rebellion of 1857.* Edwardes produced two very well done works aimed at the non-specialist. They are informative as well as entertaining. *Red Year* contains some interesting information that is not easily found elsewhere. There is an appendix consisting of a number of examples of both English and Indian poetry that treats of the Mutiny. Also included is The *Narrative of Syed Mubarak Shah* who was the chief of police in Delhi after the city had been occupied by the mutineers. The available literature of eyewitness Indian participants is limited, especially that translated into English so the Mubarak Shah monogram is quite interesting. The original of the Shah manuscript resides in the India Office at the British Library.

1973 also saw the publication of an interesting title by S.D. Singh, *Novels of the Indian Mutiny.* This is the only work devoted to a comparative study of the mass of fiction the Mutiny produced. Singh gives a short synopsis of about 50 titles and then discusses the literary merits of each and its place within the entire body of Mutiny fiction.

There was a small but useful title published in 1975 by the Indian Council of Historical Research entitled *Recent Writings on the Revolt of 1857: A Survey.* The author was Kalyan Kumar Sengupta. Dr. Sengupta discusses English language writings on the Mutiny published since Indian Independence. Entries consist of scholarly articles and books by both Indian and western writers. He discusses what new work has been published in the various fields of Mutiny study and includes a list of works in progress and new trends as well as gaps in Mutiny research.

1977, 1978, and 1979 were good years for Mutiny literature. John Pemble published a fine work on Oudh and its role in the history of the Mutiny. *The Raj, The Indian Mutiny, and the Kingdom of Oudh, 1801-1859* is a thorough study of Oudh before and during the Mutiny and the consequences of annexation upon the people of the kingdom.

Although published by Fairleigh Dickinson University Press in the United States the book is most likely a co-publishing project with an unspecified British publisher, probably Harvester Press. The author was a research fellow at the University of Leicester.

Christopher Hibbert, a well-known British historian, published *The Great Mutiny: India 1857* in 1978. This is a general work for the non-specialist. The writing and research are excellent. Hibbert, along with Michael Edwardes, Saul David, and Andrew Ward are, I believe, the best of the contemporary writers. They have the ability to generate a degree of liveliness in their work that keeps the reader's interest.

The Peasant and the Raj: Studies in Agrarian Society and Peasant Rebellion in Colonial India by Eric Stokes was an important addition to Mutiny scholarship. Although not entirely concerned with the Mutiny period there is significant focus on the subject of agrarian studies and its relation to events in 1857. Stokes, along with Jagdish Raj, was one of the first scholars to thoroughly investigate land policy and link it to civil unrest and then open rebellion in 1857. Stokes was a very influential writer and was at the top of his field when he wrote *The Peasant and the Raj*. His last book, *The Peasant Armed: The Indian Rebellion of 1857*, was published posthumously in 1986 by the Oxford University Press. Stokes died in 1981. C.A. Bayly, a respected historian as well as the co-editor of *Two Colonial Empires*, edited his last work.

In 1979 Sashi Bhusan Chaudhuri published *English Historical Writings on the Indian Mutiny 1857-1859*. Chaudhuri has made remarkable additions to Mutiny literature, first with *Civil Rebellion in the Indian Mutinies* in 1957 and then with *Theories of the Indian Mutiny* in 1965. For those scholars captivated by the literature of the Mutiny there is no finer work than *English Historical Writings on the Indian Mutiny*. This is by far the most comprehensive work on Mutiny literature and although it focuses on English works it was written by an Indian and published in Calcutta.

Chaudhuri was the first scholar to really look closely at the huge body of English literature the Mutiny produced. All of the major works are discussed, both narrative and scholarly titles. There is an excellent chapter on English women in Mutiny literature, a subject not touched upon again until the publication of Jane Robinson's *Angels of Albion* in 1996. Indira Ghose included a chapter, "Mutiny Writings by Women," in *Women Travellers in India*, Oxford University Press, 1998.

The value of the work lies in its extensive coverage of the literature and the forthright opinions offered by Chaudhuri on the value of much of what he covers. Chaudhuri's breath and depth of knowledge is certainly what makes this work so valuable to the student of Mutiny literature as well as the researcher looking for guidance in this field.

Chaudhuri includes a 50-page bibliography, an appendix listing proclamations, notifications, addresses and other state papers, an index, and a chronological table on the course of the Mutiny.

There was another notable Mutiny book in 1979. Although not a scholarly work it was of great interest to Mutiny scholars and military history specialists. Mrs. Colina Brydon, the wife of Dr. William Brydon, kept a daily diary during the siege of Lucknow. The doctor of course gained fame as the sole survivor of Elphinstone's monumental disaster in Afghanistan. Mrs. Brydon's diary had remained unpublished until it came into the hands of Major C. deL. W. fforde (sic). The major obtained the diary from Mrs. R.M. Blackburn, presumably a relation of the Brydons. deL. W. fforde himself had served at Lucknow for four years during his posting to India, 1929 to 1935.

The diary was privately published in a printing of 50 copies numbered 11 to 50. Numbers 1 to 10 were reserved for members of deL. W. fforde's family. Those copies available for sale were priced at £8.90 and were photocopies of the original typescript. Each includes three maps and nine pasted-in photographs. There are extensive notes to the text along with a chronology of events and a memoir of Arthur Frederick Dashwood, who was born at Lucknow during the siege.

Apparently deL. W. fforde experienced some problems in the publication of the book because the foreword is dated 1976 but publication was not until early 1979, as noted in private correspondence.

A curious publishing event now comes to pass: Geoffrey Moore self-publishes *Diary of the Doctor's Lady* (no date but probably 1979). This again is Colina Brydon's diary but in a smaller format and in paperback. Moore includes the entire diary but not the index, notes, or Dashwood memoir. It is assumed this was published in arrangement with Major deL. W. fforde.

The only noteworthy publications for the next few years were *The Kashmir Gate* by Roger Perkins, 1983, and *Awadh in Revolt* by R. Mukherjee, 1984.

Perkins' work is the only detailed study of the action at the Kashmir Gate and it is quite thorough in its coverage. An appendix lists all of the battles of the Mutiny with a short description of each action. Appendix J gives all of the recipients of the Delhi VC with a short biography of each medal winner.

Rudrangshu Mukherjee's study of Awadh is a highly detailed and scholarly look at Awadh both before and during the Mutiny. The central theme is the disintegration of the relationship between the peasants and the British administration due to the introduction of a new, and entirely alien, land revenue policy. When the Mutiny came to Awadh it found popular support across a wide segment of the rural population. The book grew out of a doctorate thesis. It is heavily footnoted and draws much upon Foreign Department Secret Consultations and other government publications.

1986 was a prolific year for Mutiny literature. Arguably the most important publication, at least for the researcher, was Rosemary Seton's *The Indian "Mutiny" of 1857-58*. This is a highly useful guide to the holdings of the India Office Library at the British Library, and is required reading for anyone engaged in Mutiny studies.

C.A. Bayly edited two works that saw publication in 1986. He completed Eric Stokes' *The Peasant Armed* and with D.H.A. Kolff edited *Two Colonial Empires: Comparative Essays on the History of India and Indonesia in the Nineteenth Century.*

Stokes, of course, is interested in the various rural communities and their interaction with the Raj. Some were disposed to join the Mutiny and others fought on the side of the British. The pertinent question is, what were the deciding factors in pushing one group into either camp?

Stokes always believed that, to a large degree, the Mutiny was essentially a peasant revolt: not a revolt in the sense that the peasant population was yearning to enter into a new age of land reform with the promise of prosperity and a bigger piece of the pie, but rather a peasantry that was split along economic, environmental, and social lines. Depending upon varying factors this peasantry, not by any means all farmers, cast their lot either with the British or the mutineers and the choice was often predicated upon class rivalries and social standing within their particular communities. Again, it was not just the peasants who opposed the British but often the petty landowners and higher caste groups who had seen their status threatened or destroyed by the aggressive actions of the British in Oudh.

C.A. Bayly's other work of 1986, *Two Colonial Empires*, contains an interesting essay comparing the revolt in Java, 1825-1830, with the Mutiny. Bayly points out that although the current trend is to explore the Mutiny from the perspective of agrarian studies, the political foundation should not be overlooked. The political actions of the Raj, from the Doctrine of Lapse, the seizure of Oudh, and the slow but constant erosion of honor paid to the Mughal court, all had their influences upon the eruption at Meerut. Bayly covers much more in his essay and it is quite interesting.

Dr. Joyce Lebra-Chapman has written a number of works in the field of women's history and in 1986 the University of Hawaii published her study of Lakshmibai, the Rani of Jhansi. Lebra-Chapman's work, while an excellent history of the Rani and her place in the Mutiny, is in her own words a study of "the process by which a historical figure is transformed into a legend. What is the genesis of such a process and through what stages does it pass?"

Dr. Lebra-Chapman's book was one of the earliest works to look at women during the period of the Mutiny. Later works, cited above, included Indira Ghose, Jane Robinson, and Noel Williams' chapter on "Women Face the Indian Mutineers" within *Judy O'Grady & the Colonel's Lady*.

The next few years saw the publication of several books of interest to those studying the literature and historiography of the Mutiny.

Vipin Jain produced an annotated bibliography, *The Indian Mutiny of 1857*. Entries include books of fiction, articles from journals, and books published in European languages. The final section reproduces the title pages of 16 books on the Mutiny.

The Indian Literature of the Great Rebellion by Henry Scholberg was published in India in 1993. Scholberg has done a great service to researchers in the field by producing this work concerned with purely Indian sources. He includes newspapers, archives, vernacular accounts, and "a collection of folk songs in translation which describe how the Indian people, not their Indian rulers or rebel leaders, felt. The hatred of the feringi and the awful respect the people had for his might are plainly shown in these songs."

Scholberg was born in India and as a child was quite familiar with the history of the Mutiny. He eventually came to the United States for his college education and remained to become the director of the Ames Library of South Asia at the University of Minnesota.

The Historiography of the Indian Revolt of 1857 by Snigdha Sen was published in 1992 in Calcutta. Sen states that this is an "idea specific study" as opposed to an "event specific" work. He includes studies on peasant reaction to the Mutiny, Marxist theory, the absence of any interest from the Bengali intelligentsia, Savarkar's influence, and an excellent chapter titled "The Revolt Upsurge in Bengali Writings."

P.J.O. Taylor wrote a series of somewhat related titles in the mid 1990's. All of the books dealt with the Mutiny in various degrees. Taylor is a student of the Mutiny and had a long association with India. *Chronicles of the Mutiny & Other Historical Sketches* is a compilation of articles written by Taylor that appeared in the New Delhi Statesman. Several of these pieces relate to the Mutiny and one in particular is quite interesting. Papers of a Miscellaneous Character gives the background to the publication of the 1921 Press List of Mutiny Papers.

In 1993 Taylor published *A Star Shall Fall. A Feeling of Quiet Power* followed in 1994. Two years later Taylor edited *A Companion to the Indian Mutiny, a* survey of the Mutiny with nearly 1500 entries. Taylor includes a bibliography of over 1000 entries and a glossary as well as maps, illustrations, and a day-by-day time line of the principal events of the period.

1996 was also the publication date of an extraordinarily fine work by Andrew Ward. *Our Bones are Scattered: The Cawnpore Massacres and the Indian Mutiny of 1857* is a massive work not only in the physical sense, 703 pages, but as a fine piece of research and writing. It is a great read not only for the student of the period but for the general public as well. It is the definitive history of Cawnpore and as a writer Ward ranks with Michael Edwardes, Saul David, and Christopher Hibbert in his ability to capture the raw drama of the Mutiny as it played itself out so many years ago.

Felice Beato was a photographer who visited India shortly after the Mutiny was quelled. His photographs appear in numerous Mutiny books and his name is familiar to anyone with even a minimal acquaintance with Mutiny literature. Jim Masselos and Narayani Gupta wrote *Beato's Delhi 1857, 1997*. The book was published by Ravi Dayal, Publisher, in Delhi in 2000.

Here Beato's photographs are presented in a "then and now" format: the original scene as photographed by Beato and the same scene as it appears in 1997. Each set of photographs is accompanied by explanatory text. It is a fascinating look at Delhi and an important item in any Mutiny collection.

Saul David produced *The Indian Mutiny 1857* in 2002. David is a masterful storyteller and this work is a real treat for the Mutiny student. The book runs to just over 500 pages and includes notes, appendices, bibliography, and an index. The research is quite thorough and includes numerous primary sources both published and unpublished. David has also included photographs of many of the major personalities of the Mutiny and maps and battle plans of Delhi, Lucknow, and Cawnpore.

The centenary of the Mutiny was a watershed in the literary history of the event. Historians turned their attention to the analysis of what occurred and by doing that they began to establish a body of work that will be of great value to future generations. The value lies in the fact that current research shows once again how society fractures under stress.

The broad history of the Mutiny was quite well established by 1860 but it was not until the centenary that students of the Mutiny actually looked into the underlying causes and began to question the accepted assumption that the Mutiny was clearly a military affair and nothing more. Scholars looked at much more than just what appeared on the surface. It became evident that land and social status played an important part in relation to what segments of society wished to retain the status quo, and who hoped to find a better life under an entirely new regime. Well, if not entirely new, at least not British. No doubt there was many a landowner in Oudh that supported the Mutiny solely for personal reasons and had no thought of a united India.

I believe the Mutiny still offers a fertile ground for new research, especially with primary source material located in India. I hope the sesquicentennial will produce a spate of new works reminiscent of the burst of scholarship experienced during the centennial.

Richard Sorsky
Fresno, CA
January 2007

Abbreviations used in the annotations:

Ames = Ames Library at the University of Minnesota
BL = British Library
Bod = Bodleian Library at Oxford
C = Circa
Ind Inst = India Institute at Oxford
IO = India Office at the British Library
Jain = *The Indian Mutiny of 1857* by Vipin Jain. Entry 569
Maggs = Maggs Bros. Rare Books, London
MNUA = University of Minnesota Library
NAM = National Army Museum, London
ND = No Date
NC = No City
NP = No Publisher
RAI = Royal Arsenal at Woolwich, England
RS = Held by the author
SOAS = School of Oriental and African Studies, London
Sut = Victor Sutcliffe Military Books, London
Taylor = *A Companion to the Indian Mutiny* by P.J.O. Taylor

An Annotated Checklist of English Language Books

1
BL/Ames   **A Manchester Man.** *A VOICE FROM INDIA TO THE MEN OF MANCHESTER.* Manchester: Joseph Pratt, 1858. 15pp. Pamphlet. Religious Tracts.
Written from Madras December 22, 1857. An evangelical call to service. England owes India the Gospel and the government must bring Christianity to the masses.

2
BL 9057.bb.9   **A Veteran Judicial Officer. (Samuel Da Costa).** *THE SIEGE, DEFENCE AND VICTORY OF THE ILLUSTRIOUS GARRISON OF ARRAH ZILLAH SHAHABAD IN JULY 1857-58 AD. BY A VETERAN JUDICIAL OFFICER, U.C.S., ONE OF THE GARRISON.* Mussoorie: NP. 1897. Frontis, preface, 78pp + iv pp. Index. Red paper. Jubilee edition.
Da Costa was a Eurasian clerk. The British Library gives him as the author of this work but there is some doubt as he was not a judicial officer. It may have been Arthur Littledale who was a judge in the Saran District.

3
IO/RS/   **Aberigh-Mackay, James.** *FROM LONDON*
Bod/Ames   *TO LUCKNOW: WITH MEMORANDA OF MUTINIES, MIRACLES, FLIGHTS, FIGHTS, AND CONVERSATIONS TO WHICH IS ADDED, AN OPIUM SMUGGLERS EXPLANATION OF THE PEIHO MASSACRE.* London: James Nisbet, 1859-1860. Vol.I Colored frontis, xvi & 268pp. Vol.II Folding Map xi & 269-559.
By a chaplain in H M Indian Service. Most of both volumes relate to the Mutiny. Mackay was in Ghazeepore at the outbreak. He later was stationed in Cawnpore and by January 1858 was in Futtehgurh. He meets and describes a number of prominent Mutiny personalities.

4
BL 6056.b.58   **Adam, H.L.** *THE INDIAN CRIMINAL.* London: John
Milne, 1909. Frontis, 313pp. 15 plates.
Contains one chapter on Moulvi Liaicat Ali who was
instrumental in the violence at Allahabad.

5
BL 4477.a.2   **Addams, Rev. Francis Holland.** *ENGLAND'S
INFIRMITY. A SERMON IN BEHALF OF THE
SUFFERERS FROM THE MUTINY IN INDIA.
PREACHED IN ST. PETERS CHURCH, NOTTING
HILL, ON SUNDAY MORNING, SEPTEMBER 20,
1857.* London: Bell & Daldy, 1857. 18pp.
England is being punished by the Lord. England brought
down the misfortune upon itself because it was only interested
in its own kingdom in India, not Christ's eternal kingdom.

6
IO   **Adjutant General's Office.** *THE PLATOON
EXERCISE, AND DIFFERENT FIRINGS FOR THE
ORDINARY OR RIFLE MUSKET.* Calcutta: R.C.
Lepage & Company, April 1857.
An extremely rare title. Held in the India Office.
Accession number L/MIL/17/2/506

7
RS   **Adye, General Sir John Miller.** *RECOLLECTIONS
OF A MILITARY LIFE.* London: Smith, Elder and
Co, 1895. 382pp. 11 plates, 3 plans and 1 map with 9
vignettes in the text.
Includes service in the Mutiny, about 50 pages. Adye
arrived in Calcutta on October 5, 1857 and served with
Windham and Campbell There is a good chapter on the
causes of the Mutiny and the policies of Lord Canning.

8
RS/Ames   **Adye, Lt Col John.** *DEFENCE OF CAWNPORE
BY THE TROOPS UNDER THE ORDERS OF
MAJOR GENERAL CHARLES A. WINDHAM IN
NOVEMBER 1857.* London: Longman, Brown, Green
Longmans and Roberts, 1858. iv, 58pp. 24pp Adverts.
Folding Map.
Adye defends Windham's actions when faced by the
Gwalior Contingent at Cawnpore. Day by day account from
November 9 to December 8, 1857.

9
Ames   **Ahmad Khan, Saiyid, Sir.** *POLITICAL PROFILE OF
SIR SAYYID AHMAD KHAN. A DOCUMENTARY*

RECORD. Islamabad: Islamic University, 1982. xxii & 400pp with index.

Edited by Hafeez Malik. This work discusses Ahmad Khan's thoughts on 1857 among other subjects. It includes his work on the Bijnor Rebellion, causes for the revolt in India, and "Prayer for Peace at Moradabad." This is one of the few works in English by an Indian who lived through the Mutiny. The author attempts to show that the Muslims played a minimal role in the Mutiny.

10
RS

Ahmad Khan, Saiyid, Sir. *SIR SAYYID AHMAD KHAN'S HISTORY OF THE BIJNOR REBELLION. Translated by Hafeez Malik and Morris Dembo.* Asian Studies Center, Michigan State Univ. East Lansing, Michigan: ND c. 1968. xii & 163pp.

A scholarly work on the Mutiny period in Bijnor together with a translation of Khan's "*Cause of the Indian Revolt*" and his "*Prayer for Peace at Moradabad.*"

11
Sut

Ahmad Khan, Saiyid, Sir. *THE CAUSES OF THE INDIAN REVOLT WRITTEN...IN URDOO IN THE YEAR 1858 AND TRANSLATED INTO ENGLISH BY HIS TWO EUROPEAN FRIENDS.* Benares: Medical Hall Press, 1873. 65pp.

Originally written in Urdu in 1858. It was not translated until 1860. Ahmed Khan covers the main points in the Mutiny such as the chuppatties, Russian and Persian influences, the buildup of bitterness among the sepoys, Meerut, etc. This is important because it is one of the few contemporary essays by an Indian.

12
Ames/
BL1419.b.50(3)

Ahmad Khan, Sayyid, Sir. *ACCOUNT OF THE LOYAL MAHOMEDANS OF INDIA. In Two Parts.* Meerut: J. A. Gibbons at the Mofussilite Press, ND. 1859? Part I, 82pp. Part II, 100pp. Paper.

Part one is a series of narratives setting forth the loyal acts of numerous Muslims during the Mutiny. It includes testimonials from British residents. Part two discusses the term "Jihad" as related to current events and goes on to discuss the religious and political aspects of the Mutiny as they relate to Islam.

13
Ames/RS/
BL 8220.
bbb.13(19)

Ahmad Khan, Sayyid, Sir. *AN ESSAY ON THE CAUSES OF THE INDIAN REVOLT. Translated by Captain W.N. Lees.* Calcutta: W. N. Lees 1860, 1873. viii & 80pp.

Khan attempts to vindicate the Muslims for participating in the Mutiny. Originally written in Urdu, in Agra, in 1858 or 1859, and published at the Mofussilite Press. Another edition was published in Lahore by The Book House, 1970, viii & 86pp. Khan enumerates the causes of the Mutiny and gives a point by point discussion about what went wrong in Bengal.

14
Ames

Ahmad Khan, Sayyid, Sir; *SIR SAYYID AHMAD KHAN'S HISTORY OF THE BIJNOR REBELLION. Translated with Notes and Introduction by Hafeez Malik and Morris Dembo.* Delhi: Idarah-i Adabiyat, 1982. xxi & 221pp. Bibliography and index.

A scholarly work on the Mutiny period in Bijnor together with a translation of Khan's "*Cause of the Indian Revolt*" and his "*Prayer for Peace at Moradabad.*"

15
SOAS

Ahmad, Dr. Quyamuddin. *THE WAHABI MOVEMENT IN INDIA.* Calcutta: Firma K. L. Mukhopadhyaya, 1966. xxiii & 391pp. Index and bibliography.

Ahmad deals only with the Mutiny in passing. The Wahabi's were followers of Ahmad Barelvi and were not associated with the well known movement in the Arabian Peninsula. In Mutiny literature the mention of the Wahabi's is most easily found in reference to the Patna Crisis and William Tayler. The movement was separate and distinct from the Mutiny and was active both before and after the Mutiny.

16
RS

Ahmad, Safi (ed.) *BRITISH AGGRESSION IN AVADH: BEING THE TREATISE OF MOHAMMED MASIH UDDIN KHAN BAHADUR ENTITLED, "OUDH: ITS PRINCES AND ITS GOVERNMENT VINDICATED."* London: John Davy and Sons, 1857. xv & 179pp.

Originally suppressed by the British Government. Reprinted in Meerut: Meenakshi Prakashan, 1969. Index and bibliography.

Masih Khan was the plenipotentiary of Wajid Ali Shah, the deposed King of Oudh. Upon the annexation of Oude by Dalhousie, in 1856, Masih Khan was sent to plea Oudh's case before Queen Victoria and Parliament. This book was written to acquaint England with the history of Oudh under the Nawabs. It is not directly related to the Mutiny period but was seized by the English upon the outbreak of the Mutiny and suppressed.

The original 1857 edition is very rare as most of the

copies were destroyed by the government of Great Britain. A German translation was published by Dr. V. Hoffmann in 1864 under the title: *"How Does England Make and Break Treaties? A Vindication of the Kings and Government of Oude in East India by Moulvie Museeh-oodden Khan Bahadoor, Plenipotentiary Minister of the King of Oude--After The English edition having been suppressed. Edited in German by a friend of the Indians."*

17

Aikman, Lt. W.R. *THE BENGAL MUTINY. POPULAR OPINIONS CONCERNING THE ORIGIN OF THE MUTINY REFUTED, THE REAL CAUSES CONSIDERED, WITH SUGGESTIONS FOR THE FUTURE, IN A LETTER TO VISCOUNT PALMERSTON.* London: Richardson Bros. ND. c. 1857. 32pp.
Interference of Christian missionaries and Russian intrigues.

18
Bod

Ainslie, Rev. A L. *A FEW WORDS ABOUT INDIA, AND THE MUTINIES. With a Map.* Taunton and London: Frederick May and Longman & Co., 1857. 21pp.
An informational tract for the parishoners preparatory to taking up a collection for the English in India. 2nd ed. 1857. 16pp. No map. 3rd ed. 1857. 16pp. No map.

19
IO

Aitchison, Sir Charles. *LORD LAWRENCE.* Oxford: Clarendon Press, 1892. 216pp. Folding map at front.
Rulers of India Series

20
RS

Alavi, Seema. *THE SEPOYS AND THE COMPANY. TRADITION AND TRANSITION IN NORTHERN INDIA 1770-1830.* New Delhi: Oxford University Press, 1998. xiii & 315pp. 1 map & 10 plates. Index, glossary, and bibliography.
A revised version of Alavi's doctoral dissertation this is an excellent study of the sepoy prior to the Mutiny. The concluding chapter is a discussion of the sepoys, the Company and the Mutiny.

21

Aldwell, James Skinner. *SOME REMINISCENES OF THE DEFENSE OF HOUSE NO. 5, DARAYAGANJ, DELHI, ON THE OUTBREAK OF THE MUTINY IN 1857.* NC. NP. Privately Printed, 1891.

A pamphlet cited in Stark's "*Call of the Blood*". Stark gives an extended excerpt from the book, however the actual book has not been located in any major library and there is no record of James Skinner Aldwell in various records found in the India Office. A mystery!

22

Alexander, Thomas. *THE CAUSE OF THE INDIAN MUTINY; BEING AN EXPOSITION OF THE SECOND PSALM ETC.* London: Show, 1857.

23
Bod/
BL 8022.C2

Allen, Charles. *A FEW WORDS ANENT THE RED PAMPHLET BY ONE WHO HAS SERVED UNDER THE MARQUESS OF DALHOUSIE.* London: James Ridgway, 1858. 30pp. 2nd ed. A 3rd. ed. 1858.
    Known as the yellow pamphlet, this was written in support of the policies of Dalhousie. Allen served as Foreign Secretary to the Government and then as a member of the Legislative Council.

24
IO V20463

Alli, Darogha Ubbas. *THE LUCKNOW ALBUM.* Calcutta: Baptist Mission Press, Also G.H. Rouse, Calcutta. 1874. vi & 58 pp.+ 50 mounted photographs and large folding map in pocket.
    "Containing a Series of Fifty Photographic Views of Lucknow and Its Environs Together With A Large Sized Plan of the City Executed By--To the Above is Added A Full Description of Each Scene Depicted. The Whole Forming a Complete Illustrated Guide to the City of Lucknow, the Capital of Oude."

25

Alter, James Payne. *IN THE DOAB AND ROHILKHAND: NORTH INDIAN CHRISTIANITY 1815-1915.* Delhi: NP. 1986.
    Cited in Taylor.

26
IO

Alves, Colonel Nathaniel. *INDIA: ITS DANGER CONSIDERED IN 1856. BY A RETIRED OFFICER.* Jersey: Joshua Coutanche, 1858. 52pp. Another printing in March, 1859 (England). xi & 107pp.
    The 1859 edition was titled; *India: Its Dangers, as Considered in 1856,* by A Retired Officer. With appendices and "Last Words." Alves was the Governor General's Agent in Rajputana. There were 100 copies of the 1859 edition and then a further edition was done with additions.

27
BL

An Old Quarter-master of the Bengal Army. *GAZETTEER AND GAZETTEER MAP OF THE SEAT OF REBELLION IN INDIA SHEWING THE RELATIVE POSITIONS OF THE VARIOUS CANTONMENTS WITH APPROPRIATE DESCRIPTIVE NOTICES.* London: James Madden, 1857. 24pp. Pamphlet.

Gives each town in alphabetical order with a short description. Must have been published very late in 1857 or backdated.

28
RS/Ames

An Old Resident. *BRIEF OBSERVATIONS ADDRESSED TO THE GENERAL READER ON THE BASIS OF THE REORGANIZATION OF OUR POWER IN INDIA. BY AN OLD RESIDENT IN INDIA.* London: R. C. Lepage, 1858. 14pp. Pamphlet.

The author espouses the proposition that the native of India suffers from "absolute and irremediable mental inferiority compared to the Anglo-European." This article was submitted for publication to an "Influential London Journal" but was rejected.

29
RS

Anderson, Captain R(obert) P(atrick). *A PERSONAL JOURNAL OF THE SIEGE OF LUCKNOW.* London: W. Thacker, 1858. 110pp.

Anderson was Assistant Commissioner at Lucknow at the commencement of the Mutiny. His house became one of the major outposts during the siege.

30
IO

Anderson, Captain T. Carnegy. *UBIQUE: WAR SERVICES OF ALL OF THE OFFICERS OF H.M.'S BENGAL ARMY, EXHIBITING THE RANK AND VARIOUS SERVICES OF EVERY OFFICER IN THE ARMY.* Calcutta: Privately Printed, ND. c. 1863. Reprinted 1986. xii, lxxiv & 668pp.

Useful in that it gives service records of a number of authors who subsequently wrote narratives on the Mutiny.

31

Anderson, Colonel W. *THE BLUE PAMPHLET. BY AN OFFICER ONCE IN THE BENGAL ARTILLERY.* London: 1858.

Cited in Ladendorf.

32

Anderson, George & Subadar, Manilal Bhagrandas.
*THE DEVELOPMENT OF AN INDIAN POLICY,
THE LAST DAYS OF THE COMPANY: A SOURCE
BOOK OF INDIAN HISTORY, 1818-1858.* London:
Bell and Sons, 1918. 2 vols.
Volume I. The Expansion of British India, 1818-1858.
179pp. 1918. Cited in Jain.

33

Anderson, H.S. *REMINISCENCES DURING
FORTY-FIVE YEARS SERVICE IN INDIA.* Horsham:
NP. 1903.
Cited in Hibbert and Jain.

34
BL/RS

Anderson, Maj. A.T. *A SHORT HISTORY OF
LUCKNOW.* Allahabad: Pioneer Press, 1913. ii &
142pp. Paper.
Large folding map at rear. Anderson was a major in
the Royal Field Artillery. This is a general history of the
Mutiny events surrounding Lucknow and is intended to
help the reader follow the movements on the actual ground.
Something of a guide book. Anderson mentions that Hilton,
author of "*A Tourists Guide to Lucknow*" is still alive. Anderson
includes a list of tombstones and monuments in and around
Lucknow.

35
BL

Andrews, C.F. *MAULVI ZAKA ULLAH OF DELHI.*
Cambridge: W. Heffer & Sons, 1929. xxx & 159pp.
Index, frontis and seven photos.
Gives a description of life in Delhi prior to and during the
Mutiny. Zaka Ullah was at Delhi College during the Mutiny.
He did not partake in the fighting.

36
RS

Anonymous. *1857 CENTENARY EXHIBITION
OF PRINTED BOOKS, DOCUMENTS AND
ILLUSTRATIONS AT THE NATIONAL LIBRARY,
CALCUTTA.* Calcutta: National Library, 1957. 67pp.
Paper.
A handlist of books and pictures exhibited at the library
during the centenary of the Mutiny.

37
BL

Anonymous. *A FEW REMARKS EARNESTLY
ADDRESSED TO THE MEN OF ENGLAND,
POLITICAL AND MERCANTILE, UPON THE*

PRESENT CRISIS IN INDIAN AFFAIRS. London: Darton and Co., 1857. 2nd edition. 32pp. Pamphlet.

What faults caused or permitted the sad state of affairs in India and what course will best prevent their recurrence? The Government of India should never have supported idolatry. This is a common complaint found in many of the religious pamphlets of the period.

38
IO

Anonymous. *A FORM OF PRAYER AND THANKSGIVING TO ALMIGHTY GOD TO BE USED IN ALL CHURCHES AND CHAPELS THROUGHOUT ENGLAND AND WALES, AND THE TOWN OF BERWICK ON TWEED, ON SUNDAY, THE FIRST DAY OF MAY, 1859, FOR THE SUCCESS GRANTED OUR ARMS IN SUPPRESSING THE REBELLION AND RESTORING TRANQUILITY IN H.M. INDIAN DOMINIONS.* London: George Edward Eyre & William Spottiswoode, 1859. 4pp.

39
Sut

Anonymous. *A FULL AND CORRECTED REPORT OF PROCEEDINGS OF THE PUBLIC MEETING IN HONOR OF LORD CANNING.* Calcutta: Thakoorddoss Doss at the Canning Press, 1862.

40
RS

Anonymous. *A GLANCE AT THE EAST BY A RETIRED BENGAL CIVILIAN.* London: L. Booth, 1857. 31pp.

The author was a resident in India for many years and provides a number of reasons for the crisis. Essentially the mis-rule of the British was a tremendous problem. The British simply did not know enough about the social and political structure of the sub-continent. The author also points out that rule over India must originate in India and not from a board of directors in London.

41
BL

Anonymous. *A LETTER FROM A LAYMAN IN INDIA ON THE POLICY OF THE EAST INDIAN COMPANY IN MATTERS OF RELIGION.* London: W. H. Dalton, 1858. 19pp.

Written Dec. 23, 1857. The Government of India does not lend enough support to Christian causes.

42

Anonymous. *A PERSONAL NARRATIVE OF THE SIEGE OF LUCKNOW.* See entry 121 for Huxham,

43
IO

Anonymous. *A VOLUNTEER: MY JOURNAL OR WHAT I DID AND SAW BETWEEN THE 9TH JUNE AND 25TH NOVEMBER 1857 WITH AN ACCOUNT OF GENERAL HAVELOCK'S.* See Swanston. (Entry 1013)

44
IO

Anonymous. *A WEEK IN THE MOFUSSIL IN 1857.* London: Warren Hall & James J. Lovitt, privately printed. ND. c. 1875. 77pp. See McCallan, Andrew. (Entry 740).

45
NAM 1857(54)

Anonymous. *ADDENDA TO CORRESPONDENCE REGARDING CLAIMS TO THE INDIAN MEDALS, FOR SERVICE IN WESTERN INDIA. 1857-8.* NC. Ventnor & G.M. Burt, 1865. 12pp.

46
Bod/
BL 8023.c.47

Anonymous. *CAUSE AND EFFECT: THE REBELLION IN INDIA. BY A RESIDENT IN THE NORTH WESTERN PROVINCES OF INDIA.* London: John Farquhar Shaw, 1857. 40pp.

An investigation into the causes of the Mutiny. BL gives (1859)

47
Ames

Anonymous. *CHRISTIANITY IN INDIA. PROCEEDINGS OF A PUBLIC MEETING HELD AT EXETER HALL JANUARY 5TH TO CONSIDER THE FUTURE RELATIONS OF THE BRITISH GOVERNMENT TO RELIGION IN INDIA, RIGHT HONORABLE THE EARL OF SHAFTESBURY IN THE CHAIR.* London: Reed and Pardon, 1858. 23pp. Pamphlet.

The British Government in India should discontinue all aid and support for every type of idolatry. The British should no longer maintain heathen temples, administer endowments for their support, etc.

48
RS

Anonymous. *DACOITEE IN EXCELSIS; THE SPOLIATION OF OUDE, BY THE EAST INDIAN*

*COMPANY, FAITHFULLY RECOUNTED WITH
NOTES AND DOCUMENTARY ILLUSTRATIONS.*
London: J. R. Taylor, ND. 214pp.
This work was probably written by Major R.W.Bird who
was at one time an assistant commissioner to the King of
Oude. Publication date was approximately 1857. This work
is a strong indictment of Outram, Sleeman and Dalhousie and
the manner in which the East India Company acquired the
Kingdom of Oude.

49
BL 8022.C.43   **Anonymous.** *ENGLAND'S TROUBLES IN INDIA.*

50
RS   **Anonymous.** *EX ORIENTE: SONNETS ON THE
INDIAN REBELLION.* London: John Chapman, 1858.
151pp.
Attributed to James I. Minchin. According to the
publisher's advertisement the book was written in India and
sent home for publication in November, 1857. The original
publishers declined to publish because of some unflattering
references to public figures, General Hewitt for one.
Apparently the sinking of the AVA had some effect on the
publication of this book.

51
Bod   **Anonymous.** *EXETER HALL VERSUS BRITISH
INDIA.* London: Thomas Hatchard, 1858. 20pp.
Pamphlet.
Enumerates all of the problems with India.

52
Bod   **Anonymous.** *FIVE LETTERS ON INDIAN
REORGANIZATION: TO THE EDITOR OF THE
DAILY NEWS BY C.D.L.* London: Smith Elder, 1858.
38pp. Pamphlet.
Letter I: The Question Stated and the Causes of the
Mutiny; Letter II: The Remedy That Must Not be Applied;
Letter III: The Remedy that Must Be Applied; Letter IV:
The Remedy Applied to the Actual Condition of the Patient;
Letter V: The India Bills.

53
RS   **Anonymous.** *GOLDEN COMMEMORATION OF
THE INDIAN MUTINY AT THE ROYAL ALBERT
HALL DECEMBER 23, 1907.* London: W. H. Smith
and Son, 1908. 63pp. with menu in rear.
Contains a speech by Lord Curzon and a speech by Field
Marshal Roberts. Includes a list of surviving veterans and
their regiments.

54

Anonymous. *HISTORY OF THE SIEGE OF DELHI BY AN OFFICER WHO SERVED THERE.* See Ireland, William Wotherspoon. (Entry 556).

55
Bod

Anonymous. *INDIA BEFORE AND AFTER THE MUTINY. BY A STUDENT.* Edinburgh and London: E & S Livingstone (Edinburgh) and Simpkin, Marshall & Co.(London), 1886. 136pp. 2nd ed. Revised and enlarged.
Short review of the government administration which helped form India into what it is today. (1886). The second section is a review of the economic, intellectual, and moral condition of India. This work was written by an Indian student in competition for a prize offered at the University for the best essay on "India before and after the Mutiny." This was not the winning essay.

56
IO

Anonymous. *INDIA MUTINY SERMONS BY THE AUTHOR OF NATIONAL HUMILIATION....*

57
Bod

Anonymous. *INDIA'S MUTINY AND ENGLANDS MOURNING,* NC. NP. 1857.

58
RS/
BL8022.d.69

Anonymous. *INDIA. THE REVOLT AND THE HOME GOVERNMENT.* Calcutta: Robert Hardwicke, Sept 1857. 39pp.
Pamphlet. The author is pro-John Company and Canning and is writing a rebuttal to a paper that appeared in the press titled, "The Petition of the British Inhabitants of Calcutta to the Lords and Commons of Great Britain and Ireland in Parliament assembled." Defends Canning's press laws, and a number of other policies of John Company.

59
RS

Anonymous. *INDIA: GEOGRAPHICAL, STATISTICAL, AND HISTORICAL. GIVING DISTINCT REVIEW OF THE EARLY MOHAMMEDAN INVADERS AND EUROPEAN CONQUESTS WITH A FULL ACCOUNT OF THE LATE WAR, MISSIONARY OPERATION, ETC.* London: George Watts Co., 1858. 470pp.
Compiled from the London Times correspondence. 160 pages on the Mutiny up to the relief of Lucknow.

60
IO   **Anonymous.** *INDIAN MUTINY SERMON.* London: James Darling, 1857. 15pp.

61
Ames   **Anonymous.** *INDIAN POLICY.* London: Bell & Daldy, 1858. 104pp. Pamphlet.
Puts the argument that the "Simple Solution" plan for India be reconsidered. This plan consisted of: 1) An absolute Governor General, 2) Employment of a strictly European army, 3) Complete annexation of all native states within current boundaries, excluding Nepal, 4) Various revenue plans.

62
Anonymous. *LETTERS OF THE LATE MAJOR-GENERAL R.H. HALL...WHILE SERVING UNDER GENERAL SIR HUGH ROSE.* Hitchin, 1881.
Cited in Hibbert and Jain.

63
Anonymous. *LORD CANNING, THE INDIAN MUTINIES AND THE GOVERNMENT POLICY. BY A SCOTCHMAN.* NC. NP. 1857. 24pp.
Cited by Ladendorf.

64
BL08023.aa.13 **Anonymous.** *LORD ELLENBROUGHS BLUNDER RESPECTING THE CAUSES OF THE MUTINY. SIGNED BY A.D.* Calcutta: Baptist Mission Press, 1857. 12pp.
Apparently written by an Indian loyal to Britain. States the government has done nothing to interfere with their religion. The Hindus are a tolerant people and India is not inhabited by savages and barbarians. "We hold the Christian missionaries in high regard but do not agree with their religion." This tract refutes the premise that the mutiny was caused by over zealous missionaries. This is a copy of a speech delivered to the British Indian Association.

65
RS   **Anonymous.** *LUCKNOW GUIDE, INCLUDING NOTES ON CAWNPORE, AGRA AND DELHI.*
Lucknow: American Methodist Mission Press, 1885. 76pp. One folding map of the city of Lucknow.
Paper. Good coverage of the remains of buildings of the Mutiny.
See also Hilton: *Tourists Guide to Lucknow.* (Entry 516).

66
Maggs 1985   **Anonymous.** *MEMOIR OF THE LATE MAJOR GENERAL SIR HENRY HAVELOCK K.C.B. WITH NOTICES OF HIS DEATH, EXTRACTED FROM THE LONDON AND LOCAL PRESS: AND A REPORT OF THE MEETING HELD AT SUNDERLAND, JANUARY 22, 1858 TO ORIGINATE SUBSCRIPTIONS FOR THE ERECTION OF A MONUMENT TO HIS MEMORY, IN THE PARK, AT BILDON HALL, BISHOPWEARMOUTH, WITH A LIST OF SUBSCRIBERS.* Sunderland, 1858. 40pp. 2 Plates.
Bound in is the "*Sermon on the Death of Havelock*" preached in Westminster Abbey by Dr. Richard Chenevix Trench and a 16pp biography published by the Religious Tract Society.

67
Bod   **Anonymous.** *MEMORANDUM ON THE RECONSTRUCTION OF THE BENGAL ARMY.* London: MacIntosh, Printer. 1857. 16pp.

68
Bod   **Anonymous.** *MEMORIAL CHURCH AT CAWNPORE.* NC. NP. ND. c.1857. 4 pages. Pamphlet.
Appeal for funds. Lists the committee and contributors.

69
    Anonymous. *MUTINIES AND THE PEOPLE OR STATEMENTS OF NATIVE FIDELITY EXHIBITED DURING THE OUTBREAK OF 1857-58. BY A HINDU.*
See Mukhopadhyaya, S.C. (Entries 222 and 772).

70
    Anonymous. *MUTINIES IN INDIA. Extracts of Letters From an Assistant Surgeon in the Infantry of the Hyderabad Contingent.* NC. NP. Privately printed. 1857.
Cited in Jain.

71
RS   **Anonymous.** *OBSERVATIONS ON THE LATE EVENTS IN THE BENGAL PRESIDENCY. BY AN OFFICER LATE OF THE MADRAS ARTILLERY.* Jersey: Joshua Coutanche, 1857. 51pp.
Paper pamphlet. A general exposition of the causes of the Mutiny.

72
Ames

Anonymous. *OBSERVATIONS ON THE PROPOSED COUNCIL OF INDIA.* London: William Penny, 1858. 7pp. Pamphlet.
Discusses the proposed plans for the composition of the new Council of India which is to assist the minister of the crown in governing India.

73

Anonymous. *OUR CONDUCT, AFTER THE DISAFFECTION AND MUTINY OF THE NATIVE REGIMENTS HAD BROKEN OUT, AND ITS CONSEQUENCES.* 20pp.
Cited in Ladendorf.

74
Ames

Anonymous. *PRACTICAL OBSERVATIONS ON THE FIRST TWO OF THE PROPOSED RESOLUTIONS ON THE GOVERNMENT OF INDIA.* London: William Penny, 1858. 10pp. Pamphlet.
Discusses who shall administer and govern India, a minister of the government or a commission or board of directors.

75
IO

Anonymous. *PRAYER FOR OUR CAUSE IN INDIA. A SERMON BY A LONDON INCUMBENT.* London: James Darling, 1857. 15pp.

76
Bod/Ames

Anonymous. *PRIZE MONEY; OR, THE RIGHT OF MAJOR-GENERAL WHITLOCK, K.C.B. AND HIS TROOPS, TO THE BANDA AND KIRWEE BOOTY, TRIED BY NAVAL AND MILITARY LAW, AND THE USAGE OF THE ARMY.* London: Harrison, 1862. 3rd ed. 65pp. + xlviii & folding map at rear.
This explores the question of why Whitlock's troops did not receive their share of the prize money.

77

Anonymous. *PUBLIC FEELING IN REGARD TO THE REMOVAL OF MR. W. TAYLER FROM THE PATNA COMMISSIONERSHIP AS INDICATED BY NOTICES OF THE PRESS.* Calcutta: Thacker and Co. ND.

78

Anonymous. *RED, WHITE AND BLUE SKETCHES OF MILITARY LIFE.* London: Hurst and Blackett, 1862. 3 vols.
Very critical of the British military as compared to the French. (Ladendorf)

79

Anonymous. *REMINISCENCES OF 1857, OR THE DEFENSE OF LUCKNOW BY A MEMBER OF THE ORIGINAL RESIDENCY GARRISON.* Lucknow: N. N. Sivapuri Press, 1891. Lucknow
Cited in Jain.

80

Anonymous. *REMINISCENCES OF THE GREAT AND GOOD SIR HENRY LAWRENCE AND ALSO OF THE INDIAN MUTINY OF 1857. By Y.* Dehra Dun: NP. 1893.

81
Sut

Anonymous. *RETROSPECT OF 1857.* Lahore: Punjabee Press, 1858. 82pp.

82
NAM

Anonymous. *SERVICES OF THE 31ST NLI....IN THE SAUBOZ DIST. No other information.*

83
Sut/NAM
1857(54)

Anonymous. *SERVICES OF THE LATE 31ST NOW 2ND N.I. DURING THE MUTINY AND SUBSEQUENT OPERATIONS IN 1858-1859 IN THE SAUGOR DISTRICT AND CENTRAL INDIA.* Lahore?: Kaiser Baugh Press. No imprint. ND. 39pp.
Various communications dealing with the regiment.

84

Anonymous. *SOME REMINISCENCES OF THREE QUARTERS OF A CENTURY IN INDIA.* See Churcher, E. J. (Entry 278).

85

Anonymous. *STATEMENTS OF REGIMENTS OF CAVALRY, INFANTRY AND ARTILLERY EMBARKED FOR INDIA FROM 1ST JULY 1857 TO 18TH FEBRUARY 1858.*
Cited in Ladendorf.

86

Anonymous. *THANKSGIVING THOUGHTS ON THE INDIAN MUTINY, A SERMON BY A LONDON INCUMBENT. AUTHOR OF A FASTDAY SERMON. 1859.* London: James Darling, 1859. 15pp.
Thanks God for the suppression of the Mutiny and urges the evangelization of India and the improvement of the political and social condition of the continent.

87
RS

Anonymous. *THE ANNEXATION OF THE KINGDOM OF OUDE. ONE OF THE MAIN CAUSES OF THE REBELLION IN INDIA.* NC. NP. ND. 8pp.

88
RS

Anonymous. *THE ANNUAL REGISTER OR A VIEW OF THE HISTORY AND POLITICS OF THE YEAR 1858.* London: F & J Rivington, 1859. 820pp.
Contains a history of the mutiny to the close of 1859 together with Parliamentary proceedings.

89
RS

Anonymous. *THE ANNUAL REGISTER, OR A VIEW OF THE HISTORY AND POLITICS OF THE YEAR 1857.* London: F & J Rivington, 1858. 973pp.
Contains a history of the Mutiny to the close of the year together with parliamentary debates on the subject.

90
BL 8828.c14

Anonymous. *THE ARMY PURCHASE QUESTION AND REPORT AND MINUTES OF EVIDENCE OR THE ROYAL COMMISSION CONSIDERED, WITH A PARTICULAR EXAMINATION OF THE EVIDENCE OF SIR CHARLES TREVELYAN.* London: Ridgeway, 1858. 136pp.

91
BL 9004 L3

Anonymous. *THE CAWNPORE OUTBREAK AND MASSACRE.* Calcutta: J.F. Bellamy, Englishman Press, 1857. 37pp. Paper.
Consists of a 19 page account, anonymous, of the siege at Cawnpore; another anonymous account together with a list of casualities; Nujoor Tewarree's account; Deposition of Marian, an ayah in the service of Mr. J. Greenway of Cawnpore; two poems concerning Cawnpore.

92
BL 4478b29

Anonymous. *THE CHRISTIANS OF ENGLAND, THE WATCHMEN OF INDIA. A SERMON*

*PREACHED IN AGRA...IN MARCH 1850 AND
ENGLAND IN 1852...NOW PUBLISHED AS
APPLICABLE TO PASSING EVENTS IN BRITISH
INDIA.* London: Bell & Daldy, 1857. 22pp

93
NAM1857(54)   **Anonymous.** *THE DESPATCH OF BRIGADIER*
ING   *INGLIS NARRATING THE EVENTS AT THE SIEGE
OF LUCKNOW TOGETHER WITH SELECTIONS
FROM THE SPEECHES OF SIR GEORGE COUPER.*
Cheitenham: Horace Edwards, 1896. 39pp. Pamphlet.
    Includes speeches delivered at the ruins of the Residency
for various occasions.

94
Sut   **Anonymous.** *THE FIRST BENGAL EUROPEAN
FUSILIERS IN THE INDIAN MUTINY.* London:
Blackwood's Magazine, 1858. 43pp.
    Attributed to J.P. Brougham. This is a 3 part article
totaling 43 pages extracted from Blackwood's Magazine,
1858, cloth bound. "In the Delhi Campaign" 17 pages. "After
the Fall of Delhi" 14 pages. "At Lucknow" 12 pages. The
attribution to J.P. Brougham, surgeon of the regiment, can be
found on page 144 of volume 1 of McCance's *"History of the
Royal Munster Fusiliers."*

95
BL   **Anonymous.** *THE GOVERNMENT OF INDIA AS
IT HAS BEEN, AS IT IS, AND AS IT OUGHT TO BE.*
London: Robert Hardwicke, 1858. 62pp. Pamphlet.
    A condemnation of the government of India, their entire
system, policy and principle of their rule. The difference
between the British and other foreign conquerors is that they
either departed or were absorbed, the British were neither
absorbed nor did they depart in a timely fashion. The E.I.C.
is tyrannical, rapacious, and unscrupulous.

96
BL 8023.c.50   **Anonymous.** *THE GREAT INDIAN CRISIS IN FIVE
MINUTES READING. A LETTER TO THE PEOPLE
OF GREAT BRITAIN. BY A GENERAL OFFICER.*
London: W. H. Allen, 1858. 13pp.

97
IO   **Anonymous.** *GUILTY MEN OF 1857. FAILURE OF
ENGLAND'S GREAT MISSION IN INDIA. THREE
ANONYMOUS DISCOURSES.* New Delhi: Academic
Books Corp., 1980. 72pp. Index.
    Consists of three discourses condemning the British
for the events in India. These were written anonymously

about ten years after the Mutiny. They accuse the British of betraying their Christian God by their inequities in India. Original edition "*England's Great Mission in India*" published in Lucknow by the London Printing Press, 1879. Attributed to James Bird. See entry 177 for James Bird.

98
Bod

Anonymous. *THE HISTORY OF THE BRITISH SETTLEMENTS IN INDIA; TO THE CLOSE OF THE SEPOY REBELLION.* London: The Society of Promoting Christian Knowledge, ND. c. 1860.
The last 98pp. cover the Mutiny period.

99
Bod

Anonymous. *THE INDIAN CRISIS. SPECIAL GENERAL MEETING OF THE CHURCH MISSIONARY SOCIETY AT EXETER HALL.* NC. Church Missionary Society House, 1858. 83pp. Pamphlet.
"...deals with the religion question of India...as respects -- Firstly the influence of Government upon the progress of Christianity. Secondly--The need of vernacular education for the masses of India. Thirdly--The views of the committee of the Christian duty of the Government of India...."

100
BL

Anonymous. *THE INDIAN MUTINY. THOUGHTS AND FACTS. Part I. THE PROVIDENCE OF GOD-CONSOLATION-HOPE-PRAYER. Part II. WHO ARE THE SEPOYS? CASTE- MISSION.* London: Seeley, Jackson, and Halliday, 1857. 36pp.
Mentions the story of Ensign Cheek and discusses the causes of the Mutiny, The Christian faith during times of peril, and the sepoys and caste.

101
Ames

Anonymous. *THE MORAL OF THE INDIA DEBATE.* London: William Penny, 1858. 10pp. Pamphlet.
"...how a minister governs India, when he is under no check but responsibility to Parliament, and how Parliamentary responsibility, when really enforced, is likely to work."

102
BL 8022.b.15

Anonymous; *THE MUTINY IN THE BENGAL ARMY.* London: John Chapman. 1857. 30pp. Pamphlet.
This anonymous pamphlet must have been written very soon after the outbreak. The British Library received a copy in late August 1857. The author was apparently a soldier in India and gives some explanation of what the Bengal army

was like prior to the Mutiny. The author proposes that 1) the Mutiny was not a conspiracy 2) religion and caste were the immediate causes 3) the causes of chronic disaffection were the alienation between officers and men, the increase in territory without a corresponding increase in the size of the army, and a vague fear that the government was trying to subvert religion and caste. A rather interesting pamphlet. Not to be confused with"*The Mutiny **OF** the Bengal Army*" by Malleson.

103

Anonymous. *THE NINETIETH LIGHT INFANTRY IN THE INDIAN MUTINY.*
Cited in Jain.

104
Bod

Anonymous. *THE PRESENT CRISIS IN INDIA, REFLECTIONS BY THE AUTHOR OF "North-West Frontier"* by *E.L.* London: John Chapman, 1857. 55pp.
Discusses causes of the Mutiny

105

Anonymous. *THE SEPOY MUTINIES: THEIR ORIGIN AND THEIR CURE.* See William Sinclair entry 966.

106
Bod

Anonymous. *THE STORY OF THE CAWNPORE MISSION.* Westminster: Society for the Propagation of the Gospel in Foreign Parts, 1909. xii & 207pp. Index. Frontis, title page and 38 photos.
One chapter on the Mutiny. States that Azimullah Khan had a son who later worked for the missionaries as a catechist. Azimullah Khan was a close advisor of the Nana.

107
Bod

Anonymous. *THE WHITE CROSS AT DELHI.* NC. NP. ND. 4pp.
Appeal for funds for a cross in memory of those massacred May 1857, at Delhi, in the church yard close to the road to the Cashmere Gate.

108

Anonymous. *WHAT IS HISTORY AND WHAT IS FACT? OR THREE DAYS AT CAWNPORE IN NOVEMBER 1857 UNDER THE COMMAND OF MAJOR GENERAL C. A. WINDHAM. BY A MADRAS STAFF OFFICER.* Madras: NP. 1866, 1868.
Cited in Ladendorf, Jain, and Chaudhuri.

109
RS

Anonymous (An Indian Officer). *LETTERS BRIEFLY DESCRIBING THE PROBABLE CAUSES OF THE INDIAN OUTBREAK: THE NECESSITY OF DEALING WITH IT WITH DISCRIMINATING SEVERITY; THE DANGER OF ATTEMPTING RECONSTRUCTION IN THE ABSENCE OF FULL INFORMATION; AND THE STILL....* Bombay: L M. D'Souza Press, 1858. 46pp.

A series of 16 letters published in the Daily News between October and December 1857 are collected in this work. Includes Causes, Policy, The Indian Press, Annexation of Oude, Caste, Treatment of Mutineers, Religious Intolerance, Objectionable tone of the Times. Condemns the inflammatory press, incompetent military and civil government, and the meddling of the English in the religions of their Indian subjects.

110
IO
ORW1991.a.
1929

Anonymous (Betts, Esther Anne). *REMINISCENCES OF THE INDIAN MUTINY, 1857.* Bangkok: Business Publicity Ltd., 1975. 12 leaves.

Published by the author's great grandson without formal statement of authorship. Esther Anne Betts (nee Nicholson) born 1839. Apparently the author wrote this in 1902 and it was not published until 1975. Her father was the opium agent for the Suleempore Division. She was 17 at the time and lived with her parents, two sisters and brother as well as her aunt and her two girls. This is the story of the family's escape. General John Nicholson, died at Delhi, was her father's nephew. John Nicholson was the third son lost in India. The first died in 1844 in Afghanistan at 18, another was apparently murdered. The youngest brother Charles was at Delhi with John and lost his right arm. He died some years later. Quite scarce.

111
NAM
1858-59(543)
CAD

Anonymous (By One Who Served in the Campaigns). *SORTIE FROM FORT ST. GEORGE. BEING A NARRATIVE OF THE SERVICES OF THE MADRAS TROOPS UNDER MAJOR GENERAL WHITLOCK, K.C.B., DURING THE WAR IN CENTRAL INDIA IN THE YEARS 1858-1859.* Madras: Gantz Bros, 1860. iii & 125 pp. + ix appendix.

The appendix concerns the prize money for Whitlock's force about which so much controversy evolved.

112
BL
Anonymous (By One Who Was There in 1857-58.)
(Erskine, W.C.) *CHAPTER OF THE BENGAL
MUTINY AS SEEN IN CENTRAL INDIA.* Edinburgh
& London: William Blackwood, 1871. 34pp. Folding
map at front.
Reports on Jhansee, Saugor, Nagpore, Jubulpore, etc.

113
BL9056.bbb.26 Anonymous (By a Lady Who Was One of the
Survivors) (Fanny Peile). *THE DELHI MASSACRE.
A REPRODUCTION OF THE NARRATIVE OF THE
DELHI MASSACRE, BY A LADY WHO WAS ONE OF
THE SURVIVORS, AND WHO PUBLISHED IN 1858
AN ACCOUNT OF THIS MANY-DAYED TRAGEDY.*
NC. T. J. King at the Indian News Press, 1870. 41pp.
Paper.
Peile departed Delhi with a Mrs. Patterson and a Mrs.
Wood. This is a similar story to the Wagentreiber escape.
This is a reprint of the original 1858 edition of Mrs. Peile's
book. The two plates are here omitted. See entry 846 for
Fanny Peile.

114
BL 8022.d.27 Anonymous (By an Old Bengalee. A Friend to the
Great National Cause.) *THE MUTINY AND THE
CONGRESS.* NC. Serampore Printing House, 1891.
10pp. Pamphlet.
"The abject superstition and deep ingnorance that had
taken firm hold on the minds of the Bengal Army, put the evil
propensities into play and gave birth to the Mutiny...." "The
Congress on the other hand, owes its origin to a high minded
Englishman, George Thompson."
Both Jain and Ladendorf attribute this work to
Isanachandra Mallika.

115
BL
10803.c.10(6)
Sut
Anonymous (Clyde Memorial Fund Executive
Committee). *MEMORIAL TO LORD CLYDE.* NC.
Harrison & Sons, 1864. 20pp.
Missing at the BL. Includes "Account Proceedings
13th November 1863 for the purpose of introducing the
movement...to commemorate the public services of Field
Marshal Lord Clyde."

116
BL
Anonymous (Erica) *PASSAGES FROM THE LIFE
OF A HERO, W.S.R. HODSON, OR READINGS FOR*

NIGHT SCHOOLS. London: Christian Knowledge Society, ND. c. 1863. 64pp. Paper.
A short biography based on the Reverend George Hodson's book *"Twelve Years of a Soldiers Life."*

117
RS

Anonymous (Frederic Henry Cooper). *THE CRISIS IN THE PUNJAB FROM THE 10TH OF MAY UNTIL THE FALL OF DELHI. BY A PUNJAB EMPLOYE.(sic) For the Benefit of the Lawrence Asylum.* Lahore: Punjabee Press, 1858. v & 154pp+vi page appendix. No plans. Unable to establish the spelling of Frederick or Frederic
See Fred Cooper entry 293. This is a rather scarce edition of the original London edition.

118
BL
10602.c.26(3)

Anonymous (Haldane, Julia). *THE STORY OF OUR ESCAPE FROM DELHI IN 1857.* Agra: S. Brown and Sons, 1888. 26pp.
Julia Haldane was the step-daughter of George Wagentreiber. Wagentreiber was a sub-editor at the Delhi Gazette. It is evident that Haldane's mother was very much in control of their flight. The mother was a daughter of Colonel Skinner and thus spoke the language like a native. The family owed their lives to the mother's quick wits.

119
RS/
BL 9056.a.34
and a.35

Anonymous (Harris, Mrs. G(eorgina) (Maria). *A LADY'S DIARY OF THE SIEGE OF LUCKNOW. Written for the Perusal of Friends at Home.* London: John Murray and Co., 1st ed. April 1858. 2nd July 1858. vii & 208pp. (new ed. vii & 211pp. 1858)
Mrs. Harris was the senior chaplain's wife. Taylor gives her first name, in error, as Katherine. The diary covers the period of May to December 1857. Although Harris was technically the senior chaplain at Lucknow it seems that Polehamton took it upon himself to take the lead since he had served in Lucknow longer than Harris who transferred from Peshawar. James Parker Harris died in 1864 and Mrs. Harris in 1886. The second edition contains an additional letter from the author dated Allahabad, March 7th and concerns the dress the women wore as they left Lucknow.

120

Anonymous (Hindu) *THE MUTINIES AND THE PEOPLE OR STATEMENTS OF NATIVE FIDELITY EXHIBITED DURING THE OUTBREAK OF 1857-58 BY HINDU.*
See: Mukerjee, Sambhu Chandra. (Entry 785).

121
Sut

Anonymous (Huxham, Mrs.). *A PERSONAL NARRATIVE OF THE SIEGE OF LUCKNOW DURING THE INDIAN MUTINY OF 1857.* Eastbourne: Privately printed, ND. c. 1900. 24pp. Blue card covers.
Huxham was the wife of Lt. Huxham of the 48th NI. They had two children, one of which died during the siege of Lucknow. The 48th mutinied on May 30th. They were long known as the most disaffected of the regiments stationed at Lucknow. Mrs. Huxham was born November 1829 and lived at least to 92 years of age. She was previously married to a Colonel Riddell.

122
BL
10057.bbb.36

Anonymous (J.F. Kitchen). *EXTRACTS FROM INDIAN JOURNALS.* Cheltenham: NP. ND. c. 1894. 24 pp. Pamphlet.
Narrative of the outbreak in the Goorgaon District written by J. F. Kitchen. Most of the pamphlet deals with the services of Mr. Ford, the Collector of Goorgaon and with General Van Cortlandt's movements in Rhotuck.

123
RS

Anonymous (Lowrie, John C. DD). *REVOLT OF THE SEPOYS. Reprinted from the Princeton Review.* New York: Edward Jenkins, 1858. 31pp.
Signed by James Lenox of the Lenox Collection at the New York Public Library. A general exposition on the Mutiny causes, conspiracy, etc. One of the earlier Mutiny works published in the United States.

124
BL 8022.c.4

Anonymous (Malleson, George). *MUTINY OF THE BENGAL ARMY. AN HISTORICAL NARRATIVE. BY ONE WHO HAS SERVED UNDER SIR CHARLES NAPIER. Part II The Red Pamphlet.* London: Bosworth & Harrison, 1858.
Malleson mentions there will be a third part. The book is dated India, 10th Dec. 1857. See entry 710.

125
BL

Anonymous (Monckton, Rose); *LETTERS FROM FUTTEHGURH. NC.* Clifton, Shepherd, ND. c. 1858 15pp.
Printed for private circulation. The letters were written by the wife of a Lieutenant in the Bengal Engineers, John Rivaz Monckton. They date from May 16, 1857 to May 23 and are apparently to her father. It is almost certain that immediately

after the letters were written the wife, husband, and child were murdered.

126

Anonymous (Mrs. Irwin). *OUR ESCAPE IN JUNE, 1857.* Dundalk: NP. 1862.
Cited in Hibbert and in *"Angels of Albion"* by Jane Robinson (entry 915) Also Jain.

127
Ames/
BL
8154.bbb.43

Anonymous (The Reverend William Arthur). *THE SEPOY REBELLION.* London: Alexander Heylin, 1857. 63pp. Pamphlet.
A reprint from the London Quarterly Review No. XVII, October 1857. This is a general discussion of India, the causes of disaffection, caste in India, the Brahmins and their influence, the military, etc. "God has punished England for not spreading the Gospel to India."

128
Sut

Anonymous (Tickell, Captain James E.). *RECORD OF THE SEVENTY-THIRD REGIMENT NATIVE INFANTRY AT JULPIGOREE.* Calcutta: P. M. Cranenburgh at the Military Orphan Press, ND. 26pp. Stitched as issued.

129
RS

Anonymous (Vinayak Damodar Savarkar). *THE INDIAN WAR OF INDEPENDENCE OF 1857. BY AN INDIAN NATIONALIST.* NC. NP. ND. 1909 or 1910. xii & 451pp. 1 folding map. Paper.
Originally written in 1907 and translated in 1909. The author relies heavily on the major English sources and lists those consulted for this history from the Indian point of view. Glossary. There are no notices of the publisher, city of publication or date in the book. See other entries for Savarkar, numbers 930 & 931.

130

Anonymous (William Martin). *AT THE FRONT. BEING A REALISTIC RECORD OF A SOLDIERS EXPERIENCE IN THE CRIMEAN WAR AND THE INDIAN MUTINY, BY ONE WHO WAS THERE.* Paisley: Alexander Gardner, 1915. Originally published in 1893. 261pp.
Narrative of the "Doings" of the 93rd Highlanders during the Crimean and Indian Mutiny.
Served with Campbell at Lucknow. Entered under "Front" at the BL.

131
BL
Anonymous (William Tayler). *BRIEF NARRATIVE OF EVENTS CONNECTED WITH THE REMOVAL OF W. TAYLER FROM PATNA.* NC. NP. 1857. 15pp.
Tayler was the Commissioner in Patna and was removed for his conduct which was questionable at best. He had hanged nineteen people without due process and apparently antagonized some of the large landholders in Behar who eventually turned against the British. Tayler's removal stirred a controversy because there were suspicions that it was caused by political motivations and not based entirely on the facts.

132
RS
Anson, Harcourt S. (ed). *WITH H.M. 9TH LANCERS DURING THE INDIAN MUTINY. THE LETTERS OF BREVET- MAJOR OCTAVIUS HENRY S.G. ANSON (1817-1859).* London: W. H. Allen & Co., 1896. 280pp.
O.H.S.G. Anson was the son of Sir George Anson and Frances Hamilton. This book, edited by Octavius' son Harcourt, is composed of letters written by Octavius to his wife. Many are written during the seige of Delhi and during the campagin against Lucknow. Octavius mentions General George Anson, died May 27, 1857 at Karnal. This was the father of Octavius. Also mentioned is Captain Augustus Henry Anson VC, but the relationship is not clear. Quite descriptive of daily life and combat during the Mutiny.

133
Bod
Archer, J.L. *THE INDIAN MUTINIES ACCOUNTED FOR: BEING AN ESSAY ON THE SUBJECT.* London: NP. 1857. 15pp. Pamphlet.
The author supplies his reasons for the advent of the Mutiny.

134
Jain
Ashraf, K.M. *MUSLIM REVIVALISTS AND THE REVOLT OF 1857.* New Delhi: People's Publishing House, 1957.

135
Ind Inst
Ashraf, Mujeeb. *MUSLIM ATTITUDE TOWARDS BRITISH RULE AND WESTERN CULTURE IN INDIA IN THE FIRST HALF OF THE NINETEENTH CENTURY.* Delhi: Idarah-I-adabiyat-I-Delhi, 1982. x & 326 pp. Index.
Contains a good chapter illustrating various historic views of the Mutiny. The book as a whole, is good background in Muslim thought prior to the Mutiny.

136
IO

Atkinson, Captain George Francklin. *THE CAMPAIGN IN INDIA 1857-58. FROM DRAWINGS MADE DURING THAT EVENTFUL PERIOD OF THE GREAT MUTINY, BY GEORGE FRANCKLIN ATKINSON, CAPTAIN, BENGAL ENGINEERS. ILLUSTRATING THE MILITARY OPERATIONS BEFORE DELHI AND ITS NEIGHBOURHOOD. WITH DESCRIPTIVE LETTER-PRESS.* London: Day & Son, January 1, 1859. Red Cloth blind with gold vignette. Folio.

26 full page lithos, including title page, with 19 pages text.

137
BL

Aylen, Rev. W. H. *THE SOLDIER AND THE SAINT OR TWO HEROES IN ONE. A Christian Lecture in Memory of General Havelock.* London: Judd & Glass, 1858. 12pp.

The first part of this work concerns the life of Havelock. Aylen then goes on to consider the moral of Havelock's life.

138
BL

Badger, Rev. George Percey. *GOVERNMENT IN ITS RELATIONS WITH EDUCATION AND CHRISTIANITY IN INDIA.* London: Smith, Elder, 1858. 43pp. Pamphlet.

Proposes steps the government should take in the fields of religion and education.

139

Baillie, Rev. John. *GOD'S AVENGER: OR ENGLANDS PRESENT DUTY IN INDIA.* London: Seeley, Jackson and Halliday, 1857. 23pp.

A Fast Day sermon. It is a public and religious duty to wreak vengence upon the mutineers in India.

140
Sut

Baird, J.G. ed. *PRIVATE LETTERS OF THE MARQUESS OF DALHOUSIE.* London: NP. 1911. 448pp. 11 plates.

These are letters that Dalhousie wrote to his oldest friend, Sir George Couper. In these letters he is able to give vent to his feelings that he may otherwise not have made known. Much on Oude.

141
RS

Baldwin, Reverend J.R. *INDIAN GUP. Untold Stories of the Indian Mutiny.* London: Neville Beeman, ND. c. 1890. 354pp.

Gup means gossip. Baldwin served in Lucknow in 1858 and offers numerous stories of the period, none having much to do with the Mutiny. He does mention that Kavanagh (entries 588, 589, & 590) was the most conceited person he ever knew.

142
RS

Ball, Charles. *THE HISTORY OF THE INDIAN MUTINY GIVING A DETAILED ACCOUNT OF THE SEPOY INSURRECTION IN INDIA AND A CONCISE HISTORY OF THE GREAT MILITARY EVENTS WHICH HAVE TENDED TO CONSOLIDATE THE BRITISH EMPIRE IN HINDOSTAN.* London: London Printing and Publishing Co., ND. Probably late 1859. Two volumes.

This is probably the largest work on the Mutiny as far as text is concerned. It is an immense source of original materials. For an excellent discussion of the merits of the work see S. B. Chaudhuri *"English Historical Writings on the Indian Mutiny 1857- 1859."* (Entry 269.)

143
Taylor

Banerjee, Brojendra Nath. *THE LAST DAY'S OF NANA SAHIB.* Indian Historical Records Proceedings. 1929.

144
IO

Barat, Amiya. *THE BENGAL NATIVE INFANTRY: ITS ORGANIZATION AND DISCIPLINE 1796-1852.* Calcutta: Firma K.L. Mukhopadhyay, 1962. xii & 341pp. 2 folding maps and 4 illus.

Presented as a doctorate thesis. This is an explanation of why the Bengal Army mutinied by looking back at how it was created and the process whereby it operated.

145
RS

Barker, General George Digby. *LETTERS FROM PERSIA AND INDIA 1857-1859.* London: G. Bell and Sons, 1915. 4 plates, 1 map. 183pp.

Barker arrived in India (Bombay) in 1853 at the age 20. Barker served in Persia and then under Havelock at the march to Cawnpore, the relief and defence of Lucknow, the defence of Alum Bagh and the campaign in Rohilcund.

146
IO

Barnes, George Carnac. *LETTERS FROM DELHI, 1857.* NC. NP. ND. 19pp. Two maps. Pamphlet.

These are actually letters written to Barnes, one of the Commissioners of the Punjab. The letters are those of Barnard, Greathed, Hodson, and Lawrence. All of the correspondence was written during the summer of 1857.

147
RS
Barrier, N. Gerald. *PUNJAB HISTORY IN PRINTED BRITISH DOCUMENTS. A Bibliographic Guide to Parliamentary Papers and Select, Nonserial Publications, 1843-1947.* Columbia, MO: University of Missouri Press, 1969. 108pp.
An annotated introduction to the maze of official publications of the Punjab and the parliamentary papers related to the Punjab. There is a valuable section on the historiography of the publications of the Punjab.

148
IO
Bartarya, Dr. S.C. *THE INDIAN NATIONALIST MOVEMENT.* Allahabad: Indian Press Publications, 1958. xxi & 409pp.
A very short section touches on the Mutiny.

149
RS
Barter, Richard. *THE SIEGE OF DELHI - MUTINY MEMORIES OF AN OLD OFFICER.* London: Folio Society, 1984. 130pp. 28 illus. Boxed.
Richard Barter was adjutant of the Gordon Highlanders at the outbreak of the Mutiny. He wrote his memoirs in 1869 and they were first published in this Folio Society edition.

150
RS
Barthorp, Michael and Douglas Anderson. *THE BRITISH TROOPS IN THE INDIAN MUTINY 1857-59.* London: Osprey Military, 1994. 48pp. Illus. Paper.
This is one of the Men-At-Arms Series and is useful for the information on the uniforms and weapons of both the British and the Mutineers. Contains a series of color plates showing the dress of the various parties involved.

151
RS/BL
Bartlett, D.W. *THE HEROES OF THE INDIAN REBELLION.* Columbus, Ohio: Follett, Foster & Co, 1859. 456pp. 3 plates.
Sketches and abridgements from several mutiny titles; Hodson, Polehampton, Mowbray Thompson, and others.

152
Bartrum, Mrs. Katherine Mary. *CASUAL LETTERS.* London: NP, 1929.
Vol V *India in 1857.* Cited by Jain. Unable to locate.

153
RS/BL   **Bartrum, Mrs. Robert Henry (d. 1866).** *A WIDOWS REMINISCENCES OF THE SIEGE OF LUCKNOW.* London: James Nesbit & Co., 1858. viii & 102pp.
One of the tragic stories of the siege. Katherine Bartrum was at Gonda with her husband, Robert, who was the station doctor. Robert remained at Gonda and Katherine was sent to Lucknow along with their 15 month old son, Bobbie. There she endured the siege and looked forward to being reunited with her husband. Havelock relieved the Residency on September 25-26 and Mrs. Bartrum discovered that her husband had been killed while in the city with the relief force. Her son Bobbie died in Calcutta. Katherine remarried in England and had three more children, Katherine, Bradshaw, and Jane. She died in 1866 from tuberculosis. Katherine Bartrum was 23 years old at the time of the Mutiny.

154
MNUA   **Basu, Baman Das.** *RISE OF CHRISTIAN POWER IN INDIA. 1750-1860.* Calcutta: R. Chatterjee, 1931. 1011pp. 2nd ed.
Indicts British cruelty in one chapter. (Ladendorf)

155
RS   **Battye, Evelyn Desiree.** *THE FIGHTING TEN.* London: British Association For Cemeteries in South Asia, 1984. 240pp.
A history of the ten brothers of the Battye family taken from family records recently discovered. Evelyn Battye was the wife of Stuart Battye, grandson of one of the ten brothers.
Approximately one hundred pages concern the brothers and the Mutiny.

156
BL/RAI   **Bayley, John Arthur.** *REMINISCENCES OF SCHOOL AND ARMY LIFE 1839 TO 1859.* London: Privately Printed, April 1875. vii & 206pp.
Bayley went to India as a lieutenant of the 52nd. See other titles. This work was originally intended for his nephews, nieces and such of his friends as are interested. Bayley served under Nicholson. He marched from Amritsar to Sealkote and on to Delhi and the Kashmir Gate. He led the third assault column on Delhi and was wounded at the Kashmir Gate.

157
RS   **Bayley, Major John Arthur.** *BEGINNING OF THE INDIAN MUTINY. Found within the OXFORDSHIRE LIGHT INFANTRY CHRONICLE by Lt. Col Mockler-Ferryman. Vol. XIV.* London: Eyre

& Spottiswoode, 1905. Frontis, AEG, 13 plates and photos. 301pp.
Consists of 20 pages describing Bayley's experiences. He was stationed at Sealkote and was later under the command of Nicholson. He states that Nicholson had rough manners and a "scarcely concealed contempt for European troops and their officers."

158
Bod/RS

Bayley, Major John Arthur. *THE ASSAULT OF DELHI. A vindication of H M 52nd Light Infantry and the 3rd Column of Assault from the Aspersions of Sir John Kaye in the 3rd volume of his "History of the Sepoy War."* London: William Ridgeway, 1876. 31pp. Plan of Delhi. Paper pamphlet.
Bayley was a major in the 52nd and commanded the storming party of the 3rd column. Here he refutes many comments found in Sir John Kaye's narrative of the assault in his *"History of the Sepoy War."*

159
RS

Bayly, C.A. and D.H.A. Kolff.(eds.). *TWO COLONIAL EMPIRES. Comparative Essays on the History of India and Indonesia in the Nineteenth Century.* Dordrecht, Netherlands: Kluwer Academic (USA), Martinus Nijhoff, 1986. 237pp.
This is volume six in the Comparative Studies in Overseas History, publications of the Leiden Centre for the History of European Expansion. There is an excellent essay by C.A. Bayly titled, *"Two Colonial Revolts: The Java War, 1825-1830, and the Indian "Mutiny" of 1857-59.* Bayly discusses some of the theories on the causes of the Mutiny, as well as numerous other aspects of the Mutiny.

160

Beato, Felice. *PHOTOGRAPHY.*
Felice Beato was a very early commercial photographer. He worked in China, Egypt, Japan, and India among other locales. He produced thousands of photographs and eventually some of these photos were collected by individuals and made into albums. Among the albums dealing with the Mutiny there is a copy at the Royal Artillery Arsenal at Woolwich with commentary by Colonel F. Maude VC. There are two albums in Sydney, Australia mentioned in the Masselos and Gupta book, *"Beato's Delhi in 1857, 1997"* (entry 730), there is the Younghusband Collection at the India Office and doubtless others. These are all privately produced albums.

161
RAI/IO   **Becher, Augusta. Edited by H.G. Rawlinson.**
PERSONAL REMINISCENCES IN INDIA 1830-1888.
London: Constable, 1930. xviii & 230pp. Frontis.
Approximately 20pp. on the Mutiny. Mrs. Becher was
with General Anson and on the outbreak made her way
to Bombay and thence to England. Listed as Becker in
Ladendorf.

162
BL   **Beck, Theodore of Aligarh.** *REVIEWS ON*
10604.e.17(2)   *"SYED AHMED KHAN'S LIFE AND WORKS" by*
Lieutenant-Colonel G. F. I. Graham.... Being extracts from
English and Anglo-Indian newspapers. (Edited by T. Beck).
Aligarh: Aligarh Institute Press, 1886. 3pp. + 48pp.
Yellow paper covers.
Book reviews from various newspapers. Sayed Ahmed
Khan remained loyal to the British during the Mutiny. At
the time of the Mutiny he was a judge in Bijnore. He
subsequently rose to prominence.

163
RS   **Beg, M.A.** *THE GUIDE TO LUCKNOW,*
CONTAINING POPULAR PLACES AND BUILDINGS
WORTHY OF A VISIT WITH HISTORICAL NOTES
ON MUTINY OF 1857. Lucknow: The Royal Printing
Press, 28th Feb, 1911. 6th ed. 108pp. With one folding
map.
The book consists of selections and compilations from
different guide books and Indian histories of the time. It
discusses the major points of interest from the Mutiny.

164
Bod   **Bell, Thomas Evans.** *A LETTER TO H. M. DURAND*
ESQ. C.S.I. COMMENTING ON CERTAIN
STATEMENTS IN HIS WORKS: "Central India in
1857" and "Life of Sir H. M. Durand." London: Chatto
and Windus, 1884. 64pp.
Durand accused Holkar of being in league with the
rebels. Bell has attacked Durand as an incompetent and
tries to secure for Holkar his rightful reward due him by the
government. Bell accused the government of a cover up to
save the good name of Durand and the service. This is Sir
Henry Marion Durand not to be confused with Sir Henry
Mortimer Durand, of Durand Line fame. Sir Henry Marion
married Emily the widow of Reverend H.S. Polehampton of
Lucknow.

165
IO

Bell, Thomas Evans. *HOLKAR'S APPEAL: THE OFFICE OF THE EMPIRE. Papers Relating to his Conduct During The Mutiny.* London: Privately Printed, 1881. 97pp. Index.

Bell was the "Literary and Political Executor" of John Dickinson, see "*Last Counsels of an Unknown Counsellor*" (entry 343). This is his last private appeal to clear Maharajah Holkar of any wrong doing during the "First burst of the Mutiny." He implies he will go public if the government does not rectify the situation. Colonel Durand accused Holkar of holding back support for the British.

166
IO

Bell, Thomas Evans. *THE ENGLISH IN INDIA. Letters from Nagpore Written in 1857-58.* London: John Chapman, 1859. 202pp.

Originally appeared in the "Leader" and "Daily News" newspapers. Covers: The Indian Army, the Insurrection of 1857, Policy of Annexation, Social Effects of Annexation, British Prestige, Indian Civil Service, The Oude Land Settlement, How India Must Be Governed, etc. Bell was the assistant to the Governor General's agent at Nagpore.

167
BL

Benson, A. C. (ed.). *THE LETTERS OF QUEEN VICTORIA 1837-1861.* London: John Murray, 1907 and other editions. Vol. I. 1837-1843 xciii & 641pp. Vol. II. 1844-1853 xiv & 595pp. Vol. III. ix & 660pp.

Volume 3 contains a number of letters touching on Delhi, Cawnpore, and Lucknow.

168
BL

Bernays, Leopold John. *HAVELOCK, THE GOOD SOLDIER. A Sermon Preached in the Parish Church of Great Stanmore on Sunday January 17, 1858.* London: Sampson, Low, Son & Co. 1858. 20pp. Pamphlet.

Includes a brief biography of Havelock.

169
BL
9056.bbb.26

Berncastle, Julius MD. *THE REVOLT OF THE BENGAL SEPOYS.* Sydney: Australia, J. R. Clarke, 1857. 2nd ed. 31pp.

Printed version of a lecture Dr. Berncastle delivered. He discusses the history of the British in India and causes of the Mutiny together with the grievances of Oude and the Nana. Gives extracts from General Charles Napier regarding the Indian army and its faults.

170
Ames

Bhalla, Alok & Sudhir Chandra ed. *INDIAN RESPONSES TO COLONIALISM IN THE 19TH CENTURY.* New Delhi: Sterling Publishing, 1993. 10 & 261pp. Bibliography.
 Chapter ten "The Metaphysics of Militant Nationalism" by Surjit Hans is a good discussion of V.D.Savarkar's book *"The Indian War of Independence of 1857"* (entries numbered 129, 930, 931).

171

Bhalla, Piyarelal ed. *1857 CENTENARY SOUVENIR.* Delhi: P. L. Bhalla, 1957. 230pp.
 Cited in Ladendorf.

172
RS

Bhargava, K. D. and S. N. Prasad. *NATIONAL ARCHIVES OF INDIA: Descriptive List of the Mutiny Papers in the National Archives Of India, Bhopal,* 4 vols. 1960, 1963, 1971, 1973. v & 67pp; v & 92pp; iv & 132pp; iv & 183pp.
 Vol. I May 16, 1857 to April 9, 1859. Communications between the Begam and the officers of Bhopal. Vol. II July 6, 1857 to June 27, 1858. Primarily concerns the rebellions at Sehore and Berasia. Vol. III July 18, 1857 to August 17, 1861. Primarily concerns the mutinous sepoys of the Bhopal Contingent at Sehore and Berasia.; Vol. IV January 13, 1857 to July 6, 1859. The Begam of Bhopal remained loyal to the British.

173
Ames/RS

Bhargava, Moti Lal. *SAGA OF 1857: SUCCESS AND FAILURES.* New Delhi: Reliance Publishing, 1992. xvi & 202pp. Illus. Index and Bibliography.
 Dr. Moti Lal Bhargava has done extensive research on the Mutiny and this work attempts to offer a more balanced account of the struggle. Bhargava discusses the causes of the Mutiny and devotes two chapters to Mangal Pande and other leading Indian participants. The last chapter discusses the atrocities and punishment meted out to the Indians. In addition there is a chapter on the historiography of the Mutiny.

174
RS

Bhargava, Moti Lal. *ARCHITECTS OF INDIAN FREEDOM STRUGGLE.* New Delhi: Deep & Deep, 1981. 268pp. Bibliography and index.
 Offers biographies of Nana Sahib, Azimoolah Khan, Rao Sahib, Tatya Tope, Firuz Shah, Bhai Maharaj Sing, and Rana Benee Madho Bux.

Bhargave, who edited the "*Source Material on the Freedom Movement in Uttar Pradesh*" uses a number of primary sources in this work.

175

Bhatnagar, O.P. (ed.). *PRIVATE CORRESPONDENCE OF J.W. SHERER, COLLECTOR OF FATEHPUR (19 MAY TO 28 JULY 1857).* Allahabad: 1968.
Cited in Taylor.

176
Jain

Bhojwani, Rao Bahadur Alumal Trikamdas (Trans.). *A FORGOTTEN CHAPTER OF INDIAN HISTORY AS DESCRIBED IN THE MEMOIRS OF SETH NAOMAL HOTCHAND C.S.I. OF KARACHI, 1804-1878.* NC. NP. 1915.
A record of Naomal's services to the British during the Mutiny of 1857-58.

177
RS

Bird, James. *GUILTY MEN OF 1857: Failure of England's Great Mission in India. Three Anonymous Discourses.* Delhi: Indian Bibliographies Bureau, 1985. First published 1879. 72pp. With index.
This work consists of three discourses which squarely lay the blame on the British themselves for their problems in India. They have brought their problems upon themselves because they have not propagatged the Christian faith in India as was their holy mission.
The publisher gives the author as W.J. Shepherd which is not correct. The book is also attributed to James Bird but this is not conclusive.

178
Bod

Bird, Robert Wilberforce. *THE INDIAN MUTINY. Two Lectures Delivered at the Southampton Athenaeum, February 16 and March 30, 1858.* London: Bosworth & Harrison, 1858. 37pp.
Lecture I: The Necessity of India as A Possession to Great Britain. The Causes of the Mutiny.
Lecture II: India and Its Capabilities-The Mutiny and Our Responsibilities.

179
Sut

Blake, Mrs. C. *NARRATIVE OF AN ESCAPE FROM GWALIOR.* (Agra), No imprint. (1857) 8 pp.
Mrs. Blake was the widow of Major Blake, commanding officer of the 2nd NI who was shot at the outset of the Mutiny. This work was "hastily written by request of the

Governor General's Agent at Agra to record how we got away
and the feeling of the country." This by notes in Mrs. Blake's
hand.

180
IO

Blunt, E.A.H. *LIST OF INSCRIPTIONS ON
CHRISTIAN TOMBS AND TABLETS OF
HISTORICAL INTEREST IN THE UNITED
PROVINCES OF AGRA AND OUDE.* Allahabad: Supt.
Government Press, United Provinces, 1911. 4 + 4 + 261
+ (1) + xviii. Frontis.
Gives inscription, location and, when available, a short
biography of the deceased.

181
Bod

Boileau, Colonel A Henry E. *MEMORANDUM
FOR REORGANISING THE INDIAN ARMY. With
explanatory remarks.*London: Smith Elder & Co., 1858.
39pp.

182
RS

Bonham, Colonel John. *OUDE IN 1857, SOME
MEMORIES OF THE INDIAN MUTINY.* London:
Williams & Norgate, 1928. 95pp.
Written by the last surviving officer of the Lucknow siege.
Bonham died in 1928 at age 93.
Bonham was stationed a Secrora originally. Although
Ladendorf does not accept Bonham as a useful text George
Forrest cites him a number of times in his "*History of the
Indian Mutiny.*"

183
RS

Bora, Mahendra. *1857 IN ASSSAM.* Gauhati, Assam:
Lawyer's Book Stall, 1957. 50pp.
Bora attempts to fill the gap left by both Indian and
English historians regarding the role of Assam during the
Mutiny. This book is only a very short survey of the events.

184

Bost, Isabella. *INCIDENTS IN THE LIFE OF.*
Glasgow: McNaughtan & Sinclair, 1913.
Cited in Collier, and in "*Angels of Albion*" (entry 915).

185
IO

Bourchier, Colonel George. *EIGHT MONTHS
CAMPAIGN AGAINST THE BENGAL SEPOY ARMY
DURING THE MUTINY OF 1857.* London: Smith,
Elder & Co., 1858. xii & 202pp. 16pp adverts. 4
folding maps and 3 other plans and 2 vignettes.
Bourchier marched with the Punjab Moveable Column.

He fought at Delhi, marched with Greathed to Agra and on to Cawnpore. The details from the siege of Delhi were taken from Norman's account of the siege. The rising at Cawnpore was written with information supplied by J.W. Sherer. (See "*Dailey Life During the Indian Mutiny*" entry 958)

186

Boyle, Major C.A. *THE HISTORY OF PROBYN'S HORSE. Fifth King Edward's Own Lancers.* Aldershot: NP. 1929. xvi, 98pp. 9 folding maps and 2 plates. Fine colored badge of the regiment on the cover.

187
Bod

Brackenbury, General Sir H. *SOME MEMORIES OF MY SPARE TIME.* Edinburgh: William Blackwood, 1909. xiv & 362pp. With index & frontis. Gilt vignette of sword and scabbard.
Short section on Brackenbury's Mutiny service. Not an important item.

188
IO/Ind Inst

Bradley-Birt, F.B. *CHOTA NAGPORE: A LITTLE-KNOWN PROVINCE OF THE EMPIRE.* London: Smith, Elder, 1903. xiv & 310pp. 43 illus. & folding map. Red cloth, gilt vignette & index.
25 pages on the Mutiny. 2nd edition Smith, Elder. 42 illus. With map. xviii & 327pp. Index. 24 pages on the Mutiny.

189
RS

Brantlinger, Patrick. *RULE OF DARKNESS: British Literature and Imperialism, 1830-1914.* Ithaca & London: Cornell University Press, 1988. xi & 309pp. Index and extensive notes.
Includes an interesting chapter on Mutiny literature, "The Well at Cawnpore: Literary Representations of the Indian Mutiny of 1857." This deals for the most part with fictional books on the Mutiny but it is quite well done.

190
RS

Brasyer, Jeremiah. *THE MEMOIRS OF JEREMIAH BRASYER: WHO, COMMENCING HIS SERVICE AS A PRIVATE SOLDIER ROSE TO THE RANK OF COLONEL AND COMPANION OF THE MOST HONOURABLE ORDER OF THE BATH.* London: NP. 1892. 70pp & 3 portraits. Also Bombay: Thacker and Co. 1892, 69pp and 2 pages of appendix of casualty return of the Ferozepore Regiment in the Mutiny. No portraits.

Brasyer was besieged in the Allahabad Fort. He was relieved and then marched with Renaud in the advance column to Cawnpore. He served with Havelock in the first relief of Lucknow. Upon the evacuation of Lucknow he remained at the Alumbagh and later served under Hope Grant.

191
BL

Briggs, Lt Gen John. *A LETTER ON THE INDIAN ARMY, ADDRESSED TO THE MOST NOBLE THE MARQUESS OF TWEEDDALE. May, 1842 with Notes Applicable to the Present Time.* London: Harrison & W.H. Allen, 1857. 32pp. Pamphlet.

Briggs was writing to Tweeddale with advice prior to Tweeddale proceeding to Madras as Governor and C in C. The letter shows up the problems which eventually came to the fore during the Mutiny.

192
Ames

Briggs, Lt Gen John (1785-1875). *A LETTER ADDRESSED TO THE RIGHT HONORABLE LORD STANLEY, SECRETARY OF STATE FOR INDIA. NO. II.* London: Cox and Wyman, 1859. 23pp. Pamphlet.

A look at the causes of the Mutiny.

193
RS

Brock, Reverend William. *A BIOGRAPHICAL SKETCH OF SIR H. HAVELOCK.* London: James Nisbet, 1858. 304pp. 2 folding maps.

There were numerous editions of this book. By 1858 it was in its 8th edition. In 1872 there was a 15th edition and in 1874 a 16th edition with 302pp. The 1858 edition had 288pp and a 6th edition in 1858 was xii & 302pp.

194
IO

Broehl, Wayne G. Jr. *CONTENT ANALYSIS IN PSYCHOHISTORY: A STUDY OF THREE LIEUTS. IN THE INDIAN MUTINY.* NC. Amos Tuck School of Business. 1981.

This is a reprint from the Journal of Psychohistory. Vol. 8, 1981.

195
RS

Broehl, Wayne G. Jr *CRISIS OF THE RAJ: The Revolt of 1857 through British Lieutenants' Eyes.* Hanover and London: University Press of New England, 1986. viii & 347pp. Bibliography and index. 24 illus. and 2 maps.

The letters of four British lieutenants are used to tell the story of the Mutiny. These letters were all written during the Mutiny. The authors are Frederick Roberts, George Cracklow,

Arthur Lang, and Thomas Watson. A computer program was used for content analysis of the letters and psychological profiles developed for the four authors.

196
BL

Browne, General Sir Sam. *JOURNAL OF THE LATE GENERAL SIR SAM BROWNE FROM 1840-1878.* Edinburgh: William Blackwood, 1937. 80pp. Blue cloth.
   Frontispiece portrait. About 30 pages concern the Mutiny. General Browne was awarded the VC at Seerpoorah during the Mutiny.

197
BL
09004.cc.2(2)

Browne, John. *CAWNPORE AND THE NANA OF BITHOOR.* Cawnpore: Victoria Press, 1890. 27pp. Paper.
   A history of Cawnpore during the Mutiny. Discusses the massacre, the well, and other subjects.

198

Browne, John. *LUCKNOW AND ITS MEMORIALS OF THE MUTINY.* Agra: Ornamental Job Press, 1886. iv & 48pp.
   Cited in Ladendorf. Unable to locate.

199
Bod

Buchanan, C. *CHRISTIAN RESEARCHES IN INDIA. With the Rise, Suspension, and Probable Future of England's Rule as a Christian Power in India.* London: G. Routledge & Co., 1858. 265pp.
   Edited by Rev. W. H. Foy. Frontis and 2 Engravings. Little information on the Mutiny.

200
RS

Buckland, C. E. *BENGAL UNDER THE LIEUTENANT GOVERNORS. Being a Narrative of the Principal Events and Public Measures During Their Period of Office. 1854-1898.* New Delhi: Deep Publications, 1976. 2 vols. xviii & 1130pp. 14 Illus. Index
   A chapter and appendix on the Mutiny. Covers Sir Frederick Halliday and events during the Mutiny. Includes a chronology of the case of Mr. W. Tayler of Patna.

201
IO

Buckler, F. W. *THE POLITICAL THEORY OF THE INDIAN MUTINY.* London: NP. 1922. 50pp.
   Reprinted from "Transactions of the Royal Historical Society" 4th series, Vol. V, pages 71-100. Extracts from this work can also be found in Embree: "*1857 In India*" (entry

380). Buckler feels the East India Co. derived its authority from the Firman's issued from the throne of the Mughal Emperor, not from the King or the Parliament in England.

202
Ames

Burke, S.M. & Salim al-Din Quraishi. *BAHADUR SHAH: THE LAST MOGHUL EMPEROR OF INDIA.* Lahore: Sang-e-Meel Publications, 1995. 231pp. Index. 4 Plates. Notes and references.
A scholarly biography.

203
RS

Burne, Colonel O(wen) T(udor)). *RECORD OF SERVICE OF FIELD MARSHAL LORD STRATHNAIRN, GCB, GCSI, OF STRATHNAIRN AND JHANSI, 1820-1870.* Edinburgh: HMSO, ND. c. 1885. iii & 150pp. Red cloth, folio.
Rose started his military career in Ireland closing illegal stills. During the Mutiny he led the Central Indian Field Force. About 30 pages on the Central India Field Force. Burne served as the military secretary to Sir Hugh Rose during the Mutiny.

204
RS

Burne, Major General Sir Owen Tudor. *RULERS OF INDIA. Clyde and Strathnairn.* Oxford: Oxford Press, 1891. 194pp. Folding map and two portraits. Index.
Covers the northern operations under Campbell to the reconquest of Oude and the southern operations under Rose to the recapture of Gwalior. A very popular book when published, selling about four thousand copies in a few weeks.

205
RS

Burne, Major General Sir Owen Tudor. *MEMORIES 1857-1872.* London: Edward Arnold, 1907. x & 343pp. Frontis and 16 plates with index.
Burne arrived in Calcutta in November 1857. He joined Campbell at Lucknow on March 4, 1858. The work contains little on the Mutiny.

206
Ames

Burnes, James. *SPEECH ON THE INDIA QUESTION, DELIVERED AT THE COURT OF PROPRIETORS OF INDIAN STOCK ON 27TH JANUARY 1858.* London: John Edward Taylor, 1858. 14pp. Pamphlet.
This is a reprint from the Dailey News. James Burnes is the brother of Sir Alexander Burnes and Charles Burnes, of Kabul fame. James' son was at Lucknow but it is not clear in

what capacity. Burnes speaks against the plan of putting India under Parliamentary control.

207
IO/RS
Burton, James. *SELECTIONS FROM OFFICIAL RECORDS OF THE CRIMINAL DEPARTMENT OF THE RAJPOOTANA STATES AND NORTH WESTERN PROVINCES, OF THE MURDER OF EUROPEANS BY MUTINEERS DURING THE MUTINY OF 1857, IN WHICH APPREHENSIONS OF MURDERERS HAVE BEEN MADE.* Allahabad: G.A. Savielle, 1874. 37pp. Full leather.

James Burton was Superintendent, Oudh Police, and the son of Major Charles Burton, who, along with two other sons, was murdered by mutineers. Contains the case of Salabut Khan, accused of murdering the father and brothers of James.

208
Burton, Major R. G. *THE REVOLT IN CENTRAL INDIA, 1857-1859.* (See **Government of India**. *Army Intelligence.* Entry 451)

209
BL
Butler, Lewis William George and Stewart Hare. *ANNALS OF THE KINGS ROYAL RIFLE CORPS.* London: John Murray, 1913-1932.

Volume three covers the 60th, The Kings Royal Rifle Corps. This regiment bears more honors than any other regiment.

210
RS
Butler, Rev. William D.D. *THE LAND OF THE VEDA BEING PERSONAL REMINISCENCES OF INDIA, ITS PEOPLE, CASTES, THUGS, AND FAKIRS...TOGETHER WITH INCIDENTS OF THE GREAT SEPOY REBELLION.* New York: Hunt and Eaton, also Cincinnati: Cranston and Curtis, 1895. New edition 575pp. Maroon cloth with vignette.

Originally published in 1871 from notes taken during the Mutiny. Five chapters are devoted to the Mutiny. Butler was a missionary at Shajehanpore not far from Bareilly, during the Mutiny. There was also an edition of 1872 published in New York by Carlton and Hanahan at 557pp.

211
Butler, Spencer Harcourt. *OUDH POLICY CONSIDERED HISTORICALLY.* Allahabad: NP. 1896.
Cited in Taylor.

212
IO/RS   **Buxton, Charles.** *THE QUESTIONS RAISED BY*
THE MUTINY. London: John Parker, 1857.
In "Cambridge Essays." Contributed by members of the
University. Offers causes and remedies.

213
          By A Bombay Officer. *A FEW REMARKS ON*
THE BENGAL ARMY AND FURLOUGH
REGULATIONS....
See Brig. Gen. John Jacob, entry 564.

214
Ames/   **By A Wounded Officer (Gibney, Robert D.).** *MY*
BL   *ESCAPE FROM THE MUTINEERS IN OUDH.*
12632.d.19 London: Richard Bentley, 1858. 2 volumes, 371pp.
With frontis and 360pp.
          This work appears to be fiction. From a reading of the
text it would appear the author was Philip Villars.

215
Bod/RS   **By One Who was Present.** *THE CAWNPORE*
AFFAIR ON THE 26TH, 27TH AND 28TH OF
NOVEMBER 1857 UNDER MAJOR-GENERAL
WINDHAM C.B. FULLY EXPLAINED BY ONE
WHO WAS PRESENT, WITH AN INTRODUCTION.
London: W. Jeffs, Foreign Bookseller, 1859. 31pp. Red
cloth blind. AEG.
          The Cawnpore affair dealt with the question of whether
Windham disobeyed orders when he attacked the Gwalior
Contingent on the 26th of November. Campbell's orders
to Windham were not entirely clear. This work refutes the
accusations that Windham's problems arose because of lack of
dicipline and spirit on the part of his troops.

216
BL 9056.a.13 **By One of the Besieged Party. (Boyle, Richard Vicars);**
BRIEF NARRATIVE OF THE DEFENCE OF THE
GARRISON BY ONE OF THE BESIEGED PARTY.
TO ACCOMPANY MR. W. TAYLER'S PICTURE
OF THE ATTACK. London, Calcutta, Allahabad and
Bombay: W. Thacker, 1858. 12mo. 29pp. Red paper.
AEG
          This book accompanied Mr. W. Tayler's "Picture of
the Attack." It describes the attack and defense of Arrah
House by a small group of British. This was one of the most
celebrated events during the Mutiny. The book accompanied
the 24 x 18 inch chromo-lithograph of the "Defense of Arrah

House." Boyle was the district engineer for the railway company.

217
Bod/
BL 8023.d.3

By a Barrister. *LAY THOUGHTS ON THE INDIAN MUTINY.* London: H. Sweet, 1858. 2nd ed. 41pp. Pamphlet.
Mainly concerned with religion and the introduction of religion into India from England.

218
BL

By a Civilian. *A REVIEW OF COL. ADYE'S DEFENSE OF GENERAL WINDHAM. BY A CIVILIAN.* London: Simpkin, Marshall, 1858. 12pp.
Admits Windham had a difficult task at Cawnpore but states that he was not equal to the task and it was his incompetent actions that caused so much difficulty.

219
BL

By a Former Editor of the Delhi Gazette. *THE INDIAN MUTINY TO THE EVACUATION OF LUCKNOW. TO WHICH IS ADDED A NARRATIVE OF THE DEFENSE OF LUCKNOW AND A MEMOIR OF GENERAL HAVELOCK.* London: George Routledge, 1858. 2nd ed. 198pp. Yellow pictorial covers.
Much expanded over the 1st edition, "*The Indian Mutiny to the Fall of Delhi.*" See third edition, "*The Indian Mutiny to the Recapture of Lucknow.*"

220
BL

By a Former Editor of the Delhi Gazette. *THE INDIAN MUTINY TO THE FALL OF DELHI. By a former editor of the Delhi Gazette.* London: G. Routledge & Co., 1857. 1st edition. viii & 175pp. Yellow pictorial cover. Paperback.
General narrative of events. Continues on in a 2nd and 3rd edition.

221
RS

By a Former Editor of the Delhi Gazette. *THE INDIAN MUTINY, TO THE RECAPTURE OF LUCKNOW. TO WHICH IS ADDED, A NARRATIVE OF THE DEFENCE OF THE RESIDENCY, AND A MEMOIR OF GENERAL HAVELOCK. Compiled by a former editor of the Delhi Gazette.* London: G. Routledge & Co., 1858. 3rd ed. 266pp.
Not much new material as compared to the 2nd edition.

The second edition is titled, "*The Indian Mutiny, to the Evacuation of Lucknow.*"

222
BL
8023.c.86(4)

By a Hindu (Thought to be Kishori Chand Mitra). *THE MUTINIES, THE GOVERNMENT AND THE PEOPLE. By a Hindu.* Calcutta: D'Rozario & Co. Printers, 1858. 42pp.
States the Mutiny was a military insurrection, calls for stern but discriminating justice. Mitra discusses a petition to parliament to remove the E.I.C., and Canning, and put India directly under the Crown. This is one of the few pamplets written by an Indian. The British Library gives the author as Sambhuchandra Mukhopadhyaya (i.e. Sambhu Chandra Mookerjee). The authorship of the book is not clear.

223
Bod/Ames

By a Military Officer. *THE CRISIS IN INDIA, ITS CAUSES AND PROPOSED REMEDIES. BY A MILITARY OFFICER OF 32 YEARS EXPERIENCE IN INDIA.* London: Richard Bentley, 1857. 69pp. Second ed. was 111pp.
The first edition contains ten letters. The second edition with six additional letters was previously published in one of the London newspapers. A mix of writings dealing with politics, transport, personalities, etc.

224
Bod

By a Plain Speaker. *JUSTICE FOR INDIA: A LETTER TO PALMERSTON.* London: Robert Hardwicke, 1858. 82pp. Pamphlet.
What right does England have in India? Is India worth what it has cost England? The author calls for a stop to all of the unproven tales of atrocities currently coming out of India.

225
BL

By a Retired Bengal Civilian. Author of "A Glance at the East", *INDIA AND ITS FUTURE. An Address to the People of Great Britain and Their Representatives.* London: L. Booth, 1858. 50pp. Pamphlet.
A chapter on Delhi, what sort of a man the Governor General ought to be, and chapters on opium, finance, free trade, reorganization, education and religious instruction, and the causes of the Mutiny.

226
BL

By a Roving Irishman. *A SHORT REVIEW OF THE PRESENT CRISIS IN INDIA.* Dublin: McGlashan and Gill, London: Simpkin, Marshall and Co., 1857. 15pp.
Enumerates the causes for the crisis. Government was

too lenient, the Muslims wished to re-establish their rule, the British tried to treat the Indian as if he were British. The natives no longer feared or respected the British. It was not the officers fault and it was not the lack of trained officers, as Napier stated that was conducive to mutiny. This is an example of the racist, bigoted, and inflamatory pamphlets which were so current at the time.

227
RS
By a Staff Officer (Wilson, Thomas Fourness). *THE DEFENSE OF LUCKNOW. A Diary Recording the Daily Events During the Siege of the European Residency From May 31 to September 25, 1857. By a Staff Officer.* London: Smith, Elder, 1858. 1859. iv, 224pp.
Wilson was Assistant Adjutant-General under Henry Lawrence. After Lawrence's death Wilson filled the same position under Inglis. He was highly praised by both. In the succeeding years Wilson filled a number of posts and finally was named as the Military Member of the Governor Generals Council in India. Wilson died while on a hunting expediton in the Terai.

228
BL
By and Eye Witness. *THE SEPOYS DAUGHTER: A TRUE TALE OF THE INDIAN MUTINY.* London: Henry Lea, ND. c. 1873. 870pp.
Arthur Melville had a daughter Flora. This is about Omelia the Indian companion of Flora. Edward Stanley was Omelia's fiancee. Home was Agra. Stanley was friends with Captain Sandford of the Delhi magazine explosion. The book is of questionable authenticity and probably fiction.

229
BL
By and Old Indian. *WHY IS THE NATIVE ARMY DISAFFECTED? A LETTER TO THE GOVERNOR GENERAL OF INDIA. BY AN OLD INDIAN.* Calcutta: J.F. Bellamy, Englishman Press, June 1857. 15pp. Paper pamphlet.
The army is disaffected because Leadenhall followed poor policy in India. They supported the indiginous religions, agreed that troops were not to go overseas, etc. They were not strong enough with the Sepoys. Too much power was placed in the hands of the adjutants of the regiments; many were not fit for the post.

230
BL
Caine, Rev. Caesar (ed). *BARRACKS AND BATTLEFIELDS IN INDIA. Experiences of a soldier of the 10th Foot in the Sikh Wars and Sepoy Mutiny.* York: John Sampson and London: C.H. Kelly, 1891. 131pp.

This is a biographical sketch of private Thomas Malcolm. The last 40pp concern the Mutiny. Malcolm served in Dinapore and marched with General Franks to Lucknow.

231
IO   **Cairns, Rev. John.** *THE INDIAN CRISIS, VIEWED AS A CALL TO PRAYER: A Discourse.* Berwick (Edinburgh, Glasgow and London): Melrose & Plenderleith, 1857. 16pp. 2nd thousand.
Preached August, 1857.

232
RAI   **Campbell, Col. Walter.** *MY INDIAN JOURNAL.* Edinburgh: Edmonston and Douglas, 1864. xix & 484pp. Index and frontis.
Little on the Mutiny. Describes the execution of rebels at Bangalore.

233
Bod   **Campbell, George Douglas, 8th Duke of Argyll.** *INDIA UNDER DALHOUSIE AND CANNING.* London: Longmans, 1865. viii & 143pp.
Campbell was among the men responsible for the annexation of Oude. Page 90 mentions the influence the *"Red Pamphlet"* (see Malleson, entry 710) had on the parliamentary sessions of 1857-1858. Campbell completely discredits the *"Red Pamphlet"* and justifies the actions of Dalhousie and Canning.

234
Ames/RS/   **Campbell, George Douglas, 8th Duke of Argyll.**
BL   *SPEECH OF THE DUKE OF ARGYLL ON THE*
8023.CC.2(4)   *MOTION OF LORD PANMURE FOR A VOTE OF THANKS TO THE CIVIL SERVICE, ARMY, AND NAVY, IN INDIA, IN THE HOUSE OF LORDS, ON MONDAY, FEBRUARY 8TH, 1858.* London: Edward Moxon, 1858. 19pp. Pamphlet.
An apologia for Lord Canning. Campbell was a great supporter of Canning and takes this opportunity to refute many of the charges brought against Canning.

235
                  Campbell, Robert James Roy. *INDIA, ITS GOVERNMENT, MISGOVERNMENT, AND THE FUTURE CONSIDERED IN AN ADDRESS TO THE LORDS AND COMMONS OF GREAT BRITAIN. By R.J.R. Campbell, a resident of 25 years experience in India.* London: Effingham Wilson, 1858. 44pp.
Cited in Ladendorf.

236
RS/Bod   **Campbell, Robert James Roy.** *THE INDIAN MUTINY, ITS CAUSES AND REMEDIES. A LETTER TO THE RIGHT HONORABLE LORD VISCOUNT PALMERSTON.* London: Charles Evans, 1857. 32pp.

Campbell blames much on the Commander in Chief being answerable to the Governor General and the fact that the Governor General was being manipulated by the Military Secretary. Campbell advised that corporal punishment be re-instituted. The pamphlet discusses the military aspects of the Mutiny only. An appendix gives a short history of the Indian Mutiny.

237
Bod/IO   **Campbell, Sir George.** *MEMOIRS OF MY INDIAN CAREER. Edited by Sir Charles E. Bernard.* London: Macmillan, 1893. 2 vols. ix, 733pp. with portrait. Vol. I, 305pp. Vol. II, 428pp. Index.

Vol. I has approximately 90 pages on the Mutiny. Campbell comments about a number of major British figures of the period.

238
IO   **Cardew, Francis Gordon.** *SKETCH OF THE SERVICES OF THE BENGAL NATIVE ARMY TO THE YEAR 1895.* Calcutta: Superintendent of Government Printing, 1903. 576pp.

Uses Marshman, Kaye, Malleson etc. as sources. Very little on the Mutiny.

239
IO/Ind Inst   **Cardew, Major Francis Gordon.** *HODSONS HORSE 1857-1922.* Edinburgh: William Blackwood, 1928. ix & 402pp. 9 plates and 14 maps, seven folding.

Part I covers the Mutiny in approximately 100pp.

240
BL   **Cardwell, Pamela.** *THE INDIAN MUTINY: Illustrated from Contemporary Sources.* London: Longman, 1975. 112pp. Paper.

From the "Then & There Series." A history of the Mutiny for young readers.

241
BL
09057.bb.31   **Carey, W. H.** *THE GOOD OLD DAYS OF JOHN COMPANY. Being Curious Reminiscences Illustrating Manners and Customs of British India During the Rise of the East India Company, from 1600 to 1858...Compiled*

from Newspapers.... Simla: Argus Press, 1882-1887. 3
volumes. iv & 292pp. vii & 288pp (with 7 pages of
press opinions). v & 161 pp.

242
IO   **Carey, W. H.** *THE MAHOMEDAN REBELLION ITS*
PREMONITORY SYMPTOMS, THE OUTBREAK
AND SUPPRESSION WITH AN APPENDIX. Roorkee:
The Directory Press, 1857. 261pp.
Consists of narratives culled from letters and journals
which have appeared in the newspapers of the Presidencies.
Contains many personal accounts.

243
Sut   **Carmichael-Smyth, Colonel G.** *MEMORANDUM,*
OR A FEW WORDS ON THE MUTINY. (Private, not
published). Meerut? Privately printed (A. David), 1857.
3pp.
This is something of a curosity. Carmichael-Smyth
paraded his regiment, the Third Cavalry, at Meerut and from
this open mutiny ensued. The troops made for Delhi and
the rest is history. Carmichael-Smyth states, "The chief cause
was the petting and pampering of the Sepoys, I believe the
abolition of flogging to have been the next great cause." A
scarce item.

244
IO   **Carmichael-Smyth, Major General G.** *PAPERS*
REGARDING THE INDIAN MUTINY. NP. Privately
Printed. ND. c. 1871. 26pp.
Concerns statements which appear in Kaye's "*Sepoy*
War." Carmichael Smyth was in a position of responsiblility
at Meerut during the outbreak. See Palmer "*The Mutiny*
Outbreak at Meerut."(Entry 836.)

245
Ames   **Carnegy, C.W.** *REMINISCENCES OF THE GREAT*
INDIAN MUTINY. By A Veteran of the Army of
1857-1859. Puebla, Mexico: Salesiano College, 1898.
120pp. Green paper. 12mo.
The cover of this book reads, "The Indian Mutiny
1857-1858" so there is some confusion in cataloging. Carnegy
was stationed at Salone in Oude at the outbreak. The details
of his emigration to Mexico would seem to be an interesting
story. The book was written entirely from memory some 50
years after the event. A scarce title.

246
BL08023.d.21   **Carthill, Al. (Pseud. of Bennet Christain**
Huntingdon Calcraft Kennedy). *THE LOST*

DOMINION. London: William Blackwood, 1924. vi & 351pp.

Little regarding the Mutiny. This title is listed in a number of bibliographies on the Mutiny.

247
Bod

Carus-Wilson, Rev. W. *THE SOLDIER'S CRY FROM INDIA: "Come over and Help us."* As Contained in Letters *Addressed by Them to the Rev. W. Carus-Wilson.* London: Ventnor & Portsmouth, 1858. 96pp.

Contains numerous letters extolling the religious work of the reverend and supporting his claim for the need for more scripture readers for the troops. This is listed in Taylor's *"A Companion to the Indian Mutiny"* as Wilson, W.C. (ed.).

248
Ames/RS

Case, Mrs. Adelaide. *DAY BY DAY AT LUCKNOW, A Journal of the Siege at Lucknow.* London: Richard Bentley, 1858. iv & 348pp.

Kaul gives vi & 248pp. The journal starts Thursday, May 21st, 1857 and ends Monday, December 14, 1857. Adelaide Case was the widow of Colonel Case of the Queens 32nd Artillery Regt. The Colonel was killed at Chinhat.

249
BL

Cave-Browne, John. *INCIDENTS OF INDIAN LIFE.* Maidstone: W. Dickinson, 1886, 1895. 2nd ed. 144pp. Red cloth blind.

These are a series of stories, based on fact, but with which literary license has been taken.

250
Sut

Cave-Browne, Reverend J. *THE POORBEAH MUTINY.* London: Blackwood's Magazine, 1858.

This was the journal Cave-Browne kept and had published prior to transforming it into his well known work *"The Punjab and Delhi in 1857."*

251
RS

Cave-Browne, Reverend John. *THE PUNJAB AND DELHI IN 1857. Being a Narrative of the Measures by Which the Punjab was Saved and Delhi Recovered During the Indian Mutiny.* Edinburgh: William Blackwood & Sons, 1861. 2 vols. xxii, 389pp; viii, 372pp. Two portraits, 8 plans and folding map of Delhi.

The book originated from a journal kept by the author that was subsequently expanded and published in Blackwood's Magazine in 1858. The journal was entitled *"Poorbeah Mutiny."* Cave-Browne was assistant chaplain of the Punjab

Moveable Column in 1857. Cave-Browne has been used as a
reference by many other authors.

252
IO/Ind Inst   **Cavenagh, General Sir Orfeur.** *REMINISCENCES
OF AN INDIAN OFFICIAL.* London: W. H. Allen,
1884. xi & 372pp.
    Little on the Mutiny but cited in a number of
bibliographies.

253
BL   **Cavendish, Alfred Edward John.** *THE 93RD
SUTHERLAND HIGHLANDERS, NOW 2ND
BN. THE ARGYLL AND SUTHERLAND
HIGHLANDERS, PRINCESS LOUISE'S. 1799-1887.*
London: Richard Bentley, 1883. 446pp.
    The thin red line at Balaclava and honors again at
Lucknow. Colin Campbell was commander.

254
RS/MNUA   **Chalmers, Colonel John.** *LETTERS WRITTEN
FROM INDIA DURING THE MUTINY AND WAZIRI
CAMPAIGNS.* Edinburgh: Constable, 1904. xxxii,
167pp. Portrait and folding sketch of the battles of
Noorija and Sirpooea.
    Chalmers went out to India in 1849 in the employ of the
E.I.C. He served as a Civil Engineer and raised a regiment
in the Punjab during the Mutiny. Served at Delhi and
commanded the ladder party with Nicholson's column. He
returned to England in 1880 with the majority of his sight
gone. Chalmers mentions on page 33 of finding a European
roasted and chained to a post. Page 32, his thoughts on
attacking a breach. See Terrell, Richard, entry 1052.

255
Bod   **Chamberlain, Crawford Trotter.** *REMARKS ON
CAPTAIN TROTTERS BIOGRAPHY OF MAJOR
W.S.R. HODSON.* Edinburgh: R & R Clark, 1901.
19pp.
    Chamberlain was a member of the Court of Inquiry
which investigated Hodson. He states that Trotter's book,
"A Leader of Light Horse" is very inaccurate in its defense of
Hodson. Chamberlain also discusses the Bisharat Ali affair
and Hodson's role. Bisharat Ali was a money lender that
was ordered shot by Hodson, some say so that Hodson could
escape his debt to Ali.

256
IO   **Chamier, Lieut. Edward.** *LETTERS FROM
LIEUTENANT EDWARD CHAMIER, A.D.C. AND*

PERSIAN INTERPRETER TO GENERAL SIR JAMES OUTRAM. NP. ND.
Never Published.

257
IO 9057.h.2/
RAI

Chand, Nanak. *TRANSLATION OF A NARRATIVE OF EVENTS AT CAWNPORE. NC. NP. ND.* xxxviii pp.
Chand offered evidence against prominent Indians in Cawnpore. It appears he may have wished to further his own interests by currying favor with the British. The India Office copy is bound with a number of other items as follows: *"Memorandum on the Mutiny and Outbreak at Meerut in May 1857"* by Major Williams. *"Narrative of Events Connected with the Outbreak in 1857, Which Fell Under the Observation of Major Williams in the Meerut Division." "Narrative of the Mutiny of the 29th N.I. at Morradabad." "Depositions taken at Meerut by Major G.W. Williams. Superintendent of Police NWP." "Depositions taken at Cawnpore Under the Direction of Lieut. Col. G.W. Williams Commissioner of Military Police, N.W.P."*

258
RAI/NAM

Chand, Nanak. *DIARY OF THE MUTINY AT CAWNPUR.* (sic*) Written by Nanak Chand; Mukhtar Am in the firm of Lala Ishari Pershad; Banker. Translated by Kashinath. NC. NP.* March 16, 1925. 53pp.
The translator, Kashinath, was a "very fine civil officer" who also took a... corps to France in the 1914-1918 war. His brother, Krishna Prasad, was an Indian Davis Cup player, and was Director General, Posts and Telegraphs, United Provinces. (Above information supplied by Sir Richard Burn from a copy in the NAM.) This is purported to be the translation from Urdu of a manuscript found in a heap of rubbish. There is some question as to its authenticity. Kaye did not value it, Trevelyan did use it heavily. See additional entry under Nath, Kashi, entry 586. See Mukherjee's *"Spectre of Violence,"* entry 789, for a discussion of Nanak Chand.

259
RS

Chand, Tara. *HISTORY OF THE FREEDOM MOVEMENT IN INDIA.* New Delhi: Publications Division, Government of India, Vol I xii & 344pp. 1961. Revised 1965. Reprinted 1976. xii & 344pp. Vol. II (1st published 1967) ix & 628pp. Vol. III 1972. vi & 526pp.
Vol. I covers the period 1750-1856. Vol. II deals with India's reaction to the British in the 19th century. One chapter on the Mutiny. Vol. III Covers 1905 to 1924. Vol. IV Covers 1924 to 1947.

260
RS

Chanda, S. N. *1857 SOME UNTOLD STORIES.* New Delhi: Sterling, 1976. vi & 120pp.
Sketches of some of the lesser known Indian heroes of the Mutiny. Hazrat Mahal of Lucknow, Maulvi of Fyzabad, etc.

261
Sut

Chandra, Nirmal Kanti. *HISTORY OF THE ENGLISH PRESS IN BENGAL, 1780-1857.* Calcutta: K.P. Bagchi, 1987. xxix & 511pp.

262

Chatterjee, H. P. *THE SEPOY MUTINY; A SOCIAL STUDY AND ANALYSIS.* Calcutta: NP. 1957.
The revolt was caused by discontent of both Muslim and Hindus because of the British disregard of their social and religious customs. The revolt was not a national rising.

263

Chattopadhyaya, Haraprasad. *THE SEPOY MUTINY, 1857. A SOCIAL STUDY AND ANALYSIS.* Calcutta: Bookland Private Ltd., 1957. 234pp.
Majumdar states that this gives a good treatment of the part played by the civil population. Chattopadhyaya holds essentially the same views as Majumdar. See Chatterjee, same title, entry 262.

264
RS

Chaturbhuj (ed.). *MEMOIRS OF WILLIAM TAYLER.* New Delhi: Mittal Publications, 1990. 314pp. Index.
This is the abridged and edited version of Tayler's own publication, "*Thirty Eight Years in India.*" It covers both the period before and after the Patna Crisis.

265
Ames

Chaturvedi, Jayati. *INDIAN NATIONAL MOVEMENT: A CRITICAL STUDY OF FIVE SCHOOLS.* Agra: MG Publishers, 1990. viii & 216 pp. Index, Bibliography and notes.
This is a critical discussion of five interpretations of the Indian National Movement. These schools are the Hindu, the Muslim, the Marxist, the Cambridge, and the Official Schools. The first chapter deals with 1857.

266
IO

Chaudhry, Nazir Ahmad. *THE GREAT RISING OF 1857 AND THE REPRESSION OF THE MUSLIMS.* Lahore: Superintendent of Government Printing, 1970. 70pp.
Monograph #22 Punjab Government Record Office.

Bibliography. Based on original material at the Punjab Record Office. "An attempt to collect and consolidate the data recording the repression, which followed the suppression, of the war of 1857, especially of the Muslim community."

267
RS/Ind Inst **Chaudhuri, S. B.** *THEORIES OF THE INDIAN MUTINY 1857-59. A Study of the Views of an Eminent Historian on the Subject.* Calcutta: World Press, 1965. xiii & 207pp.
Primarily a rebuttal of Majumdar's chapters on the Mutiny in his *"History and Culture of the Indian People"* in Volume IX, *The British Paramountcy and the Indian Renaissance,* Part I, 1963.
Chaudhuri includes an excellent chapter on the historiography of the Mutiny. A valuable appendix lists the contents of *"Narrative of Events Regarding the Mutiny In India of 1857-59"* (entry 448), and *"Further Papers Relative to the Mutinies in the East Indies"* (entry 462). Chaudhuri was a student of Majumdar.

268
RS/Ind Inst **Chaudhuri, Sashi.** *CIVIL REBELLION IN THE INDIAN MUTINIES 1857-1859.* Calcutta: World Press, 1957. xxiii & 367pp. 1 folding map.
An excellent treatment of the civil, as distinct from the military, rebellion during the Mutiny. This subject has been much ignored in Mutiny literature although it is now receiving more attention. Chaudhuri refutes Majumdar's thesis concerning the question of a national war of liberation.

269
RS/Ind Inst **Chaudhuri, Sashi.** *ENGLISH HISTORICAL WRITING ON THE INDIAN MUTINY 1857-1859.* Calcutta: World Press, 1979. vii & 368pp. Bibliography.
This is an excellent work covering all of the major English titles on the Mutiny. Chaudhuri offers critical appraisals and important historiography on the Mutiny. This is an essential reference for the student of the Mutiny.

270
SOAS **Chick, N(oah) A(lfred) ed.** *THE ANNALS OF THE INDIAN REBELLION.* Calcutta: Sanders, Cones, 1859. 2 vols. 932pp, xlvi. Appendix.
The full title of this work is as follows: *Annals of the Indian Rebellion: (originally published in monthly parts) containing narratives of the outbreak and eventful occurrences, and stories of personal adventures during the Mutiny of 1857-58 with and appendix comprising Miscellaneous facts, anecdotes, etc. compiled by N.A. Chick. To which is added a concise index.*

In the above title there is a printing error in the word "eventful" whereby the "T" is printed on its side.

271
RS

Chick, Noah (Alfred) Compiler. *THE ANNALS OF THE INDIAN REBELLION 1857-58.* London: Charles Knight, 1974. xxxv & 293pp. 15 illus. 1 plan and 5 maps.

Chick was at Lucknow as a sub-editor of a Lucknow newspaper. *Annals of the Indian Rebellion* was first published in 1859 and is quite rare. The book consists of first hand accounts by people directly involved in the events of the Mutiny. The 1974 edition is abridged and has some additions for continuity. The editor is David Hutchinson, who has family mentioned in the work.

272

Cholmeley, Johnstone Montague. *THE JULIUNDUR MUTINEERS: A VINDICATION.* London: 1858.
Cited in Hibbert and Jain.

273
BL

Cholmeley, R. E. *JOHN NICHOLSON: THE LION OF THE PUNJAB.* London: Andrew Melrose, 1909. 144pp. 8 colored plates.
The Worlds Heroes Series. A popular edition biography.

274
Jain

Chopra, P. N. (ed.). *WHO'S WHO OF INDIAN MARTYRS.* New Delhi: Government of India. Ministry of Education and Social Welfare, 1973.

275
IO

Choudhury, P. C. R. *1857 IN BIHAR. (Chotanagpur and Santhal Parganas).* Bihar: Gazetteers Revision Branch, Revenue Dept., 1959. xiii & 147pp. with index. 2nd ed. revised.

First edition appeared in 1957, iv (iv) 132pp. Second edition 1958 and 1959. A study of the 1857 movement from original documents and other literature.

276

Choudhury, Sujit. *THE MUTINY PERIOD IN CHACHAR.* Silchar: NP. 1981.
Cited in Taylor.

277
BL

Church Missionary Society. *THE INDIAN CRISIS. A MEMORIAL TO THE QUEEN FROM THE CHURCH MISSIONARY SOCIETY, ON THE*

*RELIGIOUS POLICY OF THE GOVERNMENT
OF INDIA WITH EXPLANATORY STATEMENT
ON THE PAST AND PRESENT POLICY OF
THE INDIAN GOVERNMENT IN RESPECT TO
RELIGION, AND THE EDUCATION OF THE
NATIVES.* NC. Church Missionary Society, 1858.
40pp.
This is an attempt to convey to Queen Victoria the
aspects of administration in India that are "at variance with the
duty of a Christian Ruler." The Indian government should
not remain neutral but should espouse Christianity.

278
RS   **Churcher, E. J.** *SOME REMINISCENCES OF
THREE QUARTERS OF A CENTURY IN INDIA.* By
a Mutiny Veteran. London: Luzac, 1909. 123pp.
Churcher served in and around Agra. The book was
written from memory 50 years after the Mutiny. Churcher's
brother was one of the survivors of Cawnpore.

279
Bod/BL   **Civicus.** *THOUGHTS ON THE INDIAN CRISIS,
AND ITS BEARINGS ON THE FREEDOM
OF THE PRESS TO WHICH IS ADDED THE
METROPOLITAN SEWAGE QUESTION.* London:
Effingham Wilson, 1857. 15pp.
A rambling essay on the Mutiny and why India is not yet
ready for freedom.

280
RS   **Clive, William.** *DANDO ON DELHI RIDGE. A Novel
of the Indian Mutiny.* London: Macmillan, 1971. 254pp.
Glossary and bibliography. Fiction.

281
RS/MNUA   **Collier, Richard.** *THE GREAT INDIAN MUTINY. A
Dramatic Account of the Sepoy Rebellion.* New York: E.P.
Dutton, 1964. 383pp. Illus. Extensive bibliography.
Recognized as one of the better books on the Mutiny. It
is a well written and researched book. Collier deals primarily
with Delhi and Lucknow. This is not a comprehensive history
of the Mutiny but rather an attempt to present a "Portrait of
the Mutiny through a handful of people--what it looked like
to them, how it felt, how it sounded and how it smelt." This
title was published in England as *"The Sound of Fury."*

282
RS   **Collier, Richard.** *THE SOUND OF FURY: An Account
of the Indian Mutiny.* London: Collins, 1963. 384pp. 19
illus. `

This title was published in the United States as "*The Great Indian Mutiny.*" Well researched with an extensive bibliography.

283
BL
10804.bbb.17
Collinson, Major General T. B. *A MEMOIR OF GENERAL SIR H.D. HARNESS, K.C.B. COLONEL COMMANDANT, ROYAL ENGINEERS.* London: Printed for private circulation 1883. Frontis, 27pp. Blue paper covers.

Harness was a Lieut-Colonel commanding the Royal Engineers at Cawnpore against the Gwalior Contingent. He subsequently went on to Lucknow.

284
BL
Collinson, Major General T. B. *A MEMOIR OF GENERAL SIR HENRY DRURY HARNESS KCB: COLONEL COMMANDANT ROYAL ENGINEERS.* London: Royal Engineers Institute Committee, 1903. vii & 295pp. Index. Maroon cloth. Two folding tables.

One chapter on the Mutiny. Harness fought at Cawnpore under Windham.

285
Collister, Peter. *HELLFIRE JACK, VC. GENERAL SIR WILLIAM OLPHERTS 1822-1902.* 1989. 182pp. 15 illustrations and 5 maps.

Olpherts saw much action with Havelock and Outram on the march to Lucknow. He was awarded the VC for action at Lucknow.

286
IO
Colvin, Auckland. *JOHN RUSSELL COLVIN THE LAST LIEUTENANT GOVERNOR OF THE NORTH WEST UNDER THE COMPANY.* Oxford: Clarendon Press, 1895. 214pp.

Rulers of India Series.

287
Combe, Charles. *LETTERS FROM INDIA AND PERSIA, 1856-1859.* NC. Privately printed. ND.

Cited in Jain.

288
Bod
Congreve, Richard. *INDIA.* London: 1907. 40pp.

A pamphlet published in 1857. Introduction by Shyamaji Krishnavarma. Condemns England's forceful acquisition of India.

289
Bod

Congreve, Richard. *INDIAN PLACARD, A PROTEST PUBLISHED AS A PLACARD.* April 19, 1859.
Indictment of the English cause in India.

290
Bod

Connon, John. *A LETTER TO R.D. MANGLES, ESQ. M.P. CHAIRMAN OF THE EAST INDIA COMPANY IN DEFENCE OF THE LIBERTY OF THE PRESS IN INDIA.* London: Algar and Street, 1857. 37pp.
A plea to abolish the press restrictions in India.

291
RS

Conran, Major H.M. *MEMOIR OF COLONEL WHELER: Afterwards Major General. With a Preface by Macleod Wylie Esq.* London: Morgan and Chase, ND. c. 1866. xxiii & 212pp.
Wheler was the Lieutenant-Colonel Commanding the 34th Regiment Native Infantry at Barrackpore when Mangal Pandy mutinied. Wheler was accused of being incompetent by Canning (see Appendix to Papers Relative to the Mutinies in The East Indies, Inclosures no. 7 to 19, page 169. Entry 462). There was also a charge of religious preaching connected with Wheler and it was thought that this incited the Sepoys. Canning called for a courtmartial.

292
Ames/
IO V6614

Conybeare, H. C. and Atkinson, Edwin. *STATISTICAL, DESCRIPTIVE, AND HISTORICAL ACCOUNT OF THE NORTH-WESTERN PROVINCES OF INDIA. Compiled by H.C.Conybeare and edited by Edwin Atkinson.* Allahabad: North-western Provinces and Oudh Government Press, 1874-1886. 14 volumes.
There are generally accounts of the Mutiny period for each district. Most information is taken from Kay and other standard works.

293
RS/IO

Cooper, Frederick. *THE CRISIS IN THE PUNJAB: From the 10th of May Until the Fall of Delhi.* London: Smith Elder, 1858. xx, 254pp. Brown cloth. 16pp of adverts. 1 folding map.
Cooper was the Deputy Commissioner of Amritsar. His harshness in dealing with the mutineers was extraordinary.

294
BL

Cooper, Frederick. *THE HANDBOOK FOR DELHI. With index and two maps, illustrating the historic remains*

of Old Delhi, and the position of the British Army before the assault in 1857. Delhi and Lahore: R. Williams at the Delhi Press, 1863 & 1865. 182pp. 3 folding maps (1863) (1865) v, 168pp. 3 folding maps.
This work illustrates the historic remains of Old Delhi with numerous references to the Mutiny. Includes a narrative on the loss and re-conquest of Delhi.

295
RS/IO   **Cooper, L.** *HAVELOCK.* London: Bodley Head, 1957. 192pp.
Bibliography, index. Frontis, 2 maps. A biography of Henry Havelock. The last 90 pages deal with the Mutiny. Uses standard references for the Mutiny period.

296
RS   **Coopland, Ruth M.** *A LADY'S ESCAPE FROM GWALIOR AND LIFE IN THE FORT OF AGRA DURING THE MUTINIES OF 1857.* London: Smith Elder and Co., 1859. iv & 316pp.
Chaudhuri states this is a very lively and exciting book. Coopland was the wife of a chaplain killed at Gwalior. Her keen perceptions are somewhat weakened by her bigotry.

297
    Cope, William. *HISTORY OF THE RIFLE BRIGADE FORMERLY THE 95TH (The Prince Consorts Own).* London: Chatto Windas, 1877. 537pp.
The 2nd Batt. won honors in the Central Indian Campaign.

298
RS   **Cork, Barry Joynson.** *RIDER ON A GREY HORSE. A Life of Hodson of Hodson's Horse.* London: Cassell and Co., 1958. 178pp. 9 pages of half tones. Provides a list of "Authorities" and an index.
A general biography of Hodson.

299
    Cosens, Francis R. and C. L. Wallace. *FATEHGARH AND THE MUTINY.* Lucknow: Newul Kishore Press, 1933. Reprinted 1978, NP. 276pp. 5 folding maps.
Cosens was a Lt.-Col. of the 10th Bn. 7th Rajput Regiment. Wallace was Collector and Magistrate at Fatehgarh.

300
IO   **Cotton, Harry Evan August.** *CALCUTTA OLD AND NEW. A Historical and Descriptive Handbook to the City.* Calcutta: W. Newman, 1907. 101pp. & xxx.

Contains one chapter on Calcutta during the Mutiny. 18pp.

301
IO

Cotton, Major General Sir Sydney. *COPIES OF SUNDRY DISPATCHES ON VARIOUS SUBJECTS CONNECTED WITH THE MUTINY REBELLION IN INDIA DURING THE YEARS 1857 AND 1858.* Roorkee: Thomason College Press. Printed for Private circulation only. 1859. 136pp.
Contains Cotton's report to the government concerning the Mutiny as it pertained to the Peshawur Frontier. Cotton was 64 years old at the time of the Mutiny but was a vigorous man and a thorough soldier.

302
Bod

Cotton, Sydney. *NINE YEARS ON THE NORTH WEST FRONTIER OF INDIA FROM 1854-1863.* London: Richard Bentley, 1868. xii & 352pp.
Cotton became a Brigadier General on June 1857 and took command of the Peshawur Division when General Reed became Commander in Chief. Three chapters on the Mutiny.

303
BL

Court, M.H. *OBSERVATIONS ON THE CIVIL, CRIMINAL, AND POLICE ADMINISTRATIONS, AS PREVALENT IN THE PROVINCES OF BENGAL, WITH SUGGESTIONS FOR ITS IMPROVEMENT....* London: W. H. Allen, 1859. 56pp. Pamphlet.
An indictment of the legal system as it stood. "The leaders of the insurrection in 1857 prominently mentioned... the administration of justice as one of the sufferings that incited them to mutiny."

304
Ames

Court, Major M. H. *THE FUTURE GOVERNMENT OF INDIA, CONSIDERED IN ITS RELATION TO A COMPACT WITH ITS NATIVE SUBJECTS.* London: W. H. Allen, 1858. 134pp. Pamphlet.

305

Cox. P. *THE RANI OF JHANSI. A Historical Play in Four Acts.* London: NP. 1933. 119pp.

306
IO

Crawford, Lt.-Colonel D. G. *A HISTORY OF THE INDIAN MEDICAL SERVICE. 1600-1913.* London: W. Thacker & Co., 1914. 2 vols. Vol. I Frontis, 1 Illus. xiv & (6) 529pp. Vol. II Frontis, 1 illus. 535 pp.

One chapter on the Mutiny gives casualties and survivors of the Mutiny to 1913.

307
IO/MNUA   **Crawshay, George (Mayor of Gateshead).** *THE IMMEDIATE CAUSE OF THE INDIAN MUTINY, AS SET FORTH IN THE OFFICIAL CORRESPONDENCE. A Lecture.* London: Effingham Wilson, 1858. 2nd ed. 1858. 28pp.
This is an expanded edition of "*The Mutiny of the Bengal Army.*"

308
IO   **Crawshay, George (Mayor of Gateshead).** *THE MUTINY OF THE BENGAL ARMY; A Lecture From Official Documents.* Gateshead: Reprinted from the Gateshead Observer, 1857. 12pp.
Discusses the question of greased bullets, events at Barrackpore, Col. Wheler's attempts at conversion, etc. A second edition, enlarged, was issued under the title *"The Immediate Cause of the Indian Mutiny."*

309
RS   **Crawshay, George.** *THE CATASTROPHE OF THE EAST INDIA COMPANY.* London: Privately Printed, 1858. 24pp.
Speeches and lectures by G. Crawshay and others.

310
Sut6/79   **Crimea and Indian Mutiny Veterans Association, Bristol. 1892-1912.** *CRIMEA AND INDIAN MUTINY VETERANS ASSOCIATION, BRISTOL. 1892-1912.* Bristol: Henry Hill, 1912. 80pp.

311
RS   **Cromb, James.** *THE HIGHLAND BRIGADE, IT'S BATTLES AND IT'S HEROES.* London: Simpkin, Marshall & Co., 1886.
Other editions; Edinburgh: Orrlock & Son, 1893 and 1897. Blue cloth with vignettes of Highlanders. Eneas Mackay, 1902, 413pp, Frontis and 8 plates. Good section on the Mutiny. The principle subject matter is the Crimean War, the Mutiny, and the Boer War.

312
BL 9057.h.3   **Crommelin, Captain William Arden.** *MEMORANDUM ON THE THREE PASSAGES OF THE RIVER GANGES AT CAWNPORE DURING THE RAINY SEASON OF 1857, BY THE OUDH FIELD FORCE UNDER COMMAND OF THE LATE*

MAJOR-GENERAL SIR HENRY HAVELOCK, K.C.B.
Calcutta: Calcutta Gazette, 1858. 11pp. Includes a large
folding map. AEG. Brown cloth blind with gilt design.
Crommelin was chief engineer with the Oudh Field
Force. A scarce title.

313
RS

Crump, Charles Wade. Lt. Madras Artillery. *A*
PICTORIAL RECORD OF THE CAWNPORE
MASSACRE. Three Original Sketches Taken on the Spot.
Drawn on Stone with Tints by Vincent Brooks. London:
Henry Graves & Co. & Calcutta: R.C. Lepage & Co.,
1858. Folio. 3 plates and one page of text. Also listed as
2pp text.
Crump was killed at Lucknow during the 1st relief. He
was previously involved in the disarming at Benares and
Havelock's march to Lucknow. He was a brilliant officer but
was killed while trying to retrieve a 24 pounder in Lucknow.
A Private Duffy involved in the same action received the VC
for his efforts. A scarce title.

314

Culrose, James. *THE MISSIONARY MARTYR OF*
DELHI. A Memoir of the Reverend John MacKay, Baptist
Missionary Who Was Killed at Delhi, May 1857. London:
J. Heaton and Son, 1860. 139pp.
Cited in Ladendorf.

315
IO

Cunningham, Henry Stewart. *EARL CANNING.*
Oxford: Clarendon Press, 1891. 220pp. Index and
folding map.
Rulers of Indian Series

316

Cureton, C. *A SHORT ACCOUNT OF THE*
SERVICES OF THE GENERAL SIR CHARLES
CURETON, K.C.B. DURING THE INDIAN
MUTINY. Colchester: NP. 1893.
Cureton served in Oude and Rohilcande.

317
Bod

Cuthell, Edith. *IN THE MUTINY DAYS. Scenes in*
a Childs Life, Founded on Fact. London: Society for
Promoting Christian Knowledge, ND.
Fiction.

318
IO

Cuthell, Edith. *MY GARDEN IN THE CITY OF GARDENS: A Memory with Illustrations.* London & New York: John Lane, 1905. Frontis & 8 photos. x & 287pp.

See also Dormer, J. Consists mostly of life in Lucknow after the Mutiny. There is no precise date given but there are references to the Mutiny and an interesting anecdote concerning women captured by the rebels and their subsequent disappearance.

This work has also been attributed to a J. Dormer. This appears to be an error.

319
RAI

D'Oyly, Major General Sir C. *THE SEPOY REVOLT IN 1857.*

320
BL

D'Oyly, Major General Sir Charles Walters. *EIGHT MONTHS EXPERIENCE OF THE REVOLT IN 1857.* Blanford: Henry Shipp, 1891. 55pp. Paper.

D'Oyly was commanding a horse depot 22 miles from Meerut on May 10th. He operated out of Meerut during most of his service during the Mutiny. This is an interesting personal account.

321
Bod

D. M. *SCENES FROM THE LATE INDIAN MUTINIES.* London: John & Charles Mozley, 1858. 18pp. Pamphlet.

This is a rather scarce work with the following coverage; "The Soldier's Death- Captain Burgess," "The Soldier's Vow-Lieut. De Kantzow," " The Boy Soldier-Ensign Arthur Cheek," and a number of poems.

322
RS

Dall, Reverend C. H. A. *PATRIOTISM IN BENGAL. Lecture on True Patriotism in Bengal Given at Chinsurah.* Calcutta; NP. 1858. 25pp.

This work is not directly related to the Mutiny but is more concerned with social issues and policy of the Indian Society and the improvement there of.

323
Sut

Dallas, A. R. *THE PRIVATE JOURNAL OF BREVET MAJOR ALEXANDER ROBERT DALLAS 1857-1858.* Wellington: New Zealand, H. Bryant, ND. c. 1910. 16pp.

Dallas was born March 17, 1819, died in camp at Chirkaree, September 16th, 1858. He served in the 1st NI with Whitlock's column. Diary entries from December 2, 1857 to April 7, 1858.

324
RS **Dalton, Colonel E. T.** *REPORT ON THE MUTINY IN CHOTA NAGPORE.* Fort William: Government Printer, 1918. 32pp.
Folio. The Government of India printed 250 copies. Dalton was the Commissioner in Chota Nagpore.

325
RS **Daly, Major H.** *MEMOIRS OF GENERAL SIR HENRY DERMOT DALY G.C.B. Sometime Commander of the Central India Horse, Political Assistant for Malwa.* London: John Murray, 1905. x & 388pp. 8vo. 22 plates. Plan and folding map.
Daly was submitted for the VC for action at Delhi. The recommendation was denied as he was an officer of the East India Co. Daly gives good character sketches of the British principals in the Mutiny. Daly was a close friend of both the Lawrences and Mansfield. He took over command of Hodson's position at Lucknow upon the formers death.

326
RS **Dangerfield, George.** *BENGAL MUTINY; THE STORY OF THE SEPOY REBELLION.* London: Hutchinson, 1933. 286pp. Also published in New York by Harcourt Brace, 1933.
A basic treatment of the Mutiny for the general reader.

327
RS **Danvers, Robert William.** *LETTERS FROM INDIA AND CHINA DURING THE YEARS 1854-1858.* London: Hazell, Watson, and Viney, 1898. 214pp. 2 portraits.
Consists of letters to his family. Danvers was in the relief column with Outram and Havelock. He remained at the Alumbagh and was thence transferred to Jalalabad, near Lucknow, as an interpreter. Danvers died in China in 1858, accidently shot on parade.
Offers good descriptions of street fighting during Havelock's relief.

328
IO **Datta, K. K.** *REFLECTIONS ON THE MUTINY.* Calcutta: University of Calcutta, 1967. iv & 82pp. Index.
Examines the Mutiny in light of some contemporary local records that have not been adequately utilized. Includes reactions abroad and effects and legacies.

Sengupta, in *"Recent Writings..."* lists this title as
"Recollections of the Mutiny."

329
IO   **Datta, K. K. ed.** *UNREST AGAINST BRITISH RULE
IN BIHAR 1831-1859.* Patna: Secretariat Press, 1957.
11 & 85pp.
Prepared in the state central records office, Political Dept.
Bihar.
Covers Kuar Singh and Amar Singh and the Mutiny
period in Bihar including the Wahabi movement.

330
RS   **Datta, Kalikinkar K.** *BIOGRAPHY OF KUNWAR
SINGH AND AMAR SINGH.* Patna: K.P. Jayaswal
Research Institute, 1957. xii & 232pp & iv. 14 plates
including a view of Arrah House, frontis and one folding
map at rear. Bibliography and index.
Kunwar Singh and his brother Amar Singh led the
Mutiny in Bihar. K. K. Datta is a well known author on the
subject and was asked by the government of Bihar to produce
this work. It is based on sources in the National Archives of
India, the State Archives of Uttar Pradesh and other sources
of original material. The appendices include a number of
statements from sepoys.

331
IO/SOAS   **Datta, Kalikinkar K.** *HISTORY OF THE FREEDOM
MOVEMENT IN BIHAR.* Patna: Government of Bihar,
1957-1958. 3 vols.
Vol. I 1857-1928. ix & 670pp. Illus. Index and
bibliography. One chapter on the Mutiny. Vol. II 1928-1941.
529pp. Illus. Index and bibliography. Vol. III 1942-1947.
478pp. Illus. Index and bibliography.

332
RS   **David, Saul.** *THE INDIAN MUTINY 1857.* London:
Viking, 2002. xxiii & 504pp. 6 maps, 32 illustrations.
An excellent account of the Mutiny. Well researched, text
notes are easily available, and the author is very knowledgeable
on the subject. Includes a glossary, extensive notes and index.
Written in an engaging style that will sustain the general
reader as well as the student of the Mutiny. David's Ph.D.
thesis was on the origins of the Mutiny. The thesis was
completed at Glasgow University.

333
          Davidson, Hugh. *HISTORY AND SERVICES OF
THE 78TH HIGHLANDERS, ROSSHIRE BUFFS,
1793-1881. Compiled from the Manuscripts of the late*

Major Colin MacKenzie and Official and Other Sources.
Edinburgh: W & A. K. Johnstone, 1901. 2 vols.
The 78th saw extensive service under Havelock and
Outram at the relief of Lucknow. Won honors at Lucknow.

334
RS/IO   **Dawson, Capt. Lionel.** *SQUIRES AND SEPOYS.*
London: P. Hollis & Carter. 1960. 98pp. Frontis and 4
portraits.
This is essentially the journal of George Blake who fought
with Neill and later was at Lucknow with Havelock. Blake
was with Neill when Neill was killed at Lucknow.

335
BL 4477.a.22 **Day, Maurice Fitzgerald, Bishop of Cashel, Emly,**
Waterford and Lismore. *THOUGHTS ON THE*
MUTINY IN INDIA, A SERMON PREACHED IN ST.
MATTHIA'S CHURCH, DUBLIN, ON SATURDAY,
AUGUST 16, 1857. Dublin: Madden & Oldham, 1857.
24pp.

336
BL 8828.b.24 **De Fonblanque, Edward Barrington.** *MONEY OR*
MERIT. THE ARMY PURCHASE QUESTION
CONSIDERED WITH ESPECIAL REFERENCE TO
THE RECENT COMMISSION OF ENQUIRY...WITH
NOTES BY SIR CHARLES E. TREVELYAN. London:
Charles J. Skeer, 1857. 46pp.

337
BL   **DeKantzow, C. A.** *RECORD OF SERVICES IN*
INDIA. 1853-1886. Brighton: T. Phillips, 1900. ix &
306pp. AEG.
DeKantzow was an officer with the 9th N.I. of
Mainpuri where he gained fame for holding the Treasury
against the mutineers. DeKantzow later received a letter of
commendation from Canning. The 9th was one of the few
regiments that did not kill their officers when they mutinied.
A very exhaustive autobiography with many notes, extracts,
and letters.

338
             DeValbezen, E. *THE ENGLISH AND INDIA. New*
Sketches. London: W.H. Allen, 1883. xv & 498pp.
Reprinted 1986.

339
Ames   **Desai, Sanjiv P. ed.** *RELATIONS OF THE RANI OF*
JHANSI: SELECTIONS FROM MAHARASHTRA
STATE ARCHIVES NO. 2., NC. Dept of Archives,

Government of Maharashtra, 1990. ii + [2] + 87pp.
Bibliography.
Papers about some ancestors and descendants in
Khandeeh and Deccan of the rulers of Jhansi, covering the
period from 1843 to 1889.

340
RS   **Devi, Ritambhari.** *INDIAN MUTINY: 1857 IN*
BIHAR. New Delhi: Chetana Publications. Also
apparently Allahabad: Chugh Pub., 1977. viii & 200.
Index, bibliography and appendices.
This work is based on contemporary newspapers,
unpublished records and official documents. Analyses is given
of the various classes of people and their support or rejection
of the Mutiny.
The author holds a doctorate in Modern Indian History
and is a professor at Magadh University in Patna.

341
BL   **Dewar, Douglas and H(erbert) L(eonard) (Offley)**
ORW1986.a.   **Garrett.** *A REPLY TO MR. F.W. BUCKLER'S*
1628   *"The Political Theory of the Indian Mutiny" WITH*
A REJOINDER BY MR. F(RANCIS) W(ILLIAM)
BUCKLER.(1891-1960) NC. Read, November 8, 1923.
34pp.
Reprinted from "Transactions of the Royal Historical
Society," 4th series, Vol. VII, pp.131-165. Buckler's theory
was that the EIC rebelled against the king of Delhi and that
the sepoys were duty bound to fight the Company. Dewar &
Garrett dismantle Buckler's theory and Buckler replies.

342
IO   **Dharaiya, Dr. R. K.** *GUJARAT IN 1857.* Ahmedabad:
Gujarat University Press, 1970, 1971, 1973. 180pp.
index. 5 Maps.

343
IO   **Dickinson, John.** *LAST COUNSELS OF AN*
UNKNOWN COUNSELLOR. London: Macmillan,
1877. Special Edition. 196pp. xxxi, appendix.
The India Office holds special edition #3. Frontis, 196pp
+ xxxi appendix. On 15 numbered copies of this edition were
printed various passages plus the additional appendix that was
not in the original.
Dickinson was a civil servant for 26 years during which
time he spoke out against the actions of the East Indian
Company. He was an early Indian reformer of some note.

344
RS   **Digby, William.** *1857 A FRIEND IN NEED. 1887 FRIENDSHIP FORGOTTEN An Episode in Indian Foreign Office Administration.* London: Indian Political Agency, 1890. 148pp. Map and plates.
Reprinted 1993 by Asian Educational Services, New Delhi. 148pp. Frontis, five portraits and folding colored map. Deals with the aid Nepal rendered to India during the Mutiny (one chapter based on Malleson) and the failure of Britain to help the Nepalese Royal Family when they were overthrown and exiled.

345
RS/BL   **Diver, Katherine Helen Maud.** *HONORIA LAWRENCE: A FRAGMENT OF INDIAN HISTORY.* London: John Murray, 1936. 524pp. Frontis with 7 illus. 1 map.
Honoria was the wife of Henry.

346
BL   **Dixon, James. D. D.** *THE SWORD OF THE LORD IN THE INDIAN CRISIS. A Fast Day Sermon. Preached in the Stocks Chapel, Manchester.* London & Manchester: John Mason, 1857. Pamphlet.
A strictly religious interpretation of the Mutiny.

347
Ames   **Dobrolyubov, Nikolai.** *THE INDIAN NATIONAL UPRISING OF 1857: A CONTEMPORARY RUSSIAN ACCOUNT.* Calcutta: Nalanda Publications, 1988. viii & 92pp. Frontis.
Translated from the Russian by Harish C. Gupta. Dobrolyubov voiced the views of the progressive elements in Russian society in relation to the Mutiny. The article was originally published in the magazine, "The Contemporary" in September, 1857 in Russian.

348
RS   **Dodd, George.** *THE HISTORY OF THE INDIAN REVOLT AND OF THE EXPEDITIONS TO PERSIA, CHINA, AND JAPAN. 1856-7-8.* London: W & R Chambers & Co., 1859. viii & 634pp. 4to. Five colored, double-page maps and over 200 woodcuts.
The author is simply listed as G.D. This is an important work and is probably the first one volume history of the Mutiny. Chaudhuri states that it contains many statistics that are not readily available elsewhere. Chaudhuri questions the date of publication as it does not seem possible that all of the

facts presented could have been gathered by 1859. Dodd is
considered one of the important early works on the Mutiny.

349
RS   **Dodgson, David Scott.** *GENERAL VIEWS AND
SPECIAL POINTS OF INTEREST IN THE CITY OF
LUCKNOW FROM DRAWINGS MADE ON THE
SPOT BY D.S.S. WITH DESCRIPTIVE NOTICES.*
Dedicated to Sir James Outram. London: Day & Son,
1860. 28 lithos, tinted on 12 plates including the frontis.
One plan of Lucknow. Folio in yellow boards.

350
RS   **Domin, Dolores.** *INDIA IN 1857-59. A Study in the
Role of the Sikhs in the People's Uprising.* East Berlin:
Akademie-Verlag, 1977. x & 375pp. Extensive notes,
bibliography, index. Map in pocket.
           Translated from the German. Vol. 17 in the series
of Studies of Asia, Africa and Latin America. Extensive
bibliography. Supports the national uprising school. The
book discusses the question of the Sikhs and their general lack
of participation in the Mutiny.

351
Exhibition of Books at the Centenary. Calcutta 1957/IO
           Dormer, J. *MY GARDEN IN THE CITY OF
GARDENS; A Memoir with Illustrations.* London: John
Lane, 1905. ix & 287pp. Plates.
           Dispatch of Major the Hon. J. Dormer A.D.C. to Sir
Colin Campbell after the Relief of Lucknow.
           See Cuthell.

352
RS   **Duberly, Mrs. Henry.** *CAMPAIGNING
EXPERIENCES IN RAJPOOTANA AND CENTRAL
INDIA DURING THE SUPPRESSION OF THE
MUTINY 1857-1858.* London: Smith Elder & Co.,
1859. viii & 254pp.
           Two maps as follows; Brigadier Smith's plan for
surrounding Tantia Tope and a map showing Duberly's route.
A fascinating book by a woman who actually accompanied her
husband on the field campaigns. In this instance the field was
Central India with Hugh Rose's Army.
           Although a highly interesting book it is full of prejudice
and invective against the rebels. Re-issued in 1974 under the
title "*Suppression of Mutiny*" by the Sirjand Press, New Delhi.

353
SOAS **Duberly, Mrs. Henry.** *SUPPRESSION OF THE MUTINY 1857-1858.* New Delhi: Sirjana Press, 1974. 168pp. 2 folding maps.
This is a reprint of Duberly's *"Campaigning Experiences."*

354
RS/BL **Duff, A.** *THE INDIAN REBELLION: ITS CAUSES AND RESULTS IN A SERIES OF LETTERS.* London: James Nisbet, 1858. iv, 383pp. Colored folding map.
There was a 2nd edition also in 1858. iv, 393pp. Dr. Duff's letters were published as they reached Scotland from Calcutta. The first letter is dated May 16th, 1857, Calcutta. Duff recounts various acts of barbarity that have been attributed to the sepoys and his letters are truly meant to inflame public opinion concerning the Mutiny. The last letter is dated 22nd of March, 1858. Duff gives an interesting chronology of how the Mutiny experience affected those in Calcutta.

355
RS/BL **Dunlop, Robert Henry Wallace.** *SERVICE AND ADVENTURE WITH THE KHAKEE RESSALAH OR THE MEERUT VOLUNTEER HORSE: During the Mutinies of 1857-58.* London: Richard Bentley, 1858. xi & 168pp. with 2 colored chromolithographs and 1 other litho. Six wood engravings.
Reprinted in 1974 by Legend Publications in India as volume 1 of *"An Eyewitness Account of the Great Indian Mutiny."* The series consisted of Vol. II, Edwards, William: *"Personal Adventures During the Indian Rebellion."* Vol.III, Majendie, V.D. Lt. *"Up Among the Pandies."* Vol. IV, Sherer, J.W., *"Daily Life During the Indian Mutiny."* Dunlop includes an appendix of Corps which have mutinied or been disbanded.

356
Bod **Durand, Sir Henry Mortimer.** *CENTRAL INDIA IN 1857. Being an Answer to Sir John Kaye's Criticisms on the Conduct of the Late Sir Henry Marion Durand, Whilst in Charge of Central India During the Mutiny.* London: W. Ridgway, 1876. 71pp.

357
BL **Durand, Sir Henry Mortimer.** *THE LIFE OF MAJOR GENERAL SIR HENRY MARION DURAND.* London: W.H. Allen, 1883. 2 vols. Portrait, viii, 476pp & viii, 487pp.
Little on the Mutiny. Durand served over forty years in India. He was the representitive of the Governor General

at Indore, the capital of Holkar in Central India when the
Mutiny broke out.

358

Durand, Sir Henry Mortimer. *LIFE OF THE RIGHT
HONORABLE SIR ALFRED COMYN LYALLL KCB.*
Edinburgh: William Blackwood, 1913. xvi & 492pp. 11
plates.
Lyall fought with the Khaki Rissala and later became the
Foreign Secretary to the Government of India.

359
IO   **East India Company.** *LETTER 235. Dated November
25th, 1857.*
From the Honourable Court of Directors, setting up a
Commission to inquire into the future of the Army in India,
with a series of questions addressed to officers in India.

360
Ames   **Eastwick, William Joseph.** *SPEECH OF CAPTAIN
EASTWICK, AT A SPECIAL COURT OF
PROPRIETORS, HELD AT THE EAST INDIA
HOUSE, ON THE 20TH OF JANUARY, 1858.* London:
Smith, Elder, 1858. 36pp. Pamphlet.
Orientals can not be measured by European standards
and that was one of the problems in India. Refutes charges
against the EIC and asks, "Has the EIC fulfilled its duty as a
Christian government?"

361

Eastwick, Edward Backhouse. (ed.).
*AUTOBIOGRAPHY OF LUTFULLAH. A
MOHAMEDAN GENTLEMAN CHIEFLY
RESIDENT IN INDIA.* London: Smith, Elder, 1858
and 1863. 411pp.
Apparently written prior to the Mutiny. Includes a trip to
London.

362
RS   **Eckford, Lieut. J.J.** *EVENTS AT MEERUT.* Meerut:
A. David, ND. 3pp.
Relates Eckford's escape from the outbreak at Meerut on
May 10th.
Eckford was the Executive Engineer at Meerut. This
appears to be a copy of his deposition found in *"Depositions
taken at Meerut"* by Major G.W. Williams.

363
RS   **Eden, Charles.** *INDIA HISTORICAL AND
DESCRIPTIVE. Revised and enlarged from "Les Voyages*

Celebres with an account of the Sepoy Mutiny in 1857-58."
London: Marcus Ward and Co., 1876. 290pp.
Colored frontis and folding map of India.

364
BL
Edwardes, Emma. *MEMOIRS AND LETTERS OF THE LIFE OF SIR HERBERT B. EDWARDES. By His Wife.* London: Kegan Paul, Trench, 1886. 2 vols.
At the outbreak of the Mutiny Edwardes was the Commissioner of the Peshawur Division. Cited in Ladendorf.

365
IO
Edwardes, Major General Sir Herbert Benjamin and Herman Merivale. *LIFE OF SIR HENRY LAWRENCE.* London: Smith, Elder, (also 3rd edition: Macmillan, 1873) 1872 and 1873. 2 Volumes, xii & 492pp. 492pp. and xii & 396pp. (Macmillan ed.: xvi & 627pp.)

366
RS
Edwardes, Michael. *A SEASON IN HELL: THE DEFENSE OF THE LUCKNOW RESIDENCY.*
London: Hamish Hamilton, 1973. 330pp. Bibliography, 20 illus. Maps and index.
A well written, well researched, and entertaining account of the siege.

367
RS/IO
Edwardes, Michael. *BATTLES OF THE INDIAN MUTINY.* London & New York: B.T. Batsford & Macmillan, 1963 216pp., 40pp.of illus., 6 maps and plans, index.
Popular treatment of the main battles on the Mutiny. Includes maps and pictures of major British figures.

368
RS
Edwardes, Michael. *RED YEAR; THE INDIAN REBELLION OF 1857.* London: Hamish Hamilton, 1973. 251pp. 28 Illus., bibliography and index.
Well written general account of the Mutiny. Has a number of very useful appendices including the text of the *"Narrative of Syed Mubarak Shah"* who was the Chief of Police in Delhi during the siege.

369
IO
Edwardes, Michael. *THE NECESSARY HELL; John and Henry Lawrence and The Indian Empire.* London: Cassel, 1958. xxi & [3] 213pp. 8 illus.
As the author states this is not a biography of the

Lawrences but rather an attempt to "place 19th century India into the perspective of the British-Indian Empire."

370
IO   **Edwardes, Michael.** *THE ORCHID HOUSE: SPLENDORS AND MISERIES OF THE KINGDOM OF OUDH. 1827- 1857.* London: Constable, 1960. 216pp.
Little on the Mutiny.

371
RS   **Edwards, Captain R.F., ed.** *PROFESSIONAL PAPERS OF THE CORPS OF ROYAL ENGINEERS.* Chatham: Royal Engineers Institute, 1897. 11 & 315pp.
Volume XXIII. Numerous large folding plans. Contains the *"Journal of the Siege Operations Against the Mutineers at Delhi in 1857"* ed. by Col. H. M.Vibart. 44pp.

372
          Edwards, William. *FACTS AND REFLECTIONS CONNECTED WITH THE INDIAN REBELLION.* Liverpool: NP. 1859. 38pp.
In Edwards' *"Reminiscences of a Bengal Civilian."* First published for private circulation. Edwards was a district magistrate in Rohilkhand and here gives his opinions on the cause of the Mutiny. Sutcliffe gives the pamphlet as published in London and 33 pages.

373
BL8022.cc.2(2)   **Edwards, William.** *NARRATIVE OF THE ESCAPE OF W.E. FROM BUDAUN TO CAWNPORE.* London: Privately printed, 1857. 35pp. Paper.
A detailed account of Edwards' travails. Quite an interesting monograph.

374
RS/RAI/Bod   **Edwards, William.** *PERSONAL ADVENTURES DURING THE INDIAN REBELLION IN ROHILCUND, FUTTEHGHUR AND OUDE.* London: Smith Elder and Co., (also Legend Publications, India, 1974) 1858. There was a 2nd and 3rd ed. of 206pp in 1858. 204pp. (iv & 206pp.)
Volume II of *"An Eyewitness Account of the Great Indian Mutiny."* See Dunlop for complete series.

375
Bod   **Edwards, William.** *REMINISCENCES OF A BENGAL CIVILIAN.* London: Smith, Elder and Co., 1866. vii, 352 pp.
With appendix: "Narrative of Rajah Misr's Sufferings

During the Rebellion." Edwards was a judge in the high
court at Agra. He traces back the disaffection in the army to
1840-41 defeats in Afghanistan. These British defeats showed
the sepoys that the British were not invincible. Edwards also
cites the withdrawal of corporal punishment, loss of power to
the central government by the various commanding officers,
and the sepoys suspicions of a British conspiracy to cause them
to lose caste and religion.

376
Bod

Elliot, Charles Alfred. *LABORIOUS DAYS. LEAVES
FROM THE INDIAN RECORD OF SIR C.A. ELLIOT,
Lieutenant Governor of Bengal, 1856-1892.* Calcutta: J.
Larkins, 1892. 107pp. and ix.
    Of little Mutiny interest.

377
IO

Elliot, Joseph A. *PADRE ELLIOT OF FYZABAD: A
MEMORIAL. Ed. By A.W. Newboult.* London: Charles
Kelly, ND. c. 1906. vii & 350pp. frontis and 19 illus.
    Elliot recounts his escape as a child during the Mutiny.
Little of interest.

378
RAI

Elliott, Major W. J. & Lieut-Colonel Knollys.
GALLANT SEPOYS AND SOWARS. London: Dean &
Son, ND. c. 1894. 176pp. 8 illus.
    Interesting. Contains a number of anecdotes on the
Mutiny.

379
BL

Elsmie, G. R. (ed.). *FIELD MARSHAL SIR DONALD
STEWART GCB. An Account of His Life Mainly In His
Own Words.* London: John Murray, 1903. xxii & 482 pp.
Portrait, 28 plates, 4 maps and plans. Index.
    Blue cloth, gilt badge on cover. Stewart was in Aligurh at
the outbreak and subsequently served in the Delhi, Oude and
Rohilkund Campaigns.

380
RS

Embree, Ainslie T. (ed.). *1857 in India: Mutiny or War
of Independence?* Boston: D.C. Heath, 1963. 101pp.
Paper.
    Excellent book covering various aspects of the Mutiny
as presented by a number of writers including Lawrence,
Disraeli, Savarkar, Marx, Buckler's *"Political Theory of the Cause
of the Mutiny"* and a number of Indian writers.

381
BL
1879.cc.14(58)

England. Proclamations 11 Chronological Series, Victoria. *BY THE QUEEN: A PROCLAMATION FOR A DAY OF SOLEMN FAST, HUMILIATION, AND PRAYER. (On the occasion of the Mutiny in India. 24 Sept. 1857).* London: G. E. Eyre & W. Spottiswoode, 1857.

382
BL

Entract, J(ohn) P(atrick). *THE DEVIL'S WIND; A CENTENARY ACCOUNT OF THE INDIAN MUTINY.* NC. NP. 1957. 19pp. 6 plates.
Reprinted from the London Hospital Gazette. Includes a photo of the Cawnpore well by Beato, 1857.

383
Not found in BL

Evans, Thomas. *THREE LECTURES ON THE REVOLT OF THE BENGAL ARMY IN 1857.* Mussoorie: NP. 1899.
Cited in Ladendorf.

384
BL

Evans, W. Downing. *ODE ON THE DEATH OF GENERAL SIR HENRY HAVELOCK, K.C.B.* London: Privately printed. Simpkin and Marshall, 1858. 15pp.

385
BL

Ewart, J. A. *STORY OF A SOLDIERS LIFE OR PEACE, WAR, AND MUTINY.* London: Sampson, Low, Martson, Searle, and Rington, 1881. 2 Vols. xi & 472pp.; viii & 368pp. 2 frontis color plates.
About 140 pages on the Mutiny. Ewart was at the first relief of Lucknow and the action against the Gwalior Contingent.

386
Taylor

Eyre, Sir Vincent. *LETTERS AND DISPATCHES.* NC. NP. ND.

387
RS

Fanshawe, H. C. *DELHI, PAST AND PRESENT.* London: John Murray and Co., 1902. xxvi & 337pp. Frontis and 50 illus. with 8 maps and plans and 2 folding maps.
Includes a list of those killed and wounded at Delhi along with a pocket containing a map of the Delhi Siege and information on the Delhi Durbar, Christmas 1902. Includes a guide to Mutiny sites.

388
NAM 92FAR   **Farquhar, Lieut. John.** *PRIVATE COPY OF LETTERS RECEIVED THURSDAY 28TH OF JANUARY FROM LIEUT. JOHN FARQUHAR 7TH B.L. CAVALRY.* NC. NP. ND. 39pp. No title page.
The letters are dated September 1, 1857, Lucknow Residency, through December 9th, 1857, at the Cawnpore camp. Most of the letters are to his mother. Presumably never published.

389
RS   **Farwell, Byron.** *ARMIES OF THE RAJ; FROM THE MUTINY TO INDEPENDENCE, 1858-1947.* London: Viking, 1989. 399pp. Index, bibliography with 41 Illustrations.
Excellent, highly readable work.

390
RS/BL   **Fayrer, Surgeon General Sir Joseph.** *RECOLLECTIONS OF MY LIFE.* Edinburgh: Blackwood, 1900 and 1930. xii and 508pp. Portrait, 23 plates and 2 plans. (Same page count in each.)
Fayrer was senior medical officer at the Residency in Lucknow during the siege. His brother, visiting from Australia, was killed in the Mutiny at the age of 23. Fayrer was 28 during the siege.

391
Sut/   **Fenwick, Captain.** *EXTRACTS FROM LETTERS*
NAM1857(54) *FROM CAPTAIN FENWICK TO HIS FRIENDS IN ENGLAND.* NC. NP. ND. 16pp. No imprint.
Pamphlet. 16 letters dated from May 1857 to July 1858.

392
RS   **Fforde, Major C(harles) del. W. (ed.).** *THE LUCKNOW SIEGE DIARY OF MRS. C.M. BRYDON.* 1979? About 132pp. Two maps and index.
Privately published in a limited edition of 50 copies. Copies 1-10 were reserved for relatives and copies 11-50 were for public sale. ND but 1979. Photocopied manuscript bound in red cloth. Nine black and white photos of Lucknow taken in 1930 and 1933 glued in front. One of the best of the diarys actually written on the spot, during the siege. The editor had the original diary to work from and was himself stationed in Lucknow from 1929-1930. See Geoffrey Moore, "*Diary of the Doctor's Lady,*" entry 773.

393
Fisher, James. *LIFE AND TRAVELS OF JAMES FISHER. SERGEANT MAJOR, SCOTS GREYS,*

Sut/
NAM 92Fish.

*MILITARY TRAIN, ARMY SERVICE CORPS. AN
AUTOBIOGRAPHY.* Toronto: The Copp, Clark
Company, 1890. 76pp. Frontis portrait.
   Contains a 24 page account of the Mutiny. Fisher
spent November 1857 with Campbell in Lucknow. He then
returned to Cawnpore and then was back in Lucknow the
following year.

394
RS

Fisher, Michael H. *A CLASH OF CULTURES.* New
Delhi: Manohar Publications, 1987. 284pp. 2 figures, 6
tables and 7 illustrations. Bibliography and index.
   Extensive use of original Persian and Urdu sources. This
is not directly concerning the Mutiny but is a valuable source
of study to understand events in Awadh previous to and
including the Mutiny.

395
RS

Fitchett, W. H. *THE TALE OF THE GREAT
MUTINY.* London: Smith, Elder & Co. 1901. 384 pp. 5
maps together with frontis and 7 portraits.
   Thompson in *"The Other Side of the Medal"* (entry 1058)
says the above title is perhaps the most contemptible of all
the histories of the Mutiny. There were also reprints in 1904,
384pp. In 1907, 485pp. 2nd ed. Enlarged. Reprinted in
1912, 1914, and 1924.

396
BL4446cc1(16)

Fletcher, Reverend W. K. *THE QUEEN IN INDIA
(Sermon).* Bombay: 1858.

397
Bod

Forbes, Archibald. *COLIN CAMPBELL, LORD
CLYDE.* London: Macmillan, 1895. 222pp., frontis of
Lord Clyde.
   English Men of Action Series

398
Bod/BL

Forbes, Archibald. *GLIMPSES THROUGH THE
CANNON SMOKE. A series of sketches.* London and
New York: George Routledge, 1880. vi & 310pp. Gilt
title with vignette of cannon.
   Written in a popular style. Contains a chapter "The
Cawnpore of Today" and a chapter "The Lucknow of Today."

399
RS/BL

Forbes, Archibald. *HAVELOCK.* London: McMillan
and Co., 1890, 1891, 1897. 223pp. frontis.
   Havelock died during Campbell's relief of Lucknow.

The frontis is claimed to be the only known photograph of Havelock.

400

Forbes, Mrs. Hamilton. *SOME RECOLLECTIONS OF THE SIEGE OF LUCKNOW.* Exminster: Edwin Snell, 1905.
Cited in Ladendorf. Unable to locate.

401
RS/IO

Forbes-Mitchell, Sgt. W(illiam). *REMINISCENCES OF THE GREAT MUTINY INCLUDING THE RELIEF AND SIEGE AND CAPTURE OF LUCKNOW AND THE CAMPAIGNS IN ROHILCUND AND OUDE.* London: Macmillan and Co., 1893 (reprinted 1894, 1895, 1897, and 1910). xii & 295pp. 1 folding map.
Forbes-Mitchell was a sergeant with the 93rd Sutherland Highlanders. He fought with Campbell at Lucknow, then Gwalior and the final siege of Lucknow. There are interesting appendices on the sword, the Neill feud and Europeans serving with the sepoys. This is one of the few books written by a soldier from the ranks who was an eye-witness to events. (See Seymour, Charles.) There is, however, some doubt as to the authenticity of the work. Ewart and Gordon-Alexander, both principals in the events at Lucknow, do not remember Forbes-Mitchell at all and there are discrepancies in a number of eye-witness accounts reported by Mitchell and Gordon-Alexander. See Mukherjee, "*Spectre of Violence*" (entry 789) for a further discussion concerning the death of Neill's son in 1887.

402
RS

Forbes-Mitchell, Sgt. W(illiam). *RELIEF OF LUCKNOW.* London: Folio Society, 1962. 159pp.
Taken from his book "*Reminiscences of the Great Mutiny.*" Edited by Michael Edwardes. In slipcase.

403
BL

Forjett, Charles. *OUR REAL DANGER IN INDIA.* London, Paris and New York: Cassell, Petter and Galpin, 1877. viii & 199pp. frontis and map.
Forjett was commissioner of police of Bombay. The author states the book is intended to explain some of the causes of the Mutiny and how the "Aggressive conduct of Russia is more than likely to occasion the most serious fear in regard to the future of India." Forjett attempts to prove that Kaye is mistaken in his assessment of the causes of the Mutiny.

404
RS   **Forjett, Charles.** *REPLY TO GENERAL JACOBS PAMPHLET.* London: NP. October, 1879. 24pp. Pamphlet. Folding map of Bombay.
Forjett, Commissioner of Police in Bombay, held the sepoy in low regard, especially when not led by Europeans. Sepoys would soon become demoralised when faced by the least check. Forjett goes on to discuss the accusation that he was not actually the Commissioner of Police and to point out how he smashed the Mutiny plot in Bombay.

405
RAI   **Forrest, George W.** *SELECTIONS FROM THE LETTERS, DISPATCHES AND OTHER STATE PAPERS PRESERVED IN THE MILITARY DEPARTMENT OF THE GOVERNMENT OF INDIA. 1857-1858.* Calcutta: Military Department Press, 1893-1912. (Reprinted 1997 Selous, Aldershot) 4 Volumes
Vol. 1: (Delhi: vi, 493pp. & clviii appendixes & ci indexes, two maps in pocket.) "British Position at Delhi" and "Map of India to Illustrate the Mutiny." Vol. 2: 1902. 420 page introduction plus 414 pages, 2 maps in rear pocket. "City of Lucknow" and "Operations in Lucknow Under Campbell." Vol. 2 covers Lucknow and Cawnpore. Vol. 3: Lucknow and Cawnpore. 1902. Pagination continues from Vol. 2 to 573 & ccclxii appendix & xvi & xxiv & xxxii & xvii & xxx & xxxv. Appendices A to G and cxvc index. Vol. 4: (scarce) Central India. 1912. 172 pp. and 177 pp. And cxix appendix A to G & lxxvii Index. With map in rear pocket.
Forrest was the son of Lieut. George Forrest VC one of the nine defenders of the Delhi Magazine. George, the father, was promoted Captain effective May 11th, 1857. He never fully recovered from his wounds at Delhi and died, age 59, at Dehra on November 3rd, 1859.

406
RS/MNUA   **Forrest, George William.** *A HISTORY OF THE INDIAN MUTINY REVIEWED AND ILLUSTRATED FROM ORIGINAL DOCUMENTS.* London and Edinburgh: William Blackwood, 1904-1912. 3 volumes
Vol. 1 (1904): Siege of Delhi, Defence of the Residency at Lucknow, Story of Cawnpore, Havelock's Campaign, xxxii & 507pp., 18 illus., 5 plans in folding pocket. Vol. 2 (1904): Havelock's Succour of the Lucknow Residency, The Second Defence, Relief by Sir Colin Campbell, Outrams Defence of the Alum Bagh, Siege and Capture of Lucknow. xvi & 415pp., 11 illus., sketch map of Cawnpore, map of India and plan of Lucknow in pocket. Vol 3: (1912) Campaign in Central India,

Rebellion in Rohilcund, Campaign in Rohilcund, Mutiny in Western Bihar, Siege and Relief of Arrah, Suppression of Mutiny in Bihar, Final Campaign in Oudh, Pursuit of Tantia Topee. xxxxix & 651pp., 10 illus., 5 maps and plans.

407
Ames/Ind Inst **Forrest, George William.** *LIFE OF FIELD MARSHAL SIR NEVILLE CHAMBERLAIN GCB.* Edinburgh & London: William Blackwood, 1909. xxii & 512pp., two portraits. Index.

Forrest uses some information regarding Delhi from his own book "*History of the Indian Mutiny.*" He also had access to a large number of family letters and documents collated by Harriet Chamberlain, Neville's sister.

Chamberlain led the Punjab Moveable Column and was later made Adjutant General of the Delhi Field Force.

408
RS/BL **Forrest, George William.** *SEPOY GENERALS. Wellington to Roberts.* Edinburgh: William Blackwood, 1901. xvi & 478pp.

Forrest was Director of Records, Government of India. Covers famous Indian generals, including Mutiny personalities Roberts and Edwardes.

409
RS/BL **Forrest, George William.** *THE LIFE OF LORD ROBERTS.* London: Cassell and Co., First ed. Sept. 1914. New edition Nov. 1914. Rept. Dec. 1914 xi & 380pp., eight plates.

This is a much more complete record of Robert's career than what Forrest published in his book "*Sepoy Generals.*" The account of Robert's service in the Mutiny is drawn largely from material in "*Sepoy Generals*" however, Roberts later career is taken from dispatches and other contemporary literature.

410
BL10816.ee.19 **Forsyth, Ethel (ed.).** *AUTOBIOGRAPHY AND REMINISCENCES OF SIR DOUGLAS FORSYTH CB.* London: Richard Bentley, 1887. v & 283pp., portrait and colored folding map.

Douglas was Deputy Commissioner of the Cis-Sutlej States. Good chapter on the Mutiny. Forsyth states there was definite information that there was to be an uprising well before Meerut.

411

Framji, Dosabhai. *THE BRITISH RAJ CONTRASTED WITH ITS PREDECESSORS; AND AN INQUIRY INTO THE DISASTROUS RESULTS*

Bod/
BL(Missing)
8023.d.

OF THE REBELLION IN THE NORTHEAST PROVINCES UPON THE HOPES OF THE PEOPLE OF INDIA. London: Smith Elder, 1858. 61pp.
This work was written by a 28 year old Parsee, apparently from a well to do family. Originally written in Guzerati and Marathi and translated by the author. A pro-British tract advising the Indians to oppose the rebels. Intro by W. H. Sykes.

412
RS/BL

Fraser, Captain Hastings. *OUR FAITHFUL ALLY, THE NIZAM BEING A HISTORICAL SKETCH OF EVENTS, SHOWING THE VALUE OF THE NIZAM'S ALLIANCE TO THE BRITISH GOVERNMENT IN INDIA, AND HIS SERVICES DURING THE MUTINIES.* London: Smith, Elder, 1895. xxviii & 507pp. Glossary.
Little on the Mutiny although there is a chapter on the services of the Nizam of Hyderabad to the British during the Mutiny.

413
IO 8831.g.20

Frere, Sir Bartle. *ANSWERS TO LETTER 235.* India Office Library.

414
BL
10804bbb17

Friend and Brother Officer. (Henry Yule). *A MEMORIAL OF THE LIFE AND SERVICE OF MAJOR GENERAL W.W.H. GREATHED OF THE ROYAL ENGINEERS (BENGAL). 1826-1878.* London: Privately Printed. 1879. Blue paper covers. Frontis of Greathed & 57pp.
William Wilberforce Harris Greathed was at the storming of Delhi. His brother Hervey was Commissioner of Meerut and his brother Edward commanded the 8th King's Regiment at Delhi. All three brothers were at Delhi during the siege.

415
BL
9056.bbb.76./
RAI

Frost, Thomas (ed.). *COMPLETE NARRATIVE OF THE MUTINY IN INDIA FROM ITS COMMENCEMENT TO THE PRESENT TIME. Compiled from the most authentic sources; including many very inte resting letters from officers on the spot.* London: Read & Co., 1857, 1858. 3rd ed. 76 pp. Paper.
8 illustrations drawn on stone. Includes numerous personal letters from witnesses of the Mutiny.

416
RAI 1857(54)   **Fulton, Captain G. W. W.** *BIOGRAPHICAL MEMOIRS WITH HIS PRIVATE JOURNAL OF HIS OWN PART IN THE SIEGE OF LUCKNOW.* Napier, New Zealand: NP. 1913. 30pp.
  Portrait, blue cloth. The journal starts on August 5th and is closed by Fulton's death on September 14th. This is cited by Forrest several times. Fulton was a Captain of Engineers, killed by a round shot at Lucknow. He was mentioned in dispatches by Inglis.

417
RS   **G. D. (Dodd).** *THE HISTORY OF THE INDIAN REVOLT AND OF THE EXPEDITIONS TO PERSIA, CHINA AND JAPAN. 1856-7-8.* London: W & R Chambers & Co., 1859. 634pp. Five colored double page maps and over 200 woodcut engravings.
  The author is simply listed a G.D. This is an important work and is probably the first one volume history of the Mutiny. Chaudhuri states that it contains many statistics that are not readily available elsewhere. Chaudhuri questions the date of publication as it does not seem possible that all of the facts presented could have been gathered by 1859.

418
Ames   **Gambier-Parry, Ernest.** *REYNELL TAYLOR CB CSI. A Biography.* London: Kegan Paul, Trench, 1888. ix & 365pp. Portrait and map. Index.
  General Taylor served at Delhi and was involved in the review of the execution of the Princes by Hodson. He was also charged with investigating Hodson's administration of the regimental chest (The Guides). He acquitted Hodson of wrong-doing. Taylor did not participate in any major Mutiny campaigns. He was stationed in Kangra.

419
IO   **Ganguly, Dr. Anil Baran.** *GUERILLA FIGHTER OF THE FIRST FREEDOM MOVEMENT.* Patna: Janaki Prakashan, 1980. x & 163pp., appendices, bibliography, index, 7 illus.
  Endorses the school of thought that the Mutiny was a national uprising. The book is basically a history of Tatya Tope and contains an interesting chapter on the question of whether Tatya Tope was actually hanged. The appendix includes the translation of Tatya Tope's "Confession and Orders" of which there is one duplicate copy in the National Archives of India, Delhi.

420
RS/BL   **Gardiner, General Sir Robert.** *CURSORY VIEW OF THE PRESENT CRISIS IN INDIA TOGETHER WITH THE MILITARY POWER OF ENGLAND, RESPECTFULLY ADDRESSED TO MEMBERS OF THE HOUSE OF COMMONS.* London: Byfield Hawksworth, 1857. 34pp.
Discusses causes and remedies of the Mutiny.

421
RS/BL   **Gardiner, General Sir Robert William.** *MILITARY ANALYSIS OF THE REMOTE AND PROXIMATE CAUSES OF THE INDIAN REBELLION, DRAWN FROM THE OFFICIAL PAPERS OF THE GOVERNMENT OF INDIA.* London: Byfield Hawkesworth, 1858. 99pp.
A monograph delivered to the House of Commons in March 1858. Gardiner supports the school of thought that the Mutiny was not only military but a social and civil rebellion as well. All of this caused by the wretched mis-rule of England.

422
Gardner, Frank M. *THE INDIAN MUTINY-A SPECIAL SUBJECT LIST.* London: Library Association, 1957. 4 pages.
Special subject list number 18.

423
Gardner, Frank M. *THE STORY OF THE INDIAN MUTINY.* London: 1957.
Considered of little significance by Sengupta in *"Recent Writings..."* Taylor shows Gardner, Frank M. and London, 1857. This is a mis-print. Ladendorf shows Gardner 1957. Ladendorf shows the book at the IO but it does not seem to be in the catalog.

424
IO/Ames   **Garrett, H. L. O. (ed.).** *PUNJAB RECORD OFFICE, PRESS LIST OF MUTINY PAPERS OF 1857-1858, IN THE PUNJAB SECRETARIAT.* Lahore: Jan. 2, 1925.
Begins May 1857 to April 1858. Offers the date, subject, address, and abstract of numerous letters. Much was previously published in 1911 in *"The Mutiny Correspondence"* by the Punjab Government. However, many have not been previously published.

425
Ames   **Garrett, H. L. O. ed.** *THE TRIAL OF MUHAMMED*
BAHADUR SHAH. NC. Punjab Government Record
Office Publications, 1932. xiv & 282pp.
Monograph 15. Edited with an introduction and notes by
H.L.O. Garrett. This is a re-editing of the trial. Garrett gives
a summary of the general evidence and has re-arranged the
material that was originally printed in 1895 as a government
blue book.

426
              Gateshead, The Mayor of. *See Crawshay, George.*

427
RS/BL   **Germon, Maria.** *JOURNAL OF THE SIEGE OF*
LUCKNOW: An Episode of the Indian Mutiny. London:
Constable, 1958. 136pp. And 5 plates.
Edited by Michael Edwardes. This text is from the
original in the India Office and has not been expurgated.

428
BL c121.aa.13 **Germon, Maria Vincent.** *A DIARY KEPT BY MRS.*
R.C. GERMON AT LUCKNOW BETWEEN THE
MONTHS OF MAY AND DECEMBER 1857. London:
Waterlow & Sons, 1870.
Captain Germon of the 13th NI commanded the Judicial
Commissioner's house during the siege. Most of the 13th
remained loyal during the Mutiny and in fact defended the
Baillie Guard at the Residency. This is an expurgated version
of the original, now located at the India Office.

429
RS   **Ghalib, Asadullah Mirza.** *DASTANBUY: A DIARY OF*
THE REVOLT OF 1857. Translated by Khwaja a Farqui.
London: Asia Publishing House, 1970. 96pp. 1 plate.
Ghalib (1797-1869) was a notable man of letters in Delhi.
When the Mutiny broke out he held a post in the court of
Bahadur Shah. The diary *"Dastanbuy"* (The Story Teller)
covers the period from the outbreak to August 1858.
Originally published in Persian in 1858.

430
RS   **Ghose, Indira.** *WOMEN TRAVELLERS IN*
COLONIAL INDIA: THE POWER OF THE FEMALE
GAZE. New Delhi: Oxford Univ Press, 1998. 2000 as a
paperback. 196pp. Good bibliography, notes and index.
Chapter 5 is "Mutiny Writings by Women." Ghose
covers the Cawnpore Massacre and "The Rape Myth" as well
as "The Tale of Miss Wheeler." Ghose discusses Coopland's
"A Lady's Escape from Gwalior and Life in the Fort of Agra

During the Mutinies of 1857" and Duberly's *"Campaigning Experiences in Rajpootana...."*

431
Ames/Ind Inst   **Gibbon, Frederick P.** *THE LAWRENCES OF THE PUNJAB. Edited by D. MacFayden.* London: J.M. Dent, 1908. xx & 305pp. Index, frontis and 6 illus.
Taken from Kaye, Bosworth and Edwardes' works on the Lawrences.

432
RS   **Gilbert, Henry.** *THE STORY OF THE INDIAN MUTINY.* New York and London: Thomas Y. Crowell, in London: G.G. Harrap, 1916. 350pp. 12 plates and 1 map, frontis.
A popular history told in a dramatic style.

433
RS   **Gilliat, Edward.** *DARING DEEDS OF THE INDIAN MUTINY.* Philadelphia and London: G.B. Lippincott and Seeley, Service and Co., 1918. 254pp. Frontis and 6 plates.
This is an abridgement of Gilliat's *"Heroes of the Indian Mutiny."*

434
RS   **Gilliat, Edward.** *HEROES OF THE INDIAN MUTINY. Stories of Heroic Deeds, Intrepidity, and Determination in the Face of Fearful Odds During the Great Mutiny.* Philadelphia: J.B. Lippincott & Co., 1914. 345pp. frontis and 7 illus., also London: Seeley, Service and Co., 1914.
Biographies of Seaton, Hodson, Edwardes, Daly, Roberts, Nicholson, Taylor, the Lawrences, Norman, Havelock, and Outram, Campbell, Hugh Rose, and others. All very laudatory.

435
RS   **Gimlette, Lieutenant-Colonel G(eorge) H(art) D(esmond) Indian Med Service.** *A POSTSCRIPT TO THE RECORDS OF THE INDIAN MUTINY. An Attempt to Trace the Subsequent Careers and Fate of the Rebel Bengal Regiments. 1857-1858.* London: H.F.& G. Witherby, 1927. 222pp. Index.
Gimlette lists all of the units of the Bengal Army and gives a short annotation of each one discussing their eventual fate. Gimlette also gives a list of those corps that did not mutiny. It is interesting to note that Stokes in *"The Peasant Armed"* states that, "Gimlete (sic.) abounds in inaccuracies,

hence his statements have to be used with caution." Stokes
was one of the pre-eminent scholars of the Mutiny.

436
Sut   **Goldsmid, Frederic John.** *JAMES OUTRAM, A*
BIOGRAPHY. London: Smith, Elder and Co., 1880,
1881. 2 volumes: xx & 434pp. and viii & 449pp.
Portrait, 4 plates, 5 maps, and 3 plans. A 2nd edition xxii
& 429pp. viii & 449pp. Portrait, 4 plates and 9 maps.
  The second edition has an additional map and some
revisions but nothing affecting the material relating to the
Mutiny.

437
RS   **Gordon, Andrew.** *1855-1885 OUR INDIAN*
MISSION. A 30 years History of the Indian Mission of the
United Presbyterian Church of North America Together with
Personal Reminiscences. Philadelphia: Published by the
author. 1886. xi & 516pp., 40 illus.
  Two chapters on the Mutiny.

438
IO   **Gordon, General Sir Thomas Edward.** *A VARIED*
LIFE. A record of Military and Civil Service, of sport and
of travel in India, Central Asia, and Persia 1849-1902.
London: John Murray, 1906. xvi & 357pp. portrait, 22
plates and two maps.
  The first chapter deals with the Mutiny. Gordon was
with the 7th Punjab Infantry, one of the new regiments raised
by Henry Lawrence. The regiment saw action in the Faizabad
and Azimgarh districts.

439
RAI   **Gordon, Surgeon General, Sir C. A.**
RECOLLECTIONS OF THIRTY NINE YEARS IN
THE ARMY: Gwalior and the Battle of Jaharajpore 1843;
The Gold Coast of Africa 1847-48; The Indian Mutiny
1857-58; The Expedition to China 1860-61; The Siege
of Paris 1870-71. London: Swan Sonnenschein, 1898.
Portrait, viii, and 320 pp.
  About 40pp. on the Mutiny. Gordon was surgeon of
the 10th during the Mutiny. Coverage of the Joonpore Field
Force, Capture of Lucknow and the Azimgurh Field Force.

440
RS/RAI   **Gordon-Alexander, Lieut. Col. W.**
RECOLLECTIONS OF A HIGHLAND SUBALTERN
DURING THE CAMPAIGNS OF THE 93RD
HIGHLANDERS IN INDIA, UNDER COLIN

CAMPBELL, LORD CLYDE IN 1857, 1858, 1859.
London: Edward Arnold, 1898. xii, 360pp., 10 illus., 9
plans, index.

Gordon-Alexander claims superior accuracy for his book
on the grounds of having witnessed or heard all of the events
in his work at the time they took place. He maintained a
personal diary throughout the Mutiny. The 93rd was one of
the most famous regiments to serve in the Mutiny. It relieved
Lucknow, returned to help Windham at Cawnpore, returned
to besiege and capture Lucknow and served with Walpole in
Rohilkhand.

441
BL   **Gorman, James T.** *THE SEIGE OF LUCKNOW.*
012211.c.2/8   Oxford: Oxford University Press, 1941. 38 pp. Paper.
            Part of the Great Exploits series.

442
RS   **Gough, General Sir Hugh Henry, VC.** *OLD
            MEMORIES.* Edinburgh: William Blackwood, 1897.
            vii, 236pp., 4 plates.

            Gough served in the 3rd Light Cavalry at Meerut at
the outbreak of the Mutiny. Fought at the Siege of Delhi
in Hodson's Horse and thence in Greathed's column and at
Lucknow. Hugh was the brother of Sir Charles John Stanley
Gough, VC and the nephew of Lord Gough. The son of
Charles was awarded the VC for bravery in Somaliland in
1903. Charles won the VC for four different acts during the
Mutiny. Hugh Gough was decorated for an action at the
Alumbagh at Lucknow.

443
RS   **Government of India.** *1857 A PICTORIAL
            PRESENTATION.* Delhi: Delhi Ministry of
            Information and Broadcasting. Publications Div., 1957.
            xv & 70pp. Illus.

444
IO   **Government of India.** *LIST OF OFFICERS OF HER
            MAJESTIES' AND THE HONORABLE COMPANY'S
            SERVICE, CIVIL SERVICE AND OTHERS WHO
            HAVE BEEN KILLED, ALSO THOSE WHO HAVE
            DIED SINCE THE 10TH MAY 1857, SERVING
            ON THE BENGAL ESTABLISHMENT, AS FAR AS
            KNOWN IN AGRA UP TO DECEMBER 15, 1857.*
            Punjab: Superintendent of Government Printing,
            December 14, 1926. 23pp.

445
IO   **Government of India.** *NARRATIVE OF*
EVENTS ATTENDING THE OUTBREAK OF
DISTURBANCES AND THE RESTORATION OF
AUTHORITY IN THE FURRUKABAD DISTRICT
IN 1857-58. Number I report by W.G. Probyn, Number II
report by C.R. Lindsay. Allahabad: Government Press,
1858. 46pp.
                      Number I includes appendix which gives names
of the Europeans at Futtehgurh who went down at the
commencement of the outbreak to Cawnpore; those that
remained at the fort, etc.

446
IO 9057.h.2   **Government of India.** *NARRATIVE OF THE*
MUTINY OF THE 29TH N.I. AT MORRADABAD.
NC. NP. ND.
                      Bound with other materials.

447
IO 9057.h.2   **Government of India (Williams, Major G. W.).**
DEPOSITIONS TAKEN AT MEERUT BY MAJOR
G. W. WILLIAMS SUPERINTENDENT OF POLICE,
N.W.P. Allahabad: Government Press, 1858. 49pp.
                      Bound with other materials.

448
IO   **Government of India.** *MUTINY IN INDIA.*
L/Mil/17/2/492 *NARRATIVE OF EVENTS REGARDING*
(51)   *THE MUTINY IN INDIA 1857-58 AND THE*
RESTORATION OF AUTHORITY. Calcutta: Foreign
Department Press, 1881. 2 Vols. 711pp. & 408pp.
                      By general order all local officers were requested to
compile narratives of events during the Mutiny in their areas.
These often contained day by day accounts and eyewitness
reports. The general order was issued April 30, 1858 and the
reports were published in 1881. This title is also listed as three
volumes in some references. For additional information see
Seton, "*The Indian Mutiny 1857-58,*" page xii. (entry 945).
The contents of the two volumes are as follows:
                      Vol. I. Narrative of Events Attending the Outbreak and
Disturbances and Restoration of Authority in the Allahabad
District 1858. From: F. Thompson, Officiating Magistrate
Allahabad to E. C. Bailey, Officiating Commissioner, 4th
Division. Narrative of Events...Shahjanpoor, 7 December
1858. From H. D. Willock, Joint Magistrate Shahjehanpoor
to C. B. Thornhill, Commissioner of Allahabad. Appendix
IV. Memorandum of the Particulars of the Escape of Mr.
Corrigan and Family...From Futtehpoor to Allahabad.

Narrative of Events...in the District of Futtehpoor in
1857- 58. Narrative of Events...in the Division of Benares
1857-58. From F. Gubbins, Commissioner 5th Division to
William Muir, Secretary to the Government, Northwestern
Provinces. Narrative of Events...in Goruckpoor 5, July,
1858. Page 2 Narrative of Events: From C. Wingfield,
Commissioner Goruckpoor to William Muir, Secretary of
Government Northwestern Provinces. Narrative of Events...
in Agra District 1857-58. From A. L. M. Phillips, Magistrate
of Agra to Commissioner of Agra Division. Narrative of
Events...District of Muttra 1857-58. From M. Thornhill,
late Magistrate of Muttra to G. F. Harvey, Commissioner
Agra Division. Narrative of Events...District of Cawnpore.
1857-58. From C. B. Thornhill, Commissioner of Allahabad
Division to Secretary of Government Northwestern Provinces.
Narrative of Events...Furruckabad District. Report by W. G.
Probyn, formerly Officiating Magistrate and Collector of that
district. Dated 3rd June, 1858. Lists those people who went
down to Cawnpore at the outbreak and those who stayed in
Furruckabad. Lists those in each boat. Page 3 Narratives of
Events.... Narrative of Events...District of Mynpoory. Dated
16 November 1858. From A. Cocks, Special Commissioner
to William Muir, Secretary to Government, Northwestern
Provinces. Narrative of Events...District of Etah. Dated
Agra 9 June 1858. From A. L. M. Phillips, Magistrate
of Agra, late Joint Magistrate of Etah. To G. H. Harvey,
Commissioner of Agra Division. Narrative of Events...
District of Allygurh. 17 November 1858. From W. J.
Bramly, Magistrate and Collector, Allygurh. To A. Cocks,
Special Commissioner. Narrative of Events...Meerut. Dated
15 November 1858. From F. Williams, Commissioner 1st
Division. To William Muir, Secretary to the Government of
the Northwestern Provinces. Contains names of those in the
volunteer force and various statesments and depositions from
both British residents and Indians. Page 4. Narratives....
Narrative of Events...Mozuffernugger. No salutation. Signed
by R. M. Edwards, Magistrate. Narrative of Events...Bareilly.
No salutation. Signed by J. F. D. Inglis. Contains a list of
European and native Christians at Bareilly on 31, May 1857
and their subsequent history.
     Narrative of Events.....Maradabad. Dated Calcutta 24
December 1858. To J. C. Wilson, Commissioner on special
duty. From G. F. Edmonstone, Secretary to Government,
Allahabad. Narrative of Events...Shahjehanpoor. Dated
9 September 1858. From G. P. Money, Magistrate and
Collector Shahjehanpoor. To R. Alexander, Commissioner
of Rohilkund. Contains a list of killed and escaped. A list of
government servants who took service with the rebels and a
list of those who did not. In addition there is a list of principal

persons not in government service who joined the rebels. Page 5 Narrative of Events. Narrative of Events...Budaon. No salutation. Signed by C. P. Carmichael, Officiating Magistrate. 23 November 1858. Narrative of Events.... Saharunpoor. Dated Saharunpoor 26 September 1857. From R. Spankie, Magistrate to F. Williams, Commissioner 1st Division, Meerut. Following appendices: Report of proceeding at Roorkee during the disturbances of 1857 & 1858 by Lieut. Colonel R. Baird Smith. Narrative of Events...Bijnour. No date. From A. Shakespear, Magistrate and Collector. To R. Alexander, Commissioner of Rohilkund, Bareilly. Narrative of Events...Kumaon. Dated Nynee Tal 22 July 1858. From Major H. Ramsay, Commissioner. To William Muir, Secretary to the Government Northwestern Provinces. Page 6. Narratives. Narratives of Events....Banda. Dated Allahabad 11 September 1857. From F.O. Mayne, Magistrate and Collector. To C. Chester, Commissioner, Allahabad Division. Narrative of Events Connected with the Mutiny at Humeerpoor. No date. Signed by George H. Freeling, Collector and Magistrate. Narrative of Events... Jhansie. No date. No salutation. Signed J.W. Pinkney Captain, Commissioner. Contains a list of Europeans and Anglo Indians murdered at Jhansie.

Narrative of Events...Jaloun. Dated Calpee 12 June 1858. From Captain A. H. Ternan. Deputy Commissioner. To Captain F. W. Pinkney, Commissioner, Jhansie Division. Narrative of Events.....Saugor and Nerbudda territories. From Major W. C. Erskine, Commissioner of Jubbulpoor Division. To William Muir. Page 7. Narratives. Special Judicial Narratives from various areas.

Volume II contains special narratives by date, commencing 9 September 1857 to 30 June 1858. Narrative of Events...Rajpootana. Dated Aboo 27 July 1858. From Brigadier General G. St. P. Lawrence, Officiating Governor General's Agent, Rajpootana State. To G. F. Edmonstone, Secretary to Government of India with the Governor General. Narrative of Events...in Central India from May 1857 to 20 June 1858. No date and no salutation. Signed by G. F. Edmonstone. Report of Major Ellis concerning services rendered by certain cheifs in Bundelcand during the disturbances, with his recommendation in each case. Page 8. Narratives. List of Europeans who have rendered good services to the government during the Mutiny. Two minutes and a dispatch complete Volume II.

449
IO   **Government of India. (Williams, G. Lieut. Col).** *SYNOPSIS OF THE EVIDENCE OF THE CAWNPORE MUTINY.* Allahabad: Government Printing Press, ND. 31pp.

Includes lists of 1) Names of those who were in Cawnpore entrenchments and names of those who perished outside of entrenchments, and 2) Names of those who left Futtehgurh on 4th June 1857 and are supposed to have perished at Cawnpore on the 12th of that month.

450
IO

Government of India. (Williams, G. Lieut.-Col.). *REVIEW OF THE EVIDENCE TAKEN AT CAWNPORE REGARDING THE REVOLT AT THAT STATION IN JUNE AND JULY 1857.* Allahabad: Government Press, 1859. 5pp.

451
RS

Government of India. Army Intelligence. (Burton, Maj. R. G. ed.). *THE REVOLT IN CENTRAL INDIA 1857-1859.* Simla: Government Monotype Press, 1908. xxi & 277 pp. 10 maps including one folding map in end pocket.

Printed for official use only. Compiled in the Intelligence Branch Division of the Chief of the Staff, Army Head Quarters, India, by Major R. G. Burton. Gives a complete history of the Mutiny in Central India. 1500 copies were originally printed. The preface to this book is written by Lieut. Colonel W. Malleson not G. B. Malleson as stated in Mythic.

452
Centennial
Exhibit/
Sut

Government of India. Imperial Record Department. *PRESS LIST OF MUTINY PAPERS, 1857. Being a Collection of the Correspondence of the Mutineers at Delhi, Reports of Spies to English Officials and Other Miscellaneous Papers.* Calcutta: Government Press, 1921. 423pp.

These are mostly translations of Urdu and Persian papers.

453
Sut

Gowan, I. G. *ACCOUNT OF MY ESCAPE FROM BAREILLY AND SUBSEQUENT OCCURRENCES TO THE PERIOD OF MY ARRIVAL AT MEERUT. Delhi:* Delhi Gazette Press, 1860. 37pp.

454
RS

Gowing, Sergeant Major T. *A SOLDIER'S EXPERIENCE: Or a Voice From the Ranks, Showing the Cost of War in Blood and Treasure. A personal narrative of the Crimean campaign, from the standpoint of the ranks, the Indian Mutiny and some of its atrocities....* Suffolk, England: NP. 1884. By the author. xv & 493pp., frontis and 16pages of plates.

New edition 1892, xvi & 585pp. With 18 plates.
Nottingham: published by the author. xvi & 585pp. With 18
plates. 1899. The 1901 edition, xvi & 628pp, was published
in Nottingham by Thos. Forman for the author. Also
1906 xvi & 628pp. Reprinted in 1954 with the title: *A Voice
From the Ranks*. Reprinted again in 1973. First edition was
1870, 274pp. Colchester. It dealt mainly with the Crimea.
Approximately 50pp on the Mutiny.

455
RS   **Grant, General Sir James Hope.** *INCIDENTS IN
THE SEPOY WAR 1857-58. Compiled from Private
Journals of General Sir Hope Grant G.C.B. Together with
some explanatory chapters by Henry Knollys.* London and
Edinburgh: William Blackwood and Sons, 1873. xvi &
380pp., folding maps of Lucknow, Delhi and the North
West Provinces.
          Another edition 1894, two volumes, xiii & 359pp; xi &
362pp. 9 plates, 7 maps. Grant saw extensive action during
the Mutiny at Delhi, Oude and Cawnpore. Chaudhuri
calls this the most famous work on the Mutiny by a military
historian.

456
BL 10816.a.23   **Grant, James P.** *THE CHRISTIAN SOLDIER.
MEMORIALS OF MAJOR-GENERAL SIR HENRY
HAVELOCK. K. C. B.* London: J. A. Berger, 1858. xii
& 91pp.
          Red cloth. Standard fare on Havelock.

457
RS   **Gray, Ernest.** *NIKKAL SEYN.* London: Collins, 1947.
239pp.
          Biography of General Nicholson.

458
IO   **Gray, Robert.** *REMINISCENCES OF INDIA AND
NORTH QUEENSLAND 1857-1912.* London:
Constable, 1913. xi & 271pp. Index, frontis and 7 illus.
1 map.
          Gray served with Campbell at Lucknow. Little on the
Mutiny.

459
RS   **Graydon, William Murray.** *THE BUTCHER OF
CAWNPORE.* New York: Street and Smith, 1896, 1897,
1900. 289pp.
          Fiction

460
Maggs   **Great Britain.** *EAST INDIA (MUTINY) RETURN OF*
Dec. 1984   *THE NAME OR NUMBER OF EACH Regiment and
                 Regular and Irregular Corps in India Which has Mutinied...
                 Since 1, January 1857. Ordered by the House of Commons to
                 be printed 15, March 1859.*, NP. Folio, 71pp.

461
Sut   **Great Britain Mutiny Return.** *EAST INDIA (NATIVE
                 CAVALRY) 1861. NUMBER 58.* London: HMSO,
                 1861. 265pp. Paper.
                 Return to an Address of the Honourable the House
                 of Commons, dated 31 January 1860- for a "Return of the
                 Number of Regular and Irregular Regiments of Native Cavalry
                 in India which have been employed upon Field Service from
                 April 1857 to December 1859, stating their respective Fixed
                 Establishments of Men and Horses; the Number of Men
                 and Horses present for Duty on the 1st and 15th day of each
                 Month in each Regiment; the Number of Horses and Men
                 sick present; and of Absentees from Head-quarters at the same
                 dates, stating causes of Absence." India Office, 18 February
                 1861. W.T. Baker Colonel, Military Secretary. Ordered by
                 House of Commons to be printed, 22 February 1861.

462
IO   **Great Britain.** *FURTHER PAPERS RELATIVE
                 TO THE MUTINIES IN THE EAST INDIES.*
                 Also *FURTHER PAPERS RELATIVE TO THE
                 INSURRECTION IN THE EAST INDIES.* London:
                 Harrison & Sons, 1858. 944 + 26 + 3 +2 + 12 + 2 + 71.
                 This volume consists of a number of reports submitted to
                 parliament during 1858. Letters to and from the Governor
                 General and the Court of Directors E.I.C. together with
                 internal correspondence between various commissions and the
                 Governor General and others.

463
Maggs   **Great Britain. House of Lords.** *EAST INDIES PRIZE
Dec. 1984   MONEY. Return to an Address of the House of Lords,
                 Calling for Copy of a Dispatch in July 1858 .... on the
                 Subject of the Delhi Prize Money. Ordered to be printed 19,
                 March 1860.* Folio. 39pp.

464
RS/RAI   **Greathed, H(ervey) H(arris).** *LETTERS WRITTEN
                 DURING THE SIEGE OF DELHI. Edited by his
                 widow.* London: Longman, Brown, Green Longmans
                 and Roberts, 1858. xxiii, 293pp., folding map.
                 Hervey Harris Greathed was commissioner at Meerut at

the outbreak of the Mutiny. He later served as Commssioner at Delhi but died before the British regained the city. He was the brother of William Wilberforce Harris Greathed and Colonel Edward Harris Greathed.

465
BL
010815.e.21

Greaves, General Sir George Richard. *MEMOIRS (1831-1922).* London: John Murray, 1924. xiii, 258pp. With 8 plates and 3 maps.
Covers service at Peshawur during the Mutiny. Greaves saw no action. Later Chief of Staff Suakin and C-in-C Bombay.

466

Green, Henry. *REPORT OF THE AFFAIRS OF KHELAT FROM 1857 TO 1860.* Calcutta: Bengal Printing, 1861.
Cited in Jain. No further information.

467

Greene, Dominick Sarsfield. *VIEWS IN INDIA FROM DRAWINGS TAKEN DURING THE SEPOY MUTINY.* London: Thomas McLean 1859. 20 plates with descriptions.
Cited in Ladendorf.

468
Bod

Grey, Leopold John Herbert. *TALE OF OUR GRANDFATHER OR INDIA SINCE 1856. Ed. By F. and C. Grey.* London: Smith, Elder and Co., 1912. 307pp. Frontis.
Originally written as letters to his grandsons in America. Approximately 20pp. on the Mutiny.
Grey arrived in India in early 1857 and was in Lahore, Delhi, and Agra. Of little value.

469
RS

Griffiths, Capt. Charles John. *A NARRATIVE OF THE SIEGE OF DELHI. With an account of the mutiny at Ferozepore in 1857. Ed. By Henry John Yonge.* London: John Murray, 1910. xiv & 260pp., 5 plates and 3 plans.
The author was a lieutenant at Ferozepore in 1857 with the 61st Foot. He later served at Delhi during the siege. Compare Griffiths' account of Delhi after the siege with Nigam's account in *"Delhi in 1857."* (Entry 802).

470
IO

Groom, Lt. William Tate. *WITH HAVELOCK FROM ALLAHABAD TO LUCKNOW. 1857.* London: Sampson, Low, Marston, 1894. xv & 110pp.

Groom died of wounds at the Residency in Lucknow on October 21, 1857. These are extracts from letters by Groom, of the 1st Madras Royal Fusiliers, to his wife.

471
RS

Gubbins, Martin Richard. *AN ACCOUNT OF THE MUTINEES IN OUDH AND OF THE SIEGE OF THE LUCKNOW RESIDENCY. With Some Observations on the Condition of the Province of Oudh and on the Causes of the Mutiny of the Bengal Army.* London: Richard Bentley, 1858. xii, 464pp. 4 colored lithos, 4 folding plans and 1 map Additional Publishing Information; 2nd edition London: 1858. xii, 484pp. The 2nd edition contains an appendix, No. 9, concerning an escape from Sultanpoor and Major Eyre's account of the Arrah Campaign. 3rd. edition London: 1858, xx, 570 pp., 4 tinted lithos, 4 folding maps and a plan. Also a reprint of the 2nd edition was printed in 1978.

Gubbins was the financial commissioner of Oude. He served through the siege at Lucknow.

Portions of the original manuscript of the book were lost with the sinking of the AVA on its return to England. This was the same ship where Lady Inglis lost part of her manuscript. Lost with the AVA was a narrative by Lt. H. M. Havelock of his father's campaign, and an account of the engagement at Chinhut in the words of Captain Hamilton Forbes who commanded the advance guard in that action. Gubbins did not get along well with Henry Lawrence and never forgave him for keeping the command of the Residency from him. The book is quite good though a number of authorities have claimed that it is biased and Gubbins is too egotistical. Gubbins returned to India from England in 1858 and became a Judge at Agra. There was an inquiry into his actions at Lucknow he again retired to England and in May of 1863 committed suicide.

Henry Marshman Havelock (afterwards Lieut.-General Sir H. M. Havelock-Allan) died December 30, 1897, shot by an Afridi sharpshooter on the NWF.

472
RS

Guha, Ranajit and Gayatri Spivak. *SELECTED SUBALTERN STUDIES.* Oxford & New York: Oxford Univ. Press, 1988. 434pp. Paper.

Ten essays from the five volume series. One of the essays, "Four Rebels of Eighteen-Fifty-Seven" by Gautam Bhadra is quite interesting. It looks at the Mutiny through the eyes of four common rebels; Shah Mal a proprietor of a portion of a village; Devi Singh, a village rebel in Mathura whose biographer was Mark Thornhill; Gonoo, an ordinary cultivator in Chotanagpore; and Maulvi Ahmaduallah Shah, known as the Maulvi of Fyzabad.

473
Ames/Ind Inst   **Gupta, Pratul C.** *THE LAST PESHWA AND THE ENGLISH COMMISSIONERS.* Calcutta: S.C. Sarkar & Sons Ltd., 1944. 113pp. Bibliography.
A scholarly study of Baji Rao II with good background for understanding the Nana Sahib.

474
RS/Ind Inst   **Gupta, Pratul Chandra.** *NANA SAHIB AND THE RISING AT CAWNPORE.* Oxford: Clarendon Press, 1963. x & 227pp., Map, plan and 9 illus., glossary, bibliography and index.
Scholarly treatment of the events at Cawnpore. Gupta uses many of the standard sources in addition to material from the National Archives of India. He lists a number of sources from the National Archives.

475
Gupta, Rajni Kant. *MILITARY TRAITS OF TATYA TOPE.* Delhi: NP. 1987.
Unable to locate.

476
Gupta, S. (ed.). *WAR OF INDEPENDENCE, CENTENARY VOLUME.* Calcutta: NP. 1957.
Collection of essays by active politicians. All stress the national character of the revolt. Cited in Sengupta "*Recent Writings.*"

477
BL 4462.d.9   **Gurney, Rev. John Hampden.** *THE MORAL OF A SAD STORY. FOUR SERMONS ON THE INDIAN MUTINY.* London: Rivington, 1857.

478
IO   **Haigh, R. H. and P. W. Turner.** *THE PUNJAB MOVEABLE COLUMN, ITS EFFECT ON THE COURSE OF EVENTS IN THE PUNJAB DURING THE INDIAN MUTINY OF 1857.* Sheffield: Sheffield City Polytechnic, Dept. of Public Sector Administration, 1977. 54pp.
This is the third in a series of occasional papers dealing with the East India Company, and the Punjab. This paper examines the role of the moveable column under Chamberlain and Nicholson.

479
IO

Haigh, R. H. and P. W. Turner. *ROUGH JUSTICE. The Administration of Bannu, the Punjab, and the Events Leading to the Outbreak of the Indian Mutiny.* Sheffield: Sheffield City Polytechnic, Dept. of Public Administration, ND. c. 1984. 44pp.

Second in a series of four occasional papers dealing with the E.I.C., the Punjab, the men and events in the decade prior to the Indian Mutiny of 1857. All of the papers have as their central character, John Nicholson. This paper examines the difference in administrative styles between Nicholson, Edwardes, and Taylor and relates this to the outbreak of the Mutiny.

480
Sut/RS

Haigh, R. H. and P. W. Turner. *JOHN NICHOLSON, THE BATTLE OF NAJAFGARH AND THE SIEGE OF DELHI.* Sheffield: Sheffield City Polytechnic, 1977. 35pp.

Fourth in the series of papers. The first paper, "*The Punjab Administration and the Events Leading up to the Second Sikh War of 1848*" has no Mutiny content.

481
RS/
BL 8022.d.69

Hale, Williams. *THE OUDE QUESTION STATED AND CONSIDERED: With Reference to Published and Official Documents.* London: Smith and Co., January, 1857. Pamphlet, 71pp.

Discusses Dalhousie's annexation of the Kingdom of Oude. An appendix was issued the following month.

482
IO

Halliday, Frederick James *MINUTE BY THE LT. GOVERNOR OF BENGAL, ON THE MUTINIES AS THEY AFFECTED THE LOWER PROVINCES UNDER THE GOVERNMENT OF BENGAL.* Calcutta: John Gray, 1858. 88pp.

Covers Bihar, Chota Nagpore, Cuttack, Bhaugulpore Division, Rajshahye Division, Nuddea, Burdwan, Dacca and Chittagong and Assam.

483
RS/
BL 9056.b.15

Halls, John James. *TWO MONTHS IN ARRAH IN 1857.* London (Calcutta): Longman, Green, Longman and Roberts (Bangabasi Office), March, 1860 (1905). 99pp. (70pp.)

Halls was the Assistant Surgeon at Arrah at the outbreak. Halls died November 6, 1860 aboard the "Ceylon" on his return to England.

484
RS/RAI

Handcock, Col. A(rthur) G(ore). *A SHORT ACCOUNT OF THE SIEGE OF DELHI IN 1857.* Simla (Allahabad): Government Central Printing Office, 1892 (1907 4th ed.). 22pp. With no appendix (25pp) 3rd ed. By Allahabad, Pioneer Press, 1899. iii, 25pp. 4th and revised ed. With folding map 1907. Originally only 2000 were printed for the first edition in Simla in 1892. To be used as a handbook for visitors to Delhi. "Consists of abbreviated extracts from works already published."

485
RS

Hannah, W. H. *BOBS: Kipling's General. The Life of Field Marshal Earl Roberts of Kandahar VC.* London: Leo Cooper, 1972. 263pp. Bibliography and index.
Five chapters on India. Roberts received his VC during the Mutiny.

486
BL

Haq, S. Moinul (Ed.). *MEMOIRS OF HAKIM AHSANULLAH KHAN.* Karachi: Pakistan Historical Society, 1958. ix & 57pp.
Ahsanullah Khan was a confidante of Bahadur Shah but he had no use for the sepoy cause and did not support it. He was in the palace during the siege of Delhi. This work also includes the journal of Kedarnath, a clerk in the Delhi Gazette Press.

487
IO

Haq, S. M. *THE GREAT REVOLUTION OF 1857.* Karachi: Pakistan Historical Society #52, 1968. xxiv & 630pp., 5pp. of illus, portraits and maps, folding map at rear, index, 5pp. corrigenda, bibliography of English and oriental sources.
Stresses the role of the Muslims in the Mutiny. Proposes to give an accurate picture of the period, not a one-sided view that has been so prevalent. States that Majumdar's book "*Sepoy Mutiny and Revolt of 1857*" and Sen's "*1857*" are the two outstanding books in English published in the post-partition period. However both authors have almost totally ignored oriental sources. Haq endorses the position that there was a conspiracy that erupted prematurely. The leaders are cited and Haq stresses that this was an attempt to liberate Hind-Pakistan from the British.

488
Jain

Harcourt, A. F. P. *THE PERIL OF THE SWORD; CONCERNING HAVELOCK'S RELIEF OF*

LUCKNOW. London: Skeffington & Sons, 1903.
364pp. 4 plates.

489
BL 10825.f.33   **Hare, Augustus and John Cuthbert.** *THE STORY OF TWO NOBLE LIVES. Being Memorials of Charlotte, Countess Canning, and Louisa, Marchioness of Waterford.* London: George Allen, 1895. 3 vols. (see below)
Vol. I: x & 381pp., Vol. II: iii & 489pp., and Vol. III: viii & 495pp. 64 illus. Vol. II has 220pp. on the Mutiny.

490
Sut   **Hare, E. C.** *MEMOIRS OF EDWARD HARE. LATE INSPECTOR GENERAL OF HOSPITALS.* London: NP. 1900. 5 plates, folding map. Blue cloth. 160pp.
Present at the siege of Delhi. About 30pp on the Mutiny.

491
RS   **Hare, Lt. Col. R. T.** *REMINISCENCES OF A MUTINY VETERAN.* Portsmouth: Charpentier and Co., ND. c. 1913. 95 pp.
Hare was a Lt. with the Bengal Horse Artillery at the siege of Delhi. He also fought with Lord Clyde at Lucknow and against the Gwalior rebels at Cawnpore.

492
RS   **Harrington, Capt. Hastings Edward, VC.** *THE LATE CAPTAIN H.E. HARINGTON, VC OF H.M. BENGAL ARTILLERY.* London: Nisbet, 1862. iv, 98pp.
Served with Nicholson and was wounded at Trimmoo Ghat. Served at the seige of Delhi and then proceeded with Greathed's column. At the relief of Lucknow he was awarded the VC and was wounded again. Was again at Lucknow and again severely wounded during the pursuit of the enemy in Rohilcund. Harington was sent home to recover. He returned to India and perished of cholera in 1861. This small book is a memoir of his services.

493
Sut   **Harrington, C. S.** *THE LATE CAPTAIN H. E. HARRINGTON, VC OF HM BENGAL ARTILLERY.* London: NP. 1862. 96pp. Thirteen thousand. Limp cloth.
Served throughout the Mutiny. Hastings Edward Harrington was elected under Rule 13 of the Warrant, to receive the VC for service during the relief of Lucknow. Harrington volunteered for duty in the Crimea and later returned to his studies at Oxford upon the conclusion of that war. He went out to India originally to work in the telegraph

service. He died at Agra in 1861. It is not clear if this is a
duplicate of entry 492.

494
RS   **Harris, John.** *THE INDIAN MUTINY.* London: Heart
Davis MacGibbon, 1973. 208pp. Select bibliography,
index.
The British at War Series. Well illustrated. General
history of the Mutiny.

495
Sut   **Harris, Major General James T.** *CHINA JIM: Being*
Incidents and Adventures in the Life of an Indian Mutiny
Veteran. London: Heinemann, 1912. Delhi and Oude xii
& 218pp. Frontis portrait.
Harris served in the Mutiny and the China War with the
Bengal Fusiliers. He got his nickname at the sack of Peking
where he acquired more loot from the Summer Palace than
any other man in the force.

496
RS   **Harrison, A. T. (ed.).** *THE GRAHAM MUTINY*
PAPERS. With an Historiographical Essay by T.G. Fraser.
Belfast: Public Record Office of Northern Ireland, 1980.
iix, 167pp., glossary and index.
The Grahams were one of a number of Irish families
deeply involved in Indian service. These are their papers and
give an important insight into what the Mutiny meant to
a middle-class Irish military family. The book contains an
introduction to the history and causes of the Mutiny. Short
discussions of the Martial Races Theory, "*The Man Who Would*
Be King" by Kipling, and a historiographical perspective of
the Graham papers. The papers consist of James Graham's
Mutiny Diary and personal correspondence from a number
of members of the family. Appendix "A" is a study of "Ulster
Attitudes to the Indian Mutiny." Editorials are presented
from the major Ulster newspapers. The role of religion and
politics is quite evident in the Irish feeling towards the British
position in India at this particular time.

497
NAM.92 HAR **Harrison, General Sir Richard.** *RECOLLECTIONS*
OF A LIFE IN THE BRITISH ARMY DURING THE
LATTER HALF OF THE 19TH CENTURY. London:
Smith, Elder & Co., 1908. vi & 382pp. Red cloth.
Frontis and 15 illustrations. Index.
Harrison served with the Royal Engineers. He arrived
in India late in 1857 and served with the 23rd in Cawnpore,
Rohilcund and Oude. About 40 pages on the Mutiny.
Harrison died at age 94 in Devon on September 28, 1931.

498
BL 8116b/13   **Harrison, John Bennett.** *THE INDIAN MUTINY.* London: Routledge, Historical Assoc. Aids for Teachers, Series No. 5, 1958. 12pp.

499
Harvey, G. F. *NARRATIVE OF EVENTS ATTENDING THE OUTBREAK OF DISTURBANCES AND THE RESTORATION OF AUTHORITY IN THE AGRA DIVISION 1857-1858.* See listing for Mutiny in India. (Entry 448)

500
Sut   **Havelock, Sir H. M.** *THREE MAIN MILITARY QUESTIONS OF THE DAY: A HOME RESERVE ARMY, THE MORE ECONOMIC MILITARY TENURE OF INDIA, CAVALRY AS AFFECTED BY BREECH LOADING ARMS.* London: Longmans Green, 1867. iii & 209pp. Red cloth. 2 folding plans.
Compares the British cavalry and their pursuit of the sepoys with the Union's cavalry and their pursuit of Confederate forces in the American Civil War. Havelock later took the additional name of Allan. He won the VC for action at Cawnpore. He was the son of Henry Havelock.

501
RS   **Hay, David.** *COPY OF LETTER WRITTEN DURING THE SIEGE OF LUCKNOW, 1857. Received by His Mother January 1858.* Edinburgh: William Blackwood and Sons, 1910. 64pp. Printed for private circulation.
Our copy has alterations showing Hay was a member of the 48th Bengal Native Infantry not the 28th. In addition, the printed lines stating, "Copied Many Years After by His Sister Susan Montagu Hay" are lined out and the following is entered, "As copied by members of his family at the time." The first letter is dated "Residency, Lucknow, July 18th, 1857." Hay remained at the Alum Bagh. The last letter is dated November 26th, 1857.

502
RS   **Headley, J.** *THE LIFE OF GENERAL H. HAVELOCK K.C.B.* New York: Low and Co. & Charles Scribner, 1859. 375pp. Frontis of Havelock. & 4 plates
The first full biography of Havelock. Headley states that he had access to all of the authentic accounts published in England and, in addition, the help of a family friend of the Havelocks and a gentleman of high position and influence in India.

503
RS
Hearn, Gordon Risley. *THE SEVEN CITIES OF DELHI.* London: W. Thacker and Co., 1906. Frontis and 19 photos, 5 folding plans, xiv & 319pp.
Good reference to find historical sights from the siege.

504
Hearsey, John B. *NARRATIVE OF THE OUTBREAK AT SEETAPORE.* Seetapore: Privately printed, 1858.
Hearsey was the cousin and brother-in-law of General John Bennet Hearsey of Barrackpore, Military commander of the Bengal Presidency. See Stark: *"Call of the Blood"* page 28. Entry 994.

505
BL 8022.c.46
Henderson, Henry Barkley. *A STATEMENT RELATIVE TO THE SUFFERERS BY THE MUTINY IN INDIA.* London: NP. 1857.

506
RAI
Herford, Capt. I. S. A. *STIRRING TIMES UNDER CANVAS.* London: Richard Bentley, 1862. xvi, 301pp., woodcut engraved frontis.
Herford marched with Campbell on the relief of Lucknow. He stayed on with Outram at the Alambagh.

507
IO
Hervey, Lt. Gen. Charles, Lt. Gen. Crommelin C.B., Royal Bengal Engineers. *A MEMOIR AND RETROSPECT. FORCING THE GANGES AT CAWNPORE AND MARCH UPON LUCKNOW--UNDERGROUND WARFARE AT THE SECOND DEFENSE OF THE RESIDENCY: IN THE YEAR OF THE MUTINY IN INDIA.* Exeter: William Pollard, 1887. 40pp.

508
RS
Hewitt, James (ed.). *EYEWITNESSES TO THE INDIAN MUTINY. (Eyewitness to History Series.).* London: Osprey, 1972. 176pp. 29 plates, 5 maps.
Extracts from letters, books, military dispatches, etc., are used to cover the events at Delhi, Cawnpore and Lucknow. A good source for descriptive quotes from many of the participants in the Mutiny.

509
RS
Hibbert, Christopher. *THE GREAT MUTINY: INDIA 1857.* New York: Viking Press, 1978. 472pp. 55 plates.
Very well written, very well researched work. There is an

extensive bibliography together with exhaustive notes. This is one of the best of the contemporary histories of the Mutiny.

510
BL

Hidayat Ali, Shaikh. *A FEW WORDS RELATIVE TO THE LATE MUTINY OF THE BENGAL ARMY AND REBELLION IN BENGAL PRESIDENCY.* Calcutta: Privately published, 1858. 20pp.
Hidayat Ali was a Subadar of the Bengal Sikh Battalion commanded by Capt. T. Rattray who translated the paper from the original Urdu.

511

Hill, J.R. *THE STORY OF THE CAWNPORE MISSION.* Westminster: NP. 1909.

512

Hill, S.C. *CATALOG OF HOME MISCELLANEOUS SERIES OF THE INDIA OFFICES RECORDS.* London: NP. 1927.
Sir John Kaye's papers are included as well as other relevant reference material.

513
IO T43549

Hilton, Edward. *THE MARTINIERE BOYS IN THE BAILEY GUARD BY ONE OF THEM.* Lucknow: Lucknow American Methodist Mission Press, 1877. 18pp. folding plan.
Includes a list of the garrison and the students at the Martiniere College during the siege. This was the first of the many incarnations of Hilton's title. A rather scarce title.

514
RS

Hilton, Edward. *THE MUTINY RECORDS: OUDH AND LUCKNOW 1856-57. By one of the beleaguered garrison. From the 7th edition.* Lucknow: NP. 1911. iii & 232pp. & xxxviii, frontis and 15 illus. with folding plan.
Reprinted by Sheikh Mubarak Ali, Lahore, Pakistan, 1975. Hilton was a student at the Martiniere at the beginning of the siege. This is a brief history of Lucknow and Oudh and a narration of events during the Mutiny. Hilton names the following as sources, Gubbins, McLeod Innes, Lord Roberts, Malleson, Marshman, and others. This title went through a number of editions and updates. Includes discussions of all of the major monuments and rulers of Oudh.

515

Hilton, Edward H. *THE MARTINIERE BOYS IN THE RESIDENCY.*
This is basically the same book as *"The Tourists Guide to Lucknow"* and *"The Mutiny Records: Oudh and Lucknow 1856-*

57." "*The Martiniere Boys in the Residency*" is mentioned in the 1916, 9th edition of the "*Tourists Guide to Lucknow*" however it is deleted from the preface of the "*Mutiny Records.*" This may be the same book as "*The Martiniere Boys*" dated 1877.

516
RS   **Hilton, Edward H.** *THE TOURISTS GUIDE TO LUCKNOW. By one of the Beleaguered Garrison.* Lucknow: London Printing Press, 1902 (4th ed.), 1916 (8th and 9th eds.), 9th ed. printed by F.W. Perry. Frontis of Hilton, 14 illus. and folding map at rear, ii & 236p
    This is essentially the same book as Hilton's "*The Mutiny Records.*"

517
RS   **Hilton, Major General Richard.** *THE INDIAN MUTINY A CENTENARY HISTORY.* London: Hollis and Carter, 1957. vi, 232 pp. Appendices and index.
    Hilton maintains the Mutiny was not a national uprising but the treatment is biased and prejudicial.

518
BL 3185.d.11   **Hoare, Edward. Canon of Canterbury.** *THE MUTINY IN INDIA, IN RELATION TO MAHOMETANISM AND ITS APPOINTED ISSUES. A LECTURE.* NC. NP. 1858

519
Bod   **Hodgson, Col. John Studholme.** *OPINIONS ON THE INDIAN ARMY.* London: W. H. Allen, 1857. 208pp.
    Originally published at Meerut in 1850 as "*Musings on Military Matters.*" Interesting because Hodgson presents many of the problems which later writers attributed to the causes of the Mutiny.

520
RS   **Hodson, Rev. George H.** *TWELVE YEARS OF A SOLDIER'S LIFE IN INDIA. Being Extracts from the Letters of Late Major W.S.R. Hodson, Including A Personal Narrative of the Siege of Delhi and the Capture of the King and Princes.* London: John W. Parker, 1859. 384pp. frontis. Also 2nd ed. London, same publisher. 3rd ed., 1859. xix & 412pp. An enlarged edition attempting to clear Hodson's name. (3rd. ed. Boston: Ticknor and Fields, 444pp. 1860) The 3rd edition has additional chapters on Shower's and Seatons's operations. Also

a 4th ed., 1882, London: Kegan Paul Trench. Also
5th ed., Kegan Paul Trench, xxiv & 300pp. Contains a
vindication of the attack of Mr. Bosworth Smith.
Reverend George Hodson was the brother of W.S.R.
Hodson who was killed in the second relief of Lucknow.
The murder of the princes of Delhi caused a controversy and
impugned Hodson's name. Hodson was chief of intelligence
at the siege of Delhi and the commander of Hodson's Horse.

521

Hoey, W. (Translator). *MEMOIRS OF DELHI AND
FAIZABAD.* Allahabad: NP. 1887.
Noted in Taylor. Unable to locate.

522
BL
10347F14(13)

Hogarth, George, Vicar of Burton-upon-Humber.
THE MUTINY IN INDIA, A SERMON. Hull: J.W.
Leng, 1857. 19pp.

523

Holcomb, James Foote. *JHANSI HISTORY AND THE
RANI OF JHANSI.* Madras: M.E. Press, 1904. 73pp.
Cited in Ladendorf.

524
IO

Holloway, John. *ESSAYS ON THE INDIAN MUTINY.*
London: Dean and Son, 1865? xv & 366pp. Printed
by the author.
Written by a survivor of Lucknow. Holloway had been
separated from his wife and she eventually died at the siege at
Cawnpore. The book describes the events at Lucknow.

525
Bod

Holmes, Frederick Morell. *FOUR HEROES OF
INDIA: CLIVE, WARREN HASTINGS, HENRY
HAVELOCK, JOHN LORD LAWRENCE.* London:
S.W. Partridge, 1892. 176pp.
Short biographical sketches.

526
RS

Holmes, T(homas) R(ice) E(dward). *A HISTORY
OF THE INDIAN MUTINY AND OF THE
DISTURBANCES WHICH ACCOMPANIED IT
AMONG THE CIVIL POPULATION.* London: W.H.
Allen, 1883. 2 maps and 6 plans, xx & 576pp.
2nd rev. ed. London: W.H. Allen, xx & 576pp. 2 maps
and 6 plans. 3rd ed. London: W.H. Allen. 582pp. 2 maps and
6 plans. 1888. 4th ed. London: W.H. Allen, 1891. 2 maps and
6 plans, xx & 582pp. Also London: MacMillan & Co. 1898
and 1904, xxiv & 659pp., revised and enlarged. 6 folding battle

plans and 5 maps. London: MacMillan & Co. 1913, 659pp. as above.

Holmes wrote one of the standard one volume works on the Mutiny and it proved very popular and long lived as evidenced by its publishing history. The *"Oxford History of India"* states that Holmes is "The best book on the subject for most readers." Holmes was the headmaster at various grade schools in England. Chauduri feels it is quite a good work if not entirely impartial.

527
Bod

Holmes, T(homas) R(ice) E(dward). *FOUR FAMOUS SOLDIERS: Sir Charles Napier, Hodson of Hodson's Horse, Sir W. Napier, Sir. H. Edwardes.* London: W.H. Allen, 1889. 344 pp. 3 folding maps.
Good biographical sketch of Hodson.

528
RS

Home, Surgeon General Sir Anthony Dickson. *SERVICE MEMORIES, ed. By Charles H. Melville.* London: Edward Arnold, 1912. vii & 340pp. Red cloth.

90 pages on the Mutiny. Home was with the 90th Light Infantry at Lucknow. He was in the party with Thornhill when they were attempting to bring Outram's rear guard up to the Residency. This was the action in which so many of the wounded were left in their litters to be killed by the enemy.

Home was in charge of the wounded in the rear guard and he and his party were separated from the main column. He was awarded the VC for the ensuing action.

529
Bod

Hood, Edwin Paxton. *HAVELOCK: THE BROAD STONE OF HONOUR.* London: John Snow, 1858. 68pp.
Originally delivered as a funeral discourse.

530
Bod

Hoseason, Commander John Cochrane, R.N. *REMARKS ON THE RAPID TRANSMISSION OF TROOPS TO INDIA AND THE PRACTICABILITY OF PROMPTLY ESTABLISHING EFFECTUAL MEANS OF CONVEYANCE BETWEEN THE SEA COAST AND THE INTERIOR BY THE NAVIGATION OF THE GREAT RIVERS BY STEAM.* London: Edward Stanford, 1858. 48pp. Folding map.

531

Hoskins, Lt. Col. *BRITISH ROUTE TO INDIA.* NP. ND.
Cited in Chudhuri: *"English Historical Writings."*

532
BL
08023.aa.13(12)

Hough, W. Lieut-Colonel. *HINTS REGARDING THE REORGANIZATION OF THE BENGAL ARMY AND AS TO THE BEST MEANS OF PREVENTING MUTINIES IN THE INDIAN ARMY.* London: Benton Seeley, 1857. 26pp.

533
RS

Hughes, Derrick. *THE MUTINY CHAPLAINS.* Salisbury, England: Michael Russell, 1991. 192pp. (2 pp of photos)
This book attempts to tell the story of the Indian Mutiny through the eyes of the East India Company's chaplains. Through the book is woven a short account of the Chaplains' Service, until the moment of its abolition in 1858.
Includes some information from the unpublished Peppin diary.

534
Sut

Hughes, Major General B. P. *THE BENGAL HORSE ARTILLERY 1800-1861.* London: Arms and Armour Press, 1971. 184pp. 24 plates, 14 maps.

535
RS

Humphrey, Rev. J. L. M.D. *TWENTY ONE YEARS IN INDIA.* Cinncinati: Jennings and Graham, 1905. 283pp. Frontis and 11 plates.
Humphrey left New York in 1857 just as the Mutiny broke out, bound for missionary service in India. He located in Oude and describes the work of the church in India from shortly after the Mutiny. Interesting for the missionary view of the period. Little material actually concerning the Mutiny.

536

Hungerford, Townsend. *REPORT OF OCCURRENCES AT MHOW DURING AND SUBSEQUENT TO THE MUTINY OF NATIVE TROOPS AT THAT STATION IN JULY 1857.* Mhow? Privately published. January 1858. 21cm. [v], [4] 57pp. 3 plates.
Green quarter leather and marbled boards. Preface-- "The following report has been printed to save me the trouble of writing a number of copies, which my friends wished me to give them. It will, I hope, speak for itself; and if those who read it be convinced by it how zealously and creditably the Mahajara of Indore has upheld his character as a friend and ally to the British Government, and how desirous the small number of men composing the garrison of Mhow in July 1857 were of serving their Government advatageously, I shall be contented." Townsend Hungerford, Bengal Artillery. Not

found in any other source. Hungerford assumed authority in the district during the Mutiny. Durand felt that Hungerford should not have done this. Hungerford defends the Maharajah of Indore as being a friend of England. This title is not listed in Ladendorf and appears to be quite rare.

537
NAM 1857(54)   **Hunter, Colonel Charles.** *PERSONAL REMINISCENCES OF AN INDIAN MUTINY VETERAN.* Brighton: H&A Horton-Stephens, 1911. 38pp. Paper with colored frontis.

Hunter served in the Bengal Horse Artillery and saw action at the siege of Delhi. This book is mentioned in Lt. Col. R.T. Hare's *"Reminiscences of a Mutiny Veteran."*

Hunter states that he has lost his original diary and at the age of 77 is trusting to a treacherous memory. He mentions Nicholson's part in the unfortunate death of a soldier.

538
Bod   **Hunter, Lt. Col. William.** *SUGGESTIONS RELATIVE TO THE REORGANISATION OF THE BENGAL ARMY.* London: Acton Griffith 1858. Pamphlet 34pp.

539
RS   **Husain, Mahdi.** *BAHADUR SHAH II AND THE WAR OF 1857 IN DELHI WITH ITS UNFORGETTABLE SCENES.* Delhi: Atma Ram & Sons, 1958. lxxv & 451pp. Frontis, folding genealogical history of Bahadur Shah and two folding maps and fifteen plates.

Covers Delhi from the arrival of troops from Meerut to its fall. Rejects Majumdars contention that there was communal strife in Delhi. The book is based on primary sources, published and unpublished.

540
RS/RAI   **Hutchinson, Capt. G.** *NARRATIVE OF THE MUTINIES IN OUDE: Compiled From Authentic Records.* Calcutta & London: P.M. Craneburgh, also Smith Elder. 1859. iii & 182pp. Folding plan. London ed. 256pp.

Hutchinson was Military Secretary to the Chief Commissioner of Oude. Montgomery, the Chief Commissioner of Oude directed this book to be written "with the object of affording, to all, who may have lost friends or relations in Oude, the most accurate and complete information that the Local Government has been able to collect."

541
Sut/IO T35367 **Hypher, P.P.** *DEEDS OF VALOUR OF INDIAN
SOLDIERS WHICH WON THE INDIAN ORDER
OF MERIT DURING THE PERIOD FROM 1837 TO
1859.* Simla: The Times Press, 1925. v & 204pp.

542
Ames   **India. Imperial Record Department.** *PRESS LIST OF
MUTINY PAPERS 1857. BEING A COLLECTION OF
THE CORRESPONDENCE OF THE MUTINEERS
AT DELHI, REPORTS OF SPIES TO ENGLISH
OFFICIALS AND OTHER MISCELLANEOUS
PAPERS.* Calcutta: Superintendent of Gov't Printing,
1921. 423pp.
Papers are arranged chronologically.

543
RS   **Indian News (The).** *A COMPLETE LIST OF
DEATH CASUALTIES AMONGST THE EUROPEAN
POPULATION IN DISTURBED DISTRICTS OF
INDIA THAT HAVE OCCURRED SINCE THE
COMMENCEMENT OF THE SEPOY REVOLT.* NC.
The Indian News, ND. c. 1857. 16pp.
Presented to subscribers with no. 373 of the Indian News.
Includes "Distribution of the Indian Armies on Completion of
the Relief for 1857-8. The Bengal Army, The Madras Army,
and the Bombay Army." Shows regiments and where they
were stationed.

544
    Indophilus. (See Trevelyan, Charles Edward).

545
Ames   **Indumati, Sheorey.** *TATYA TOPE.* New Delhi:
National Book Trust, 1973. 112pp. Bibliography.
Part of the National Biography Series. An appendix
addresses the question "Was Tatya Tope Really Hanged?" The
author concludes that there is ample evidence to question the
validity of the identiy of the executed man.

546
    Inge, Dennison M. Lt. Col. *A SUBALTERN'S
DIARY, CONSISTING OF SCRAPS FROM 17
YEARS OF A SUBALTERN'S LIFE AT HOME AND
ABROAD IN THE 31ST REGIMENT, 8TH HUSSARS
AND INNISKILLING DRAGOONS.* London: Rait,
Henderson & Co., 1894. 123pp.
Approximately three chapters concern the Mutiny period.

547
BL 898f3 (1)   **Inglis, Honorable Julia.** *LETTER CONTAINING EXTRACTS FROM A JOURNAL KEPT DURING THE SIEGE OF LUCKNOW.* London: Privately printed, 1858.
Cited in Collier.

548
Sut   **Inglis, J.W. et. al.** *REPORTS ON THE ENGINEERING OPERATIONS DURING THE DEFENCE OF LUCKNOW.* Woolwich: Royal Engineers Institution, 1860. 19pp.
    Consisting of extracts from reports of Major General Sir John Inglis, Lieut. J.C. Anderson, Major General Sir James Outram, Major Crommelin, and Lieut. G. Hutchinson. Paper 9, Professional Papers of the Royal Engineers Volume 10.

549
   Inglis, John E.W. *REPORTS ON THE ENGINEERING OPERATIONS DURING THE DEFENSE OF LUCKNOW IN 1857. Being extracts from the Report of Major General John Inglis, on the Defense of the Residency at Lucknow, September 26, 1857.* NC. NP. 1857. 40pp.
    Upon the death of Henry Lawrence on July 4th, 1857, the military command at Lucknow passsed to Brigidier Inglis. Major Banks became the chief civil authority. Cited in Ladendorf.

550
RS   **Inglis, Lady (Julia Selina).** *THE SIEGE OF LUCKNOW: A DIARY.* London: James R. Osgood, Macvillaine, 1892. viii, 240pp.
    There was an edition of 1893, 224pp, and Leipzig: Tauchnits, 1892. 255pp. Julia Inglis was the wife of Brigadier John Inglis who succeeded to command at Lucknow after the death of Sir Henry Lawrence. She was thus the senior woman at the siege. Important work by one of the survivors. It is interesting to compare this book with Mrs. Case's work "*Day by Day at Lucknow.*" Mrs. Inglis died in 1904.

551
Ames/   **Innes, Lieut. John James McLeod VC.** *ROUGH*
BL copy   *NARRATIVE OF THE SIEGE OF LUCKNOW.*
9056.bb.39   Calcutta: NP. 1857.
is missing   Innes was a Lieutenant of the Engineers during the Mutiny. He was awarded the VC for action at the Battle of Sultanpore. Innes captured a gun single handedly and held it against great odds until relieved.

552
RS

Innes, Lt. General John James McLeod. *LUCKNOW AND OUDE IN THE MUTINY. A NARRATIVE AND A STUDY. With Views, Maps and Plans.* London: A.D. Innes & Co., 1895. xxvi & 340pp. 4 large folding maps, sketch map, 8 double spread plates, table.

There was a new and revised editon in 1896 that added an index and a glossary of terms and made corrections to the account of Chinhut and General Wheeler. This book was highly rated by Holmes and other Mutiny historians. See T.R.E. Holmes, *"History of the Indian Mutiny."* Valuable maps that show the various positions at Lucknow.

553
RS

Innes, Lt. General John James McLeod. *THE SEPOY REVOLT; A CRITICAL NARRATIVEE.* London: A.D. Innes, 1897. xii, 319pp. 4 folding plans, 3 folding maps (2nd ed. 1897. xxiii, 303pp. 6 maps)

A good work on the Mutiny by a capable writer and military author. In the preface to the second edition Innes clarifies some of the conclusions drawn from the first edition. Specifically the responsibility Dalhousie may bear for the causes of the Mutiny, some comments on Lord Lawrence, and the disaffection that prevailed prior to Meerut.

554

Innes, Lt. General John James McLeod. *SIR HENRY LAWRENCE THE PACIFICATOR.* Oxford: Clarendon Press, 1898. 208pp. Portrait.

555
RS/Ames

Innes, Percival Robert. *HISTORY OF THE BENGAL EUROPEAN REGIMENT, NOW THE ROYAL MUNSTER FUSILLIERS AND HOW IT HELPED TO WIN INDIA.* London: Simpkin, Marshall and Co., 1885. xii & 572pp. (2nd ed. 1885. Colored frontis, x & 572pp. 7 sketch maps.)

About 90 pages cover the Mutiny.

556
SOAS

Ireland, William Wotherspoon. *HISTORY OF THE SIEGE OF DELHI. By an Officer Who Served There With a Sketch of the Leading Events in the Punjab Connected with a Great Rebellion of 1857.* Edinburgh: Adam & Charles Black, 1861. xii & 331pp. Folding map of Delhi, Index, Vocabulary.

Ireland was in the Indian Medical Service. Kaye made use of this book in his work and quotes it a number of times.

Chaudhuri does not believe it is better than any of the other histories of the siege such as Ball and Dodd.

557
RS

Jackson, Alice F. *A BRAVE GIRL; A True Story of the Indian Mutiny.* London: Society for Promoting Christian Knowledge. ND. c. 1909. 127pp.
The story of two young girls and their father, a military man, and the mutiny at Mhow. Written as a novel but probably based on fact judging from the title.

558
RS

Jackson, Sir Charles. *A VINDICATION OF MARQUIS OF DALHOUSIE'S INDIAN ADMINISTRATION.* Allahabad: Chugh Publications, 1975. First Indian Edition. 179pp
Discusses major policies during Dalhousie's administration. The Doctrine of Lapse, Annexation of Oude, the Nana's claims etc.

559
RS

Jacob, Brig. Gen. G. Le Grand. *ENGLISH GOVERNMENT OF INDIA.* London: Smith, Elder, and Co., 1860. 19pp.
"...on the principles laid down in Her Majesty's proclamation to its chiefs and people, shown to be necessary; the danger of underrating the events of 1857-58...." A letter addressed to a dignitary of the Church of England. Originally published in the Daily News. Jacob believes the Christian missionaries and their evangelical fervor helped to instigate the Mutiny. The church dignitary was Jacob's brother.

560
IO

Jacob, Brig. Gen. John. *ANSWERS TO LETTER 235.*

561
Sut

Jacob, Brig. Gen. John. *A FEW REMARKS ON THE BENGAL ARMY, AND FURLOUGH REGULATIONS WITH A VIEW TO THEIR IMPROVEMENT. By a Bombay Officer.* London & Bombay, Smith Taylor, 1857. 25pp.
Reprinted from the 1851 edition with corrections.

562
Ames

Jacob, Brig. Gen. John. (b. Jan. 11, 1812 d. Dec 5, 1858). *TRACTS ON THE NATIVE ARMY OF INDIA, ITS ORGANIZATION AND DISCIPLINE.* London: Smith Elder & Co., 1857, 1858, 1859. 70pp. Pamphlet.
Most of this is pre-Mutiny. Jacob died of brain fever in 1858.

563
Ames   **Jacob, Brig. Gen. John.** *OBSERVATIONS ON A SCHEME FOR THE RE-ORGANIZATION OF THE INDIAN ARMY.* London: Smith, Elder, and Co. 1857 18pp. Pamphlet.

564
Ames   **Jacob, Brig. Gen. John.** *THE VIEWS AND OPINIONS OF BRIGADIER GENERAL JOHN JACOB. Corrected and edited by Captain Lewis Pelly.* London: Smith, Elder & Co., 1858. 2nd ed. 467pp. with index.

Jacob was a harsh critic of the seniority system prevelant in the Bengal Army. He wrote many letters and pamphlets on the state of the Bengal Army. Jacob commanded two regiments of irregulars and found himself in Persia under Outram when the Mutiny broke out. Neither of his regiments, the 1st and 2nd Scinde Irregular Horse were disloyal during the Mutiny. Jacob was a very energetic officer combining military skills with diplomatic and practical skills. He did a vast amount of work on firearms and invented a type of rifle with which he armed his two regiments.

565
BL   **Jacob, Major General Sir George Le Grand.** *LETTER TO THE MEMBERS OF THE EAST INDIA UNITED SERVICE CLUB VINDICATING THE NATIVE ARMY OF INDIA FROM THE CHARGES OF COWARDICE, MADE BY C. FORJETT IN "Our Real Danger in India."* London: C. Kegan Paul, 1878. 6 pp. Pamphlet.

566   **Jacob, Major General Sir George Le Grand.** *THE CAUSES OF THE CRISIS 1857-1858.*
          Cited in Ladendorf.

567   **Jacob, Major General Sir George Le Grand.** *CORRESPONDENCE REGARDING AN OMISSION IN A PARLIAMENTARY RETURN AND ON THE CLAIM TO THEM ETC. OF TROOPS SERVING UNDER MAJ. GENERAL G. LE GRAND JACOB DURING THE INDIAN MUTINY AND REBELLION.* NC. Ventnor. 1865.

568
RS   **Jacob, Major General Sir George Le Grand.** *WESTERN INDIA BEFORE AND DURING THE MUTINIES: PICTURES DRAWN FROM LIFE.*

London: Henry S. King & Co., 1871. (1872 ed. viii & 262pp.) (Rept. Delhi: Majpur Productions, 1985.) viii & 262pp.

569
RS

Jain, Vipin. *THE INDIAN MUTINY OF 1857: AN ANNOTATED AND ILLUSTRATED BIBLIOGRAPHY.* Haryana: Vintage Books, 1993. 174pp.
Contains works of fiction, articles, and books published in European languages. Includes 16 illustrations of title pages from some of the well-known books on the Mutiny.

570
RS

Jenkins, L. Hadow. *GENERAL FREDERICK YOUNG FIRST COMMANDANT OF THE SIRMOR BATTALION 1786- 1874. The Life Story of One of the Old Brigade in India: 1786-1874, Including Reminiscences of Ireland and of India in the 'Fifties.* London: George Routledge & Sons. New York: E.P. Dutton & Co., 1923. 268pp. Portrait.
Mrs. Jenkins, the daughter of General Young, has several chapters on her own Mutiny experiences including the siege of Agra. This is an interesting bit of biography concerning General Young, who retired before the Mutiny and left for Ireland, and Mrs. Jenkins' experiences in Agra during the Mutiny. Mrs. Jenkins is one of the most even-handed biographers of the period.

571
RS

Jenkins, Rev. John. *MARTYRS OF THE MUTINY OR TRIALS AND TRIUMPHS OF CHRISTIANS IN THE SEPOY REBELLION IN INDIA.* Philadelphia: Presbyterian Publication Committee, 2nd ed. 1860. 234pp. 12mo. Frontis and two illustrations.
Composed of material from Owen's *"Memorials of Martyrs in the Indian Rebellion."* Walsh's *"A Memorial of the Futtegurh Mission,"* and Brock's *"Life of Havelock."*

572
RS

Jennings-Bramly, William. *REMINISCENCES OF THE INDIAN MUTINY.* Dublin: Hodges, Figgis, & Co., 1899. 39pp. Printed for private circulation.
Bramly was in the civil service at Shajehanpoor when the Mutiny broke out. He quickly left for Futehghur and then Etah to restore order. Later events took him to Agra. Bramly discusses charges made in Mark Thornhill's book, *"Indian Mutiny"* (entry 1061) regarding events at Agra. He goes on to defend the actions of the commanding officers at Agra.

573
BL
Jervis-Waldy, W. T. *FROM EIGHT TO EIGHTY: The Life of a Crimean and Indian Mutiny Veteran.* London: Harrison & Sons, 1914. 224pp.
Little of interest on the Mutiny.

574
Jivanalala, Rai Bahadur. *SHORT ACCOUNT OF THE LIFE AND FAMILY OF RAI JEEWAN LAL BAHADUR, WITH EXTRACTS FROM HIS DIARY RELATING TO THE MUTINY. 1857.* Delhi: I.M.H. Press, 1902. (2nd ed. Lahore: Tribune Steam Press, 3rd ed. 1911. 218pp.)
Cited in Ladendorf.

575
RS
Jocelyn, Col. Julian R. J. *THE HISTORY OF THE ROYAL AND INDIAN ARTILLERY IN THE MUTINY OF 1857.* London: John Murray, 1915. xxvi & 520pp. Frontis & 8 half tones, 6 engravings in the text. 28 plans in text.
MacMunn, in the introduction to "*The Indian Mutiny in Perspective*," (entry 685) states this book contains better tables and orders of battle than any other book published on the Mutiny.

576
Ames
John Company. *FAMILIAR EPISTLES OF MR JOHN COMPANY TO MR. JOHN BULL.* London: William Blackwood & Sons, 1858. 119pp. Pamphlet.
This is a reprint from Blackwoods Magazine. It is an interesting work where in John Company defends itself from blame in the Mutiny. The author contends that parliament should not act in haste to legislate in regards to India. John Company knows best.

577
RS/RAI
Johnson, Major W(illiam) T(homas). *TWELVE YEARS OF A SOLDIERS LIFE. From the letters of Major W. T. Johnson. Edited by his widow.* London: A.D. Innes, 1897. 215pp. Portrait.
Johnson served at Lucknow in the 1st Cavalry under Daly, later General Sir Henry Daly. About half of the book deals with the Mutiny.

578
RS
Jones, Captain Oliver John RN. *RECOLLECTIONS OF A WINTER CAMPAIGN IN INDIA IN 1857-1858.* London: Saunders & Otley, 1859. (rept. 1989. 17

plates. 213pp. London Stamp Exchange) xvi & 213pp. Frontis, 14 lithos and 2 plans.

Jones went to India as a civilian because he could not obtain an appointment in the Navy. He received a year's leave from the Admiralty for his trip to India. He sailed with Captain Mansfield from Suez to Calcutta. Mansfield was the brother of Colin Campbell's Chief of Staff. Once in India he fought under Campbell when Lucknow was re-taken. He blames the Mutiny on want of British discipline among the sepoys. This caused a loss of respect and resultant mutiny. It was not the abuse of British power but rather the lack of application of that power which caused the Mutiny. Excellent lithos.

579
Ames

Jones, Earnest Charles. *THE REVOLT OF HINDOSTAN, OR THE NEW WORLD. Ed. With an new introduction and other prose writings of the Poet on the Revolt of 1857.* Calcutta: Eastern Trading Co., 1957. iv & 55pp.

This is a reprint of the 1857 edition of Effingham, London. The author was a leader of the Chartist's in England. The poem was written in 1848-1849 and was published in 1857. Two appendices include statements on the Mutiny.

580
RS

Jones, Gavin Sibbald. *THE STORY OF MY ESCAPE FROM FATEHGARH.* Cawnpore: Pioneer Press, 1913. (1933 with 33pp) 79pp.

Gavin and his brother Thomas were both at Fatehgarh. Thomas was killed and Gavin, about 20 years old at the time, managed to escape by boat towards Cawnpore. He left the boat party before they eventually were captured by the Nana.

581
RS

Jopling, L. M. *NOTE OF THE MUTINY FIGHTING AT LUCKNOW.* Lucknow: Government Branch Press, October, 1923. 8pp.

Jopling was the Commissioner of the Lucknow Division in the Indian Civil Service. This appears to be a pamphlet handed out to visitors to Lucknow. There is a short history of Lucknow during the Mutiny.

582

Joshi, P. C. (Compiled). *1857 IN FOLK SONGS.* New Delhi: 1994. 175pp.

The voice of the rebels recaptured from the oral tradition.

583
RS

Joshi, P. C. ed. *REBELLION 1857. A Symposium.* New Delhi: People's Publishing House, 1957. 355pp.

Fifteen articles on various aspects of the Mutiny. Part II deals with literature and the Mutiny, part III with the foreign community and the Mutiny.

584
BL   **Jourdain, Lieut. Colonel Henry F. N. and Edward Fraser.** *THE CONNAUGHT RANGERS. 1st BATTALION, FORMERLY 88th FOOT.* London: Royal United Service Institution, 1924-1928. 3 vols.
The 1st Batt. Won honors in Central India. Vol. 1. 1924. xxviii & 616pp. Index, colored frontis, 39 plates & 32 maps and plans. Vol. 2. 1926. xxiii & 544pp. Index, colored frontis, 62 plates, 35 maps and plans. Vol. 3. 1928. xvi & 590pp + 6 frontis, 64 plates and 16 maps and plans.
Vol. 2. has some coverage of the 88th when it was with Windham at Cawnpore.

585
RS   **Joyce, Michael.** *ORDEAL AT LUCKNOW: The Defence of the Residency.* London: John Murray, 1938. ix & 396pp. Three maps, bibliography, index.
Quotes many letters and dispatches and has some interesting notes on the text.

586
NAM 1857(54)   **Kashinath. (Trans.).** *DIARY OF THE MUTINY AT CAWNPUR. WRITTEN BY NANAK CHAND; MUKHTARAM IN THE FIRM OF LALA ISHARI PERSHAD, BANKER.* NC. NP. 1925. 53pp.
See Nash, Kashi and Chand, Nanak entries. See Mukherjee: *"Spectre of Violence"* for a discussion of Nanak Chand.

587
RS   **Kaul, H. K.** *EARLY WRITINGS ON INDIA. A Union Catalogue of Books on India in the English Language Published up to 1900 and Available in Delhi Libraries.* London: Curzon Press, 1975. 324pp.

588
BL d.6605.bb.9   **Kavanagh, Thomas Henry VC.** *THE VERDICT T.H.K. Late Deputy Commissioner, Oudh. (Being Memorials, Correspondence, etc, Relating to His Removal from Office.).* NC. American Methodist Mission Press, 1877. iii & 27pp. Part II
Quite rare. The British Library had a copy but it was destroyed during bombing in WW II.

589
BL   **Kavanagh, Thomas Henry, VC.** *GUILTY OR NOT*
1414.h.18(11)   *GUILTY, OR CONDUCT UNBECOMING AN*

OFFICER AND A GENTLEMAN? Lucknow: The American Methodist Mission Press, 1876. 54pp. Pamphlet.

Part I. Correspondence relating to the bestowal of the VC. Part II. Statement of the case of Sir George Couper against Mr. Kavanagh, and his refutation. Part III. Correspondence with the local and supreme government referred to in part II. In 1874, Sir George Ebenezer Couper, Chief Commissioner of Oude, accused Kavanagh, at that time serving as a deputy commissioner of Pertabgurh, of certain financial improprieties. The government of India supported Crouper.

590
IO/RS   **Kavanagh, Thomas Henry, VC.** *HOW I WON THE VICTORIAN CROSS.* London: Ward and Lock, 1860. x & 219pp., frontis, paper covers.

Kavanagh was the first civilian to earn the Victorian Cross. He died at Lord Napier of Magdala's house on Gibralter in 1882. Kavanagh was reported to have been a near-do-well. The Rev. Baldwin mentions in his book *"Indian Gup"* that Kavanagh was one of the most conceited persons he had ever met. He reported Kavanagh had VC on his slippers as well as all other articles in ordinary use. Kavanagh's daughter, Mrs. Kathleen Haynes, died November 1935. Another daughter, Mrs. Long died in 1934.

591
IO   **Kaye and Malleson.** *HISTORY OF THE INDIAN MUTINY OF 1857-1858. Edited by Col. Malleson. Cabinet edition.* London: W.H. Allen, 1889. 6 vols.

This work contains Kaye's first two volumes, Malleson's three volumes and Pincott's Index.

Vol. I: xx & 454pp. Vol. II: xxiv & 506pp., 3 folding maps. Vol. III: xxii & 388pp., 1 woodcut, 1 folding plan. Vol. IV: xix & 412pp., 4 folding maps. Vol. V: xxiv & 362pp., 4 maps. Vol. VI: Index, xv & 442pp., 1 map. 2nd ed. 1891.

592
RS   **Kaye, J. W.** *A HISTORY OF THE SEPOY WAR IN INDIA 1857-1858* London: Allen and Co., 1864-1876. 3 vols.

This work, together with Malleson is the standard history of the Mutiny. Numerous editions have been published by W.H. Allen and Longmans & Green. 1872-1876, 3 vols., 656pp., 686pp., 684 pp. 1878-1880, 3 vols., xvi & 656pp., xvii & 692pp., xvi & 702pp. 1874-1877, 7th ed., iil, 2032pp., 6 folding maps and plans. 1876, 2nd ed., includes new information. 1880, 9th ed. 1896, Longman & Green Co. W. Malleson, 6th ed., 3 vols., xiv & 656 pp., xvi & 692 pp., xiv & 702 pp., 6 folding maps. 1897-1898, with Malleson.

Sir John William Kaye (1814-1876) served in the Bengal
Artillery and retired in 1841. By 1844 he established the
Calcutta Review, where he remained for a number of years.
    In 1856 he entered the service of the East India Company
and in 1858 served in the Secret Dept. of the India Office.
Kaye was the author of a number of books including the
"History of the War in Afghanistan." Kaye and Malleson's
"History of the Indian Mutiny" is the standard work on
the Mutiny and is of greatest value when obtained in the
combined edition with the Pincott index.

593
RS   **Kaye, John William.** *LIVES OF INDIAN OFFICERS:*
          Illustrative of the History of the Civil and Military Services
          in India. London: W.H. Allen, 1867. Vol. I xiv &
          489pp., Vol. II 502pp.
              Those covered include James Neill, Sir Henry Lawrence
          and Brig. Gen. John Nicholson. Also published by A.
          Strahan and Bell and Daldy, London, 1867. Half red
          morrocco.

594
          Kaye, John Williams and Col. George Bruce
          Malleson. *A HISTORY OF THE SEPOY WAR IN*
          INDIA 1857-1858.
              Numerous editions. Malleson alone as follows: *HISTORY*
          OF THE INDIAN MUTINY 1857-1858, first published in
          1878-1880, 2nd ed., 1700pp., 9 maps and plans, W. H. Allen
          and Co., 1878. 3 vols., xxxi & 575pp., xxxvi & 602pp., xxxi &
          524pp., 1878-1880, 9 folding maps.
              In February 1896 the rights to the combined Kaye and
          Malleson history were transferred to Longman, Green, and
          Co. There was a Silver Library edition in August 1897,
          reprinted in June 1898 and re-issued in a new style in July
          1898. This was reprinted again in January 1906, March
          1909, and January 1914. All were six volume editions. Kaye
          and Malleson: *HISTORY OF THE INDIAN MUTINY OF*
          1857- 1858, 6 vols., New York: Longman, Green and Co.,
          1909-1914, 2564pp., index, includes Pincott Index. Vol. I,
          1897, 1898, 1906, 1909, xx & 453pp. Vol. II, 1897, 1898,
          1906, 1910, xxiv & 506pp., 3 folding maps. Vol. III, 1897,
          1898, 1906, 1909, xxiii & 388pp., 1 illus. And 1 folding map.
          Vol. IV, 1897, 1898, 1907, 1911, xxxvi & 412pp., 2 sketches,
          2 folding plans. Vol. V, 1897, 1898, 1907, 1911, xxiv &
          362pp., 4 maps. Vol. VI, 1914, xv & 442pp., 1 folding map.
          Malleson's history begins at the close of the second volume of
          Sir John Kaye's history. Malleson defends this action in his
          preface. Here he states that the third volume of Kaye did not
          do justice to the actors in the drama of the Mutiny. It was not
          impartial and was not accepted as a history by a broad segment

of the military and political establishment. Chuadhuri, while finding fault with a number of aspects of Malleson's scholarship does state that his work is the most exciting in Mutiny literature.

George Bruce Malleson (1825-1898) served in the Bengal Infantry, saw action in the Second Burmese War 1852-53 and later served in a number of official positions in India. He wrote a history of Afghanistan and other books dealing with the sub-continent. Quentin Battye of the guides was Malleson's brother-in-law. Battye died on the ridge before Delhi.

595
RS/Ames   **Keene, Henry George.** *1857, SOME ACCOUNT OF THE ADMINISTRATION OF INDIAN DISTRICTS DURING THE REVOLT OF THE BENGAL ARMY.* London: W.H. Allen and Co., 1883. xii & 145pp.

Used as a source by Malleson. Much of the material has been drawn from narratives furnished to the Government of the North West Provinces by the Collectors and Commissioners. This book is an account of how the administrators of the various districts helped the military and worked to restore order after the Mutiny. Reprinted in New Delhi by Inter-India Publications under the title *"British Administration During the Revolt of 1857."*

596
Ames   **Keene, Henry George.** *A SERVANT OF JOHN COMPANY: Being the Recollections of an Indian Official.* London: W. Thacker, 1897. xviii, 337pp., portrait and six other plates.

Keene was the chief civil authority in the District of Dehra Dun. About 13 pages on the Mutiny.

597
Ames   **Kelly, Charles.** *RELIEF OF ARRAH.* Melbourne, Australia: NP. 1860.

Originally published as a privately printed pamphlet called *"The Great Britain Magazine."* Kelly accompanied the relief force to Arrah as a volunteer. Written while sailing to Australia on the "Melbourne."

598
     Kelly, Sophia. *THE LIFE OF MRS. SHERWOOD, CHIEFLY AUTOBIOGRAPHICAL WITH EXTRACTS FROM MR SHERWOOD'S JOURNAL DURING HIS IMPRISONMENT IN FRANCE AND RESIDENCE IN INDIA.* London: Darton And Co., 1957. ix & 573pp.

Edited by his daughter. Cited in Jain.

599

Kennedy, James. *LIFE AND WORK IN BENARES AND KUMAON. 1839-1877, with an introductory note by Sir W. Muir.* London (New York): T. Fisher Unwin (Cassell and Co.), 1884 (1885). 392pp.
Ladendorf lists two chapters on the Mutiny. Kennedy was a missionary.

600
Bod

Kennedy, James. *THE GREAT MUTINY OF 1857, ITS CAUSES, FEATURES AND RESULTS.* London: Ward and Co., ND. c. 1858. 70pp.

601
IO

Khadgawat, Nathu Ram. *RAJASTHAN'S ROLE IN THE STRUGGLE OF 1857.* Jaipur: General Administrative Department, Government of Rajasthan, 1957. ix & 198pp.
A state sponsored publication. "The work is based mainly on the Rajputana Residency Records, British authors and indigenous records."

602

Khairabadi, Fazl Haq. *Bagh-i-Hindustan.* NC. NP. ND. 36pp. Typescript.
This was originally written in Arabic. Khairabadi wrote it while a prisoner in the Andamans sometime before 1859. There is a typescript translation in the P.C. Joshi archives at the Jawaharlal Nehru University Library. (Noted in Scholberg: *"The Indian Literature of the Great Rebellion."*)

603
Ames

Khilnani, Niranjan. *BRITISH POWER IN THE PUNJAB 1839-1859.* New York: Asia Publishing House, 1972. xi & 288pp. Index and bibliography.
The last chapter, covering 23 pages, concerns the Mutiny. A scholarly work employing many sources.

604

Khobrekar, V. G. ed. *MAHARASHTRA ARCHIVES, BULLETIN OF THE DEPARTMENT OF ARCHIVES NOS. 9 AND 10. THE LEGEND OF NANA SAHEB.* Kolhapur: Government Printing Press, ND (1973). x & 216pp.
This is the last in a series of bulletins published by the department on the hunt for Nana Saheb.

605
Ames

Kincaid, Charles Augustus. *LAKSHMI BAI, RANI OF JHANSI AND OTHER ESSAYS.* London: Published by the author. ND. 1943. 102pp. Blue paper.
This was an article in the Journal of the Royal Asiatic Society, April 1943. Approximately 14 pages discuss the Rani of Jhansi.

606
Bod

King, Edward, Lt. *A BIRDS EYE VIEW OF INDIA SHOWING OUR PRESENT POSITION, ITS DANGER AND REMEDY.* London: Partridge & Co., 1857. 63pp.
Espouses primarily a religious cure for England's crisis in India.

607

King, Theodore. *THE GREAT REBELLION.*
Cited in Nigam.

608
Bod

Kinloch, Charles W. *THE MUTINIES IN THE BENGAL ARMY.* London: Simpkin, Marshall and Co., 1858. 34pp.
Six letters relating to the Mutiny originally published in the "Cape Argus." Published to raise money for the India Relief Fund.

609
RAI

Kinlock, Rev. A. *INSTRUCTIONS ON BEHALF OF SIR G.C. WHITLOCK, K.C.B., AND THE TROOPS ENGAGED UNDER HIS COMMAND AT BANDA AND KIRWEE. The Plaintiffs in the cause, to the Solicitors in the case of the Banda and Kiwee Prize Money.* London: Harrison & Sons, 1865. 150pp. Folding map at front.
See Lushington. (Entries 674 & 675)

610
RS

Kinsley, D. A *THEY FIGHT LIKE DEVILS: STORIES FROM LUCKNOW DURING THE GREAT INDIAN MUTINY, 1857-58* New York: Sarpedon, 2001 (6) 224pp. 3 maps and 25 photographs. Bibliography and index.
Each of the fourteen chapters is an extract, or a number of extracts, from literature on the siege at Lucknow. There is a short author introduction to each chapter. Some of the sources are Lieutenant Harry Havelock, Henry Willock, Ensign William Tweedie, General Outram, and many others. Each chapter deals with a particular aspect of the siege such as Havelock's advance, the street fighting, the action at the

Secunder Bagh, the recapture of Lucknow by Campbell, storming the Kaiser Bagh, etc.

611

Kittermaster, F. W. *THE MUSLIM AND THE HINDOO. A POEM ON THE SEPOY REVOLT.*

612
BL   **Kittermaster, Rev. Fred. Wilson.** *A FUNERAL SERMON ON THE DEATH OF THE REVEREND HENRY STEDMAN POLEHAMPTON, M. A. Late Chaplain to the H E I C at Lucknow. Preached in St. Chad's Church, Shrewsbury.* London: Wertheim, MacIntosh and Hunt, 1858. 31pp.
Kittermaster was a classmate of Polehampton at Oxford. An appendix includes the last days of Polehampton at Lucknow.

613

Knight, Robert. *THE INAM COMMSSION UNMASKED.* London: Effingham Wilson, 1859. 120pp.
This was an infamous commssion consisting of mostly military officers that over a period of years wreaked havoc in the Bombay presidency by confiscating land under the guise of reform. The commssion was established in 1852.

614
Ames   **Knollys, Capt. Henry, ed.** *LIFE OF GENERAL SIR JAMES HOPE GRANT With Selections from his Correspondence.* Edinburgh: William Blackwood, 1894. 2 vols, xiii & 359pp., and xi & 362pp., 8 plates, 5 folding battle plans and 3 folding maps.
Also 1 vol. 1873 William Blackwood, xvi & 380pp., 3 folding maps. Contains the complete chronology of Grant's actions during the Mutiny. Delhi, the first relief of Lucknow, Cawnpore, second action at Lucknow, etc.

615
Ames   **Knollys, Lt. Col. William Wallingford.** *THE VICTORIAN CROSS IN INDIA.* London: Dean and Son, ND. c. 1865. 2nd ed., viii & 142pp., 14 plates.
The exploits of those officers and men who won the VC in the Mutiny. 1857-1859.

616
Ames/RS   **Kumar, Nagendra.** *INDIAN NATIONAL MOVEMENT WITH SPECIAL REFERENCE TO THE DISTRICT OF OLD SARAN, BIHAR,*

1857-1947. Patna: Janaki Prakashan, 1979. x & 270pp.
Index and bibliography.
The first chapter discusses the Mutiny in the district of
Saran. Hostilities erupted on July 23rd.

617
RS   **Kumar, Purushottam.** *MUTINIES AND
REBELLIONS IN CHOTANAGPUR. 1831-1857.*
New Delhi: Janaki Prakashan, 1991. xv & 324pp.
Bibliography and index.
    A poorly edited work but interesting in its subject matter.
This book was a result of Kumar's doctoral thesis. The author
states that much of the book is based on unpublished material
in various Indian libraries. Kumar states that the foundation
of the Mutiny was laid in Chotanagpur. The author's name is
mispelled on the dust jacket.

618
IO   **Kyne, J.** *A CHAPLAIN AT THE INDIAN MUTINY.*
NC. NP. 1960.

619
RS   **Ladendorf, Janice M.** *THE REVOLT IN INDIA
1857-58. An Annotated Bibliography of English Language
Materials.* Zug, Switzerland: Inter Documentary
Company, 1966. v & 191pp.
    Ladendorf wrote the first annotated bibliography on
Mutiny literature. For the first time the immense body of
literature on the subject was collected in a useful manner.
Ladendorf covers manuscripts, both private and public, as well
as newspapers and maps. Source locations are listed and an
index is provided. Still a valuable work, useful to scholars and
collectors alike.

620
    Lal, Jivan. *A SHORT ACCOUNT OF THE LIFE AND
FAMILY OF RAI JEEWAN LAL BAHADUR. Late
Honorary Magistrate of Delhi with Extracts from His Diary
to the Time of the Mutiny 1857.* Delhi: I.M.H. Press,
1902. 2nd ed., ix & 218pp. With a genealogical foldout
at rear.
    Appendix "A" contains extracts from the Mutiny Diary,
approx. 22pp. There was a third edition of 218pp, 1911,
Lahore: Tribune Steam Press.

621
Nigam   **Lal, Kanhaya.** *HISTORY OF THE INDIAN MUTINY.*

622
    Lall, Peary. *CENTENARY SOUVENIR.* Delhi: NP.
1957.

Considered of little significance by Sengupta in *"Recent Writings."*

623
Ames/
BL 010058f5

Landon, P. *UNDER THE SUN.* London (New York): NP. (Doubleday,Page) 1906 (1907). 288pp., illus. Frontis & 65 illus.

Impressions of Indian cities with a chapter dealing with the later life of Nana Sahib. Well illustrated with photographs.

624
IO

Landon, Perceval. *"1857" In Commemoration of the 50th Anniversary of the Indian Mutiny.* London: W.H. Smith & Son, 1907. 140pp., map, 12 plates.

With appendix containing the names of the survivors of the officers, non-commisioned officers and men who fought in India in 1857. (Includes some civilian survivors as well.)

625
Sut

Lang, Arthur Moffatt. *DIARY AND LETTERS OF LT. A. M. LANG* London: Society of Army Historical Research, 1857-1859.

Lang was a Bengal engineer at the Siege of Delhi. He was in the first ranks at the Kashmir Gate. Lang's diary was published in Journal of the Society for Army Historical Research edited by J.H. Leslie and Colonel F.C. Molesworth, issues 35, pages 1 to 26; issue 36, pages 72 to 97; issue 38, pages 189 to 213; issue 39A, pages 69 to 108; issue 39B, pages 129 to 142; issue 40, pages 195 to 206; and issue 41, pages 1 to 25. Vols 9-11.

626
RS

Lang, Arthur Moffatt. *LAHORE TO LUCKNOW: The Indian Mutiny Diary of Arthur Moffat Lang.* London: Leo Cooper, 1992. 190pp. Illus.

Lang, of the Bengal Engineers, fought at Delhi and Lucknow. This work was taken from his journals and edited by a grandson, David Blomfield. Lang was given orders to inspect the breaches near the Kashmir Gate to determine the prospects of a successful attack. He was recommended for the VC three times. This is an interesting work that incorporates material not readily available elsewhere. Parts of the journals were published in 1930 by the Society for Army Historical Research.

627
Ames

Lang, John. *WANDERINGS IN INDIA AND OTHER SKETCHES OF LIFE IN HINDUSTAN.* London: Routledge, Warne, and Routledge, 1859. 415pp.

Lang met with the Rhani of Jhansi. He discusses a

number of other points of interest in relation to the Mutiny, the Nana, Bhitoor, and Tantia Tope.

628
IO

Langdon-Davies, John. *THE INDIAN MUTINY, A Collection of Contemporary Documents.* London: Jonathan Cape, 1966.
Jackdaw Series No. 22. Part of a series of teacher's aids. Contents: Sheet with table of contents. 1a. Letter smuggled out of Cawnpore. 1b. Transcript of above letter. 2. Page from General Neill's Diary. 3. Four pages from the Times dated 8/31/57. 4. Letter from Agra to General Neill at Cawnpore. 5. Eight pages from Atkinson's "The Campaign in India." 6. Muslims and Hindu's: An outline of religious beliefs and the Caste System. 7. Photographs taken in India. 8. Six broadsheets as follows: A. India in 1857. B. The Mutiny. C. Cawnpore. D. The two sides. E. The British Reaction. F. The Results of the Mutiny.

629

Laurence, Thomas Benson. *SIX YEARS IN THE NORTH-WEST, FROM 1854 TO 1860; Being Extracts from a Private Diary, With a Glimpse of the Rebellion of 1857-1858.* Calcutta: NP. 1859. 119pp.
Cited in Ladendorf.

630
RS

Laverack, Alfred. *A METHODIST SOLDIER IN THE INDIAN ARMY. HIS PERSONAL ADVENTURES AND CHRISTIAN EXPERIENCE.* London: T. Woolmer, ND. 265pp.
Very little of value concerning the Mutiny.

631
Ames

Lawrence, Lt. General George. *REMINISCENCES OF FORTY THREE YEARS IN INDIA. Including the Cabul Disasters, Captivities in Afghanistan and the Punjab, and a Narrative of the Mutinies in Rajputana.* London: John Murray, 1874. xiii, 315pp. (2nd ed. 1875, 303pp.)
Edited by W. Edwards from letters and diaries entrusted to him for the purpose. The last two chapters give some information concerning Lawrences' career during the Mutiny.

632
BL

Lawrence, Sir Henry Montgomery. *ESSAYS ON THE INDIAN ARMY IN OUDH.* Serampore: Friend of India Press, 1859. 354pp.
Five essays contributed to the Calcutta Review by Henry Lawrence. They have been republished because of new interest since the Mutiny. The essays date from 1844 to 1856

and are as follows: I: Military Defence of our Empire in the
East; II: Lord Hardings Administration; III: The Indian
Army; IV: Indian Army Reform; V: The Kingdom of Oude.

633
BL   **Lawrence, Sir Henry Montgomery.** *ESSAYS,*
MILITARY AND POLITICAL WRITTEN IN INDIA.
London: W.A. Allen, 1859. 483pp.
  Lawrence died at the siege of Lucknow. Most of the
material deals with army organization. All of the essays
pre-date the Mutiny.

634
Ames/RS   **Lawrence, Sir Henry Montgomery.** *LETTERS OF*
SIR HENRY MONTGOMERY LAWRENCE. Selections
from the Correspondence of Sir Henry Montgomery
Lawrence During the Siege of Lucknow. From March to
July, 1857. Edited by Sheo Bahadur Singh Ph.D. New
Delhi: Sagar Publications, 1978. xi & 80pp. Index.
  Contains correspondence to and from Canning, Herbert
Edwardes, J. Colvin, General Wheeler, Col. Neill, Patrick
Grant, and Havelock.

635
IO SB VI/31   **LeBas, C.** *HOW WE ESCAPED FROM DELHI.* NC.
NP. 1858

636
RS   **Leasor, James.** *THE RED FORT.* London: Werner
Laurie, 1956. 383pp. map and 21 illus. bibliography and
index. Good photo of Hodson.

637
RS/
BL ORW
1991.1.1915   **Leather, G. F. T. ed.** *ARRAH IN 1857. Being an*
Account of the Splendid Defense of Arrah House During
the Indian Mutiny. Dover: George W. Gregg, 1893.
Privately printed. 137pp. 103 copies were printed.
Frontis of Arrah House.
  Reprinted from a pamphlet by John James Halls; " to
which is added an account of the gallant relief of the same
by a company and a half of the 5th Fusilliers, under Major
Vincent Eyre, of the Bengal Artillery, and Captain Ferdinand
L'Estrange, of the 5th Fusilliers, by Charles Kelly.

638
RS   **Lebra-Chapman, Joyce.** *THE RANI OF JHANSI. A*
Study of Female Heroism in India. Honolulu: University
of Hawaii Press, 1986. 199pp. one frontis, 3 photos and
2 maps, glossary, notes, index, & bibliography.

The author studies the genesis of the legend of the Rani. There is a good section on the historiography of the literature on the Mutiny. This is a very well researched book using both British and Indian sources.

639
RS/SOAS

Leckey, Edward. *FICTIONS CONNECTED WITH THE INDIAN OUTBREAK OF 1857 EXPOSED.* Bombay: Chesson and Woodhall, December, 1859. xxi & 178pp.

A compilation, with author comments, of 81 extracts from writings on the Mutiny.

An expose on the lack of accurate, factual, writing on the Mutiny. Leckey exposes inaccuracies in Mead's *"The Sepoy Revolt,"* Rev. A. Duff's *"The Indian Rebellion,"* Chamber's *"The History of the Revolt in India,"* and a number of other works on the Mutiny. Discusses numerous sordid cases of mutilation. Approximately 365 copies were printed.

640
RS/
BL
09059.aaa.26

Lee, J(oseph) F. *THE INDIAN MUTINY: A NARRATIVE OF THE EVENTS AT CAWNPORE. By one who was present two hours and ten minutes after the butchers completed their sanguinary work in the "House of Massacre."* (Cawnpore), NP. June and July, 1857 [21] 40 pp. [19]. Also Cawnpore: Victoria Press, 1893, 55pp. Also bound with *A NARRATIVE OF MY TRAVELS AND OF MY VISIT TO ENGLAND AND AMERICA IN 1883....* 40 + 20pp., NP. ND. c. 1893.

Lee was a sergeant who served in the 53rd regiment of Shropshire Light Infantry. He came out to India in 1844 and remained. He was present just after the Cawnpore massacre. There was also a printing in 1886. It seems there was some question if Lee actually participated in the events he describes. William Forbes-Mitchell confirmed Lee's participation but then there is also doubt as to Forbes-Mitchell's veracity.

641

Lee, J(oseph) F. And Captain F.W. Radcliffe. *THE INDIAN MUTINY UP TO THE RELIEF OF LUCKNOW.* Rawalpindi: Privately printed 1918. (1857/1858) ND. 97pp. Map.

Chaudhuri credits this as being the first book on the Mutiny. He assigns it a date of late 1857 to early 1858, while Ladendorf puts it at 1918. Chaudhuri gives high marks to this work and notes that it discusses many of the questions that were to gain such prominence in later works. This work is very scarce and there is some doubt as to the actual publication date. There does not appear to be a copy in either the IO or the BL. The Ladendorf copy is located at the Imperial Library, Calcutta.

642
RS   **Lee-Warner, Sir W.** *MEMOIRS OF FIELD MARSHAL SIR HENRY WYLIE NORMAN.* London: Smith, Elder, 1908. xv & 327pp., 2 portraits, 2 folding maps and plans.
 Norman was the Adjutant General of the Delhi Field Force. Six chapters on the Mutiny. Includes some of Norman's correspondence.

643
Ames   **Lee-Warner, Sir William.** *THE LIFE OF MARQUISE OF DALHOUSIE.* London: MacMillan, 1904. Vol. I xxi+446pp. Frontis, 3 plates & 3 folding maps. Vol. II xiii+450pp. One folding map, 1 plate. Index.
 One chapter on the Mutiny. In addition, there are chapters on military affairs and the annexation of Oude.

644
RS   **Lennox, Chas. Wm.** *MEMOIR OF MAJOR GENERAL WILLIAM GEORGE LENNOX.* Lerwick: Privately printed, 1894. 16pp. Paper.
 Lennox commanded the 22nd NI at Faizabad and this is an account of events at that station.
 Reprints Lennox's statement to the "Times" dated 29th September 1857.
 Charles William, the author, is the son of Major General William George Lennox. The author was assisted by William George Lennox, Solicitor, Lerwick, the Major-General's grandson.

645
Ames   **Lewin, Lt. Col. Thomas H.** *A FLY ON THE WHEEL: Or How I Helped to Govern India.* London: W.H. Allen, 1885. 9 plates and two folding maps, vii & 466pp. Constable and Co., 1912. 2nd ed., 466pp. Also reprinted from the 1912, 2nd ed. by Aizawl, 1977. xi & 318pp.
 Lewin arrived in Calcutta in late 1857, a raw cadet. He fought at Cawnpore with Windham and then on to Lucknow and finally Central India. Approximately sixty pages on the Mutiny.

646
BL 8022.b.58   **Lewin, M. (ed.).** *CAUSES OF THE INDIAN REVOLT. By a Hindu of Bengal.* London: NP. 1857.

647
Bod

Lewin, Malcolm. *HAS OUDE BEEN WORSE GOVERNED BY ITS NATIVE PRINCES THAN OUR INDIAN TERRITORIES BY LEADENHALL STREET?* London: James Ridgeway, 1857. 26pp.
   Compares the condition of Oude in its Police and Revenue Administration with that of other territories under the E.I.C. Indicts the annexation of Oude.

648

Lewin, Malcolm. *THE GOVERNMENT OF THE EAST INDIAN CO. AND ITS MONOPOLIES OR THE YOUNG INDIA PARTY AND FREE TRADE.* London: James Ridgeway, 1857.
   Cited in Ladendorf

649
RS

Lewin, Malcolm. *THE WAY TO LOSE INDIA WITH ILLUSTRATION FROM LEADENHALL STREET.* London: NP. 1857. 31pp.
   This piece went through a third edition in 1857, it obviously was a popular paper. Lewin was judge in Madras. This was written shortly before the Mutiny and enumerates all the wrongs England has heaped on India.

650
Bod

Lewin, Malcolm. *THE WAY TO REGAIN INDIA.* London: James Ridgeway, 1858. 30pp.
   Lewin assumes that the Mutiny was actually an insurrection of the inhabitants. Compare this with "*Theories of the Indian Mutiny.*" (Entry 267)

651
RS

Lewis, Sir George. *SPEECH OF SIR GEORGE LEWIS ON THE INTRODUCTION OF THE BILL FOR THE BETTER GOVERNMENT OF INDIA. FEB. 12, 1858.* London: James Ridgeway, 1858. 48pp.
   Discusses the actions of the EIC, Board of Directors, Court of Control etc. in regards to India.
   Interesting section on "Patronage."

652
RS

Llewellyn, Alexander. *THE SIEGE OF DELHI.* London: McDonald and James, 1977. 182pp. 23 illus. 2 maps.
   Rejects the revolutionary aspect of the Mutiny. Independence was not the goal of the Sepoys.

653
RS

Llewellyn-Jones, Rosie. *A FATAL FRIENDSHIP: The Nawabs, the British and the City of Lucknow.*

Delhi: Oxford University Press, 1985. xii & 284pp.
Bibliography and index. 19 plates.
An extensive and scholarly study of Nawabi Lucknow. A
fine source for the study of the architecture of the city. Some
coverage of the Mutiny.

654
RS   **Llewellyn-Jones, Rosie.** *ENGAGING SCOUNDRELS:*
TRUE TALES OF OLD LUCKNOW. New Delhi:
Oxford University Press, 2000. xvi & 196pp.
Bibliography and index. 12 illus and 4 color plates.
Very interesting work on mostly pre-Mutiny Lucknow
though there is and interesting chapter on post-Mutiny
Lucknow with information not easily available elsewhere.

655
BL 4477.c.59   **Lloyd, Julius.** *THE MUTINY OF THE BENGAL*
ARMY. A SERMON. London: NP. 1857.

656
        Lockwood, E. *THE EARLY DAYS OF*
MARLBOROUGH COLLEGE. London: Simpkin,
Marshall, Hamilton, Kent, 1893. xvi & 234pp.,
numerous illus.
Presents material on Patna during the Mutiny.

657
        Login, Lady. *SIR JOHN LOGIN AND DULEEP*
SINGH. London: W.H. Allen, 1890. xx & 580pp.,
portrait, large folding map of the Punjab.
Includes material on the Punjab during the Mutiny.
Login was an assistant surgeon of the Bengal Army. Duleep
Singh was put under Login's tutelage in 1849.

658
        Looker, Edith C. *SIR HENRY HAVELOCK AND*
COLIN CAMPBELL, LORD CLYDE. London: Cassell
& Co., 1885. 128pp.
The Worlds Workers Series. See E.C. Phillips. (Entry
855)

659
Bod   **Low, Charles Rathbone.** *A MEMOIR OF LT*
GENERAL SIR GARNET J. WOLSELEY. London:
Richard Bentley, 1878. Also 2nd ed. 1 vol. xvi &
482pp. With frontis. 2 vol. ed. Vol. I x & 280pp. Vol.
II iv & 299pp.
Wolseley, who was a captain during the relief of
Lucknow under Colin Campbell, later succeeded the Duke of
Cambridge as the Commander-in-Chief of the British Army.
Approximately 80pp on the Mutiny.

660
IO

Low, Charles Rathbone. *SOLDIERS OF THE VICTORIAN AGE.* London: Chapman and Hall, 1880. 2 vols. Vol. I xxiii & 347pp; Vol. II viii & 446pp.
Includes General George Whitlock, General George Macgregor, General Evelyn Wood, General Vincent Eyre, General Herbert Edwardes, General Durand, General Outram, Field Marshal Lord Strathnairn, General Neville Chamberlain, General Hope Grant, General Lord Napier of Magdalla, Field Marshal Lord Clyde.

661
Ames

Low, Lt. Charles Rathbone. *HISTORY OF THE INDIAN NAVY 1613-1863.* London: Richard Bentley, 1877. Vol I xx & 541pp. Vol. II vi & 596pp.
Two chapters cover the Mutiny. About 97 pages.

662
Ames

Low, Ursula. *FIFTY YEARS WITH JOHN COMPANY. From the Letters of Gen. Sir John Low of Clatto, Fife. 1822-1858.* London: John Murray, 1936. xxvii & 434pp. Index. Frontis and 11 illus.
Low had seen extensive action in India. In 1856 he was on the Supreme Council in Calcutta along with Dorin, Grant, and Peacock. About forty pages on the Mutiny. Two chapters on the Mutiny, one of which traces the fate of friends and relatives.

663
RS

Low, W.D. *LIEUTENANT COLONEL GOULD HUNTER-WESTON OF HUNTERSTON, ONE OF THE DEFENDERS OF LUCKNOW DURING THE INDIAN MUTINY, 1857-8. A BIOGRAPHICAL SKETCH.* Selkirk: The Scottish Chronicle, 1914. xii & 154pp., 12 Plates, 3 maps.
Commanded the outpost at Fayrer's house during the siege at Lucknow. Stayed on at the Alum Bagh and worked in Special Intelligence. There is much written on the defence of Fayrer's house and thus the actions of Weston. The book contains a few photos taken by Ahmad Ali, the Court Photographer at Lucknow. Weston had found these at Ali's house after the siege.

664

Lowe, E.D. *LETTER FROM LUCKNOW AND CAWNPORE.* Greenwich: NP. 1858.
According to Michael Joyce, author of *"Ordeal at Lucknow"* this was written by E. Delaney Lowe of the 32nd Foot. Confirmed by Chaudhuri.

665
RS   **Lowe, Thomas.** *CENTRAL INDIA DURING*
                THE REBELLION OF 1857 AND 18588. London:
                Longman, Green, Longman and Roberts, 1860. xiii &
                369pp. + 24pp. 1 folding map.
                A narrative of operations of the British Forces from the
                suppression of the Mutiny in Aurungabad to the capture of
                Gwalior under Major General Sir Hugh Rose and Brigadier
                Sir C. Stuart, K.C.B. Lowe was medical officer to the Madras
                Sappers and Miners.

666
NAM 1857(54) **Luard, Major C. E.** *CONTEMPORARY NEWSPAPER*
                ACCOUNTS OF EVENTS DURING THE MUTINY
                IN CENTRAL INDIA 1857-59. Allahabad: Ram Nath
                Bhargava, 1912. 50pp.
                Prints the article and cites the newspaper and date.

667
Bod   **Luaro, Robert Davies.** *AN ADDRESS TO THE*
                RECONSTRUCTORS OF OUR INDIAN EMPIRE.
                London: Effingham Wilson, 1857. 32pp.
                Pamphlet.

668
RS   **Lucas, J.J.** *MEMOIR OF REV. ROBERT STEWARD*
                FULLERTON American Presbyterian Missionary In
                North India 1850-1865. Allahabad: The Christian
                Literature Society, 1928. 268pp. Frontis and 4 plates.
                Index.
                Primarily concerned with the Mutiny and includes
                correspondence and a 100 page appendix of narratives of the
                Mutiny in Agra and surrounding regions.

669
IO   **Lucknow State Library.** *PHOTOS OF LUCKNOW*
                FROM 1858. Lucknow: NP. 1920.

670
Bod   **Ludlow, John Malcolm.** *BRITISH INDIA, ITS*
                RACES AND ITS HISTORY CONSIDERED WITH
                REFERENCES TO THE MUTINIES OF 1857. A series
                of lectures addressed to the students of the Working Mens
                College. Cambridge: Macmillan, 1858. Vol.1, xvi & 390
                pp., frontis. Vol. 2, viii & 390pp. Index.
                Vol. 2, lecture xxi discusses England's responsibility for
                the causes of the Mutiny. England did not set a good example
                for the peoples of India.

671

Ludlow, John Malcolm. *THE WAR IN OUDH.*
Cambridge: Macmillan, 1858. 58pp.
Cited in Ladendorf.

672
RS

**Lumsden, General Sir Peter S(tark) and George R.
Elsmie.** *ROBERT LUMSDEN OF THE GUIDES.
A Sketch of the Life of Lieut.-Gen. Sir Harry Burnett
Lumsden, K.C.S.I., C.B., With Selections From His
Correspondence and Occasional Papers.* London: John
Murray, 1899. xvi & 333pp. Frontis, 13 plans and
illustrations, 1 folding map.
    Lumsden and his brother Peter were in Kandahar during
much of the Mutiny treating with Dost Muhammad and the
Afghans.

673
RS

Lunt, J. (ed.). *FROM SEPOY TO SUBEDAR. Being the
Life and Adventures of Subedar Sita Ram, A Native Officer
of the Bengal Army, Written and Related by Himself.*
    See Norgate (Entry 806)

674
RS

Lushington, Right Honourable Stephen. *BANDA
AND KIRWEE BOOTY.* London: HMSO, 1866. 79pp
with folding map.
    Bound with five related papers. House of Commons
paper number 298 of 1869 which has 112 pages of financial
papers relating to the amounts realized on account of the prize
fund and four more papers on the correspondence about the
Banda and Kirwee Booty.
    The question of division of booty arose because
Whitlock's column captured so much more than either Rose's
or Roberts' columns in Central India. A proposal to split
the booty among the three field forces gave way to the legal
proceeding which was finally settled in 1875.

675
Stanford Lib.,
Palo Alto, Calif.

Lushington, Stephen. *BANDA AND KIRWEE
BOOTY. Judgement of the Hon. S. Lushington Delivered
in the High Court of Admiralty of England.* London:
Harrison and Sons, 1865. Documents in six vols.
    Also: Proceeding and Judgement, London: Eyre and
Spotiswood, 1866. map and 1150pp. & 79pp.

676
BL

Lutfullah, Syed. *AZIMULLAH KHAN
YUSUFZAI: THE MAN BEHIND THE WAR OF
INDEPENDENCE 1857.* Karachi: Mohamedali

Education Society, 1957. 2nd ed. photo & 197pp.
Bibliography and index.
A biography of Khan who served as minister of the Nana.
This work is distinctly from the Indian (or Pakistani) point of
view.

677
RS   **M.W. (Macleod Wylie).** *THE THOUGHTS OF*
A NATIVE OF NORTHERN INDIA ON THE
REBELLION, ITS CAUSES AND REMEDIES. WITH
A PREFACE BY MACLEOD WYLIE. London: W. H.
Dalton, 1858. 37pp.
The writer states the Mutiny was not a national revolution
nor a concerted plan. The main point of contention with the
Hindu sepoy was not religion but the idea that government
was causing them to lose caste. The complete and utter lack of
understanding of Indian social, political and moral values and
the lack of any "mix" between English and native was the root
of the unrest in India.

678
            MacCarty, J. *THE INDIAN MUTINY.* Leipzig, NP.
1887
            Cited by Domin in "INDIA IN 1857-59."
            Unable to locate.

679
            MacCrea, R. *TABLETS IN THE MEMORIAL*
CHURCH, CAWNPORE. Calcutta: Thacker Spink,
1894.
            Cited Ladendorf.

680
RAI   **MacGregor, Charles Metcalf.** *LIFE AND OPINIONS*
OF MAJOR GENERAL C.M. MACGREGOR
QUARTERMASTER- GENERAL IN INDIA. Edited by
Lady MacGregor. Edinburgh: William Blackwood, 1888.
2 vols. xviii & 367pp., x & 438pp. Frontis portrait, 6
folding maps.
            Approximately 100 pages on the Mutiny. Ferozepore,
Delhi, and Trans-Gogra.

681
Ames/BL/   **MacIntyre, James J.** *A PLAN FOR THE MILITARY*
Bod G.Pamph   *SEIZURE AND OCCUPATION OF THE TEMPLE*
2479 (7)   *AND CITY OF MECCA, AS A DEFENSIVE AND*
OFFENSIVE MEASURE FOR THE WAR IN ASIA,
ETC. London: Charles Westerton & Edward Stanford,
1858. 37pp. Pamphlet.
            This is a military plan for the occupation of Mecca in

retaliation for the Mutiny in India. MacIntyre feels the
Muslims are being helped financially from Mecca and that all
Muslims aid each other and are thus responsible as a group for
the atrocities of the Mutiny.

682
RS

MacKenzie, Mrs. C. *SIX YEARS IN INDIA: Delhi the
City of the Great Mogul With an Account of the Various
Tribes in Hindostan, Hindoos, Sikhs, Affghans, etc. A new
edition of "The Mission, The Camp and the Zenana."*
London: Richard Bentley, 1857. xvi & 288pp.
  Mentions the Mutiny only in the preface where she
emphatically states it is a mutiny, not an insurrection. Believes
the Mutiny can be blamed on the intrigues of the Prince's and
the desire of the Muslims to regain their supremacy. The book
covers 1846-1852.

683
Centenary
Exhibit
Calcutta

MacLean, J. *THE RANE: A LEGEND OF THE
INDIAN MUTINY. 1857-58.* London: Gustavus
Cohen and Co., 1887.
  Written under the name Gillean. The author states he
witnessed many of the occurrences described in the book.

684
RS

MacLeod, Norman D.D. *DAYS IN NORTH INDIA.*
Philadelphia: J.B. Lippincott, 1870. Frontis with
numerous plates, two folding, 188pp.
  A travelogue through north India. Macleod visits
Benares, Allahabad, Delhi, Cawnpore, Lucknow and Agra.
He visits and discusses the Mutiny sites in each locale.

685
RS

MacMunn, Sir George. *THE INDIAN MUTINY IN
PERSPECTIVE.* London: G. Bell and Sons, 1931. xii
& 276pp., 23 illus., 6 maps.
  MacMunn treats the Mutiny from a strictly military point
of view. He feels previous authors did not fully understand
the military aspects. Chaudhuri does not feel MacMunn is
entirely accurate.

686
RS

MacMunn, Sir George. *VIGNETTES FROM THE
INDIAN WARS* London: Sampson Lowe, ND. c. 1932
x & 214pp., folding map and 19 illus.
  Reprint 1978, x & 214pp. Offers one chapter on the
Mutiny. "Dawn At Delhi, May 11th, 1857" and "The Master
Gunner," a tale about Patrick Delahaney, a gunner forced to
serve the mutineers.

687

BL 4463.d.22/   **MacNeile, Hugh, et. al.** *THE FAST DAY SERMONS.*
Bod   *THE INDIAN MUTINY. 12 Sermons Revised by the*
100.i(40)(24)   *Authors Hugh MacNeile, John Cumming and others.*
London: J.A. Berger, Partridge & Co., Manchester:
Bremner & Co., 1857. 148pp.

> "12 sermons, delivered on October 7, 1857, being the day
> appointed as a national fast and humiliation."
> Author spelled as MacNeele in Ladendorf.

688

RS   **MacPherson, Lorne C.** *DAMN TIGHT PLACE(S)*
(with apologies to Rudyard Kipling). Magog, Quebec,
Canada: MacPherson Lumber Inc., 1994. xxviii [2]
& 214pp. Frontis, 4 maps, 85 photographs, 2 drawings,
bibliography.

> The memoirs of Nicholas Marshall Cummins. In 1902
> Cummins wrote his memoirs about his experiences in the
> Mutiny. Some of the accuracy may be suspect but it is an
> interesting story. He went out to India in the employ of the
> East Indian Railway and eventually became a soldier of the
> Queen. The memoirs start just as the mutineers arrive from
> Meerut on May 11th. The Cummins memoirs now reside in
> the India Office Library.

689

NAM   **MacPherson, Maj. Samuel Charters.** *Charteris:*
MEMORIALS OF SERVICE IN INDIA. From the
Correspondence of the Late ... Political Agent at Gwalior
During the Mutiny, and Formerly Employed in the
Suppression of Human Sacrifices in Orissa. Ed. By his
brother, William. London: John Murray, 1865. xii &
[47] + 400pp. 5 plates with map of Orissa at rear.

> MacPherson was the Resident at the Court of Sindhia at
> Gwalior. Two chapters on the Mutiny. (Approx. 30 pages)

690

Bod   **MacQueen, Kenneth.** *WHO IS TO BLAME FOR*
THE INDIAN MUTINIES? Edinburgh: Thomas
Constable, 1857. 30pp.

> Pamphlet.

691

NAM   **Macbean, Major N. I.** *VIEWS IN LUCKNOW; FROM*
1857(54)MAC   *SKETCHES TAKEN DURING THE SIEGE.* London:
J. Hogarth, May 1858. Title Page, Intro, list of plates.(i)
(ii)(iii)(iv)(v)(vi)(vii)(viii) 15 photographic plates, 2 hand
colored. Photographed by J. Hogarth Jr.

> An extremely scarce book on the Indian Mutiny.

Neither the India Office nor the British Library has it. The introductry note reads: "In presenting these views to the public, the publisher begs to say that these are facsimiles of the original sketches by Major Macbean, executed by the photographic process; and he feels assured they will be more interesting and valued as perfect transcripts of the spirited, though hasty, productions of a Military man himself an actor in the scenes he represents, than they would have been, if he had placed them in the hands of an artist for revisal at the risk of sacrificing fidelity to pictorial effect."

692
BL4767.de.8(1) **Mackee, Reverend James.** *OBSTACLES TO THE PROGRESS FOR CHRISTIANITY IN INDIA. A LECTURE.* Belfast: Newsletter Office, 1858. 24pp.

693
RS **Mackenzie, Alexander R. D.** *MUTINY MEMOIRS, BEING THE PERSONAL REMINISCENCES OF THE GREAT SEPOY REVOLT OF 1857.* Allahabad: Pioneer Press, 1891. (2nd ed. 1892. 214pp. 5 plates by Bourne and Shepherd) iv & 211pp. Index.
Mackenzie commanded the 8th Irregular Cavalry posted at Bareilly, the capital of Rohilcund and seat of the Commissioner. The 8th mutinied May 31, 1857. They did not kill their officers.

694
Bod **Mackenzie, James Thompson.** *SUGGESTIONS FOR THE RECONSTRUCTION OF THE GOVERNMENT OF INDIA; WITH SOME REMARKS UPON IT'S MONETARY, COMMERCIAL, SOCIAL, AND RELIGIOUS ASPECTS.* London: NP. 1857. 56pp.
Pamphlet.

695
Bod **Mackenzie, W. B.** *INDIA'S TROUBLE: IS THERE NOT A CAUSE?* London: Seeley, Jackson and Halliday, 1857. 20pp.
Pamphlet.

696
RS **Maclagan, Michael.** *CLEMENCY CANNING, CHARLES JOHN 1ST EARL CANNING, GOVERNOR GENERAL AND VICEROY OF INDIA. 1856-1862.* London: MacMillan, 1962. xvi & 420pp., index, bibliography, frontis, 10 illus., 8 maps and plans.
Appendix 1 gives table of office holders in India and England 1856-1862. Appendix 2 is a full text of the

Clemency Resolution. This work was written by a relative of
Canning with full access to his papers.

697
RS   **Macleod, Major Gen. A.** *ON INDIA.* London:
Longmans, Green, 1872. iv & 198pp.
Includes an essay on the causes of the Mutiny.

698
Ames   **Madras Military Male Orphan Asylum.** *NARRATIVE
OF THE INDIAN MUTINIES OF 1857 COMPILED
FOR THE MADRAS MILITARY MALE ORPHAN
ASYLUM FOR THE BENEFIT OF THIS "HOME" OF
THE ORPHANS OF THE SOLDIER, ALL PROFITS
OF THE SALE WILL BE APPROPRIATED.* Madras:
Printed at the Asylum Press, Mount Road, by William
Thomas. 1858. 196pp.

699
RS   **Mahdi, Husain** No entry.

700
RS   **Majendie, Lt. V(ivian) D(ering).** *UP AMONG THE
PANDIES.* London: Routledge, Warne, and Routledge,
1859. 360pp. Red cloth. Frontis of Iron Bridge at
Lucknow.
Reprinted 1974, Legend Publications, India, xii & 360pp.
Majendie fought at the final siege of Lucknow in 1858 with
Campbell. His book is known as one of the most savage
though Chaudhuri states he is generally reliable and was one
of the first to write on the Mutiny.

701
Ames   **Majumdar, J. K. ed.** *INDIAN SPEECHES AND
DOCUMENTS ON BRITISH RULE 1821-1918.*
Delhi: Kanti Publications, 1987.
Originally published Calcutta: Longman Green & Co.
1937. Contains a number of speeches related to the Mutiny.
1) Letter of the British Indian Association to the
Governor General in Council on the breaking out of the
Sepoy Mutiny, 23, May, 1857.
2) Proceedings of a meeting of the Mahomedans of
Calcutta on the breaking out of the Sepoy Mutiny 27, May,
1857.
3) The Gengalies Address to the Governor General
in Council on the re-taking of Delhi....1857. In all about 9
documents related to the Mutiny.

702
RS

Majumdar, Ramesh Chandra *HISTORY OF THE FREEDOM MOVEMENT IN INDIA.* Calcutta: Firma K.L. Mukhopadhyay, 1962-1963. 1st ed, 3 vols. Also: 2nd rev. ed. 1971 to 1977, Vol. I xx & 471pp., Vol. II, xxiv & 509pp., Vol. III, xxx & 759pp. This work was written partially because Majumdar did not agree with the work of the same name, by Tara Chand. Volume I, chapter seven covers the Mutiny.

703
RS

Majumdar, Ramesh Chandra *SEPOY MUTINY.* Calcutta: Firma K.L. Mukhopadhyay, 1957. xviii & 289pp. (2nd ed. 1963. xxiv & 503pp)
The 2nd ed. Gives details of local risings and includes a map and bibliography which is not contained in the 1st edition. This is one of the basic works on the Mutiny. Majumdar withdrew from the government sponsored history of the Mutiny because he felt the government had preconceived ideas on how the history should read. The book is regarded as one of the first really scholarly works on the Mutiny. Majumdar does not believe the Mutiny was a war of independence, nor does he believe there was a general conspiracy. Sengupta states that Majumdar seems to have written this book with the idea of destroying certain notions regarding the Mutiny. See Sengupta, entry 944, page 10.

704

Majumdar, Ramesh Chandra, ed. *THE HISTORY AND CULTURE OF THE INDIAN PEOPLE.* Bombay: Bharatiya Vidya Bhavan 1951-1963.
Vol. 9 discusses the causes of the Mutiny. This is rebutted by Chaudhuri in his *"Theories of the Indian Mutiny"* (entry 267).

705

Malcolm, Henry Frederick. *HISTORY OF THE WAR IN INDIA INCLUDING THE COMPLETE HISTORY OF BRITISH INDIA FROM THE EARLIEST TIMES TO THE PRESENT DAY ALSO A SKETCH OF GENERAL HAVELOCK.* Philadelphia: John E. Potter and Co., 1859.
About one third of the book deals with the Mutiny.

706
RS

Malcolm, Henry Frederick. *INDIA AND THE INDIAN MUTINY: COMPRISING THE COMPLETE HISTORY OF HINDOSTAN, FROM THE EARLIEST TIMES TO THE PRESENT DAY; with full particulars*

of the recent Mutiny in India. Philadelphia: J.W. Bradley, 1858. 456pp. Blue cloth blind. Numerous woodcuts.
Approximately 100 pages deal with the Mutiny. The work saw a second edition in 1859 published by John E. Potter Co. This work was titled *"History of the War in India...."* and included three additional chapters covering the capture of Calpee and Gwalior, the change in the Government of India, and a memoir of General Havelock.

707

Malcolm, Thomas (See Caine, Rev. Caesar).
BARRACKS AND BATTLEFIELDS IN INDIA: EXPERIENCES OF A SOLDIER OF THE 10TH FOOT NORTH LINCOLN IN THE SIKH WARS AND SEPOY MUTINY.
Cited in Ladendorf.

708
RS

Malgonkar, Manohar. *THE DEVIL'S WIND: Nana Saheb's Story.* New Delhi: Penguin Books, 1972, 1988. 315pp.
Fiction.

709

Malik, Salah-uddin. *MUTINY: REVOLUTION OR MUSLIM REBELLION, BRITISH PUBLIC REACTION TOWARDS INDIAN CRISES OF 1857.*
Cited in Jain

710
RS/
BL8022.c.4

Malleson, Capt. G. B. *THE MUTINY OF THE BENGAL ARMY: An Historical Narrative by One Who Has Served Under Sir Charles Napier.* London: Bosworth and Harrison, 1857-1858. Part I, 1857. 46pp. Part II, 1857. London: John Chapman. 38pp.
This work was later known as the "Red Pamphlet." Chaudhuri assigns the first part of the book a date of July 2nd 1857 and the 2nd section a date of early 1858. This work is arguably the most famous work in Mutiny literature. Upon publication it caused an immediate storm and brought a quick response from Charles Allen. The indictment of Dalhousie caused particular reaction in some quarters. Malleson refers to him as "a man of paltry littleness and petty jealousy." The third part of this book was lost in a shipwreck and so never published.

711
RS

Malleson, Col. George Bruce. *THE INDIAN MUTINY OF 1857.* London: Seeley & Co. and New

York: Scribner & Welford, 1891. xiv & 421pp. 4
portraits and 3 plans.
This title went through numerous editions. 1891 2nd
& 3rd ed. (Charles Scribner, New York) and limited large
paper edition of 250 copies. 1892 4th ed. 1898 7th ed. xvi
& 421pp; 1901;1906;1912 10th ed. Seeley Service & Co.
The book was written as part of a series, "Events of Our Own
Time" published by Seeley and Co. Each has a large paper
limited edition as well as a standard edition.

712
Ames

Malleson, G. B. *ESSAYS AND LECTURES ON
INDIAN HISTORICAL SUBJECTS. HAVELOCK,
ROSE, ETC. BY AN OFFICER OF THE BENGAL
STAFF CORPS.* London and Calcutta: Trubner & Co.
and R. C. Lepage (Calcutta), 1866. iv & 347pp.
Contains an 80 page essay on Havelock and a 68 page
essay on Sir Hugh Rose.

713

Malleson, George Bruce. *See HISTORY OF THE
INDIAN MUTINY under Kaye*
Malleson, George Bruce 1825-1898. Served in the
Bengal Native Infantry, fought in the Second Burmese War,
wrote the *"Red Pamphlet"* 1857-58. He was Chief of the
Commissariat Dept at Cawnpore when Outram entered
Oude to depose the King in 1856. Two months later he was
appointed to the Military Audit Dept in Calcutta. 1866-68
Sanitary Commissioner for Bengal; Controller, Military
Finance Dept. 1868-69. Guardian of the young Maharaja of
Mysore, 1869-77.
Malleson was a prolific writer on India and Afghanistan.

714
Ames

Malleson, George Bruce. *AMBUSHES AND
SURPRISES: Being a Description of Some of the Most
Famous Instances of the Leading into Ambush and the
Surprise of Armies, from the Time of Hannibal to the period
of the Indian Mutiny.* London: W. H. Allen, 1885. x,
434pp.
With a Portrait of General Lord Mark Kerr. Chapter X
discusses the activities at Arrah and the events in Azamgarh
and Kunwar Singh.

715
Bod

Malleson, George Bruce. *RECREATIONS OF AN
INDIAN OFFICIAL.* London: Longman, Green, 1872.
xii & 467pp.
Biographical sketches including Sir Vincent Eyre, Lord
Lawrence and Sir Bartle Frere.

716
RS

Mansfield, H. O. *CHARLES ASHE WINDHAM. A Norfolk Soldier (1810-1870).* Suffolk: Terence Dalton, 1973. 239pp. Plates and index.
Most of the work deals with Windham's career prior to the Mutiny.

717
Bod
100i38 (9)/
BL

Margolioth. *THE QUARREL OF GODS COVENANT, A FASTDAY SERMON.* London: Wertheim & MacIntosh, 1857. Pamphlet.

718

Mariwalla, C. L. *WHEN THE STORM CAME 1857.* Bombay: K.W. Dwani, 1957. 311pp.
Considered of little significance by Sengupta in *"Recent Writings...."*

719
RS

Marshman, John Clark. *MEMOIRS OF MAJOR GENERAL SIR HENRY HAVELOCK.* London: Longmans Green, 1860, 1861. 426pp.
3rd ed. 1867. frontis. 457pp. Written by Havelock's brother-in-law.

720
BL
4412.ee.18(1)

Marston, Louise *HEALED & SAVED: A STORY OF THE LUCKNOW MEDICAL MISSION.* NC. NP. 1890.

721
Bod

Martin, Major W. *WHO SHALL REGENERATE INDIA?* London: William H. Allen, 1859. Pamphlet.
How to proceed in India in the aftermath of the Mutiny.

722
RS

Martin, R. Montgomery. *THE INDIAN EMPIRE WITH A FULL ACCOUNT OF THE MUTINY OF THE NATIVE TROOPS.* London: London Printing and Publishing Co., 1858-1861. 3 vols. 1278pp. 111 engravings. Folding Map. 582pp. vii & 504pp. vii & 192pp.
According to Chaudhuri this work could not have been written before 1860-61. This is one of the major works on the Mutiny. Martin was a member of the Court of Directors of the East India Co. Martin (1803? - 1868) went out to India as a surgeon, botanist and naturalist. His work does not go into great depth, however it is without much of the prejudice of later works.

723
RS   **Martin, Robert Montgomery.** *RISE AND PROGRESS OF THE INDIAN MUTINY, A FULL EXAMINATION OF THE ALLEDGED CAUSES OF THE INSURRECTION AND AN ADDRESS TO LORD STANLEY ON THE CONDITION OF OUR EASTERN EMPIRE.* London: London Printing and Publishing Company, 1859. Frontis of Lucknow, vi & 124pp.
     This appears to be a separate edition of the introductory chapter to Martin's book "*The Indian Empire.*" If so it would seem to prove that "The Indian Empire" was not first published in 1857.

724
         Martin, W. *A FEW WORDS ON GENERAL JACOB'S SCHEME FOR THE REORGANIZATION OF THE INDIAN ARMIES.* London: W. H. Allen & Co, 1858. 22pp.
     See John Jacob, *"The Views and Opinions of Brig. Gen. John Jacob."* Edited by Capt. Lewis Pelly. (Entry 564)

725
Bod   **Martin, William.** *MEMORANDUM ON THE RECONSTRUCTION OF THE BENGAL ARMY.* London: NP. 1857.
     There is an 1858 edition that is the 2nd edition and considerably enlarged with an appendix which contains thoughts on Indian Patronage. London: W. H. Allen & Co., 1858.

726
Bod   **Martin, William.** *WHY IS THE ENGLISH RULE ODIUS TO THE NATIVES OF INDIA?.* London: W. H. Allen, 1858. 75pp.
     Calls for the reform of the civil and judicial systems as well as equal rights and opportunities for the native

727
RS   **Marx, Karl and Frederick Engels.** *THE FIRST INDIAN WAR OF INDEPENDENCE 1857-1859.* Moscow: Foreign Languages Publishing House, 1959. 2nd impression 253pp, another edition, ND. 245pp.
     Based on articles in the New York Daily Tribune.

728
RS   **Mason, Philip.** *A MATTER OF HONOUR: An Account of the Indian Army, Its Officers and Men.* London: Jonathan Cape, 1974. 580pp. plates, bibliography and index.

A study of the Indian Army from its earliest days.
Includes two sections which cover the sepoy army and the
Mutiny.

729
RS   **Mason, Philip Woodruff.** *THE MEN WHO RULED
INDIA.* New York: St Martins Press, 1954. 2 vols.
402pp. 6 plates & 8 maps; 385pp. 8 plates & 4 maps.
This work consists of two titles: "The Founders" and "The
Guardians." An excellent work giving the story of British rule
in India.

730
RS   **Masselos, Jim and Narayani Gupta.** *BEATO'S DELHI
1857, 1997.* New Delhi: Ravi Dayal, 2000. 115pp.
Bibliography. Oblong.
A wonderful work showing side by side comparisons of
Felice Beato's photographs of Mutiny scenes in Delhi in 1857
and the same scene photographed in 1997. Text accompanies
each photo.

731
Bod/RS   **Matthews, Charles Richard.** *THE FIRST SHOT IN
1857. By an Indian Colonel.* NC. NP. Privately printed.
ND. c. 1914. 40pp.
Red Leather. Matthews was with the 43rd Bengal Light
Infantry. He was Regimental Subaltern on the day when
Mangal Pande mutinied at Barrackpore. This is an account of
that incident.

732
RS   **Maude, Captain Francis Cornwallis, V.C. and John
Walter Sherer.** *MEMORIES OF THE MUTINY.*
London: Remington, 1894. 2 vols. Vol I 14 plates and
frontis. Vol II 15 plates with folding map of Lucknow.
Maude commanded the artillery of the Havelock column.
The work also incorporates the personal narrative of John
Sherer formerly Magistrate of Futtehpore and afterwards of
Cawnpore.
Maude was Consul-General at Warsaw from 1876 to
1886. He also served in Madagascar as a director of the
Madagascar Timber Company. He died at Windsor Castle on
October 19, 1900.

733
RS   **Maude, Col. E.** *ORIENTAL CAMPAIGNS AND
EUROPEAN FURLOUGHS. The Autobiography of a
Veteran of the Indian Mutiny.* London: T. Fisher Unwin,
1908. xx & 292pp. Portrait.
Maude served in the Persian Campaign and then returned
to serve in the Central Indian Campaigns.

734
RAI   **Maude, Col. F. C. (VC)**; *INDIAN VIEWS DURING THE MUTINY.* NC. NP. ND. 37 photos.
This is a photo album with explanatory notes by Col. Maude. Lucknow, Wheelers Entrenchments, Mowbray Thompson before the Entrenchments, Dilkoosha, inside the Secundra Bagh, Imam Bara, a good panorama of Lucknow. Quite a rare album. Contains photography by Felice Beato.

735
RS   **Maunsell, General Sir Frederick Richard K.C.B.**
THE SIEGE OF DELHI. A Record by a Survivor Who Filled an Important Post at the Glorious Siege. London: Simpkin, Marshall, Hamilton, Kent & Co., 1912. 23pp. Pamphlet.
This is a reprint of two articles which originally appeared in the R. E. Journal July 1911, and in the "Nineteenth Century and After," October 1911. Maunsell, commander of the Sappers at Delhi, wrote these articles to publicize the work of General Sir Alexander Taylor at Delhi. Although Baird Smith was the Chief Engineer it was Taylor who took on the actual duties and developed the plans for the siege.

736
Maurice, Maj. Gen. Sir F. and G. Arthur. *THE LIFE OF LORD WOLSELEY.* London: William Heinemann, 1924. xxiii & 375pp. 16 plates, 4 maps.
Includes service in the Mutiny.

737
Jain   **Mawe, Mrs.** *NARRATIVE OF THE MUTINY OF THE 12TH N.I. AT NAWGONG.*,
Cited in Jain. Unable to locate.

738
Mayne, F.O. *NARRATIVE OF EVENTS ATTENDING THE OUTBREAK OF DISTURBANCES AND THE RESTORATION OF AUTHORITY IN THE DISTRICT OF BANDA IN 1857-58. Part I and Part II.*, See listing for *"Mutiny in India"* (Entry 448)

739
McAree, James Gregory. *THE PASSAGE OF THE GOVERNMENT OF INDIA BILL OF 1858.* Minneapolis: University of Minnesota, 1961. 300pp. Ph.D. Thesis cited in Ladendorf.

740
IO

McCallan, Andrew. *A WEEK IN THE MOFUSSIL IN 1857.* London: Warren Hall and James J. Lovitt, ND. c. 1875. 77pp.

Originally printed in Allahabad in 1857. Recounts the events which befell Mr. McCallan at Allahabad upon the outbreak of the Mutiny. Rather well written.

741
RS

McGovern, Joseph Henry. *HOW ONE OF THE MCGOVERN CLAN WON THE VICTORIA CROSS IN THE INDIAN MUTINY WITH A SKETCH OF ITS TRIBAL HISTORY: Armorial Bearings, and Plan of the Barony of Tullyhaw, Co. Cavan, Ireland.* Liverpool: Printed at the "Daily Post" and "Echo" Offices, Victoria Street. 1889. 37pp.

McGovern was an architect by trade. This is the history of Sergeant John McGovern of the 1st Bengal Fusiliers. McGovern was awarded the VC for action during the siege at Delhi.

742
RS

McKenzie, Captain Thomas. *MY LIFE AS A SOLDIER.* New Brunswick, Canada: J & A McMillan, 1898. xi & 202pp. Frontis.

McKenzie served in Persia and then was shipped directly to Bombay and on to Calcutta. He marched up to Allahabad and then to Cawnpore with Havelock. McKenzie was field bugler with Havelock. He went on to Lucknow and back to Cawnpore with Campbell. There are about 60pp on the Mutiny.

743
RS

Mead, Henry. *THE SEPOY REVOLT: Its Causes and Its Consequences.* London: John Murray, 1857. viii & 398pp. A New Edition 1859. 378pp. viii & 398pp. and a 2nd ed. enlarged, iv & 378pp London: G. Routledge 1858.

According to Chaudhuri this is one of the, if not the, earliest work on the Mutiny.

Mead was a journalist in India for many years. He was very critical of the Canning Government. He was the editor of "The Friend of India."

744
RS

Mecham, C. H. *SKETCHES AND INCIDENTS OF THE SIEGE OF LUCKNOW With Descriptive Notices by George Couper.* London: Day & Son, October 1, 1858. Imperial folio. 27 tinted lithos on 18 plates. The drawings were made during the siege. 12 pages of text.

Clifford Henry Mecham was a Lieut. in the Madras

Army. At the time of the Mutiny he was the adjutant of the 7th Regiment Oude Irregular Infantry. Mecham saw extensive action in and around Lucknow. He owed his life to his coolness under pressure on two different occassions.

745
RS

Medley, Capt. J. G. *A YEARS CAMPAIGNING IN INDIA. From March 1857 to March 1858.* London: W. Thacker, 1858. xii & 213pp. Chromolithographic frontis of an officer of the Muzbee Sikhs. Folding map and three plans.

Medley was a Captain in the Bengal Engineers and garrison engineer of Lucknow. The narrative embraces an account of the Bozdar Expedition in the Derajat Hills, in March 1857; the Siege and Capture of Delhi, in September 1857; Colonel Seaton's Campaign in the Doab, in December of the same year; and the Siege and Capture of Lucknow, in March, 1858. The Bozdar Expedition has no relation to the Mutiny.

746
RS

Meek, Rev. R. *THE MARTYR OF ALLAHABAD. Memorials of Ensign Arthur Marcus Hill Cheek of the 6th Bengal Native Infantry. Murdered by the Sepoys at Allahabad.* London: James Nisbet, 1857. vi & 70pp. Portrait.

This was reprinted in 1858 with iv & 86pp.

747
RS/IO

Mehta, Asoka. *1857, THE GREAT REBELLION.* Bombay: Hind Kitab, 1946. 81pp. Paper.

Considered of little significance by Sengupta in *"Recent Writings...."*

748
IO

Melville, S. S. *EXPERIENCES OF LIFE IN INDIA IN 1857-1858.* NC. Privately Printed 1912. 47pp.

Account of the Delhi Campaign. Includes service with the Meerut Volunteer Cavalry.

749
BL

Mercer, Edward Smyth. *A LETTER TO RT. HON. THE EARL OF ELLENBOROUGH ON THE MILITARY, RELIGIOUS AND EUROPEAN SETTLEMENT QUESTION IN THE EAST INDIES.* London: Edward T. Whitfield, 1861. 11pp. Pamphlet.

Causes of the Mutiny i.e. nepotism; friction between the new Young Indian Party & the conservatives; interference of government in religious matters; a more even hand where

religion is concerned, both native and Christian. Mercer goes
on to make a number of other recommendations.

750
RS   **Metcalf, Thomas R.** *THE AFTERMATH OF
REVOLT IN INDIA. 1857-1870.* Princeton: Princeton
Univ Press, 1964. rept 1990, Manohar Books, Delhi,
With new introduction. xi & 352pp bibliography, index.
        Examines how the Mutiny shaped the later history of
India. The author gives the terms of office of various Indian
administrators 1850-1870 and biographical notes on some
of the famous figures of the Mutiny. This is a very well
researched work concentrating on the post-Mutiny decade.
The Introduction and Chapter II, "The Mutiny and Its
Causes," are especially valuable. The Manohar edition suffers
from poor proofing.

751
RS   **Metcalfe, Charles Theophilus.** *TWO NATIVE
NARRATIVES OF THE MUTINY IN DELHI.*
London: Archibald Constable, 1898. 259pp. 2 plates.
Another edition, Sema Publications, India: 1974. 259
pp.
        This is an important work and is used as a reference by
many writers on the Mutiny. The book contains the narratives
of Al-Din Hasan Khan Muin, who held an Inspectorship
of Police at Delhi, and Munshi Jeewan Lal, a resident at the
court in Delhi during the siege. Lal was a writer by caste and
profession. The work was compiled by Metcalfe who was the
Magistrate in Delhi at the time of the outbreak. Metcalfe
was said to have hung numerous rebels from the rafters of his
burned out mansion in Delhi.
        Charles was the elder brother of Sir Thomas Theophilus
who was Commissioner at Delhi. Sir Thomas died in 1853,
possibly by poison. Sir Thomas was the builder of Metcalfe
House, of Mutiny fame.
        Sir Charles (1785-1846) was Resident at Delhi
1811-1819, and 1825-1827, Governor of Agra 1834-35,
Governor of Canada 1843-45.
        The translator of *"Native Narratives"* was Charles
Theophilus Metcalfe, son of Thomas and nephew of Charles
Theophilus the first.

752
RS   **Miles, A. H. and A. J. Pattle.** *FIFTY TWO STORIES
OF THE INDIAN MUTINY AND THE MEN WHO
SAVED INDIA.* London: Hutchinson, 1895. 440pp.
Illus.
        A popular history of the Mutiny taken from
Cave-Browne, Holmes, Kaye, Malleson and others.

753
BL 8022.d.46   **Mills, A.** *INDIA IN 1858.* NC. NP. 1858.

754
RS   **Milman, Lieut-General G. Bryan.**; *MAURITIUS TO INDIA, 1857-8-9. From the Journal of Lieut-General Bryan Milman. Late of the 5th Fusiliers. Major and resident Governor of the Tower.* Dover: G.W. Grigg, 1899. 62pp. Eight plates and one map. Green cloth with vignette.
    Milman served at the Alam Bagh. Includes a long poem titled "To the Young Ladies of Mauritius: A Slight Account of the 1st Batt. 5th Fusiliers in the Oude Campaign, Christmas, 1858."

755
RS   **Minturn, R. B.** *FROM NEW YORK TO DELHI: By Way of Rio De Janeiro, Australia and China.* London: Longman, Brown, Green, Longmans and Roberts, 1858. xv & 466pp.
    Minturn was a missionary and very opinionated and critical of the Indian. Very racist.

756
BL 9056.aa.19   **Misr, Koonwar Gunga Pershad.** *PARTICULARS OF THE MUTINY OF 1857 IN BAREILLY AND BUDAEON WITH AN ACCOUNT OF THE SERVICES RENDERED TO THE BRITISH GOVERNMENT BY KOONWAR GUNGA PERSHAD MISR.* Bareilly: Regimental Press, (5th Fusiliers) 1872. 80pp.
    Printed for private circulation. The author came from a family of bankers in Bareilly and states that much of the European military in the area banked with them. Apparently the author was familiar with much of the local European population.

757
BL   **Misr, Rajah Byjenath.** *NARRATIVES OF RAJAH BYJENATH MISR'S SUFFERINGS DURING THE REBELLION.* London: Smith Elder & Co., 1866. 352pp.
    Cited in William Edward's "*Reminiscences of a Bengal Civilian.*" (Entry 375)

758
IO/RS   **Misra, Anand Swarup.** *NANA SAHIB PESHWA AND THE FIGHT FOR FREEDOM.* Lucknow: Information Dept, 1961. xxviii & 636pp. Appendices, bibliography, index, frontis, illustrated.

Massive work covering not only the Nana, with an
attempt to restore his good name, but also including a survey
of the entire Mutiny. Interesting chapters on the last days
of some of the leaders of the Mutiny. The later history of
the Cawnpore Well Memorial is covered as well as brief
personality sketches of some Indians and Europeans of the
period. A glossary of military and special terms is found at the
rear. A useful work.

759
IO   **Mistry, Homi D.** *REBELS OF DESTINY.* Bombay:
Hind Kitabs Ltd., 1959. xvi & 212pp. Index.
The first abridged edition was published in 1957 in Blitz
Magazine.
Interesting format. The book is done in the form of a
trial with Winston Churchill as prosecution and Netaji Bose as
defense. Their dialogue, as well as all others, are exact quotes
from their own writings and speeches. The book supports the
idea that the Mutiny was a war of Independence.

760
Bod   **Mitchell, Rev. J. Murray.** *INDIAN MISSIONS;
VIEWED IN CONNEXION WITH THE MUTINY
AND OTHER RECENT EVENTS.* London: James
Nisbet, 1859. 31pp. Pamphlet.
Discusses the lessons which can be learned from the
Mutiny.

761
RS   **Mohan, Krishan.** *REVOLT OF 1857 AND THE
INDIAN FREEDOM MOVEMENT.* Jaipur: Book
Enclave, 1999. vi & 272pp. Index.
A major portion of the book is a chapter titled "An
Analysis of the Revolt of 1857" in which Mohan covers all of
the major causes of the Mutiny.

762
RS   **Mollo, Boris.** *THE INDIAN ARMY.* London:
Blandford Press, 1981, and London: New Orchard
Editions, 1986. The 1986 ed. is illustrated with a
glossary, bibliography and an index of Indian regimental
names. 191pp.
A well illustrated work. One chapter on the Mutiny.

763
Molloy, Maj. G. M. *THE HISTORICAL RECORDS
OF THE 34TH (Prince Albert Victor's Own) POONA
HORSE.* London: Hugh Rees, 1913. x & 139pp. 3rd
ed.
Includes Mutiny material.

764
BL   **Moncrieff, Alexander Scott.** *LETTERS OF ALEXANDER SCOTT MONCRIEFF.* London: William Blackwood & Son. Printed for private circulation. 1914. 229pp with folding map.

About 60pp on the Mutiny. Moncrieff was stationed in Chota Nagpore.

765
        Moncrieff, Ascott Robert Hope. *THE STORY OF THE INDIAN MUTINY 1857-1858.* Edinburgh: W.P. Nimmo Hay & Mitchell, 1898. 224pp.

Of little value and of questionable origin. See Chaudhuri *"English Historical Writings..."* page 306, note. There was a Robert Hope Moncrieff Aitken who won the VC for various acts during the defense of the Residency at Lucknow. It is not known if there was a relation with the author.

766
BL   **Money, Reverend C.F.S.** *THE INDIAN MUTINY OR INDIA'S IDOLATRY AND ENGLAND'S RESPONSIBILITY. A SERMON PREACHED ON THE FAST DAY, OCTOBER 7, 1857.* London: Wertheim and MacIntosh, 1857. Pamphlet. 15pp.

Money states that there is a connection between the religion of the Hindus and the atrocities during the Mutiny. An account is given of human sacrifice and there is a general discussion of the debasement of the Hindu religion in the eyes of the Christians.

767
BOD/   **Montagu, Rear-Admiral Victor Alexander.** *A*
BL 010817h8 *MIDDY'S RECOLLECTIONS 1853-1860.* London: A.C. Black, 1898. xi & 206pp. Frontis and 7 illus.

Montagu arrived in Calcutta in 1857 (August) on the "Pearl" and served with the Naval Brigade.

768
RS   **Montalembert, M. Le Comte De.** *A DEBATE ON INDIA IN THE ENGLISH PARLIAMENT.* London: Office of the Continental Review, Bedford St, Strand, 1858. 64pp.

Translated from the "Correspondent" Oct. 29, 1858. This originally appeared in the "Correspondent" a publication of the Liberal Catholic Party in France. The author and the "Correspondent" were indicted by the government of France for the publication of this pamphlet.

769
RS
Montgomery, Brian. *MONTY'S GRANDFATHER. Sir Robert Montgomery GCSI, KCB, LLD 1809-1887. A Life's Service for the Raj.* Poole, Dorset UK: Blandford Press, 1984. xix & 140pp. Two maps and 12 photos. Bibliography and index.

The author is the brother of Lord Montgomery of Alamein (Monty). Good coverage of the Mutiny period. Sir Robert Montgomery served as the Judicial Commissioner of the Punjab, Chief Commissioner of the Punjab and Lieutenant Governor of the Punjab from 1859-1865.

770
RS
Montgomery, Robert. *SELECTIONS FROM THE PUBLIC CORRESPONDENCE OF THE ADMINISTRATION FOR THE AFFAIRS OF THE PUNJAB.* Lahore: Chronicle Press, 1859. 197pp. Folding statement.

Vol. IV No. 1 Punjab Mutiny Report. A detailed report of occurrences in the Punjab during the Mutiny. Montgomery was the Judicial Commissioner in the Punjab and later the Commissioner of Oude.

771
IO
Moody, Rev. N. J. *INDIA'S PAST AND FUTURE AND ENGLAND'S DUTY. A Sermon for the Times, Preached in St. Clements Church, Oxford, Sept. 20, 1857.* Oxford: H. Hamman's and in London: Wertheim & MacIntosh, 1857. 22pp.

Blames the Muslims for a conspiracy. The Hindus would not have acted had not the Muslims conspired to restore the Mughal Empire.

772
RS/
IO 8023.b.45
Mookerjee, Sambhu Chandra (also known as Mukharji). *MUTINIES AND THE PEOPLE OR STATEMENTS OF NATIVE FIDELITY EXHIBITED DURING THE OUTBREAK OF 1857-58 by a Hindu.* Calcutta: I.C. Bose & Co. Stanhope Press, 1859. i & 196pp. 2 plates

There is much confusion on this title. Chaudhuri states that the author is Mukhopadhyaya and there seems to be some evidence that the book was published originally in England in 1857. There is also an edition printed in Calcutta: Bangabasi Office, 1905, iv & 332pp. Another edition was printed in 1863, xviii & 175pp. All of these books are one and the same.

The book was originally printed anonymously by "A Hindu." It has been established that the author was Mookerjee who was a college graduate and later in life a leading Indian politician and writer. This title was written when Mookerjee was 18 years old and consists of material compiled from a number of current newspapers. There seems to be evidence that Malcolm Lewin, another student of the Mutiny, helped with an earlier edition in London in 1857. In *"The Growth of Nationalism"* Haridas Mukherjee discusses this title.

773
RS   **Moore, Geoffrey (compiler).** *DIARY OF THE DOCTOR'S LADY.* England: Published by the compiler. ND. c. 1979. 64pp.
The doctor is William Brydon, sole survivor of Elphinstone's diastrous retreat from Kabul in 1842. This is the diary his wife, Colina, kept during the siege of Lucknow after which the family eventually returned to Calcutta and Scotland. Brydon retired from the East India Company in 1859 and his spirit bloomed for departure in 1873.

774
NAM 92LAW **Morison, J. L.** *LAWRENCE OF LUCKNOW. 1806-1857. Being the Life of Sir Henry Lawrence.* London: Bell, 1934. 348pp. 8 plates and 2 maps. Index.
A general biography.

775
RS   **Morrison, Rev. C. (compiler).** *SIEGE OF LUCKNOW: BRIGADE ORDERS ISSUED BETWEEN OCTOBER 2ND AND NOVEMBER 18TH, 1857.* London: Richard Clay, 1897. 51pp.

776
Bod   **Morrison, Rev. W. Robert.** *FACTS FOR A CHRISTIAN PUBLIC. AN EARNEST APPEAL TO THE PEOPLE OF ENGLAND CONCERNING OUR FUTURE CONDUCT IN INDIA.* London: Wertheim, MacIntosh & Hunt, 1859. 59pp. Pamphlet.
Blames government for its position of religious neutrality as being the key to the Mutiny.
Morrison gives five specific charges regarding the religious problems in India.

777
BL   **Mouat, Fred J.** *THE BRITISH SOLDIER IN INDIA.* London: R.C. LePage, 1859. viii & 87pp.
A monograph aimed at improving the condition of the British soldier in India. Covers clothing, equipment, barracks, food, family, etc.

778
RS   **Muddock, J. E.** *THE GREAT WHITE HAND OR THE TIGER OF CAWNPORE: A Story of the Indian Mutiny.* London: Hutchinson and Co., 1896. xii & 356pp.
             Fiction.

779
Kaul   **Muddock, Joyce Emerson.** *THE STAR OF FORTUNE. A STORY OF THE INDIAN MUTINY.* London: George Bell and Sons, 1894. viii & 320pp.
             Fiction.

780
             Muin, Al-Din Hasan Khan. *TWO NATIVE NARRATIVES OF THE MUTINY IN DELHI.* London: 1898.
             See Metcalfe: "Two Native Narratives" (Entry 751)

781
Kaul/Maggs.   **Muir, Sir William**; *AGRA CORRESPONDENCE DURING THE MUTINY.* Edinburgh: T & T Clark, 1898. 109pp.
             Extracts of Muir's letters to his family take up the main portion of this book. Extracts from the Intelligence Department's Records are also included. Muir's letter to Canning about the "dishonour of the European females" is included.

782
RS/   **Muir, Sir William.** *AGRA IN THE MUTINY AND*
NAM   *THE FAMILY LIFE OF W & E MUIR IN THE FORT.*
1857(54)MUI *1857, A Sketch for Their Children.* NC. NP. 1896. 59pp.
             3 photographic plates.
             There was an edition published in Edinburgh in 1898 with 109pp but not illustrated. The 1898 edition is smaller and contains extracts from the records of the Intelligence Dept. There is also a copy in the NAM with no publisher, no date, and no title page.

783
RS   **Muir, Sir William.** *RECORDS OF THE INTELLIGENCE DEPARTMENT OF THE GOVERNMENT OF THE NORTH-WEST PROVINCES OF INDIA DURING THE MUTINY OF 1857. Including Correspondence with the Supreme Government, Delhi, Cawnpore, and Other Places.* Edinburgh: T & T Clark, 1902. 2 volumes, ii & 559pp; vi & 398pp.
             Contains extracts from Muir's book *"Agra in the Mutiny."*

Muir was the Secretary to the Government of the Northwest Provinces. In 1857 he was the head of the Intelligence Department in Agra. By 1865 he was the Foreign Secretary to the Government of India and from 1868 to 1874 was the Lieutenant Governor of the North-Western Provinces.

784
Ames

Mujeeb, Muhammad. *ORDEAL 1857: A Historical Play.* Bombay: Asia Publishing House, 1958. 78pp.
The author has excluded "All that could cause hatred between the nations concerned...."

785
RS

Mukerjee, Sambhu Chandra. *THE MUTINIES AND THE PEOPLE OR STATEMENTS OF NATIVE FIDELITY EXHIBITED DURING THE OUTBREAK OF 1857-58. By a Hindu.* Calcutta: Sanskrit Pustak Bhandar, 1969. Also Calcutta: NP. 1905. 332pp. 175pp.
Originally printed by I.C. Bose & Co. Stanhope Press, Calcutta, 1859.
The author was born 1839 and died 1894. Mukerjee was a journalist and was 18 years old when he wrote this.

786

Mukharya, P. S. *THE REVOLT OF 1857: SAUGOR.* Delhi: Sharada Publications, 2001. xiv & 296pp. Folding map.

787
Ames

Mukherjee, Haridas and Uma Mukherjee. *THE GROWTH OF NATIONALISM IN INDIA 1857-1905.* Calcutta: Presidency Library, 1957. xix & 166pp.
A few pages on the Mutiny.

788
RS

Mukherjee, Rudrangshu. *AWADH IN REVOLT 1857-58. A Study of Popular Resistance.* New Delhi: Oxford Univ Press, 1984. xvi, 219pp. Bibliography, index
A scholarly study which grew out of an Oxford Ph.D. thesis. The author discusses the peasant-talukdar relationship and the British intrusion into this relationship. He then turns his attentionn to both the Summary Settlement of 1856 and the actual events of the Mutiny.

789
RS

Mukherjee, Rudrangshu. *SPECTRE OF VIOLENCE. THE 1857 KANPUR MASSACRES.* New Delhi:

Penguin Books, 1998. xiii & 217pp. Bibliography and index.
A very close study of the events at Cawnpore together with a look at the literature of the period and how to interpret that literature.

790

Munro, Sir Thomas. *DISAFFECTION IN THE NATIVE ARMY* 1857.
Cited in Mason.

791
Sut

Munro, Surgeon General William. *RECORDS OF SERVICE AND CAMPAIGNING IN MANY LANDS.*
London: Hurst & Blackett, 1887. 2 vols. xvi & 363 pp. x & 426pp. Red cloth.
The second volume deals with service during the Mutiny. Lucknow, Rohilcund and Oudh.

792
Sut

Munro, Surgeon General William.
REMINISCENCES OF MILITARY SERVICE WITH THE 93RD SUTHERLAND HIGHLANDERS.
London: Hurst & Blackett, 1883. xii & 330pp. Red cloth with regimental crest in gold.
Munro kept a journal throughout the Crimean War and the Mutiny. He served as a surgeon of the 93rd from 1854 to 1866.

793
RS

Muter, Mrs. (Dunbar Douglas).(Elizabeth McMullin)
MY RECOLLECTIONS OF THE SEPOY REVOLT 1857-58. London: John Long, 1911. xv & 266pp. Frontis, folding plan of Meerut, and 16 plates. Index.
Mrs. Muter was married to Captain Muter of the 60th Rifles stationed at Meerut at the outbreak. He later served in the assult of Delhi with the fourth column. Mrs. Muter claimed to be the first woman to enter Delhi after it was taken by the English. Just outside of Portsmouth the Muter's ship "The Eastern Monarch" exploded. Both escaped with their lives. Mrs. died in 1914. Some authorities have questioned the accuracy of this work as it was published so long after the events.

794
Ames

Muter, Mrs. (Dunbar Douglas) (Elizabeth McMullin).
TRAVELS AND ADVENTURES OF AN OFFICER'S WIFE IN INDIA, CHINA AND NEW ZEALAND.
London: Hurst & Blackett, 1864. 2 vols. Vol I xi+324pp. Vol. II vi+314pp. Red cloth blind.

First nine chapters deal with the Mutiny. Muter's husband was a captain in the Royal Rifles stationed at Meerut on May 10th. After Meerut she followed her husband to Delhi.

795
Ames

Napier, Lt. Colonel Henry Dundas. *FIELD MARSHAL LORD NAPIER OF MAGDALA: A MEMOIR BY HIS SON.* London: Edward Arnold & Co., 1927. ix & 368pp. Portrait, 2 views, 3 maps. Index.

56pp on the Mutiny and an appendix "Report of the Engineer Operations at the Siege of Lucknow." Also Central India Campaign.

796
Sut

Napier, Robert Cornelis (1810-1890) Afterward Field Marshal. *REPORT ON ENGINEERING OPERATIONS AT THE SIEGE OF LUCKNOW.* Chatham: NP. 1860.

This is Paper 5 of Papers of the Royal Engineers, volume 9. Paper 5 by Brigadier General Sir Robert Napier has 22 pages with 3 folding plans and contains:1) Memorandum on the Military Occupation of Lucknow. 2) Memorandum by Major Crommelin on the Military Works that have been executed at Lucknow. 3) Reports on the Forts at Lucknow by Major Greathed et al.

797
RS

Napier, Sir Charles James, Lt.-Gen. *DEFECTS, CIVIL AND MILITARY OF THE INDIAN GOVERNMENT.* London: Charles Westerton, 1853. xii & 437pp.

Good explanation of problems in India before the Mutiny.

798
Sut

Nash, John Tullock. *VOLUNTEERING IN INDIA: OR AN AUTHENTIC NARRATIVE OF THE MILITARY SERVICES OF THE BENGAL YEOMANRY CAVALRY DURING THE INDIAN MUTINY AND THE SEPOY WAR.* London: George Philip, 1893. 136pp. Frontis of uniform. Red cloth with gilt vignette.

799

Nath, Kashi (Translator). *DIARY OF THE MUTINY AT CAWNPUR (sic) (written by Nanak Chand).* Fyzabad: NP. March 16, 1925. 53pp.

Note in NAM copy. "The editor, Kashi Nath, was a "Very fine provincial civil service officer who took a ??? to France in the 1914-1918 war. His brother Krishna P??? was a Davis Cup tennis player and the late Director General Posts & Telegraphs U.P." The diary is the translation of a Urdu ms. found in Cawnpore in a heap of rubbish. Kaye did not put much store in the diary because Chand states he saw Havelock & Neill ride into Cawnpore together. Actually Neill came a few days after Havelock. The translation does not include the many marginal entries found in the original Urdu ms. The lists of men who participated in the rebellion are omitted. The second chapter of the original ms. is omitted. This chapter dealt with the rioting in Cawnpore during the fight with the Gwalior Contingent. NAM copy.

800

Nicholl, Lt. General T. *SAUGOR: A STORY OF 1857.* Woolwich: Royal Artillery Institution, 1894.
Cited by Collier.

801
RS

Nicholson, Rev. Maxwell. *BRITAIN'S GUILT & DUTY WITH REFERENCE TO HER INDIAN EMPIRE.* Edinburgh: Paton & Ritchie, 1857. 23pp.
A sermon delivered on the day of national humiliation. England did not rule India in a Christian manner, they did not bring Christianity to the native with the vigor required and this is why England now faces the mutiny in Bengal.

802
RS

Nigam, N. K. *DELHI IN 1857.* Delhi: S. Chand, 1957. ix & 188pp. 2 portraits and 12 plates.
The Mutiny was an organized national uprising that began prematurely. Because no strong leader emerged the Mutiny was doomed. Nigam made use of material collected by researchers under the auspices of the Committee for the History of the Freedom Movement in Delhi State. An interesting book with an extensive bibliography and some unusual photography. Includes a good description of Delhi after the British recapture.

803
RS

Nilsson, Sten and Narayani Gupta. *THE PAINTER'S EYE. EGRON LUNDGREN AND INDIA.* Stockholm: Stockholm National Museum, 1992. 158pp. Illus. Bibliography. ISBN 91-7100-441-6
Lundgren was a young painter who arrived in Calcutta in 1858. This book offers many of his illustrations together with extracts from his diary. Lungren travelled with Russell and Beato for a time. The diary extracts are quite interesting and include his experiences in Lucknow.

804
Bod

Nolan, Edward H. *THE HISTORY OF THE BRITISH EMPIRE IN INDIA AND THE EAST FROM THE EARLIEST TIMES TO THE SUPPRESSION OF THE SEPOY MUTINY IN 1859.* London, James S. Virtue ND. c. 1860. 2 vols. Vol. I 804pp. Vol. II 774pp. Illus. With numerous steel engravings.
Approximately 60pp on the Mutiny.

805
Bod

Nolan, Edward H. *THE ILLUSTRATED HISTORY OF THE BRITISH EMPIRE IN INDIA AND THE EAST FROM THE EARLIEST TIMES TO THE SUPPRESSION OF THE SEPOY MUTINY IN 1859. WITH A CONTINUATION TO THE END OF 1878.* London: Virtue & Co., 1878-79 3 vols. Vol. I 804pp. Vol. II 774pp. Vol. III 392pp. With index.

806
RS

Norgate, Lt. Col D. C. ed. *FROM SEPOY TO SUBADAR: Being the Life and Adventures of a Native Officer of the Bengal Army. Trans. By Lt. Col. James Thomas Norgate.* Lahore: NP. 1873.
This title was referred to in the London Times as early as 1863. Norgate received it from the author, Seetaram Sitaram in 1861. It was reprinted in Lahore in 1880 and; 3rd ed. Calcutta: Baptist Missionary Press, 1911. 130pp London: Routledge Kegan Paul, 1970 xxix & 186pp. 4 maps. James Lunt (ed.) The book was highly thought of by Kitchener. Seetaram retired shortly after the Mutiny after about 50 years service. There is some question as to the authenticity of this book. See Mason: *"A Matter of Honor"* 208ff. (Entry 728)

807
RS

Norman, General Sir Henry Wylie and Mrs. K. Young Ed. *DELHI 1857: THE SIEGE, ASSAULT AND CAPTURE AS GIVEN IN THE DIARY AND CORRESPONDENCE OF THE LATE COLONEL KEITH YOUNG. Judge-Advocate General, Bengal.* London & Edinbrugh: W. & R. Chambers. 1902. xxvi & 371pp. Frontis and 29 plates and large folding map. Index and Glossary
One of the detailed accounts of the siege. Young died at the age of 54, exhausted from his service in India. Includes a color plate of suggestions for the design of the Mutiny medal.

808
IO ORW
1986.a.5557.kkk

Norman, H. W. *LORD LAWRENCE AND THE MUTINY.*

809
BL
9056.bbb.26

Norman, Sir Henry Wylie. *A LECTURE ON THE RELIEF OF LUCKNOW, DELIVERED IN THE SIMLA INSTITUTE ON THE 7TH AUGUST, 1867.* Simla: Station Press, 1867. Red paper. ii & 35pp. Frontis and folding map.
Also published in London by Dalton & Luey, 1867.

810
RS/
BL
9056.bbb.26

Norman, Sir Henry Wylie. *A NARRATIVE OF THE CAMPAIGN OF THE DELHI ARMY.* London: W. H. Dalton, 1858. 64pp.
Norman was Deputy Adjutant General of the Bengal Army and saw extensive action during the Delhi siege. Later Norman marched with Greathed's column and on to Lucknow. He retired as a Field Marshal.

811
RS

North, Major (Charles Napier). *JOURNAL OF AN ENGLISH OFFICER IN INDIA.* London: Hurst & Blackett, 1858. viii & 280pp. Frontis.
North served in the 60th Rifles and was an aide to Havelock. In the preface North states that no record, at least as of August 1858, had been given of Havelock's march on Lucknow. North arrived in Calcutta May 14th and received word of Meerut on the 16th.

812
RS

Norton, John Bruce. *THE REBELLION IN INDIA: How to Prevent Another.* London: Richardson Brothers, 1857. xii & 244pp.
Norton was an officer in the Bombay Presidency. He suggests putting India under direct control of the Queen. See article in Hodgson Pratt.

813
Bod

Norton, John Bruce. *TOPICS FOR INDIAN STATESMEN.* London: Richardson Brothers, 1858. viii & 407pp.
Norton's position was that the outbreak was not merely a military mutiny, but a full scale rebellion. Topics include the character of the rebellion, was there warning?, should the annexation policy be continued?, what form of home government should India have, proselytism.

814
IO RL115

O'Callaghan, Daniel. *SCATTERED CHAPTERS: The Fatal Falter At Meerut.* Calcutta: Privately Printed. 1861.

815
Sut

Oatts, L. B. *A PRIVATE SOLDIER IN CENTRAL INDIA.* London: 1952. 8pp.
An article which appeared in the JRUSI for February 1952. This is the Journal of Private John Watt of the 71st HLI.

816
RS

Oldenburg, Veena Talwar. *THE MAKING OF COLONIAL LUCKNOW 1856-1877.* Delhi, India: Oxford University Press, 1989. 287pp. Illus.
This was originally published in 1984 by the Princeton University Press, Princeton, New Jersey.
Oldenburg argues that although the British generally followed the principle of non-interference in the post Mutiny era, they did in fact intrude extensively into the social fabric of India in very subtle ways as demonstated by their absolute regulation of city life through innumerable bylaws and committees.

817
IO

Oliver, John Ryder. *CAMPAIGNING IN OUDE.* London: Privately printed, 1860. 76pp. Two hand-drawn maps. Blue cloth blind.
Oliver rewrote his Mutiny experiences for United Service Magazine in 1895. Published by them in monthly parts, the text totals 64pp. (Sutcliffe)

818
Bod

Orlich, Leopold Von. *THE MILITARY MUTINY IN INDIA ITS ORIGIN AND ITS RESULTS.* London: T & W Boone, 1858. 31pp.
Translated from the German, with observations, by Major-General Sir W.M.G. Colebrooke.

819
BL
9056.bbb.26(5)

Orr, A. P. See Wylie, Macleod. *THE ENGLISH CAPTIVES IN OUDE, AN EPISODE IN THE HISTORY OF THE MUTINIES OF 1857-1858.* Calcutta: NP. ND.
Edited by MacLeod Wylie. See Kaye Vol. III, page 257 n. This was probably Patrick Orr not Phillip Orr as mentioned in Holmes.

820
RS

Outram, Lieut.-General Sir James. *LIEUT.-GENERAL SIR JAMES OUTRAM'S CAMPAIGN IN INDIA 1857-58. Comprising General Orders and Despatches Relating to the Defense and Relief of the Lucknow Garrison, and Capture of the City, by the*

*British Forces; also, Correspondence Relating to the Relief,
Up to the Date When that Object was Effected by Sir Colin
Campbell.* London: Smith, Elder and Co., Printed for
Private Circulation Only, 1860. xi & 412pp.

This title was produced from the records of Outram by
his publishers who in turn hired an un-named gentleman of
military knowledge to edit the papers. Sir James Outram
(1803-1863) was the Resident at Lucknow from 1854 to 1856.
In 1856 he became Commissioner of Oudh and from 1858 to
1860 served on the Governor General's Council. His military
experience included the Command of the Persian Expedition
shortly before the Mutiny. In this campaign Havelock was
his subordinate. At the conclusion of the Persian Campaign
Outram returned to Calcutta and was given command
of the Dinapur and Cawnpore Divisions. He marched
with Havelock to the relief of Lucknow and graciously
subordinated himself to Havelock until they reached Lucknow.
Havelock died at Lucknow, Outram remained to hold the
Allumbagh and with Colin Campbell reclaimed the city.

821
RAI
     Outram, Mary Frances. *MARGARET OUTRAM
1778-1873.* London: John Murray, 1932. xii & 358pp.
12 plates.

Margaret was the mother of Sir James. Includes letters to
and from James Outram.

822

     Outram, Sir James; *GENERAL ORDERS AND
DISPATCHES RELATING TO THE RELIEF OF
THE GARRISON OF LUCKNOW, THE DEFENSE
OF THE ALLUMBAGH POSITION AND THE SIEGE
AND CAPTURE OF THE CITY OF LUCKNOW
1857-1858.* Calcutta: Military Orphan Press, 1857.
Cited in Ladendorf. Unable to locate.

823
Ames
     Ouvry, Col. Henry A. *CAVALRY EXPERIENCES
AND LEAVES FROM MY JOURNAL.* Lymington:
Chas.T. King, 1892. vii & 235pp 3 maps and 8
illustrations.

Published privately after his retirement to Canada.
Commanded 9th Lancers during the siege at Delhi. Includes
his diary and letters. Ouvry went on to Cawnpore and Agra
after Delhi.

824
IO
     Ouvry, Mrs. Matilda H. *A LADY'S DIARY BEFORE
AND DURING THE INDIAN MUTINY.* Lymington:
Charles T. King, 1892. 166pp. frontis.

About 40pp. on the Mutiny. Mrs. Ouvry was at Ambala at the outbreak.

825
IO

Owen, Arthur. *RECOLLECTIONS OF A VETERAN OF THE DAYS OF THE GREAT INDIAN MUTINY. Being an autobiographical sketch of his life and work during sixty years in India.* Lucknow: Murray's Printing Press, 1916. 189pp. Portrait. 3rd ed. 250 copies
Approximately 50 pages on the Mutiny. Owen served with Havelock in the first relief of Lucknow. A previous edition was published in Lahore: George Mission Printing Works, 1915. Also Simla, 1914, 193pp. No edition stated. Owen acquired some fame at the Delhi Durbar where he paraded as "the blind veteran." Considered to be disappointing as it was written long after the events and there are inaccuracies.

826
RS

Owen, Sidney. *ANGLO-INDIAN RULE HISTORICALLY CONSIDERED. A Lecture Delivered at Taylor Institution April 28, 1876.* London: James Parker & Co., 1876. 23pp.
A very short history of the Indian sub-continent and England's involvement there.

827
IO

Owen, Rev. William. *MEMORIALS OF CHRISTIAN MARTYRS AND OTHER SUFFERERS FOR THE TRUTH IN THE INDIAN REBELLION.* London: Simpkin, Marshall, 1859. ix & 236pp. Engraved frontis and pictorial title page of the Cawnpore Well.
A British missionary's memoirs of the Mutiny with a description of the part played by Indian Christians during the Mutiny.

828
Bod

Owen, Rev. William *THE GOOD SOLDIER, A MEMOIR OF MAJOR GENERAL SIR HENRY HAVELOCK. His Military Career, Campaigns, Engagements, and Victories: His Domestic, Social, and Religious Character.* London: Simpkin, Marshall, ND (1858) 236pp. Green boards with portrait on cover. A biography.

829
Bod

Owen, Rev. William *THE MARTYRS OF THE INDIAN REBELLION.* London: Ward, Lock & Co. ND. (1891) vii & 144pp. Frontis and engraved title page.

Reports on the martyred missionaries in Delhi, Lucknow, Meerut, Agra, Cawnpore, etc.

830
IO   **Paget, Mrs. Leopold.** *CAMP AND CANTONMENT. A Journal of Life in India in 1857-1859. With Some Account of the Way Thither. To Which is Added, A Short Narrative of the Pursuit of the Rebels in Central India, by Major Paget.* London: Longman Green et al., 1865. viii & 469pp. Colored frontis.
    The main point of interest in this work is the appendix by Major Paget, "How I helped in the pursuit of Tantia Topee." 34pp.

831
    Pal, Dharm. *TATYA TOPE, THE HERO OF INDIA'S FIRST WAR OF INDEPENDENCE 1857-1859.* New Delhi: Hindustan Times, 1957.
    According to Sengupta, *"Recent Writings..."* this is a disjointed biography.

832
RS   **Pal, Dharm.** *THE POORBEAH SOLDIER. THE HERO OF INDIA'S WAR OF INDEPENDENCE 1857.* Delhi: A. Ram, 1957. 63pp.
    Describes the Mutiny as the first Indian War of Independence.

833
    Pal, Kristo Das. *NATIVE FIDELITY.*
    Mentioned in Mukherjee's *"The Growth of Nationalism in India."*

834
Ames   **Palande, M. R. Executive Secretary.** *SOURCE MATERIAL FOR A HISTORY OF THE FREEDOM MOVEMENT IN INDIA. COLLECTED FROM BOMBAY GOVERNMENT RECORDS.* Bombay: Government Central Press, 1957. 2 vols. Vol. I, xiv & 397pp. Vol. II (1958) xxvi & 1015pp.
    Volume I covers the period 1818 to 1885. Volume II 1885-1920. Proposed volume III 1920-1947. Includes a proclamation from Nana Sahib as defender of the Hindu religion as well as other documents related to the Mutiny period in Bombay Presidency.

835
NAM 92   **Palmer, General Henry.** *INDIAN SKETCHES*
PALMER   *1816-1866. WRITTEN EXPRESSLY FOR MY FRIENDS.* Mussoorie: Mafasilite Printing Works, ND but 1888. iv & 68pp. 6 plates.

Quite Scarce. Not in BL. Palmer wrote this 31 years after he lost his notes when his house burned in Lucknow at the outbreak. He served at Chinhut and commanded the Muchee Bhawan at Lucknow.

836
RS

Palmer, J. A. B. *THE MUTINY OUTBREAK AT MEERUT IN 1857.* Cambridge: Cambridge Univ Press, 1966. xi & 175pp. Notes and index. Folding map of Meerut.

This is part of the South Asian Studies Series. It is the definitive study of the sequence of events at Meerut. Palmer was a solicitor by profession and went out to Bombay and Delhi in 1937. Work began on this book in the late 1950's. Palmer was related to Sir Peter Melvill, Military Secretary to the Bombay Government in the 1840's and 1850's.

837
IO

Panikkar, Kavalam Modhava. *IN 1857.* Ahmedabad: Harold Laski Institute of Political Science, 1957. 8 pp.

Panikkar was the Indian Ambassador to France. Capsule view of the Mutiny.

838
BM/RS

Parker, Neville Thornton. *A MEMOIR OF MEERUT (Notes and Accounts From Contemporary Accounts of Events in Meerut During the Indian Mutiny of 1857).* Meerut: O'brien's Press, 1904. The 1914 date of the preface appears to be in error. 1 + 1 + 39pp. 8 illustrations.

By 1914 there were 5 printings and 1000 copies printed. This work contains extracts from various letters and reports written in or about Meerut. Includes statements of eye-witnesses to the Mutiny.

839
BL

Parkinson, Yehza-en-Nasr (ed). *INVERSION OF TIMES. AN APPEAL FOR THE ERECTION OF A MEMORIAL AT RANGOON TO ABU-ZAFAR BAHADUR SHAW, MOGUL EMPEROR....EDITED WITH ALTERATIONS AND ADDITIONS BY YEHZA-EN-NASA PARKINSON.* London: Luzac & Co., 1911. 22pp.

840
Ames /
NAM 92 JON

Parry, Captain Sidney Henry Jones. *AN OLD SOLDIER'S MEMORIES.* London: Hurst & Blackett, 1897. x & 290pp. Frontis.

Jones-Parry came up through Cawnpore and fought in the relief of Lucknow from October to November with Colin

Campbell. His Mutiny experiences are rather interesting.
About 30 pages on the Mutiny.

841
RAI   **Parsons, Richard.** *A STORY OF JUGDESPORE, 1858.*
London: Army and Navy Cooperative Society, 1909.
52pp.
   Jain cites this book as "A Journal of Jugdespore."

842
RS   **Paske, Major A. G.** *SIXTY YEARS AGO. The Story of
Major-General William Paske's Services in India During
the Mutiny, in the Bengal Presidency, and His Experiences
and Trying Adventures for Many Years.* London: NP.
1907. 32pp.
   Paske arrived in Madras in 1845 and then went up to
Calcutta. He fought in a number of campaigns and was in the
Punjab at the outbreak. He served under Nicholson.

843
Bod   **Pearse, Colonel Hugh.** *THE HEARSEYS, FIVE
GENERATIONS OF AN ANGLO INDIAN FAMILY.*
Edinburgh: William Blackwood, 1905. xi & 410pp.
Frontis.
   The last chapter covers the Mutiny at Barrackpore which
General John Hearsey put down.

844
RS   **Pearse, Major Hugh ed.** *THE CRIMEAN DIARY
AND LETTERS OF LIEUTENANT GENERAL SIR
CHARLES ASH WINDHAM. With Observations Upon
His Service During the Indian Mutiny and an Introduction
by Sir William Howard Russell.* London: Kegan Paul, et
al. 1897. xi & 272pp. Portrait.
   Windham was left to guard Cawnpore while Colin
Campbell relieved Lucknow. Cawnpore was besieged by
Tantia Tope and the Gwalior sepoys. Eventually Windham's
conduct caused some dismay among later historians. The
cover and spine of the book are titled "Redan Windham."

845
RS   **Pearson, Hesketh.** *THE HERO OF DELHI: The Life of
John Nicholson, Saviour of India and a History of His Wars.*
London: Collins, 1939. 291pp. Frontis and 5 plates.
Bibliography and index.
   Uses the standard sources and, in addition, the
unpublished autobiography of a Major Angelo who served
with Nicholson during the Mutiny.

846
BL
9056.bbb.26
& 9056.aaa.6
(Liverpool)

Peile, Mrs Fanny. *HISTORY OF THE DELHI MASSACRE, ITS SUPPOSED ORIGIN AND THE MEANS BEING ADOPTED TO AVENGE THE MURDER OF THE BRITISH SUBJECTS. By a Lady, The Wife of an Officer in the Bengal Army, and a Sufferer in the Late Tragedy.* Liverpool: C. Tinling, 1858. iii & 92pp. Blue cloth blind. 2 lithos.

Fanny was the wife of a Lieut. of the 38th NI. He is reputed to be the last Englishman to leave Delhi on May 11th. Many of the major bibliographies omit the 1858 edition. See Edward Vibart, *"The Sepoy Mutiny as Seen by a Subaltern from Delhi to Lucknow,"* for an account of Mrs. Peile's escape from Delhi.

847
RS

Pemble, John. *THE RAJ, THE INDIAN MUTINY, AND THE KINGDOM OF OUDH 1801-1859.* US: Farley Dickinson Univ Press, 1977. 303pp.

Index and bibliography. 3 maps and 4 pages of photos. There was most likely a UK edition of this work however it is not indicated on the copyright page of this edition.

Pemble discusses the history of Oude and how such anti-British feeling was produced in this region during the Mutiny. "...a full analysis of annexation and its impact on Oudh metropolitan and rural society."

848
RS

Perkins, Roger. *THE KASHMIR GATE. Lieutenant Home and the Delhi VC's.* Chippenham: Picton Publishing, 1983. xiii & 161pp. Illus.

Detailed discussion of the officers and men assigned to destroy the Kashmir Gate during the assult on Delhi. There are also short descriptions of the other Delhi VC winners.

849
BL

Pershad, Issoree. *CASE OF ISSREEPERSAUD.* NC. NP. 1861.14pp + 18pp.

This is an appeal to Canning for recompense for his losses during the Mutiny. Pershad supplied the commissariat department at Cawnpore and advised General Wheeler and others that the Nana was not to be trusted. "But nothing was done, on the contrary, implicit faith was reposed in the Nana...."

Pershad states what his services to the English consisted of and what he wants in return.

850
IO

Persico, Right Rev. Dr. *INDIA: APPEAL TO THE CHARITY OF THE CATHOLICS OF GREAT*

*BRITAIN AND IRELAND FROM THE RIGHT
REVEREND DR. PERSICO, BISHOP AND VICAR
APOSTOLIC OF HINDUSTAN, IN BEHALF OF
THE SUFFERING CATHOLICS OF BRITISH INDIA
CONFIDED TO HIS CARE.* London: Keating &
Dillon, 1858. 16pp.

851
Bod

Peter the Pearker. *CASTE IN INDIA. CASTE
EVERYWHERE. HOW TO KEEP OR LOSE AN
EMPIRE.* London: J. Heaton & Son, 1858. 24pp.
Pamphlet.
Discusses caste. False principles of government have
endangered India. The empire is in danger. Speaks of the
duty of the British Christian.

852
Ames

Philips, Cyril Henry ed. *HISTORICAL WRITINGS
ON THE PEOPLES OF ASIA. Vol. 1, Historians of
India, Pakistan, and Ceylon.* London: Oxford Univ Press,
1961. ix & 504pp. Index.
Contains a paper on the historiography of the Mutiny
by Surendra Nath Sen. Excellent presentation. Discusses a
number of the major works in the field.

853

Phillipps, Alfred. *ANECDOTES AND
REMINISCENCES OF SERVICE IN BENGAL.*
Inverness: Courier Office, 1878.

854

Phillips, A. L. M. et al. *COMMUNICATIONS AND
TESTIMONIALS SHOWING THE LOYAL CONDUCT
OF THE LATE MUNSHI RAJA RAN, KOTWAL AND
RAIS OF AGRA, DURING THE MUTINY OF 1857.*
Agra: NP. 1906. 15pp.

855
BL

Phillips, E. C. *SIR HENRY HAVELOCK AND COLIN
CAMPBELL, LORD CLYDE. The World's Workers
Series.* London: Cassell & Co., 1885. 128pp.
A popular issue biography.

856
RS

Picton-Turberville, Edith. *THE STORY OF ALGAR
TEMPLE AND THE INDIAN MUTINY.* Cardiff:
Western Mail and Echo, ND. c. 1958. 71pp.
The letters of Algar Temple written from India
1856-1860. Temple served at the siege of Delhi and

eventually died of wounds received there. The book is composed of his letters home.

857
RS

Pincott, Frederick. *ANALYTICAL INDEX TO SIR JOHN W. KAYE'S HISTORY OF THE SEPOY WAR AND COLONEL G.B. MALLESON'S HISTORY OF THE INDIAN MUTINY.* London: Longmans and Green also W. Allen, 1880, 1896. 201pp.

858

Pinkney, F. W. *NARRATIVE OF EVENTS ATTENDING THE OUTBREAK OF DISTURBANCES AND THE RESTORATION OF AUTHORITY IN THE DIVISION OF JHANSI IN 1857-58.*
See listing for *"Mutiny in India"* (entry 448)

859
IO

Pitt, F. W. ed. *INCIDENTS IN INDIA AND MEMORIES OF THE MUTINY. With Some Records of Alexander's Horse and the 1st Bengal Cavalry.* London: Kegan Paul, Trench, Trubner, 1896. vi & 151pp.
Incidents in the life of General W. R. E. Alexander commander of the 1st Bengal Cavalry. About one half deals with the Mutiny.

860
RS

Polehampton, Reverend Henry Stedman. *A MEMOIR, LETTERS AND A DIARY OF THE REV. HENRY S. POLEHAMPTON M.A. CHAPLAIN OF LUCKNOW.* London: Richard Bentley, ND.(1859) 440pp. Frontis. Also 2nd ed. London, xii & 414pp., four woodcuts, and 3rd ed. London, xii & 368pp. Frontis. 1859?
Polemhampton was the junior chaplain during the siege of Lucknow and did not survive the siege. Mrs. Polehampton later married Sir Henry Durand, Lt. Governor of the Punjab in 1859. This was Durand's second marriage. Mrs. Polehampton died of heart failure March 29, 1905.

861
RS

Pollack, J. C. *WAY TO GLORY. THE LIFE OF HAVELOCK OF LUCKNOW.* London: John Murray, 1957. x & 270pp. 10 Illus. 2 maps.

862
BL 4477.a.89

Porter, John Leech. *NATIONAL CHRISTIANITY FOR INDIA, OR, NATIONAL ACTS AS NATIONAL DUTIES VIEWED IN CONNECTION WITH THE*

SEPOY MUTINIES. A FAST DAY SERMON. London: NP. 1857.

863
Bod/Ames/RS   **Poynder, John.** *EXTRACTS FROM THREE SPEECHES DELIVERED BY THE LATE JOHN POYNDER AT THE EAST INDIA HOUSE IN THE YEARS 1830, 1836, AND 1839 DEMONSTRATING THE DIRECT SUPPORT AND ENCOURAGEMENT GIVEN BY THE COMPANY TO IDOLATRY.* London: Wertheim & Macintosh, 1857. Written in late 1857. 55pp.
Pamphlet. Edited by G. Poynder. Includes extracts from other sources on the subject of idolatry, and the Indian Mutinies, with remarks by the editor.

864
RS   **Prasad, Bisheshwar.** *BONDAGE AND FREEDOM 1707 TO 1947.* New Delhi: Rajesh Publications, 1977 and 1979. 2 vols. Vol. I, 586pp. Bibliography and index. Vol. II, 619pp. Bibliography and index.
The first volume has a long chapter on the Mutiny. Prasad feels there was a conspiracy.

865
Ames   **Prashanto, K. Chatterji.** *THE MAKING OF INDIAN POLICY 1853-65.* Burdwan: University of Burdwan, West Bengal, 1975. vx & 409pp. Index and folding map of India.
A study on the Charter Act of 1853 and the Charter Act of 1858 and how they affected policy making with the Court of Directors and the India Council and how they affected the roles of Home Government and the Indian government. There is one chapter, about 22 pages, dealing specifically with the Mutiny. This book grew out of a Ph.D. thesis at Cambridge.

866
Ames   Pratt, Hodgson. SELECTION OF ARTICLES AND LETTERS ON VARIOUS INDIAN QUESTIONS. Including Remarks on European Parties in Bengal, Social Policy and Missions in India and the Use of the Bible in Government Schools. London: Chapman and Hall, November 1857. 47pp
Contains 8 articles including a review of *"Rebellion in India"* by John Norton, and an article on the causes of the Mutiny.

867
RS
Prichard, Iltudus Thomas. *THE MUTINIES IN RAJPOOTANA BEING A PERSONAL NARRATIVE OF THE MUTINY AT NUSSEERABAD. With Subsequent Residence at Jodhpore, and Journey Across the Desert into Sind, Together with an Account of the Outbreak at Neemuch, and Mutiny of the Jodhpore Legion at Erinpoora and Attack on Mount Aboo.* London: John W. Parker and Son. Shabd Sanchar. 1860 vii & 311pp. Reprinted in Rajasthan in 1876.
   Prichard served with the 15th NI in Rajputana. According to Malleson, Prichard became disgusted with the military and left his regiment in 1858. Apparently he became a capable literary talent during his years in India.

868
IO
Probyn, W. G. *NARRATIVE OF EVENTS ATTENDING THE OUTBREAK OF DISTURBANCES AND THE RESTORATION OF AUTHORITY IN THE FURRUCKABAD DISTRICT IN 1857-58.* Allahabad: Government Press, 1858. 46pp.
   See listing for *"Mutiny in India."* (Entry 448)

869
IO
Punjab. *DELHI RESIDENCY AND AGENCY. 1806-1857. (I).* Lahore: Superintendent, Government Printing, Punjab. 1915. 402pp.

870
IO
Punjab. *RECORDS OF THE DELHI RESIDENCY AND AGENCY. (I).* Lahore: Superintendent, Government Printing, Punjab, 1911. v & 488pp.

871
Centennial
Exhibit
of Books
Punjab. *SELECTIONS FROM THE RECORDS OF THE GOVERNMENT OF THE PUNJAB AND ITS DEPENDENCIES. NEW SERIES. NO. VIII.* Lahore: Punjab Printing Co. Ltd., 1879. 298pp. xxxi.
   Related to the trial of Muhammad Bahadur Shah, Titular King of Delhi, for rebellion against the British government and murder of Europeans during 1857.

872
IO
Punjab. *TRIAL OF MUHAMMAD BAHADUR SHAH, TITULAR KING OF DELHI, AND OF MOGAL BEG, AND HAJEE, ALL OF DELHI, FOR REBELLION AGAINST THE BRITISH GOVERNMENT, AND MURDER OF EUROPEANS*

DURING 1857. Lahore: Punjab Civil Secretariat Press, 1870. 298pp.& xxxi.

873
RS

Punjab Record Office. *SELECTIONS FROM THE RECORDS. VOL. VIII. PART I and PART II.* Lahore: Punjab Government Press, 1915. Part I 408pp. 3 plates. Part II 371pp + 18page index. 2 plates
Parts I and II contain reports from 1857 submitted in 1858 by Commissioners of Divisions and District Officers to R. Montgomery, Judicial Commissioner of the Punjab. Also includes a reprint of the Punjab Mutiny Report. Originally published in 1911. Reprinted c. 1979 by Al-Biruni. Lahore.

874
RS

Punjab Record Office. *SELECTIONS FROM THE RECORDS. VOLUME VII, PART I AND PART II.* Lahore: Punjab Government Printing Press, 1911, 1915, rept 1979. Part I: Frontis 445pp. 6 plates. Part II: Frontis 410pp. 26pp index. 5 plates.
Volume VII consists of dispatches from John Lawrence to the Government of India together with some replies. Edited by Mr. A Raynor. This work was reprinted c. 1979. 2 vols. Al-Birunoi, Lahore Vol. I 408pp. No plates. Vol. II 371pp & 18 page index. No plates.

875
IO

Punjab. *CHIEF COMMISSIONERS ADMINISTRATION, PUNJAB, FROM 10TH FEBRUARY 1853 TO 31ST DECEMBER 1858: POLITICAL DEPARTMENT (XIII).* Lahore: Superintendent. Government Printing, Punjab, 1922. 616pp.

876
BL 8022.b.74

Qui Hi. *WHAT IS TO BE DONE WITH THE BENGAL ARMY?* London: Effingham Wilson, Royal Exchange, 1857. 96pp.
The present calamity is devine judgement because Britain has not properly carried out it's duty in India. They have not fulfilled their Christian duty. Dalhousie provoked the war by his aggressive policies. The Crown should have at least 20 regiments posted to India and the Court of Directors and Board of Control should be abolished. The author has strong opinions and presents them in a straight forward manner. Additional comments include discussion of the proper pay for officers as well as keeping officers in service when they are no longer fit for duty.

877
RS   **Rahim, M. A.** *LORD DALHOUSIE'S ADMINISTRATION OF THE CONQUERED AND ANNEXED STATES.* Delhi: Chand & Co., 1963. vi & 396pp. Bibliography and index.
Doctoral thesis at University of Nagpur, India. Good background on the period leading up to the Mutiny.

878
   Rahman, B. Abdur. *THE INDIAN REVOLUTION 1857.* Bangalore: Modi Power Print Works, 1957. 94pp.
Considered of little significance by Sengupta in "*Recent Writings...*"

879
RS   **Raikes, C.** *NOTES ON THE REVOLT IN THE NORTH WESTERN PROVINCES OF INDIA.* London: Longmans, Brown, Green, et al. 1858. viii & 195pp. 24pp of advertisments. Folding statistical return.
Raikes was the Judge of the Sudder Court at Agra and previously Commissioner at Lahore. He held the view that the hostilities were a military mutiny and not a civil rebellion.

880
BL   **Raines, General Sir Julius.** *THE 95TH (THE DERBYSHIRE) REGIMENT IN CENTRAL INDIA.* London: Swan Sonnenschein, 1900. xiv & 90pp.
Portrait, sketch map. Red cloth. 2nd Batt. Won honors in Central India.

881
Ames/   **Rait, Robert Sangster.** *THE LIFE OF*
BL   *FIELD-MARSHAL SIR FREDERICK PAUL HAINES.*
010854.g.16   London: Constable, 1911. xiv & 366pp. Portrait with 2 maps.
Served as Military Secretary to the C in C Madras during the Mutiny. He did not see active duty during the Mutiny. The book covers material on the period from June 17 to August 13, 1857 when Patrick Grant was acting C in C at Calcutta and Haines was his Military Secretary.

882
RS   **Raj, Jagdish.** *THE MUTINY AND THE BRITISH LAND POLICY IN NORTH INDIA 1856-1868.* NC. Asia Publishing House, 1965. xv & 191pp, Index.
Discusses the nature and variation of land policy in North India. The period discussed spans the terms of Dalhousie, Canning, Elgin, and Lawrence.

883
RS
Ram, Moti, ed. *TWO HISTORIC TRIALS IN THE RED FORT: AN AUTHENTIC ACCOUNT OF THE TRIAL BY GENERAL COURT MARTIAL OF CAPT. SHAH NAWAZ KHAN, CAPT. P. K. SAHGAL AND LT. G.S. DHILLON: AND THE TRIAL BY A EUROPEAN MILITARY COMMISSION OF EMPEROR BAHADUR SHAH.* New Delhi: M.L. Sabbarwall, Roxy Printing Press, 1946. 6pp & 422pp and 11 plates.
Covers the first I.N.A. trial and the trial of the last Mughal Emperor.

884
Ram, Sita. *SEE LT. COL. D.C. NORGATE. (Entry 806)*

885
BL
Ramsay, Lieut-Colonel Balcarres Dalrymple Wardlaw. *ROUGH RECOLLECTIONS OF MILITARY SERVICE AND SOCIETY.* Edinburgh & London: Blackwood and Sons, 1882. Vol. I xiii & 294. Vol. II vii & 98pp. Index.
Personal experiences in Calcutta.

886
RS
Rawding, F. W. *THE REBELLION IN INDIA. 1857.* NC. Cambridge Univ Press, 1977. 48pp
Gives a good synopsis of the Mutiny.

887
Rawlins, Major-General J. S. *THE AUTOBIOGRAPHY OF AN OLD SOLDIER.* Weston-Super-Mare, 1883.
Cited in Hibbert

888
Raychawdhury, P. C. *1857 IN BIHAR.* Bihar.
Cited in Sengupta, *"Recent Writings...."* See entry 921.

889
Read, Rev. Hollis. *INDIA AND ITS PEOPLE: Ancient and Modern With a View of the Sepoy Mutiny: Embracing an Account of the Conquests in India by the English Their Policy and its Results also, ...* Columbus, OH: J. & H. Miller, 1858, 1859. 384pp. Frontis, numerous illus.
Hollis was an American missionary to India. As expected the book is very judgemental.
Enumerates the causes of the Mutiny, "What God is bringing out of the Sepoy mutiny,and what will probably be the final results." Two chapters of interest.

890

Reade, Edward A. *DESCRIPTION OF THE MEASURES TAKEN AT AGRA DURING THE INDIAN MUTINY.* Agra: NP. 1857. 66pp.
Reade was the senior member of the Board of Revenue at Agra. Cited in Ladendorf.

891
BL

Reade, Edward A. *SELECTION OF PAPERS FROM THE OFFICE OF COMMISSIONER OF FINANCE & SUPPLIES, NO. 11, BLOCK G, AGRA FORT. DURING PART OF 1857 & 1858.* Allahabad: Mission Press, ND. 64pp.

892
BL
8023.dd.16

Reade, Edward A. *SELECTION OF PAPERS ON VARIOUS SUBJECTS. AGRA 1857, 1858.* Allahabad: Mission Press, 1859. 77pp.
All deal with Agra during the Mutiny.

893
BL
4920.f.25(14)

Reed, Andrew. The Younger. *A GOOD SOLDIER. A SERMON ON THE OCCASION OF THE DEATH OF MAJOR- GENERAL SIR H. HAVELOCK.* London: NP. 1858.

894
RS/Ames

Rees, L. E. Ruutz. *A PERSONAL NARRATIVE OF THE SIEGE OF LUCKNOW FROM ITS COMMENCEMENT TO ITS RELIEF BY SIR COLIN CAMPBELL.* London: Longman, Brown, Green, et al., 1858. xx & 380pp. Frontis and folding map. Red cloth blind.
This book went through 3 editions between January 25th and March 1858. Rees was a Calcutta civilian who found himself at Lucknow during the siege. He made some use of information from Lady Inglis' Journal. Rees died in London, March 28, 1909 at the age of 80.

895
Bod

Rees, L. E. Ruutz. *OUDE: ITS PAST AND ITS FUTURE.* London: Longman, Brown, Green, Longmans & Roberts, 1859. 10 & 34pp.
This is a republication of an article from the Calcutta Review, June 1856, published under the title, "Physical Capabilities of Oude."

896
RS

Reid, Colonel Charles. *EXTRACTS FROM LETTERS. NOTES WRITTEN DURING THE SIEGE*

OF DELHI IN 1857. London: Henry S. King & Co.,
ND. c. 1895. iv & 93pp. 1 plate. Also, Smith, Elder &
Co., 1861. (81pp)
Major Reid led the Gurkha's to Meerut directly after the
outbreak. The battalion saw extensive action at Delhi. Reid
commanded the fourth column during the assult. Reid's daily
reports from the ridge were written in pencil and thus rejected
by General Wilson because they were not written in regulation
form. Because of this many gallant actions by the men and
officers under Reid went unrewarded. See note in Kaye and
Malleson.
A copy in the NAM (1857 (54))

897
NAM 1857(54) **Reid, Colonel Charles.** *RECORD OF SERVICES IN
THE FIELD.* London: NP. 1861. 19pp.
Reid commanded the Sirmoor Rifles.

898
Sut   **Reid, General Sir Charles.** *2nd KING EDWARD VII's
OWN GOORKHA RIFLES (THE SIRMOOR RIFLES)
1857 CENTENARY 1957 OF THE SIEGE OF DELHI;
THE DEFENCE OF THE MAIN PICQUET AT
HINDOO RAO'S HOUSE AND OTHER POSTS ON
THE RIDGE AS RECORDED BY MAJOR REID
COMMANDING THE SIRMOOR BATTALION.*
Kings Langley: Privately Printed, 1957. (ii) 61pp.
Color plate, 4 plates, 2 folding maps. Half red and green
cloth.
Mainly a reprint of General Sir Charles Reid's *Extracts
from Letters and Notes* published by Henry King circa
1890. Front cover reads, 1857 1957 Sirmoor Rifles, Delhi,
Centenary, The Diary of Major Reid. Does not agree with
title page.

899
NAM 92PAS **Reilly, Patrick.** *DEPUTY SURGEON-GENERAL
CHARLES THOMAS PASKE 1830-1920.* NC. Private
Circulation, NP. 1982. Frontis and 42pp. Paper.
Little relative to the Mutiny.

900
             Renaud, George. *BRITAIN CAUGHT IN THE
SNARE, A SERMON PREACHED AT ST. ANDREW'S
CHURCH, HERTFORD ON WEDNESDAY,
OCTOBER 7, 1857. The Day Appointed as a Day of
Solemn Fast, Humiliation and Prayer on Account of the
Troubles in India.* Hertford: Stephen Austin, 1857.
Pamphlet.

901
BL

Reynolds, Reginald. *THE WHITE SAHIBS IN INDIA.* London: Martin, Secker and Warburg, 1937. 1st. ed.; 1938 2nd ed.; 1946 3rd revised ed. Socialist Book Center 1946 ed. xv & 242pp. Index.
One chapter on the Mutiny.

902
RS/
BL
10055.aaa.45

Rich, Capt Gregory. *THE MUTINY IN SIALKOT WITH A BRIEF DESCRIPTION OF THE CANTONMENT FROM 1852 TO 1857.* Sialkot: P. N. Handa, 1924. v & 80pp. Red Cloth. 1st ed. of 1000 copies.
Rich attempts to preserve what information remained concerning events at Sialkot. He made extensive use of Gordon's "*Our India Mission 1855-1885*," Montgomery's "*The Mutiny at Sialkot*" and Ball's "*History of the Indian Mutiny*" as well as some primary sources.

903
BL
9058.a34bm

Richardson. *THE INDIAN MUTINY OF 1857 AFTER HERODUTUS.* Oxford: Blackwell, 1926. 38 pp.
In Greek.

904
RAI

Ricketts, George H. M. *EXTRACTS FROM THE DIARY OF A BENGAL CIVILIAN 1857-59.* NC. NP. Privately Printed, 1893.
Ricketts was deputy commissioner at Loodhianah in the Punjab and shared in the suppression of the Mutiny there. (Ladendorf)

905
RS

Riddick, John F. *A GUIDE TO INDIAN MANUSCRIPTS. MATERIALS FROM EUROPE AND NORTH AMERICA.* Westport: Connecticut & London, Greenwood Press, 1993. xiii & 266pp. Sources and index.
The guide is organized on a geographical basis and gives the location, institutes name and the relevant information regarding the type and extent of the manuscript collection. Thus we see that in Leicester, at the Leicesterhire Record Office there is a holding of a diary of Henry Eyrl, Member of the 19th Regiment, Bengal Army, 1855-62.

906
BL

Ritchie, John Gerald. *THE RITCHIES IN INDIA. Extracts from the Correspondence of William Ritchie, 1817-1862; and Personal Reminiscences of G. Ritchie.*

Compiled and edited by Gerald Ritchie. London: John
Murray, 1920. xvi & 398pp. Frontis and 24 illus.
Folding map and family table at rear.
Little on the Mutiny. William Ritchie was Advocate
General of Bengal. The book includes a few letters written to
his children, in England, that touch on the Mutiny.

907
IO   **Rizvi, S. A. and M. L. Bhargava. Ed.** *FREEDOM
STRUGGLE IN UTTAR PRADESH.* Lucknow:
Uttar Pradesh Publications Bureau, Information Dept.
1957-1959. 5 vols.
Vol. I. Source Material. 514pp. 21 plates. Index. A
collection of published and unpublished material related to the
Mutiny. Vol. II. 1958. Source material relating to Awadh.
vi & 736pp. Index. Vol. III. 1959. Covers Bundelkhand
and adjoining territories. 15pp & 767pp. Index. 1857-1859.
1 picture. Vol V. 1960. Western Districts and Rohilkhand.
1857-59. 17pp & 1108pp and index. 8 folding maps. 8
plates. Required reading for any serious study of the Mutiny.
Sengupta in *"Recent Writing..."* states that this work is the
most important collection of Mutiny documents published in
India.

908
RS   **Robb, Alexander.** *REMINISCENCES OF A
VETERAN. Being the Experiences of a Private Soldier
in the Crimea and During the Indian Mutiny.* Dundee:
W.& D.C. Thomson, 1888. vi & 128pp.
Decorative paper cover, 12mo. Alexander Robb was a
member of the 42nd Highlanders, The Black Watch. The
book discusses duty in the Crimea and the Mutiny. Robb,
known as Sandy, arrived in India in late 1857 and moved
up to Cawnpore and eventually marched on Lucknow with
Campbell. Robb was a private soldier and this is one of the
few accounts available from a man of the ranks.

909
RS   **Roberts, Field Marshal Sir Frederick.** *FORTY ONE
YEARS IN INDIA.* London: Bentley & Son, 1897. 2
vols xx & 511p and xii & 522pp. 23 plates and 9 maps.
One volume edition Macmillan, 1898. xxii & 601pp. 6
folding maps. 41 illus. Also NY, 1897. 2 vols. 1033pp. 20
illus. 9 maps with appendix and index. Also 1898 Longmans
Green and Co. 29th ed. 597pp.
The first volume deals with the Mutiny and covers the
causes, the actions at Delhi and Lucknow.

910
RS

Roberts, Lt. Fred. *LETTERS WRITTEN DURING THE INDIAN MUTINY.* London: Macmillan, 1924. (Rept. 1979. New Delhi, Lal Pub. xxiii & 169pp. No pictures.) xxiv & 169pp. 5 plates and 2 plans and map.

Roberts, later Field-Marshal Lord Roberts of Kandahar, saw much action during the Mutiny and received the VC in India. He became one of Englands most beloved generals. The book consists of thirty letters by Roberts and gives his personal views on a large number of matters including some of his fellow officers. Roberts was the most celebrated English general of his time. Roberts' son, Lieut. F. H. S. Roberts was recommended for the VC in 1899 but died of his wounds.

911
RAI/RS

Robertson, Colonel James P. *PERSONAL ADVENTURES AND ANECDOTES OF AN OLD OFFICER.* London: Edward Arnold, 1906. xv & 284pp. Frontis and portrait.

Robertson served at Lucknow under Campbell and remained at the Alum Bagh under Outram. Approximately 75pp. on the Mutiny. Taylor lists this incorrectly as Roberts, N. J. P. *"Personal Adventures...."*

912
RS

Robertson, Henry Dundas. *DISTRICT DUTIES DURING THE REVOLT IN THE NORTH WEST PROVINCES OF INDIA IN 1857: With Remarks on Subsequent Investigations During 1858-1859.* London: Smith, Elder & Co., 1859. xvi & 238pp folding map.

Robertson was in the Bengal Civil Service as Joint Magistrate in the Saharunpore District in the North West Provinces. The subsequent investigations referred to in the sub-title concern the investigation and trial of cases connected with the Mutiny and rebellion. Robertson served on a commission with jurisdiction over the North West Provinces, Oude, Bengal Proper, and Central India.

913
BL

Robertson, Lieut-General Alexander Cunningham. *MEMORIALS OF GENERAL SIR EDWARD HARRIS GREATHED.* London: Harrison & Sons, 1858. viii & 95pp. Frontis of Greathed and one additional portrait.

Greathed, commander of the 8th, (Kings) Regiment of Foot, was dispatched by Wilson to clear the Doab after the fall of Delhi. His brothers Hervey and Wilberforce also served at Delhi.

914
Bod

Robertson, Reverend A. *A SERMON UPON THE INDIAN OUTBREAK CONTAINING NOTICES OF THE PEOPLE, DRAWN FROM PERSONAL OBSERVATION, PREACHED IN THE MOLYNEUX ASYLUM CHAPEL ON SUNDAY EVENING, OCTOBER 11, 1857.* Dublin: William Carson, 1857. 23pp.
The war is the result of sin. The English have become more heathen than the Indians have become Christian. Robertson takes an extremely bigoted view of the Hindu.

915
RS

Robinson, Jane. *ANGELS OF ALBION. WOMEN OF THE INDIAN MUTINY.* London & New York: Penguin Group, 1996. xx & 298pp. Index, bibliography and notes. 34 plates.
Very interesting. Discusses all of the major characters including those that later wrote books on their experiences.

916

Robson, Brian (ed.). *SIR HUGH ROSE AND THE CENTRAL INDIA CAMPAIGN. 1858.* London: Army Records Society, 2000. 323pp. Index.
198 documents relating to the campaign.

917
Sut

Rogerson, Colonel William. *HISTORICAL RECORDS OF THE 53RD SHROPSHIRE REGIMENT, NOW THE 1ST BATTALION THE KINGS SHROPSHIRE LI. FROM THE FORMATION OF THE REGIMENT IN 1755 DOWN TO 1889.* London: Simpkin, Marshall, Hamilton, Kent, 1891. xxii & 248pp. 9 plates, 4 in color.
The first battalion won honors at Lucknow.

918
RS

Roseberry, J. Royal III. *IMPERIAL RULE IN PUNJAB 1818-1881.* Delhi: Manohar Publications, 1987. 285pp.
A meticulously researched book on the interaction of the British and the local leadership in the Punjab, specifically in the city of Multan. One chapter on the Mutiny as it relates to the area.

919
RS

Rotton, John Edward Wharton. *THE CHAPLAIN'S NARRATIVE OF THE SIEGE OF DELHI: From the Outbreak at Meerut to the Capture of Delhi: With a Plan of the City.* London: Smith Elder, 1858. vi, 357pp. & xvi.

Folding plan. Appendices of Return of Killed, Wounded and Missing
> The reader can not forget that the author is a priest. Rotton was chaplain to the Delhi Field Force.

920
RS   **Rowbotham, Commander W(illiam) B(evill) R.N. ed.** *THE NAVAL BRIGADES IN THE INDIAN MUTINY 1857-1858.* London: Naval Records Society, 1947. 332pp. 1 folding map. There were at least two separate binding styles.
> Based upon information found in *"The Shannon's Brigade in India"* by Verney, *"Recollections of a Winter Campaign in India 1857-58"* by Jones, and *"The Cruise of the Pearl"* by Williams. In addition there are about 150 pages of official correspondence together with a number of private letters never before published.

921
Roy, Choudhury. *1857 IN BIHAR.* Patna: Revenue Dept of Bihar, 1957, 1959. 147pp.
> Cited in Ladendorf.

922
Roy, Tapti. *SEPOY MUTINY AND THE UPRISING OF 1857 IN BUNDELKHAND.* Calcutta: 1991.
> Taylor cites this as an excellent study by a gifted historian.

923
Roy, Tapti. *THE POLITICS OF A POPULAR UPRISING: BUNDELKHAND IN 1857.* Delhi: NP. 1994.
> Taylor cites this as an outstanding study. Includes an index and bibliography.

924
Royal   **Royal Artillery.** *OCCASIONAL PAPERS OF THE*
Artillery   *ROYAL ARTILLERY INSTITUTION. DESPATCHES*
Institute   *OF ARTILLERY OFFICERS RELATIVE TO THE INDIAN MUTINY.* Woolwich: Royal Artillery Institute, 1860. Vol. 1
> Dispatches are about 15 pages.

925
RS   **Ruggles, Major General J.** *RECOLLECTIONS OF A LUCKNOW VETERAN 1845-1876.* London: Longmans and Green, 1906. xv & 185pp.
> Ruggles wrote this some 60 years after the Mutiny and relies on Martin Gubbins work, *"An Account of the Mutinies in Oude...."* together with Ruggles own notes. When the

book was written there were still at least 25 survivors at the Lucknow Dinner.

926
RS/IO

Russell, William Howard. *MY DIARY IN INDIA IN THE YEAR 1858-59.* London: Routledge, Warne & Routledge, 1860. Vol. I, Frontis, xvi & 408pp, 4 plates and 1 folding map. Vol. II, Frontis, xii & 420pp.

Originally issued as a one volume book. 1859, 425pp. Rept in London: Cassell, 1957. xxvii & 288pp. Edited by Michael Edwardes.

Russell was the first war correspondent. He wrote for the London Times. This is a very well known book on the Mutiny.

927
IO/Ames

Sahai, Jawala, Nazim of Bharatpur. *THE LOYAL RAJPUTANA: Or a Description of the Services of the Rajputana Princes to the British Government Rendered During the Mutiny of 1857.* Allahabad: Indian Press, 1902. 346 pp.

Gives brief history of the Indian Mutiny and Part II covers the history of the Mutiny in Rajputana.

928
BL

Salmond, Albert Louis. *SALMOND OF WATERFOOT. A FAMILY HISTORY.* London: Walter Eyre, 1887. Frontis and two photos. Family pedigree and 35 illus. xi & 125pp, index of illustrations.

Contains the letters of Charles James Salmond who served in the Second Cavalry, Gwalior Contingent. Born 1833 died 1857. Salmond served at Agra and the Alumbagh. He was an orderly officer to General Hope Grant. Salmond apparently killed at least 30 men in single combat. His unfortunate death came when, suffering from sun stroke, he stopped to rest under a tree. He was found murdered by unknown assailants.

929
RS

Sattin, Anthony (ed.). *AN ENGLISHWOMAN IN INDIA. The Memoirs of Harriet Tytler. 1828-1858.* Oxford: Oxford Univ Press, 1986. xxiii & 229pp. Glossary and Index. 22 photographs and illus. Two maps.

Edited by Anthony Sattin. This is the first full publication of Harriet Tytlers memoirs of which the original manuscript is in possesssion of the editor. Tytler was one of the few women who witnessed the entire siege of Delhi from the ridge. The work was written late in life and one authority commented that it is, "a rather disappointing collection of second hand stories."

930

Savarkar, Vinayak Damodar. *THE VOLCANO, OR, THE FIRST WAR OF INDEPENDENCE.* Kuala Lumpur: Jayamani S. Subhramanyan, ND.
Vipin Jain cites this as the first edition of Savarkar's famous book *"Indian War of Independence."* There seems to be various editions of this work in the early instance and descriptions are not in agreement though they all appear to be the same work, i.e. Savarkar's *"Indian War of Independence."*

931

Savarkar, Vinayak Damodar (1883-1966). *THE INDIAN WAR OF INDEPENDENCE 1857.* NC. England: 1909, xxi & 451pp. Folding map, 2 plates.
Originally published in England in 1909. 2nd ed. Holland 1910, 3rd ed. U.S.A. 1912, 4th ed. Lahore 1928 also 4th ed. (iii) viii & 487pp Bombay 1946. 5th ed. Japan 1944, 6th ed. Bombay 1947 Phoenix Publications xxvi & 552pp. Abridged edition xx & 180pp Bombay 1960. 7th ed. Poona 1963. 8th ed. xxiv & 558pp. 7 plates, New Delhi 1970. 9th ed. 1970, xxvi & 558pp. Ram Tirath Bhatia. New Delhi 10 pages of plates.
This book was banned by the British authorities, who apparently never saw a copy at the time of banning, from 1909 to 1944. It is quite important in the historiography of the Mutiny due to its very existence as the first outburst of Indian Nationalism in regards to Mutiny literature. Savarkar was believed to have been involved in the assassination of Ghandi.

932
RS

Scholberg, Henry. *THE INDIAN LITERATURE OF THE GREAT REBELLION.* New Delhi: Promilla & Co, 1993. 125pp.
The book is divided into three parts. Part One is a bibliography of published works in various languages of the Indian sub-continent. Part Two is concerned with primary source material in the vernacular. Part Three is a collection of folk songs, in translation, concerning the Mutiny.
The author was born in India and later served as the director of the Ames Library at the University of Minnesota.

933
BL

Schorn, J. Arnold. *TALES OF THE EAST AND NARRATIVES OF THE INDIAN MUTINY WITH INTERESTING ACCOUNTS FROM THE DIARY OF A DECEASED OFFICER OF THE LATE H.E.I. CO'S.*

SERVICE. Allahabad: Pioneer Press, 1893. 113pp. 2nd
ed.
Contains 1) "Lucille's Watch" a tale of Cawnpore. The
author's father was Brian Chapman of Cawnpore. 2) The
Sepoy Rebellion of 1857 as related by "B.P." Pensioned
drummer of the Khelat-i-Ghilzie Regiment. 3)From Agra
to Umballa in a Bombay Shigram after the fall of Delhi in
1858 and 4) Simla, before, in and after 1857. (Notes from a
deceased officer's diary).

934

Scot, Patrick G. *PERSONAL NARRATIVE OF
THE ESCAPE FROM NOWYONG TO BANDA AND
NAGODE.* Dumfries: Herald Office, 1857.
No further information. Cited in Jain and Ladendorf.

935
BL

Scrutator. *ENGLISH TENURE OF INDIA.
PRACTICAL REMARKS SUGGESTED BY THE
BENGAL MUTINY.* London: Privately Printed for the
author by Smith, Elder, 1857. Pamphlet 31pp.
The Mutiny was not pre-planned. "At the bottom of
all, beyond question, lies the entire want of any feeling of
attachment or loyalty on the part of the people of India
towards their foreign rulers." Discusses all of the problems
that led up to the Mutiny.

936
IO

Scrutator. *THE INDIAN MUTINY.* London: W. Kent
& Co., 1857. 29pp.
Indicts those in power for not forseeing the Mutiny.
States that caste alone is what preserved Englands supremacy
in India. It fractured Indian society. Calls for army reform
and offers various programs.

937
RS

Seaton, Major-General Sir Thomas. *FROM CADET
TO COLONEL, A Record of A Life of Active Service.*
London: Hurst and Blackett, 1866. (1877, 2 vols. xix
& 663pp.; 1880 one vol. 435pp. 6 plates.)
Seaton commanded the 60th NI which mutinied at
Umballah originally on May 10th. Seaton saw many years
of action in India. He served at the Siege of Delhi and
afterwards in the Doab and Rohilcund. Seaton was a good
friend of Hodson. Approximately seven chapters on the
Mutiny.

938
RS

Sedgwick, F(rancis) R. *THE INDIAN MUTINY OF
1857. Sketch of the Principal Military Events.* London:

Foster Groom & Co., 1908 rept. 1909, 1919, 1920 160pp.
Includes five maps in rear pocket. General Map of India, Plan of Delhi, Plan of Lucknow, Plan of Cawnpore, and Theatre of War. This is not a history of the Mutiny but rather an account of the military events. Sedgwick used Kaye and Malleson, Forrest, Roberts' *"Forty-one Years in India"* and material at the India Office as source material for this publication.

939
RS   **Sellar, Edmond Francis.** *THE STORY OF LORD ROBERTS.* London: T.C. & E.C. Jack and New York: E.P. Dutton & Co. ND either edition. vii & 119pp
Frontis and 7 pictures. The Children's Heroes series.

940
        Sen, Ashoka Kumar. *THE POPULAR UPRISING AND THE INTELLIGENTSIA: BENGAL BETWEEN 1855-73.* Calcutta: 1992.
Cited in Taylor.

941
IO T25250   **Sen, Mohit.** *THE INDIAN REVOLUTION, VIEWS AND PERSPECTIVES.* New Delhi: NP. 1970.

942
Ames/RS   **Sen, Snigdha.** *THE HISTORIOGRAPHY OF THE INDIAN REVOLT OF 1857.* Calcutta: Sankar Kumar Bhattacharya, 1992. xi & 304pp with index and bibliography.
Discusses the major questions concerning the Mutiny;
1) Was it a mutiny or war of independence.
2) Participation of the civil population.
3) Ideology.
4) Centenary writings. This is a scholarly look at both Indian and British perspectives and writings on the Mutiny.

943
RS   **Sen, Surendranath.** *EIGHTEEN FIFTY-SEVEN.* New Delhi: Publications Division, Ministry of Information and Broadcasting, 1957. xxv & 468pp. 8 illus. Reprinted 1958 with 2 folding maps. xxvii & 466pp. 8 pages of illus and 3 folding maps. Bib., glossary, index. Also a 3rd reprint 1977.
Chaudhuri credits this with the first real bibliography of the Mutiny. Sen does not support the conspiracy theory. Sengupta calls it perhaps the best one volume study of the Revolt.

944
RS

Sengupta, Kalyan Kumar. *RECENT WRITINGS ON THE REVOLT OF 1857. A Survey*. New Delhi: Indian Council of Historical Research, 1975. viii & 70pp.

An important work covering historical writings on the revolt of 1857 published since Indian Independence and written in English. Includes bibliography, list of works in progress as of 1975, new trends in research. A valuable and useful research tool but poorly proof-read. Some errors in dates.

945
RS

Seton, Rosemary. *THE INDIAN MUTINY 1857-58. A Guide to Source Material in the India Office Library and Records*. London: British Library, 1986. xvi & 99pp. Index and 10 plates.

A very important work for the study of the Mutiny. Seton covers the whole range of material available in the India Office. From the contents of Parliamentary papers to the telegram and photo collections of the India Office Library and Records. This work is especially helpful in determining material of primary source value. A long section lists and describes the contents of the Board of Control's collection of relevant material.

Political and Secret Department Records, Records of the various Residencies and Government of India Records are also presented.

946
IO

Seton-Karr, George Berkeley. *AN EPISODE OF THE INDIAN REVOLT*. Bombay: NP. 1862. 30pp.

An extract from the Overland Telegraph and Courier. Bombay, February 27th, 1861.

Seton-Karr was the political agent in Southern Maharastra. He discusses the Inam Commission, the Doctrine of Lapse, and other causes of the Mutiny.

947
Sut

Seton-Karr, Walter Scott. *A SHORT ACCOUNT OF EVENTS DURING THE SEPOY MUTINY OF 1857-8 IN THE DISTRICT OF BELGAUM AND JESSORE*. London: NP. For private circulation, 1894. 30pp.

Seton-Karr was Civil Judge at Jessore and his brother was Political Agent at Belgaum. Seton-Karr was requested to write this narrative for a collection of accounts by members of the Indian Civil Service during the Mutiny. There was no rising in either district but there was much anxiety.

948
Jain

Sevestre, Allan Alexander. *A SHORT AND USEFUL COMPILATION FROM THE CALCUTTA GOVERNMENT GAZETTE ABOUT THE FALL OF DELHI.* Calcutta: NP. 1858.

949
NAM
92McCAB

Sewell, Colonel J. W. *A RECORD OF THE LIFE AND TIMES OF CAPTAIN BERNARD McCABE.* No imprint., NP. ND. 16pp. 2 plates.
McCabe was a captain and was killed at the siege of Lucknow.

950

Sewell, J. C. *THE JOURNAL OF A SOLDIER DURING THE CAMPAIGNS OF 1857-1858.*
Cited by Chaudhuri in *"English Historical Writing..."* Page 325n

951
IO

Seymour, Charles Crossley. *HOW I WON THE INDIAN MUTINY MEDAL: AND HOW THINGS WENT AFTERWARDS.* Benares: Medical Hall Press, 1888. 195pp. 1 map.
Seymour was a private in the Agra Militia. See Forbes-Mitchell's claim regarding his work as being the only book on the Mutiny written by an enlisted man. Interesting work.

952
RS

Shadwell, Lt. Gen. *THE LIFE OF COLIN CAMPBELL, LORD CLYDE. Illustrated by extracts from His Diary and Correspondence.* Edinburgh, William Blackwell, 1881. Vol. I, xvii & 457pp and 6 maps (1 folding in rear pocket) and frontis. Vol. II. xi & 489pp. with 10 maps and plans.
A good part of volume two covers the Mutiny period. Shadwell includes the correspondence betweeen Campbell and Canning concerning their difference of opinion on how to conduct the campaign after Campbell's relief of Lucknow.

953
Sut

Shakespear, Lt. Col. J. *JOHN SHAKESPEAR OF SHADWELL AND HIS DESCENDANTS 1619-1931.* Newcastle-upon-Tyne: Private, 1931. 407pp. 47 plates. 4to. Green cloth.
140 copies were printed. 62 pages on the Mutiny with chapters covering Edward Thackeray.
Alexander Shakespear was Collector of Bijnaur near Meerut from where he and his treasure were rescued by Hugh

Gough, Malcolm Low and Sir Richmond Shakespear who was Resident at Baroda.

954
IO   **Sharma, Benudhar.** *THE REBELLION OF 1857 VIS-A-VIS ASSAM.* Calcutta, NP. 1958. 86pp.

955
SOAS/RS   **Shastitko, Pyotr**; *NANA SAHIB: An Account of the Peoples Revolt in India, 1857-1859.* Pune: Shubhada-Saraswat Publications, 1980. xii & 178pp. Bibliography, Glossary.
          Translated by Savitri Shahani. Gives account of the causes of failure of the Mutiny. Shastitko aims to "acquaint the reader with some dramatic and heroic events of Indian History; with the first Great Liberation War of the people of the Indo-Pakistan sub-continent." The author is a Russian professor of Indian history in Moscow.

956
RS   **Shepherd, J. W.** *A PERSONAL NARRATIVE OF THE OUTBREAK AND MASSACRE AT CAWNPORE: During the Sepoy Revolt of 1857.* Agra: Wm. Deugo, Delhi Gazette Press, 1862. (500 copies) 201pp.
          First published under the title *"Brief Account of the Outbreak at Cawnpore"* in the Calcutta and London Papers in 1857. In January, 1862 the Delhi Gazette published it as *"Narrative of Events at Cawnpore."* In 1879 it was published in Lucknow under the present title. See Chaudhuri *"English Historical Writings"* p. 63.
          A 2nd ed., Lucknow: R. Craven, 1879, revised and corrected. 2 plates vi & 161 & 70pp & xxix. A 3rd ed. Lucknow: Methodist Publishing House, 1886, liii & 203pp. 8 illus. 4 plans. Revised and enlarged. A 4th ed. revised. Lucknow: 1894. 213pp.7 illus. 3 maps. (1 folding).
          Shepherd was a Eurasian clerk of the Commissariat Department. He was one of the few survivors of the massacre at Cawnpore. His book was used as source material by many Mutiny historians.

957
          Sherer, G. M. *BRIEF NARRATIVE CALLED FOR BY SIR JAMES OUTRAM SHOWING HOW THE 73RD NATIVE INFANTRY WAS SAVED.* Jersey: NP. 1860.
          Cited in Ladendorf.

958
RS   **Sherer, J. W.** *DAILY LIFE DURING THE INDIAN MUTINY. Personal Experiences of 1857.* London: Swan Sonnenschein & Co., 1898. viii & 197pp. Frontis. (1910, ix & 197pp. London.)

Originally part of Colonel Maudes' *"Memories of the Mutiny."*

959
RS

Sherer, J. W. *HAVELOCK'S MARCH ON CAWNPORE 1857. A Civilian's Notes.* London: Thomas Nelson. ND. Another ed. New York: 1898. xiv & 366pp. Portrait.
This title is the same as *"Daily Life During the Indian Mutiny."*

960

Sherer, John Walter. *AT HOME AND IN INDIA. A Volume of Miscellanies.* London: W. H. Allen, 1883. 330pp.
Cited in Ladendorf.

961
RS

Sherring, Mathew Atmore. *THE INDIAN CHURCH DURING THE GREAT REBELLION. An Authentic Account of the Disasters Which Befell It. Its Sufferings, and Faithfulness unto Death of Many of Its European and Native Members.* London: James Nisbet, 1859. 355pp.
This is a history of the various missions such as Delhi, Bareilly, Allahabad, Meerut, 21 in all, and what befell them during the Mutiny. The book contains a list of Missionaries, Chaplains, and their families killed during the Mutiny. In addition there is a list of native Christian Catechists and teachers killed during the Mutiny.

962
RS

Showers, Lt. General C. L. *A MISSING CHAPTER OF THE INDIAN MUTINY.* London: Longmans Green, 1888. viii & 214pp. Frontis, 2 plates and folding map at rear.
Showers was the political agent in Rajputana. He refers to this as a missing chapter because it includes information not included in his official reports to the government. Includes final operations and execution of Tantia Topee. Showers feels that Malleson did not write an accurate history of the Mutiny and strongly takes him to task in his final chapter.

963
RS

Showers, Major-General Charles Lionel. *THE INDIAN HISTORY AND COLONEL G.B.MALLESON, C.S.I.; Being a Correspondence between the Author of "Kaye Rewritten" and Major General C. L. Showers.* London: Reeves and Turner, 1881. 18pp.
Showers feels that Malleson was out to rehabilitate reputations damaged by Kaye. However Malleson's

scholarship does not hold up to close scrutiny according to
Showers.

964
RS

Sieveking, I. G. *A TURNING POINT IN THE
INDIAN MUTINY.* London: David Nutt, 1910. xii &
226pp. 14 plates. Index.
Discusses the relief of Arrah House. Contains some of
the correspondence of General John Nicholson.

965
BL 8831.d.40

Simcox, Arthur Henry Addenbrooke. *A MEMOIR
OF THE KHANDESH BHIL CORPS 1825-1891.
COMPILED FROM ORIGINAL RECORDS.* Bombay:
Thacker & Co, 1912. Frontis, v & 281pp. Folding map
in rear pocket and 4 illus.
James Outram founded the Bhil Corps in 1825. They
mutinied but apparently were not connected with the other
mutineers in Upper India.

966
Bod/
BL 8022a36

Sinclair, William. Rector of Pulborough. *THE
SEPOY MUTINIES: Their Origin and Their Cure.
By and Old Servant of the Hon. East India Company.*
London: Wertheim and Macintosh, 1857. 22pp.
Discusses the causes of the Mutiny and how to prevent
another.

967
IO

Singh, Balbhadra. *BRIEF SURVEY OF
RAGHOGARH STATES SERVICES DURING THE
INDIAN MUTINY. 1858-1859.* Ajmer: Imprint, 1937.
23pp.
A testamonial to the loyalty of Raghogarh State during
the Mutiny. Presents various letters from responsible persons
attesting to that fact. Includes a brief history of the state.

968
IO

Singh, Ganda. *THE INDIAN MUTINY OF 1857 AND
THE SIKHS.* Delhi: Gurdwara Parbandhak Committee
Sisganj, 1969. 40pp.
Consists of two parts. Part I was originally published by
the Tribune in Ambala, India on August 15, 1957. This was
a rebuttal of the charge that the "Indian struggle for freedom
failed as the Sikhs betrayed and sided with the British." Part
II was published in the same journal on October 6, 1957 and
is a defense and clarification of Part I.

969
Jain

Singh, Govind. *1857.* Varanasi: Sohan Ram and Sons,
1957.

970
SOAS   **Singh, Shailendra Dhari.** *NOVELS OF THE INDIAN MUTINY.* New Delhi: Arnold Heinemann, 1973. 248pp. Map. Bibliography and index.
Originally published as a thesis at the Patna University, this is a chronological study of English novels dealing with the Mutiny. Singh states there are at least fifty novels by English men and women which are set during the Mutiny. Short, critical analysis' are given for many of them.

971
RS   **Singh, Sheo Bahadur.** *LETTERS OF SIR HENRY MONTGOMERY LAWRENCE, Selections from the Correspondence of Sir Henry Montgomery Lawrence (1806-1857) During the Siege of Lucknow from March to July 1857.* New Delhi: Sagar Publications, 1978. xi & 80pp. Index.
See Lawrence, Sir Henry.

972
    Sinha, Dr. S. N. (ed). *MUTINY TELEGRAMS.* 1988. Cited by Jain.

973
    Sinha, R. M. *1857 IN JABALPUR DISTRICT.* Jabalpur: NP. 1957.

974
RS   **Sinha, S. N.** *RANI LAKSHMI BAI OF JHANSI.* Allahabad: Chugh Publishers, 1980. 134pp. Bibliography, inde and frontis.
This is a well documented work based on a number of primary sources.

975
IO ORW   **Sinha, S. K.** *GREAT WARRIOR.* 1997.
1998.A.1774

976
IO T44917   **Sinha, S. N.** *REVOLT IN 1857.*

977
BL   **Small, E. Milton.** *TOLD FROM THE RANKS: RECOLLECTIONS OF SERVICE DURING THE QUEEN'S REIGN BY PRIVATES AND NON-COMMISSIONED OFFICERS OF THE BRITISH ARMY.* London: Andrew Melrose, 1897. Frontis and 5 plates and 219pp. Red title with colored vignette on cover.
Includes Mutiny narratives by Sergeant J. Palmer of the 20th and by Gunners MacCallam and Cox of the Royal

Artillery. MacCallam was at Meerut on the 10th and then went to join the Central India Field Force. He served at Kirwee and mentions the massacre of about 300 prisoners and the Kirwee prize money. Cox was a gunner and driver in the Artillery. He served with Campbell at Lucknow as did Sergeant Palmer.

978
RS
Smith, Juliet. *ESCAPE FROM MEERUT.* London: William Collins, 1971.
Fiction.

979
RS
Smith, R. B. *LIFE OF LORD LAWRENCE.* London: Smith Elder, 1883. 5th ed.; 1885, 6th ed.; Vol. I, xiii & 536pp. Vol. II, vi & 654pp.(6th ed. Revised. Vol. I, xiii & 542pp. Folding map at rear, frontis. Vol. II, xv & 557pp.) A further edition, London: Smith Elder, 1901. xiv & 542pp. and xiv & 557pp.

980
RS
Smyth, Sir John. *THE REBELLIOUS RANI.* London: Frederick Muller, 1966. 224pp. 8 plates 5 maps. Frontis. Bibliography and index.
Includes photos that do not appear in other books on the Rani.

981
BL
Somerville, E. and Martin Ross. *WHEEL TRACKS.* London: Longmans, Green. 1923. x & 284pp. Frontis and 31 illus.
The author's uncle served at the Delhi ridge. His letters are briefly quoted including his account of the storming of the city.

982
Soppitt, Elizabeth. *DIARY.*
A title mentioned in the fifth edition of Fitchett, "*The Tale of the Great Mutiny.*" Unable to locate.

983
Sorsky, R. *1857 THE INDIAN MUTINY. A Short Price Guide to Mutiny Titles.* Fresno, CA: Linden Pub, 1979. 16pp. Paper.

984
RS
Spear, Percival. *TWILIGHT OF THE MUGHULS. Studies in Late Mughul Delhi.* London: Cambridge University Press, 1951. xi & 270pp. Bibliography, index and frontis. Folding Map of Delhi. Also Karachi:

Oxford University Press, 1973. New introduction, xix & 270pp. with folding map, index and bibliography.
One chapter on the Mutiny. Glossary. Useful reference work to events and personalities before the Mutiny. Spear is often cited by later historians of the Mutiny.

985
RAI/
BL
YA1991.a.9682

Spencer, Margaret. *PERSONAL REMINISCENCES OF THE INDIAN MUTINY.* Clifton and London: Clifton: S. Baker & Son. London: Dawson & Co. ND. c. 1916 or Clifton: 1905 84pp.
Spencer was the daughter of a missionary stationed at Benares.

986
NAM 92
SPOT

Spottiswoode, Col. Robert Collinson D'esterre. *REMINISCENCES.* Edinburgh: Privately printed. Edinburgh Press, 1935. Frontis & portrait. 158pp. Cloth.
Believed to be the last Mutiny combatant. Spottiswoode died in December 1936 at age 94. He was 16 years old when he served as a cadet in the 3rd Bengal European Cavalry.

987
RS

Sprot, Captain A. *A CONTINUATION OF THE HISTORICAL RECORDS OF THE VI DRAGOONS CARABINIERS.* Chatham: England, Gale and Polden, 1888. 76pp.
About 20 pages relate details of action during the Mutiny.

988

Squire, E. B. *GODS PROLONGED CONTROVERSY WITH BRITAIN.* Swansea: Cambrian Office, 1857.
Cited by Ladendorf.

989
RS

Srivastava, Harindra. *FIVE STORMY YEARS: SAVARKAR IN LONDON.* Calcutta: Allied Publishers, 1983. xii & 326pp. Frontis of Savarkar and 8pp of plates.
Two chapters cover material of Mutiny interest. Chapter two details golden jubilee celebrations of the Mutiny and chapter three discusses the writing of Savarkar's highly influential book *"The Indian War of Independence."*

990
RS

Srivastava, K. L. *THE REVOLT OF 1857 IN CENTRAL INDIA-MALWA.* Bombay: Allied Publishers, 1966. xiv & 310pp. Index. 1 folding map, maps and photos of the principal characters

This was presented as a doctoral dissertation. Excellent bibliography.

991
IO

Srivastava, M. P. *THE INDIAN MUTINY 1857.*
Allahabad: Chugh Publications, 1979. x & 243pp.
With index and bibliography.
Based on a doctoral dissertation, *"The Role of Allahabad Division in the Revolt of 1857."*

992
IO/RS

Staff Officer. *REMINISCENCES OF THE INDIAN REBELLION, 1857-58. BY A STAFF OFFICER (E.A. THURBURN).* London: Army & Navy Co-operative Society, 1889. 2nd ed. Revised with additions. First issue 1868. 120pp
First written for a relative of the author and published in 1868. In 1856 the author was appointed magistrate of Fyzabad and Oude. Included in appendices are; 1) Regards the Spread of Chuppaties 2)Regards Henry Lawrence; 3) Regards Occupants of Four Boats Which Left Fyzabad On June 9th 1857. (One person killed by alligator one later committed suicide). 4) Regards the actions of the Indian ringleaders 5) Notes on a voyage by steamer from Calcutta to Allahabad in 1858 by K.T. 6) Regards Allahabad and the story of young Mr. Cheek. See Meek, *"The Martyr of Allahabad"*(entry 746). 7) No interest 8) Mahomdee District During the Mutiny. 9) No interest. 10) Calls for a larger foreign element in the Indian Army. 11)List of regular regiments of the Bengal Army that mutinied or were disbanded or disarmed in 1857. 12) No interest.

993
Bod

Stanley, Right Honorable Lord, Secretary of State for India. *SPEECH IN THE HOUSE OF COMMONS ON THE FINANCIAL RESOURCES OF INDIA ON THE 13TH OF FEBRUARY, 1859. REVISED AND CORRECTED.* London: Smith, Elder, 1859. 56pp. Pamphlet.
Information and comparisons of pre and post Mutiny finances.

994
RS

Stark, Herbert Alick. *THE CALL OF THE BLOOD OR ANGLO-INDIANS AND THE SEPOY MUTINY.* Rangoon: British Burma Press, 1932. iv & 172pp. 10 illustrations and frontis of Mutiny medal.
Stark recounts the loyalty of the Anglo-Indians during the Mutiny. He traces a number of incidents involving Anglo-Indians. Includes a photo of George Brendish, one of

the telegraph operators at Delhi who received the first news of Meerut.

995
BL
Steel, Flora Annie. *THE GARDEN OF FIDELITY. BEING THE AUTOBIOGRAPHY OF FLORA ANNIE STEEL 1847-1929.* London: Macmillan, 1929. Frontis and plates, xi & 293pp.
Little about the Mutiny.

996
RS
Steel, Mrs. Flora. *ON THE FACE OF THE WATERS.* London: Heinemann, 1897. 432pp.
Reprinted by Heinemann in Delhi 1984 also New York, Macmillan, 1897, 475pp. Recognized as the best novel dealing with the Mutiny.

997
Sut
Stent, George Carter. *SCRAPS FROM MY SABRETASCHE BEING PERSONAL ADVENTURES WHILE IN THE 14TH KINGS LIGHT DRAGOONS.* London: W. H. Allen, 1882. iv & 276pp. Red cloth, with blind stamped vignette.
Last half deals with the Central India Campaign.

998
RS
Steuart, Lt. Colonel Thomas Ruddiman. *THE REMINISCENCES OF ...ed. by his wife.* Edinburgh: Privately Printed, 1900. xx & 218pp. Frontispiece.
Includes some information on the Mutiny. Steuart was stationed at Shirkapore in Scinde. There are approximately 25 pages on the Mutiny.

999
Bod
Stewart, Charles Edward. *THROUGH PERSIA IN DISGUISE WITH REMINISCENCES OF THE INDIAN MUTINY.* London: George Routledge and Sons, 1911. xxii & 430pp. 17 plates (2 color) 6 text illus. Maps of Khorassan and India.
Taken from Stewart's diaries. Stewart commanded the 1st Sikh Irregular Cavalry under Sir Hope Grant. Then, as adjutant of the 5th Punjab Infantry, under Lord Clyde and later commanded the force which killed Bukht Khan in May 1859. Forty three pages on the Mutiny.

1000
RS
Stokes, Eric. *THE PEASANT ARMED. The Indian Rebellion of 1857.* Oxford: Clarendon Press, 1986. 261pp. Index, bibliography and extensive notes.
Edited by C.A. Bayly. This work represents a substantial part of what would have been Stokes position on the social

origins of the Mutiny. Stokes, one of the leading English
scholars on India, died in 1981. Stokes discusses the
pre-disposition to disorder among the various classes in India
at the time of the Mutiny. Stokes believed environment and
ecology played an important part in the forces which led to
either participation or withdrawal from involvement in the
Mutiny. This was, in a significant sense, a peasant rebellion.
Excellent and important study. Very interesting discussion as
to why the Indians could not take advantage of their numerical
superiority.

1001
RS

Stokes, Eric. *THE PEASANT AND THE RAJ. Studies
in Agrarian Society and Peasant Rebellion in Colonial
India.* Cambridge: Cambridge Univ. Press, 1978. viii &
308pp. Glossary and index.

Part of the Cambridge South Asian Studies series. Four
of the twelve studies deal with the Mutiny. 1) Traditional
resistance movements and Afro-Asian nationalism: the
context of the 1857 Mutiny Rebellion 2) Nawab Walidad
Khan and the 1857 Struggle in the Bulandshahr district 3)
Rural revolt in the Great Rebellion of 1857. Saharanpur and
Muzaffarnagar districts 4) Traditional elites in the Great
Rebellion of 1857...upper and central Doab.

1002
Ames

Stokes, William. *INDIAN REFORM BILLS; OR,
LEGISLATION FOR INDIA, FROM 1766 TO 1858,
ALSO AN ARGUMENT FOR A REPRESENTATIVE
GOVERNMENT IN INDIA.* London: A. W. Bennett,
1858. 48pp. Pamphlet.

1003
Bod

Stoqueler, J. H. *INDIA: ITS HISTORY, CLIMATE,
AND PRODUCTIONS: WITH A FULL ACCOUNT OF
THE ORIGIN, PROGRESS, AND DEVELOPEMENT
OF THE BENGAL MUTINY AND SUGGESTIONS
AS TO THE FUTURE GOVERNMENT OF INDIA.*
London: G. Routledge, 1857. viii & 219pp. Illus.
12mo.

A history for the layman. The last chapter offers
suggestions on the future rule of India.

1004
RAI

Stoqueler, J. H. *THE TRUE CAUSES OF THE
REVOLT OF THE BENGAL ARMY.* London: Charles
Evans, ND. c. 1858. 32pp.

Blames the Mutiny on the mal-administration of the
E.I.C. and the Board of Directors.

1005
Ames

Strachan, J. M. *A LETTER TO CAPTAIN EASTWICK, OCCASIONED BY HIS SPEECH AT A SPECIAL COURT OF PROPRIETORS HELD AT EAST INDIA HOUSE ON THE 20TH OF JANUARY 1858.* London: Seeley, Jackson & Halliday, 1858. 48pp.
Strachan promotes the religious aspect of British power in India. It is the duty of England to spread the gospel.

1006
RS

Strang, Herbert. *STORIES OF THE INDIAN MUTINY.* London: Hodder and Stoughton, ND. c. 1915. 160pp. Colored frontis and three colored plates with one map.
This work consists of extracts and narratives from a number of well known mutiny works.
"*Cawnpore*" by Trevelyan, "*Personal Adventures During the Indian Rebellion*" by William Edwards, "*A Widow's Reminiscences of the Siege of Lucknow*" by Bartrum, "*How I won the Victoria Cross*" by Kavanagh, "*Hodson of Hodson's Horse*" by Hodson, "*A Chaplain's Narrative of the Siege of Delhi*" by Rotton.

1007

Strang, Herbert. Ed. *THE PIONEER SERIES. DUTY AND DANGER IN INDIA.* London: Oxford Univ Press, Rept 1916 vi & 320pp. Frontis and 7 plates and 2 maps.
Juvenile book consisting of extracts from famous Mutiny literature, i. e. Trevelyan, Hodson, Dunlop, Kavanagh, etc.

1008
RS

Strange, General Thomas Bland. *GUNNER JINGO'S JUBILEE: An Autobiography.* London: Remington, 1893. A 3rd ed. London: J. Macqueen, 1896. 546pp. Illus.
Supposedly an autobiography. Of little value for its material on the Mutiny.

1009
Bod

Stuart, W. K. Col. *REMINISCENCES OF A SOLDIER.* London: Hurst and Blackett, 1874. 2 vols. Vol. I, xvi & 309pp. Vol. II, viii & 307pp.
Includes material on the Central India Campaign. Approximately two chapters on the Mutiny. Stuart led an interesting life, apart from his Mutiny experiences.

1010
IO

Stubbs, Major-General Francis William. *EXTRACTS FROM THE DIARY OF LT. F.W. STUBBS, BENGAL*

ARTILLERY, IN 1857-58. Woolwich: NP. 1894. 29pp. Blue paper. Illus. With two fold out maps.

This work is a reprint from "Proceedings, Royal Artillery Institution, Vol. 21, No. 11-12.

Stubbs was in Meerut on May 10th. The diary skips from May 26th to December 3rd. The majority of the diary is from 1858.

1011
BL

Sturges, Octavious. *IN THE COMPANY'S SERVICE: A Reminiscence.* London: W. H. Allen, 1883. iv & 332pp. Red cloth.

Fiction.

1012
Bod

Sulivan, Reverend Henry. *REST IN THE LORD. A SERMON PREACHED IN YOXALL CHURCH ON SUNDAY MORNING 13TH SEPTEMBER, 1857, FOR SUFFERERS IN THE INDIAN MUTINIES.* London: Rivingtons, Hatchards, 1857. 14pp.

1013
IO

Swanston, Major-General William Oliver. *MY JOURNAL OR WHAT I DID AND SAW BETWEEN THE 9TH JUNE AND 25TH NOVEMBER 1857 WITH AND ACCOUNT OF GENERAL HAVELOCK'S MARCH FROM ALLAHABAD TO LUCKNOW BY A VOLUNTEER.* Calcutta: Baptist Mission Press, 1858. 60pp. Also 1890 Uxbridge: Hutchings Printing Works. 66pp.

Swanston served with the volunteer cavalry on Havelock's march to Lucknow.

1014
Ames

Sykes, Colonel W.H. *SPEECH OF COLONEL SYKES IN THE HOUSE OF COMMONS, ON THURSDAY FEBRUARY 18TH 1858, ON THE PROPOSED INDIA BILL. With notes and appendices.* London: Smith, Elder, 1858. 67pp.

An apologia for the Court of Directors of the EIC.

1015
RS

Sylvester, Deputy Surgeon General John Henry. A. McKenzie Annand (ed.) *CAVALRY SURGEON. THE RECOLLECTIONS OF DEPUTY SURGEON-GENERAL JOHN HENRY SYLVESTER, F.G.S.* London: Macmillan, 1971. 336pp. 15 plates. 2 maps. Index.

Uses Sylvester's *"Recollections..."* as source material for the Mutiny period. Sylvester served in Hugh Rose's campaign in Central India. Extensive footnotes. The editor points out that this is not an exact reprint of Sylvester's previous work *"Recollections of the Campaign in Malwa and Central India Under Major General Sir Hugh Rose, G.C.B."* New material is added and some material in the first book is omitted from *"Cavalry Surgeon."*

1016
RS

Sylvester, John Henry. Assistant Surgeon.
RECOLLECTIONS OF THE CAMPAIGN IN MALWA AND CENTRAL INDIA UNDER MAJOR GENERAL SIR HUGH ROSE, G.C.B. Bombay: Smith, Taylor, 1860. 266pp. Folding map at front.
Originally published as articles in the Bombay Standard. After the final pursuit and capture of Tantia Tope it was published. Reprinted as *"Cavalry Surgeon"* and edited by A. McKenzie Annand. London 1971. It should be noted that "Cavalry Surgeon" is not an exact reprint of *"Recollections."* Sylvester served with the Central India Field Force and saw action against the Ranee of Jhansi at Gwalior and the pursuit and capture of Tantia.

1017
RS

Tahmankar, D. V. *THE RANEE OF JHANSI.* London: MacGibbon and Keye, 1958. 178pp. 10 illus.
An attempt to clear the Rani of complicity in the Jhansi massacre.

1018
RS

Taqui, Roshan. *LUCKNOW 1857: THE TWO WARS OF LUCKNOW. THE DUSK OF AN ERA.* Lucknow: New Royal Book Co., 2001. xvi & 297pp. Hard cover. Bibliography and notes. 16 pages of plates.
Taqui uses a variety of sources from Michael Edwards to P.J.O. Taylor, Gubbins, Urdu sources and some first hand information handed down from participants to their relations. Unfortunately the book is so poorly edited that it is difficult to follow in places and there are factual errors. For example, Dr. Brydon did not die in Lucknow. The book is essentially a day by day (March 1856 to March 21, 1858) account of Lucknow in the Mutiny, told from the Indian point of view. There is an interesting section concerning the extensive looting that went on after the fall of Lucknow.

1019
IO

Tavender, I. T. *CASUALTY ROLE FOR THE INDIAN MUTINY.* Polstead, Suffolk: J.B. Hayward & Son, 1983. 205pp. Bibliography.
Includes chronological precis of events. The book was originally written for medal collectors.

Lists all of the units involved in the Mutiny and their
casualties with circumstances.

1020
From an
announcement
found in
Anderson:
*"A Personal
Journal of
The Siege of
Lucknow."*

Tayler, W. *A VIEW OF THE DEFENCE OF ARRAH
HOUSE AGAINST THE DINAPORE MUTINEERS
UNDER LOER SING. From a Picture by W. Tayler esq.
Bengal Civil Service. Accompanied by a small pamphlet
containing a Narrative of the Siege.* London: Thacker and
Co., 1858.
"This picture shows the exact position of the attacking
party, the house of which the Mutineers took possession,
and from which they attacked the besieged; and the small
building from which the garrison defended themselves against
8000 men." "The picture is prepared in the finest style of
Chrome-Lithography." This announcement presumably refers
to entry 216.

1021
IO

Tayler, William. *A BRIEF SUMMARY OF THE
FACTS CONNECTED WITH MY REMOVAL FROM
THE COMMISSIONERSHIP OF PATNA.* Calcutta:
P.S. D'Rozario, 1869. 15pp. Also 1871, 21pp.

1022
IO

Tayler, William. *A NARRATIVE OF EVENTS
CONNECTED WITH MY REMOVAL FROM THE
PATNA COMMISSIONERSHIP IN 1857.* Calcutta:
NP. 1867-1868. 3 parts. Part I. viii & 164pp continous
pagination. Part II. 165-279pp.
Appendix containing letters and reports from Mr. W.
Tayler to Government in 1857 extracted from the "Blue
Book." 1868. Iv & 79pp.

1023
RS

Tayler, William. *COPY OF A MEMORIAL
ADDRESSED TO THE SECRETARY OF STATE
FOR INDIA BY MR WILLIAM TAYLER, LATE
COMMISSIONER OF PATNA, BEING HIS REPLY
TO A MINUTE OF SIR FREDERICK HALLIDAY ON
THE SUBJECT OF THE INDIAN MUTINY.* London:
House of Commons, 1880. March 18. 68pp.
This is Tayler's refutation to Halliday's memorandum
which accused Tayler of a number of charges, among them
panic and incompetence. Tayler lays out his defense point by
point and offers a number of testimonials in his behalf.

1024
IO
Tayler, William. *CORRESPONDENCE CONNECTED WITH MY FIRST MEMORIAL. To the Right Honorable Sir Stafford Northcote, Secretary of State for India.* NC. NP. 1867. 30pp + 19pp. + 6pp. And bound with a copy of his book, *"Addenda to the Correspondence Relative to the Removal of Mr. W. Tayler from the Commissionership of Patna."*

1025
IO
Tayler, William. *CORRESPONDENCE CONNECTED WITH THE REMOVAL OF MR. WILLIAM TAYLER FROM THE COMMISSIONERSHIP OF PATNA.* Calcutta: John Gray, 1858. 189pp. + 40pp. + 22pp. + v.
Correspondence connected with the arrest and trial of Ali Khan, a banker in Patna. Mr. Tayler's orders under which the officers at Gaya, Muzumfferpore, Barth, Mowada, Shergholty, and Chumparun abandoned their stations. Remarks by Mr. Samuells on Mr. W. Taylers *"Brief Narrative of Events"* connected with his removal.

1026
RS
Tayler, William. *FACT v. FALSEHOOD. Being a Brief Summary of Mr. W. Tayler's Refutation. Presented March 15, 1880, in Reply to the Memorandum to The House of Commons (24th June, 1879) by Sir Frederick Halliday.* London: M. Walbrook, ND. viii & 66pp.
Tayler recounts a short history of his problems and removal.

1027
Tayler, William. *MAGNA EST VERITAS.*
See William Tayler, *"History of the Press on the Case of Mr. William Tayler, Late Commissioner of Patna."*

1028
IO
Tayler, William ed. *SELECTION OF LETTERS FROM DISTINGUISHED INDIAN STATESMEN AND OTHERS REGARDING MY SERVICES DURING THE REBELLION OF 1857. Series 1-2.* Calcutta: P.S. D'Rozario, 1869. Section I: 32pp. Section II: 13pp.

1029
Tayler, William ed. *SELECTIONS FROM LETTERS ON TAYLER'S REMOVAL FROM THE COMMISSIONERSHIP OF PATNA.* 1868. 38pp.
Cited in Ladendorf.

1030
IO

Tayler, William, ed. *ADDENDA TO THE CORRESPONDENCE RELATIVE TO THE REMOVAL OF MR. W. TAYLER FROM THE COMMISSIONERSHIP OF PATNA.* Calcutta: John Gray, 1857.

Consists of two appendices: Appendix V contains 4pp and appendix VI contains 5pp.

1031

Tayler, William. *DEFENSE OF ARAH HOUSE AGAINST THREE MUTINOUS REGIMENTS AND A LARGE BODY OF INSURGENTS UNDER KOER SINGH.* London: Maclure & Co.

Cited in Ladendorf. Unable to locate.

1032
Bod

Tayler, William. *HISTORY AND THE PRESS ON THE CASE OF MR. WILLIAM TAYLER, LATE COMMISSIONER OF PATNA.* London: Henry Sotheran, 1876. 51pp.

Essentially the same format as Tayler's other writings; letters, testimonials, extracts from newspaper and books. All supporting his claims.

1033
Bod

Tayler, William. *JUSTICE IN THE NINETEENTH CENTURY, AN APPEAL TO BRITISH HONOR.* London: William Ridgway, 1885. 4+11+8+7+43+7+8+4 +25+4+11

This is a series of letters and extracts which Tayler collected in his ongoing attempt to clear his name. Included are extracts from letters Tayler received from many well known people of the time supporting his claim. In addition there are extracts from Kaye and Malleson and the leading journals of the day.

1034
RS

Tayler, William. *THE PATNA CRISIS OR THREE MONTHS IN PATNA DURING THE INSURRECTION OF 1857.* London: James Nisbet, 1858. Also 1882.

An edition was published by Thacker & Co. in Calcutta in 1858 entitled *"Our Crisis or Three Months in Patna."* 73pp. Tayler was the Commissioner of Patna and was removed under much controversy.

1035
Bod

Tayler, William. *VERITAS VICTRIX. Being letters and testimonials relating to the conduct of W. Tayler in the Indian Mutiny.* London: Ridgeway, 1878. 109pp. Pamphlet.
Contains many testimonial letters, extracts from Kaye and Malleson and generally the same type of discussion as his other books.

1036
IO

Tayler, William. *WHAT IS TRUTH?.* London: E. Westerton, 1872. viii & 65pp.
Contains four statements:
A. Parallel columns giving Halliday's official version and Tayler's "facts." Halliday was Tayler's immediate superior.
B. Extracts from letters of local citizens.
C. Extracts from letters of officials.
D. Extracts from periodicals, newspapers, etc.

1037
Bod

Tayler, William. Late Commissioner of Patna. *THIRTY EIGHT YEARS IN INDIA. From Juganath to the Himalaya Mountains.* London: W. H. Allen, 1881, 1882. 2 volumes. Vol. I, viii & 516pp. With 100 illus by the author. Vol. II, xv & 565pp. With frontis and 14 lithos.
An autobiography. See author Chaturbhuj (entry 264).

1038
RS

Taylor, A(licia) Camero. *GENERAL SIR ALEX TAYLOR. His Times, His Friends, and His Work. By his daughter.* London: Williams and Norgate, 1913. 2 volumes. xvi & 325pp. and xii & 325pp. 2 portraits and 8 folding maps.
Taylor was the directing engineer at the siege of Delhi. Good coverage of the Mutiny period.

1039
Bod

Taylor, Col. Philip Meadows. (ed. By Henry Bruce). *THE STORY OF MY LIFE.* Edinburgh & London: William Blackwood, 1877, 1878, 1882. Another edition London, 1920, edited by his daughter. xlvi & 500pp. Frontis, 1 plate and folding map at rear.
Approximately 60 pages on the Mutiny. Taylor served at Hyderabad.

1040
BL
080233.aa.13

Taylor, Colonel Philip Meadows. *LETTERS FROM MEADOWS TAYLOR, DEPUTY COMMISSIONER OF THE CEDED DISTRICTS IN THE DECCAN,*

WRITTEN DURING THE INDIAN REBELLION.
1857. London: John E. Taylor, 1857. 26pp.
Letters dated June 21, 1857, July 6 (from Nuldroog in
the Deccan), September 7 and 26 from Berar where he was
Deputy Commissioner.

1041
Bod
Taylor, Lucy. *SAHIB AND SEPOY OR, SAVING AN*
EMPIRE. London: John F. Shaw: ND. c. 1898. 368pp.
Fiction

1042
Bod
Taylor, Lucy. *THE STORY OF SIR HENRY*
HAVELOCK, THE HERO OF LUCKNOW. London, T.
Nelson & Sons 1894 72pp
Part of the "Stories of Noble Lives" series.

1043
Bod
Taylor, Lucy. *THE STORY OF SIR HENRY*
LAWRENCE; DEFENDER OF LUCKNOW. London:
T. Nelson & Son, 1894.
A popular biography of Lawrence. Part of the series,
"Stories of Noble Lives."

1044
RS
Taylor, P. J. O. *A FEELING OF QUIET POWER.*
Delhi: Harper Collins, 1994. 163pp. Paper.
A study of the siege of Lucknow. Taylor has a deep
knowledge of the Mutiny and has written a number of works
on the subject.

1045
RS
Taylor, P. J. O. *A STAR SHALL FALL.* New Delhi:
Harper Collins, 1993. 269pp. Paper. Illus.
A very well researched book on various aspects of
the Mutiny. This is not a general history but rather an
investigation and explanation of a number of events associated
with the Mutiny. A discussion of Europeans who turned
against the British, Leckey's book of fictions connected with
the Mutiny, Amy Horne, and some of the other famous
victims of the Mutiny.

1046
RS
Taylor, P. J. O. *CHRONICLES OF THE MUTINY*
& OTHER HISTORICAL SKETCHES. New Delhi:
Harper Collins, 1992. 184pp. Paper. Illus.
Approximately 15 sketches on various aspects of the
Mutiny. The sketches were all articles that appeared in the
New Delhi "Statesman." Sample chapters: "A Point of View
on the Mutiny," "Rani Lakshmibai of Jhansi," "Loyalty II,"
"The Tantalyzing Case of Tatya Topi," and others.

1047
RS
Taylor, P.J.O. *WHAT REALLY HAPPENED DURING THE MUTINY. A Day-by-day Account of the Major Events of 1857-1859 in India.* New Delhi: Oxford University Press, 1997. 323pp. Index, illustrations and an extensive bibliography.
Contains valuable information, however the day-by-day arrangement does not seem to be particularly useful for research purposes. Taylor has written extensively on the Mutiny and has produced a number of valuable works for the student of the period.

1048
RS
Taylor, P.J.O. (ed.). *A COMPANION TO THE INDIAN MUTINY OF 1857.* Delhi: Oxford University Press, 1996. x & 415pp. Numerous maps and illustrations
Excellent resource for study of the period. This is an attempt to provide an extensive collection of information on every aspect of the Mutiny. Entries include people, battles, cities, and annecdotal material on various aspects of the Mutiny. There are nearly 1500 main entries together with a checklist of about 1000 titles. The value of the work is enhanced by the inclusion of color plates showing some of the landmarks of the period.

1049
RS
Temple, Sir Richard. *LORD LAWRENCE.* London: Macmillan, 1889 & 1890. 203pp. Frontis. Men of Action Series.

1050
BL
Temple, Sir Richard. *MEN AND EVENTS OF MY TIME IN INDIA.* London: John Murray, 1882. xvii & 526pp. Index.
Temple was the Finance Minister of India, Lieut-Governor of Bengal and Governor of Bombay.
He mentions that it was his duty to inquire into the truth or error regarding the treatment of the European victims of the mutineers. He found the cases of outrage were often exaggerated and at times baseless. The work contains some interesting Mutiny material.

1051
Bod
Temple, Sir Richard. *THE STORY OF MY LIFE.* London: Cassell & Co., 1896. 2 vols. Vol. I, frontis, xvi & 299pp. Vol. II, xi & 331pp. with index.
One chapter regarding the Mutiny. Temple served under Sir John Lawrence, as his secretary, however he did not arrive back in India, having been on furlough, until late 1857.

Temple later became commissioner of the Lahore Division shortly after the Mutiny.

1052

Terrell, Richard (ed.). *JOHN CHALMERS, LETTERS FROM THE INDIAN MUTINY 1857-1859* Norwich: Michael Russell, ND. Frontis, table, map & 4 plates. Index. 192pp.
This is an updated version of Chalmers 1904 book, *"Letters Written from India During the Mutiny and Waziri Campaigns."* Terrell has omitted the letters concerned with the Waziri Campaign.
The editor offers the letters and usually a commentary on the important points found within the letters.

1053
IO

Thackeray, Brevet Colonel C. B. (ed.) *A SUBALTERN IN THE INDIAN MUTINY. Containing Some Letters of Lieut. Edward Talbot Thackeray, Bengal Engineers, Afterwards Colonel Sir E. T. Thackeray, VC. 1836-1927.* NC. NP. ND. Rept from the Royal Enginners Journal 1930-1931. VI parts.
Part I. Meerut 13pp. Part II Delhi Ridge. 14pp. One folding map. Part III Delhi-The Assault. 14pp. Frontis, Two photos and one folding map. Part IV Delhi to Lucknow 9pp. Frontis. Part V Lucknow to Bareilly-The Last Phase. 14pp. Three plates and one folding map. Part VI Five Victoria Crosses. 14pp. 2 plates.

1054
IO

Thackeray, Col. E. T. *TWO INDIAN CAMPAIGNS IN 1857-58.* Chatham: Royal Engineers Institute, 1896. vii & 130pp. 2 portraits, 11 folding plans maps and views, the latter from original Beato photos.
Thackeray served at Delhi, Lucknow in 1858, and the Rohilcund Campaign.

1055
IO

Thackeray, Edward Talbot. *REMINISCENCES OF THE INDIAN MUTINY (1857-1858) AND AFGHANISTAN, (1879).* London: Smith, Elder & Co., 1916. vi & 181pp.
Most of the information in this book had been published earlier. Contains *"Recollections of the Siege of Delhi,"* which is a memoir of General Sir Alexander Taylor and also a memoir of Hodson. Includes the capture of Lucknow in April of 1858.

1056
Taylor

Thatcher, M. and L. Carter (ed.). *CAMBRIDGE SOUTH ASIAN ARCHIVE: RECORDS OF THE*

BRITISH PERIOD IN SOUTH ASIA HELD IN
THE CENTRE OF SOUTH ASIAN STUDIES,
UNIVERSITY OF CAMBRIDGE. London: 1973,
1980, 1983, and 1987?

1057
RS
Thomas, Henry Harington. *THE LATE
REBELLION IN INDIA, AND OUR FUTURE
POLICY.* Exeter: William Clifford, 1858. 31pp.
Absolves the Hindus of a conspiracy on the grounds they
were not intelligent enough. The real blame rests with the
Mahomedans. The author states, "In short, I do not hesitate
to declare my belief that our Christian Missionaries would be
found, on the strictest enquiry, to have been held in general
respect, if not affection, by the Natives of India." Thomas was
in the Bengal Civil Service.

1058
RS
Thompson, Edward John. *THE OTHER SIDE OF
THE MEDAL.* London: Hogarth Press, 1925. 143pp,
also a 1930, 3rd edition.
This work is well known in Mutiny literature. The author
claims the Indians are, as a whole, unable to write their view of
the Mutiny, so Thompson will act as their voice. Thompson
is highly critical of the British and the early Mutiny literature.
Includes a short historiography on the Mutiny and a section of
personal notes on some of the major British figures.

1059
RS
Thomson, Captain Mowbray. *THE STORY OF
CAWNPORE: By One of the Only Two Survivors of the
Cawnpore Garrison.* London: Richard Bentley, 1859.
vii, 262pp Frontis, folding plan and 2 plates.
A title of major importance in Mutiny literature.
Thomson escaped the massacre at Cawnpore via the Ganges.
His book vividly describes the condition of the British forces
in the entrenchments during the siege. Although events are
not presented in an absolutely chronological order the work is
generally considered quite accurate.
Thomson died with the rank of General in Reading,
England, February 24, 1917, at the age of 86.

1060
BL
Thorburn, Septimus S. *THE PUNJAB IN PEACE
AND WAR.* Edinburgh: William Blackwood & Son,
1904. vi & 358pp. 6 folding maps at rear. Bibliography.
Two chapters on the Mutiny. Thorburn was a retired civil
servant and late Commissioner of the Punjab.

1061
RS

Thornhill, Mark. *THE PERSONAL ADVENTURES AND EXPERIENCES OF A MAGISTRATE DURING THE RISE, PROGRESS AND SUPPRESSION OF THE INDIAN MUTINY.* London: John Murray, 1884. vi & 334pp. Frontis of the Great Ghaut at Muttra. Plate and folding plan of Agra Fort.

Thornhill was the magistrate and collector at Muttra (Mathura) in the Agra division. Malleson made extensive use of the book and states, "Of all the books written regarding the Mutiny not one is more interesting than that in which Mr. Thornhill records his personal adventures and experiences as a magistrate in 1857-58."

1062
Maggs 1991

Thornton, Dep. Surgeon General James Howard. *MEMORIES OF SEVEN CAMPAIGNS. A Record of Thirty-five Years service in the Indian Medical Department in India, China, Egypt, and Sudan.* London: Archibald Constable, 1895. xxviii & 359pp.

Thornton was attached to HM 5th at the Relief of Arrah. Subsequently he joined the 1st Bengal Europeans.

1063
Sut

Thornton, Thomas Henry. *GENERAL SIR RICHARD MEADE AND THE FEUDATORY STATES OF CENTRAL AND SOUTHERN INDIA.* London: NP. 1898. 390pp. Portrait, map, and 16 plates.

Sixty pages on the Mutiny. Discusses Gwalior to its recapture and the pursuit and capture of Tantia Tope.

1064

Thurburn, E. A. *REMINISCENCES OF THE INDIAN REBELLION.*

See entry for Staff Officer (Entry 992).

1065
NAM
Ind.Inf.7 Regt.

Tindall, Captain John William Brooke. *THE SEVENTH RAJPUT REGIMENT IN THE INDIAN MUTINY OF 1857.* Ahmednagar: S.P.G. Mission Printing Press, Nov. 20, 1936.

The author was killed November 25, 1936 on the North Western Frontier. A note in the NAM copy states that Michael Joyce drew most of his information concerning the Indian regiments serving during the Mutiny from this book.

1066
Bod

Tisdall, Evelyn Ernest Percy. *MRS. DUBERLY'S CAMPAIGNS. An English Woman's Experiences in the*

Crimean War and Indian Mutiny. London & Chicago: Rand McNally, 1963. 224pp. 12 Illus.
A biography of Mrs. Dubberly using her published journals and letters to her sister Selina. The majority of the book deals with the Crimean War. Her experiences of the Mutiny was with the Rajputana Column.

1067
NAM
92 TOM

Tombs, Henry VC. *MEMOIR OF MAJOR GENERAL SIR HENRY TOMBS.* Woolwich: Royal Artillery Institution, 1913. xii & 88pp. Frontis & 5 illus. Appendix.
Tombs commanded the artillery at Meerut during the uprising. Later he proceeded to Delhi where he commanded number four battery at the siege. Tombs was awarded the VC for gallentry at Delhi in a famous action with Lt. Hills. Includes about thirty pages on the Mutiny.
Finely engraved gilt title. Badges front and rear. Full blue calf.

1068

Tracy, Louis. *RED YEAR.* London: F. V. White, 1908. 329pp.
Also New York: Edwards Clode. 1907. Fiction.

1069
NAM 1857(54)

Travers, Lieut. Gen. Jas. *THE EVACUATION OF INDORE 1857 BY LIEUT. GEN. JAS. TRAVERS, VC, VERSUS THE HISTORY OF THE SEPOY REVOLT BY SIR JOHN KAYE.* London: Henry S. King & Co., 1876. 24pp.
Refutes Kaye's version of events at Indore. Travers was in command at Indore. Travers also defends Durand's actions.

1070
Ames

Trevelyan, Charles Edward. (Indophilus). *THE LETTERS OF INDOPHILUS TO "THE TIMES."* London: Longman, Brown, Green, Longmans, and Roberts, January, 1858. 2nd ed. With additional notes. 97pp.
Fifteen letters including: 1) Retribution-Delhi 2) Reconstruction of the Bengal Army 5) Causes of the Mutiny 6) Patna 7) Transportation of the Surviving Mutineers 14) The Evangelization of India.

1071
RS

Trevelyan, George Otto. *THE COMPETITION WALLAH.* London: Macmillan, 1864. ix & 452pp.
A work very biased in nature. Originally published in Macmillan's Magazine, it consists of twelve letters written to

the editor of Macmillan Magazine by a civil servant in India by the name of H. Broughton (Trevelyan). Letter IV is "A Story of the Great Mutiny" which concerns events at Arrah. Letter IX is "British Temper Towards India, Before, During, and Since the Mutiny." Trevelyan has often been recognized as a highly skilled writer.

1072
RS

Trevelyan, Sir George (Otto). *CAWNPORE*. London: Macmillan, 1865. 2nd ed. v & 342pp. 1866, 3rd edition also 4th ed. 1894, 280pp.

George Otto Trevelyan was the son of Charles Trevelyan, past Governor of Madras and Finance Member of the Governor General's Council 1862-1865. "*Cawnpore*" was written from information supplied by witnesses in depositions given to Colonel Williams, Commissioner of Police in the Northwestern Provinces. The book is known for its literary value however, great doubt has been placed on its accuracy by both Majumdar in "*Sepoy Mutiny*" and Sen in "*Eighteen Fifty Seven.*" Interesting comments on this book may be found in Brantlinger, "*Rule of Darkness*" pages 202-204 (Entry 189).

1073
Ames

Trevor, George. [A Man of York]. *THE COMPANY'S RAJ*. Edinburgh & London: William Blackwood & Sons, 1858.

Discusses the religious questions in India. England has a duty to convert the heathen.

1074
RS

Trotter, Capt. L. *A LEADER OF LIGHT HORSE. Life of Hodson.* Edinburgh: William Blackwood & Sons., 1901. xii & 396pp. Portrait and folding map.

Rept. Everymans Library 1910.

1075
RS

Trotter, Captian Lionel J. *THE BAYARD OF INDIA: A Life of General J. Outram.* Edinburgh: Blackwood, 1903. x & 320pp. Also 1906, 1909, 1913. All with 240pp. Frontis and one plate. Index.

Trotter states that this is not to be considered merely an abridgement of Goldsmid's biography of Outram.

1076
RS

Trotter, L. J. *THE LIFE OF JOHN NICHOLSON.* London: John Murray & Co., 1897. 1st and 2nd ed. xii & 333pp. 3 plates and 3 maps. 3rd through 7th ed. 1898. 8th ed. 1900 9th ed. 1906 xii 333pp. 3 folding maps. There was a reprint in 1978 and 1987 ed. x & 332pp. 1 plate and 3 folding maps.

Standard biography of Nicholson. Nicholson lost two brothers in India, Alexander and William. Alexander murdered by Afghans and William under mysterious circumstances. His brother Charles lost an arm at Delhi and of course John was shot and killed at Delhi.

1077
RS

Trotter, Lionel James. *LORD LAWRENCE: A SKETCH OF HIS PUBLIC CAREER.* London: W. H. Allen & Co., 1880. vi & 132pp. Frontis. A short biography.

1078
Bod

Trotter, Lionel James. *LIFE OF THE MARQUIS OF DALHOUSIE.* London: W. H. Allen & Co., 1889, 1895. xiii & 235pp.
A general biography. Part of the Statesmen series.

1079
BL
10815.bbb.18

Trotter, Lionel James. *WILLIAM TAYLOR OF PATNA: A BRIEF ACCOUNT OF HIS SPLENDID SERVICES, HIS CRUEL WRONGS, AND HIS THIRTY YEARS STRUGGLE FOR JUSTICE.* London: S. Sidders, 1887. Paper. 49pp.
Brief extracts from letters received from 1857 to 1884.

1080

Tucker, Henry Carre. *A LETTER TO AN OFFICIAL CONCERNED IN THE EDUCATION OF INDIA.* London: W.H. Dalton, 1858. 14pp.
Tucker was the rather controversial commissioner at Benares in 1857. Cited in Ladendorf.

1081
Bod

Tucker, Henry Carre. *A LETTER TO THE RT. HON. LORD STANLEY, MP, SECRETARY OF STATE FOR INDIA.* London: W. H. Dalton, 1858. 15pp.
Discusses education, government,efforts to expose Christianity to the populace and the effect this exposure will have on the Indians.

1082
RS

Tucker, Major General H. T. *A GLANCE AT THE PAST AND THE FUTURE IN CONNECTION WITH THE INDIAN REVOLT.* London: Effingham Wilson, 1857. 41pp.
Tucker served in the Bengal Army. He advocates a number of measures which he feels will prevent another mutiny. Tucker feels that the English were too easy with the Indians and that they should have been treated with more vigour. The natives are not to be trusted, especially

the Muslims. Tucker also claims that Colonel Birch, the Secretary to the Government in the Military Department, was unfit for the job and held too much power. In 1853 Tucker was Adjutant General of the Bengal Army. He advised the government against the use of the greased cartridges which had been sent out in 1853 as an experiment. This warning was not acted upon by the Commander-in-Chief. There were no problems experienced with the cartridges at this time.

1083
RS

Tuker, Lt. General Sir F. ed. *THE CHRONICLE OF PRIVATE HENRY METCALFE OF HM 32ND REGIMENT OF FOOT TOGETHER WITH LT. JOHN EDMONSTONE'S LETTER TO HIS MOTHER OF 4TH JANUARY 1858.* London: Cassell, 1953. x & 117pp. 2 colored plates, 4 other plates and a plan.
The journal of a private soldier at Lucknow.

1084
Bod

Turnbull, Brevet Major John Robertson. *SKETCHES OF DELHI TAKEN DURING THE SIEGE.* London: Maclean, 1858. 14 plates and title page.
Folio. Title page: The Selimghur Bridge. 1) British camp from left rear. 2) The General's tent. 3) The Ridge. 4) Delhi from the Flagstaff Tower. 5) The Flagstaff Tower. 6) Hindoo Rao's House. 7) General Barnard's Grave. 8) The Mound Battery 9) The Sugzee Mundee from the Mound. 10) The Sugzee Mundee pickets. 11) Breach in the curtain Cashmere Bastion. 12) Breach in the curtain Water Bastion. 13) Lahore Gate of the palace. 14) Easy times. With descriptive text.

1085
BL
9056.bbb.26

Turnbull, Lt.-Colonel John Robertson. *LETTERS WRITTEN DURING THE SIEGE OF DELHI.* Torquay: Directory Printing Works, 1876 & 1883 30pp.
Turnbull was a Lieutenent in H.M. 75th and ADC to General Barnard, General Reid, and General Wilson.

1086
RS

Tweeddale, Lord ed. *LETTERS FROM THE FIELD DURING THE INDIAN REBELLION.* London: Waterlow & Sons, 1907 [6] & 73pp.
Tweeddale was the Governor and the Commander-in-Chief of the Madras Government in 1844. At the time of the letters, May 1857, Tweeddale was Deputy Commissioner of Simla and Superintendent of Hill States. The letters are from Lieut. Macdowell of the Bengal Fusiliers; Major Tombs, Bengal Horse Artillery; Captain Coghill of the

2nd Bengal and Col. G. Campbell, H.M. 52nd Regiment.
Each of these men served during the Delhi siege.

1087
RS   Tyler, R. A. J. *BLOODY PROVOST.* NC. Phillimore,
1980. 245pp. Index.
A history of the Provost Marshals and military police.
Two chapters on India related to Delhi during the Mutiny.

1088
IO   Tyrrell, Lieut. General F. H. *IN PIAM MEMORIAM:
THE SERVICES OF THE MADRAS NATIVE
TROOPS IN THE SUPPRESSION OF THE MUTINY
OF THE BENGALI ARMY.* NC. NP. ND. (1907).
39pp.

1089
RS   Tyrrell, Isaac. *FROM ENGLAND TO THE
ANTIPODES AND INDIA-1846 TO 1902, With
Startling Revelations, or Fifty Six Years of My Life in the
Indian Mutiny, Police, and Jails.* Madras: Thompson &
Co., At the Minerva Press, 1902. Ladendorf gives this
as 1904. There were apparently two editions, 333pp. &
342pp.
Quite an interesting day by day account of life in the
armed services in pre and post Mutiny India. Tyrrell served in
the Central India Campaign. Tyrrell was involved in events
at Banda and discusses some of the treasure found in the area.
There are about three chapters that deal with the Mutiny.

1090
IO   Urquhart, David. *THE REBELLION OF INDIA.*
London: D. Bryce, 1857. 45pp.
Part I: Mr. Disraeli; A Speech Reviewed. II: The
Illegality of the Acts of Abolishing Native Customs. III:
The Wonderous Tale of the Greased Cartridges. In
section I Urquhart discusses the faults of Britain in India's
administration. Suggests that India be brought directly
under a Minister and that European troops be substituted for
Indian troops. Section II is an indictment against the EIC for
backing laws which were inimical to good relations with the
Indians. Section III was originally published separately and
consists of 15pp.

1091
NAM 92USH   Usherwood, Charles William. *SERVICE JOURNAL
OF CHARLES WILLIAM USHERWOOD, 19TH
FOOT & 8TH FOOT, 1852-1864.* NC. Never
published, 1981.
A typed journal, photo-copied, in the National Army

Museum. About 92pp. concern the Mutiny. There is a
forward written by Kenneth Usher-Wood and dated 1981.
Part I Crimea 1-165pp. Part II Indian Mutiny 1-92pp.
Career Notes pages 93-99.

1092
IO   **Valbezen, Eugene de.** *THE ENGLISH AND INDIA.*
New Sketches. Translated by a Diplomate. (Holysley).
London: W.H. Allen & Co., 1883. xv & 498pp.
    Chaudhuri in *"English Historical Writings..."* states that
the book is "A familiar product of a western mixture of
colonialism and racialism which unfolds the romance of the
British Empire...." The book extolls the English in India and
denigrates the Asian in comparison to the European. It seems
a strange book coming from a French author especially since
the French were at one time in opposition to the English in
India. It appears more of a plea to recognize the benefits of
European colonial rights. This work had at least two editions
in France prior to 1878. Reprinted 1986, Gian Publishing,,
Delhi.

1093
BL   **Vansittart, Jane. Ed.** *FROM MINNIE, WITH LOVE.*
THE LETTERS OF A VICTORIAN LADY 1849-1861.
(MARIA LYDIA WOOD NEE BLANE). London: Peter
Davies, 1974. 188pp. 11 photos. Index.
    Maria Wood was a woman of 22, stationed at Jhelum
with her husband, Captain Wood. The letters, written by
Maria and her husband, are quite interesting.

1094
    Vaughan, John Luther. *MY SERVICES IN THE*
INDIAN ARMY AND AFTER. London: Archibald
Constable, 1904. 304pp
    Cited in Ladendorf.

1095
    Verner, Col. W. *THE MILITARY LIFE OF H.R.H.*
GEORGE, DUKE OF CAMBRIDGE. London: John
Murray, 1905. 2 vols, xl & 917pp. Eleven plates.
    Includes some Mutiny material.

1096
RS   **Verney, Lieut. Edmund Hope.** *THE SHANNON'S*
BRIGADE IN INDIA. Being Some Account of Sir William
Peel's Naval Brigade in the India Campaign of 1857-1858.
London: Saunders, Otley & Co., 1862. xiv & 153pp.
Frontis of William Peel and 2 folding maps.
    Peel was present at Lucknow. He was very highly thought
of by all who knew him. He died at the age of 33 of smallpox
at Cawnpore in 1858. Peel received the VC for bravery during

the Crimean War. Peel was the son of a past Prime Minister of Great Britain.

1097
RS

Verney, Major General G. L. *THE DEVIL'S WIND. The Story of the Naval Brigade at Lucknow. From the Letters of Edmund Hope Verney and Other Papers Concerning the Enterprise of the Ship's Company of H.M.S. Shannon in the Campaign in India 1857-58.* London: Hutchinson & Co., 1956. 176pp. Frontis and 11 illus. Two maps, bibliography and index.

The author was the nephew of Edmund Hope Verney author of "*The Shannons Brigade in India.*" Edmund's step-mother's younger sister was Florence Nightengale and Brig. Adrian Hope was a second cousin of Edmund's.

1098
RS

Vibart, Col. H(enry) M. *RICHARD BAIRD SMITH: The Leader of the Delhi Heroes in 1857.* London: Archibald Constable, 1897. xii & 172pp. Portrait and large folding map of Delhi.

"Private correspondence of the commanding engineer during the siege and other interesting letters hitherto unpublished." Many of the letters from Smith to his wife are reproduced here.

1099
RS

Vibart, Colonel Edward *THE SEPOY MUTINY: As Seen by a Subaltern From Delhi to Lucknow.* London: Smith, Elder, 1898 & Scribner NY, xi & 308pp. 12 plates and 1 folding map.

Vibart was stationed at Delhi when the Mutiny broke out. Vibart includes a chapter on the telegraph. A second edition of the book appeared in 1899. Vibart's parents, Major Edward Vibart and Emily Vibart were killed at Cawnpore.

1100
Sut

Vibart, Colonel Henry M. *THE LIFE OF GENERAL SIR HARRY N. D. PRENDERGAST, THE HAPPY WARRIOR.* London: NP. 1914. 445pp. 25 plates, 3 maps.

60 pages on Malwa and Central India during the Mutiny.

1101
Sut/Nigam

Wagentreiber, Florence. *REMINISCENCES OF THE SEPOY REBELLION OF 1857.* Lahore: Civil and Military Gazette, 1911. vi & 57pp.

Florence Wagentreiber was the grand-daughter of Colonel James Skinner the half-caste leader of Skinner's Horse. Skinner (1778-1841)had fourteen wives and was almost a legend in India at the time. This monograph relates the family's escape from Delhi on May 11, 1857.

1102
Sut   **Wagentreiber, George.** *OUR ESCAPE FROM DELHI.* Delhi: Indian Punch Press, ND. 7 pp. Pamphlet.
    No title page. Printed at the Indian Punch Press by Dabee Sahay. Bound in blue cloth by A. J. Combridge of Bombay and Madras.

1103
BL 9008.c.33   **Wagentreiber, Miss. (Florence).** *THE STORY OF OUR ESCAPE FROM DELHI IN MAY 1857. FROM PERSONAL NARRATIONS BY THE LATE GEORGE WAGENTREIBER AND MISS HALDANE.* Delhi: Imperial Hall Press, 1894. 39pp. 1 drawing.
    Much is copied from Haldane's earlier work. See Haldane, Julia. (Entry 118)

1104
Bod   **Wakefield, Lieut-Col Henry Funj.** *SOME OF THE WORDS, DEEDS, AND SUCCESS OF HAVELOCK IN THE CAUSE OF TEMPERANCE IN INDIA.* London: William Tweedie, 1861. 16pp.
    The effects of alcohol on the men and how Havelock was a driving force for temperance in the army. Apparently Wakefield was a very old friend of Havelock.

1105
RS   **Walker, Col. T. N.** *THROUGH THE MUTINY: Reminiscences of Thirty Years Active Service and Sport in India 1854-1883.* London: Gibbings & Co., 1907. xxi & 203pp. Portrait and 11 illus.
    Walker served at the seige of Delhi and Rohilcund Campaign.

1106
BL   **Wallace, Charles Lindsay.** *FATEHGARH CAMP, 1777-1857.* Lucknow, K. D. Seth, 1934. 243pp. Frontis and two folding maps.
    A history of Fatehgarh camp with some mention of the effects of the Mutiny.

1107
    Walmsley, Joshua. *HINTS ON THE REORGANIZATION OF THE INDIAN ARMY. Being Extracts From A Series of Letters Addressed to Sir Joshua Walmsley By an English Officer.* London: Chapman and Hall, 1858. 32pp.
    Cited by Ladendorf.

1108
RS   **Walsh, Rev. J. Johnston.** *A MEMORIAL OF THE*
FUTTEHGURH MISSION AND THE MARTYRED
MISSIONARIES. With Some Remarks on the Mutiny In
India. Philadelphia: Joseph Wilson & Co. London:
James Nesbit Co., 1858. 338pp. Frontis and 11
illustrations and 2 maps.
        This title was also published by Nisbet in London in
1859 and again in Philadelphia in 1859 by the Presbyterian
Board of Publication. The title page states Walsh was the sole
surviving member of the Futtehgurh mission of the Board of
Foreign Missions of the Presbyterian Church.

1109
RS   **Ward, Andrew.** *OUR BONES ARE SCATTERED.*
THE CAWNPORE MASSACRES AND THE INDIAN
MUTINY OF 1857. New York: Henry Holt, 1996.
xxviii & 704pp. Bibliography and index. 40 illus.
        This is the definitive work on the events at Cawnpore. A
massive book with years of research behind it. Extensive notes
and an excellent bibliography complement this particularly
well written account. The author lived in India and had a
deep knowledge of the Mutiny and Cawnpore. The book
suffers from a mediocre index.

1110
NAM 92 UTT   **Ward, Beatrice (ed.)** *LETTERS OF EDWIN*
UTTERTON FROM THE CRIMEA AND THE
INDIAN MUTINY. Gibralter: NP. ND. c. 1964. iii &
186pp. Portrait and folding genealogical chart at rear.
        Utterton arrived at Calcutta on September 9, 1857.
He served with the 23rd Foot, Royal Welsh Fusiliers. By
December he was at Cawnpore and by March, 1858, was on
his way to Lucknow and served there at least through January,
1859.

1111
IO/RS   **Waterfield, Arthur J.** *CHILDREN OF THE MUTINY.*
A Record of Those Now Living Who Were in India During
the Sepoy War. 1857-9. Worthing, UK: Caxton Printing,
November 1935. 14pp.
        The copy in the India Office includes a supplementary list
of April 1936.

1112
IO   **Watson, Bruce.** *THE GREAT INDIAN MUTINY.*
Colin Campbell and the Campaign at Lucknow. New York
and London: Praeger, 1991. xv & 138pp. Index and
bibliography.
        A general work.

1113
Bod
Watson, Edward Spencer. *JOURNAL. INDIA: With H.M.S. "Shannon," Naval Brigade, From August 18th, 1858.* Kettering: W.E. and J. Goss, 1858, 1890. Reprinted in 1989 by the London Stamp Exchange. 131pp.

1858 is a mis-print and has been corrected in the India Office to read 1857. The Shannon arrived in 1857. Watson went through the entire Shannon Brigade experience.

Selina Charlotte Evans (nee Watson) daughter of the author, wrote an errata slip dated 1932 which appears in the Bodleian copy. Watson was 15 years old when he accompanied the Shannon Brigade.

1114
Sut
Weston, Major C. S. *KAZAN SINGH. An Episode of My Life.* NC. Privately printed, ND. c. 1898. 14pp.

From Sutcliffe: Not cited by Ladendorf. Affectionate memories of the Sikh servant Weston found in a Calcutta jail and who saved his life at the assault of Chandipore in the Mutiny. Weston's little pamphlet ends where he recommends Kazan Singh to his brother-in-law Captain Robert Godby who had been ordered to China.

1115
Sut
Weston, Major C. S. *PRIVATE MEMORANDA OF THE SECOND PUNJAB WAR OF 1848 AND OF THE MUTINY IN INDIA, 1857.* NC. Privately printed. ND. c. 1910. 82pp with three actual photographs of pen & ink maps of the Sikh War.

From Sutcliffe: The first 62 pages are on Weston's regimental service in the Second Sikh War. (36th NI). The rest of the book concerns his services in the Mutiny in which he served with the Gurkha contingent in the Sarun Field Force under Colonel Rowcroft until he was wounded at Chandipore. The photographs are albumen prints which suggests an earlier date than 1910 but the editor refers in her notes to incidents (pp 68) almost up to the end of her father's life. Not in Ladendorf

1116
Bod
Wheeler, Edmund H. *WHAT SHALL WE DO AT DELHI? An Englishman's Letter to the Humanitarians.* London: Daniel F. Oakey, 1857. 34pp.

A very black and white view of the need for retribution in the reconquest of Delhi. The siege of Delhi is God's work and Wheeler offers four proofs or chapters for the right of the British to take Delhi and destroy the sepoys. A very inflamatory work full of indignation.

1117
RS

White, Col. Samuel Dewe. *COMPLETE HISTORY OF THE INDIAN MUTINY.* Weston-Super-Mare: J. Marche, 1885. iv & 275pp. No illustrations.
White was stationed in Agra. He states he is the only participant in the Mutiny to write a general history of the war. His sources include Shadwell's *"Life of Lord Clyde,"* Goldsmid's *"Life of Sir James Outram,"* and Smith's *"Life of Lord Lawrence."* In addition he had access to the notes of General Sir Charles Reid who fought at Delhi. White states that he has written "the truth, the whole truth, and nothing but the truth...."

1118
RS

White, Michael. *LACHMI BAI, RANI OF JHANSI.* New York: J.F. Taylor, 1901. Frontis and five plates, 297pp.
An historical novel.

1119

White, Samuel Dewe. *INDIAN REMINISCENCES.* London: W.H. Allen. 1880. 263pp.
Cited in Ladendorf.

1120
RAI

Whitton, Lieut-Colonel F. E. *THE LAST OF THE PALADINS.* NC. NP. 1934. 28pp.
Reprinted from a periodical, title unknown. June 1934. A short essay on the career of Hugh Rose through the Mutiny.

1121
Maggs

Wigram, Francis Spencer. *MUTINY AT MEERUT, 1857-58. Being Extracts from Letters from the Joint-Magistrate of that Station. For Private Use.* Southampton, England: Privately Printed, ND. c. 1860. 56pp.
Wigram and Robert Dunlop were Joint-Magistrates in Meerut.

1122
RS

Wilberforce, Reginald Garton. *AN UNRECORDED CHAPTER OF THE INDIAN MUTINY. Being the Personal Reminiscences of Reginald G. Wilberforce Compiled From a Diary and Letters Written on the Spot.* London: John Murray, 1894. xix & 235pp. 8 plates; 2nd ed. 1894. xviii & 234pp. 8 plates; 3rd ed. 1895. xviii & 240pp.
Wilberforce served in the 52nd Light Infantry as a boy of 19. He marched down to Delhi with Nicholson's column. He is quite complimentary towards Nicholson. After publication there were strong attacks on the accuracy of the work and even upon the veracity of the author.

1123
Wilkinson, Osborn and Johnson Wilkinson.
MEMOIRS OF THE GEMINI GENERALS,
PERSONAL ANECDOTES, SPORTING
ADVENTURES, AND SKETCHES OF
DISTINGUISHED OFFICERS. London: A. D. Innes,
1896. 491pp.
Little on the Mutiny.

1124
RS
Wilkinson-Latham, Christopher. Color plates by
G. A. Embleton. *THE INDIAN MUTINY.* London:
Osprey Publishing, 1977. 40pp.
Contains color plates of the uniforms of the various
regiments that served in the Mutiny. Osprey "Men at Arms"
Series.

1125
IO ORW.   **Williams, Donovan.** *AN ECHO OF THE INDIAN*
1997.a.1344(b) *MUTINY, THE PROPOSED BANISHMENT OF*
BAHADUR SHAH II TO THE CAPE COLONY, 1857.
NC. NP. 1972. Pages 265-268.
An offprint from Historia Vol. 17 Num. 4, Dec. 1972.

1126
IO
Williams, Rev. Edward Adams *THE CRUISE OF*
THE PEARL ROUND THE WORLD. With an Account
of the Operations of the Naval Brigade in India. London:
Richard Bentley, 1859. xii & 311pp. Frontis.
The Pearl was assigned to the South American and Pacific
Stations but eventually reached China and was thence ordered
to India where its crew took part in Mutiny operations. They
were in several operations with the Ghurkas.

1127
IO/   **Williams, Frederick Smeeton.** *GENERAL*
BL10817.h.2 *HAVELOCK AND CHRISTIAN SOLDIERSHIP.*
London: Judd & Glass, 1858. 12pp.

1128
IO 9057.h.2 **Williams, George Walter.** *MEMORANDUM ON*
THE MUTINY AND OUTBREAK AT MEERUT.
Allahabad: Government Press, 1858. 49 pages.
See Mutiny in India. Bound with other material.

1129
RS
Williams, Noel St. John. *JUDY O'GRADY & THE*
COLONEL'S LADY: THE ARMY WIFE AND CAMP
FOLLOWER SINCE 1660. London: Brassey, 1988. xii
& 269pp.Notes and index. Frontis & 42 illus.

Includes a chapter "Women Face the Indian Mutineers."

1130
IO 9057.h.2   **Williams. F.** *NARRATIVE OF EVENTS ATTENDING THE OUTBREAK OF DISTURBANCES AND THE RESTORATION OF AUTHORITY IN THE DISTRICT OF MEERUT IN 1857-58.* Allahabad: Nov. 15, 1858. 68pp.
   See Mutiny in India. (Entry 448)

1131
IO   **Williamson, George M. D.** *NOTES ON THE WOUNDED FROM THE MUTINY IN INDIA WITH A DESCRIPTION OF THE PREPARATIONS OF GUNSHOT INJURIES CONTAINED IN THE MUSEUM OF FORT PITT.* London: John Churchill, 1859. iv & 124pp. 11 plates.
   The appendix contains a plate and information on the use of the dooley. Describes in detail the various types of wounds and their treatment.

1132
Bod   **Williamson, John Vaughan.** *FALLEN HEROES OF THE INDIAN WAR. A POEM. IN MEMORY OF HAVELOCK AND OTHER BRITONS GLORIOUSLY FALLEN IN DEFENCE OF ENGLAND'S SUPREMACY IN ASIA DURING THE SEPOY REBELLION OF 1857-8.* London: S. H. Lindley, 1858. 96pp.
   The actual poem is 51pp. The remainder of the book consists of notes on Nicholson, Neill, William Williamson (the author's brother), Major General C. S. Fagan and his brother Lieut-Col James Fagan, Captain Robert Fagan, Captain James Fagan and Lieut. Sanders.

1133
RS   **Wilson, Archdale.** *ARCHDALE WILSON'S LETTERS DURING THE MUTINY.* NC. NP. 1916. 118pp.
   Wilson was the commander at the Siege of Delhi. The book contains privately typed letters beginning May 2nd, 1857 to March 18th, 1858.

1134
Bod   **Wilson, Daniel. Bishop of Calcutta.** *HUMILIATION IN NATIONAL TROUBLES. A SERMON DELIVERED AT ST. PAUL'S CATHEDRAL, CALCUTTA ON FRIDAY, JULY 24TH 1857. BEING A DAY APPOINTED FOR HUMILIATION*

THROUGHOUT BRITISH INDIA. London: Seeley, Jackson & Halliday, 1857. 22pp.

All the Christians of India must offer humiliation, repentance and hope for the terrible judgement which the Lord has visited upon India. Some of the British sins in India are: 1) Too close connection with the vices and idolatry of Brahmanism 2) The connection of the Government with the opium trade 3) The favor shown to the anti-social and anti- Christian civil system of caste 4) The profanation of the Lord's Day.

1135
Bod

Wilson, Daniel. Bishop of Calcutta. *PRAYER, THE REFUGE OF A DISTRESSED CHURCH. A SERMON DELIVERED AT ST. PAUL'S CATHEDRAL, CALCUTTA ON SUNDAY, JUNE 28TH, 1857, ON THE OCCASION OF THE RECENT MUTINIES.* London: Seeley, Jackson & Halliday, 1857. 24pp.

Discusses what types of prayer to offer for the relief of India.

1136

Wilson, Francesca Henrietta. *RAMBLES IN NORTHERN INDIA.* London: Sampson Low, Marston Low and Searle, 1876. 86pp. Frontis. Some plates colored.

"With Incidents and Descriptions of Many Scenes of the Mutiny, Including Agra, Delhi, Lucknow, Cawnpore, Allahabad, Etc. With Twelve Large Photographic Views." Cited in both Kaul and Jain.

1137
RS/Ames

Wilson, John Cracroft. *NARRATIVE OF EVENTS ATTENDING THE OUTBREAK OF DISTURBANCES AND THE RESTORATION OF AUTHORITY IN THE DISTRICT OF MORADABAD IN 1857-58.* London: Privately printed at the "Anglo-American Times Press" Strand, 1871. [4] 33 [14] Folio. Folding map, glossary.

Originally published in Calcutta in 1859 by order of Lord Canning. This apparently was a very limited printing and soon became unavailable. Wilson moved to New Zealand and died there in 1881. The appendix contains a number of facsimiles of various correspondence. Wilson was a Sessions Judge at Moradabad at the outbreak of the Mutiny. He had served the government at least 30 years prior to the Mutiny. The Ames Library 1871 edition has two plates of Wilson at the front of the book. One dated 1857 and one dated 1871.

Another color plate dated 1872 is also of Wilson. Also see listing for Mutiny in India.(Entry 448)

1138

Wilson, John.; *THE INDIAN MILITARY REVOLT VIEWED IN ITS RELIGIOUS ASPECTS.* Bombay: Smith, Taylor and Co., 1857. Pamphlet.
Cited in Ladendorf. Unable to locate.

1139
Bod

Wilson, Minden. *HISTORY OF THE BEHAR INDIGO FACTORIES; Reminiscences of Behar; Tirhoot and its Inhabitants of the Past; History of the Behar Light Horse.* Calcutta: Calcutta General Printing Co., 1908. viii & 334pp.
Apparently this is composed of four previous works. The author lived in Behar and offers reminiscences of the Mutiny and the defence of Arrah House. This portion was written in 1887.

1140
RS

Wimberley, Douglas. *SOME ACCOUNT OF THE PART TAKEN BY THE 79TH REGIMENT OR CAMERON HIGHLANDERS IN THE INDIAN MUTINY CAMPAIGN IN 1858.* Inverness: Northern Chronicle Office, 1891. 82pp.
Reprinted from the Highland Monthly Magazine, 1891. Contains a folding general map of Northern India in rear pocket.

1141
NAM1857(54)   **Windham, Lieut. General Charles Ash. K.C.B.** *OBSERVATIONS SUPPORTED BY DOCUMENTS BEING A SUPPLEMENT TO COL. ADYE'S DEFENSE OF CAWNPORE.* London: Longman, Green, Longman, Roberts & Green, 1865. 31 pp. 1 map.
Windham states that this late entry in his defence is because he now had permission to publish certain letters that Adye could not publish when he wrote his book. A marginal note in the NAM copy states that the army at Cawnpore was very anti-Windham.
See Adye, *"The Defence of Cawnpore"* (Entry 8).

1142
BL

Winslow, Octavius. *HONORING GOD AND ITS REWARD. A LESSON FROM THE LIFE OF THE LATE GENERAL SIR HENRY HAVELOCK. K.C.B.* London: Bath, 1858. 50pp.
Published in paper and cloth. About one half of the

pamphlet illustrates the proposition that man should honor God. The remaining portion uses Havelock as an example of a man that honored the devine and as a "Beautiful illustration of the great truth that we have been expounding--Them that honor me I will honor."

1143
Bod

Wintringham, Thomas. *MUTINY. Being a Survey of Mutinies from Spartacus to Invergordon.* London: Stanley Nott, 1936. 355pp. US edition by Fortuny's, New York.
    One chapter on the Mutiny. 53pp. Wintringham gives a rather balanced historical account.

1144

Wise, James M.D. *DIARY OF A MEDICAL OFFICER DURING THE GREAT INDIAN MUTINY OF 1857.* Cork: Guy & Co., 1894. v & 377pp.
    Wise went out to India in the service of the East India Company in 1856. He was appointed as a surgeon of artillery at Meerut. The book is a fine, detailed diary of his service. Wise is another to report that when Hodson captured the Princes he also captured a European, thought to be the Quarter-Master Sergeant of the 28th NI. He was captured wearing native dress. From Delhi Wise went on to Cawnpore and Lucknow. Cited in Ladendorf.

1145
RS

Witts, The Rev. B. L. *THE WORDS SHE WROTE: Or the Blood Stained Leaf. A True and Touching Story of a Young Lady; and Two Highlanders at Lucknow.* London: NP. 1859, 1860. vi & 101pp.
    Contains the story of the religious awakening of two Highlanders. Most of the book however is a religious tract not pertaining to Lucknow.

1146
RS

Wolseley, Field Marshal Garnet Joseph 1ˢᵗ Viscount, Baron Wolseley of Cairo and of Wolseley *THE STORY OF A SOLDIERS LIFE.* London: Archibald Constable, 1903. NY: Scribner, 1903. 2 vols. Vol. I, Frontis, xi & 398pp. 2 plans. Vol. II. Frontis, xi & 383pp. 1 plate.
    The set contains nine chapters on the Mutiny. Both volumes are indexed separately.

1147

Wood, Field Marshal Sir Henry Evelyn. VC. *THE REVOLT IN HINDUSTAN 1857-59.* London: Metheun, 1908. xvi & 367pp. 8 plates and 5 folding maps.

This work originally appeared as articles in the "Times" in October 1907. Mainly descriptive of military movements. Written many years after Wood took part in the suppression of the Mutiny. Wood eventually reached the rank of Field Marshal, together with his Mutiny contemporaries Roberts and Wolseley. Wood is quite free from bias in this book although he is not analytical but merely descriptive of events.

1148
Sut

Wood, Field Marshal Sir Henry Evelyn. VC. *WINNOWED MEMORIES.* London: Cassell, 1917, 1918. xii & 406pp. 8 portraits. 1918 (407pp.).
A collection of essays that includes some work on the Mutiny.

1149
Sut

Wood, Field Marshal Sir Henry Evelyn. VC. *FROM MIDSHIPMAN TO FIELD MARSHAL.* London: Methuen, 1906. 2 vols. xiv & 322pp; vii & 299pp. 24 illus. And maps.
Volume I contains about 45 pages on the Mutiny.

1150
RS

Wrench, Lieut. Colonel Edward Mason. *NOT TO REVENGE BUT TO PROTECT.* London: National Army Museum, 1907. Photocopy. Never published. 18pp + 15pp.
Photocopy of a typescript concerning the escape of Brevet Major Henry Kirke from the rebels at Nowgong in Central India. Written by his cousin Edward Wrench. The Major dies shortly after the escape but his son, Henry, continues on with the small party. Wrench, the author, also served during the Mutiny and gives his personal experiences. The last two pages concern the reunion at the Albert Hall of the Mutiny veterans. Attached is a copy of Lord Roberts speech to the reunion.

1151
Bod

Wright, Rev. Charles H(enry) H(amilton). *MEMOIR OF JOHN LOVERING COOKE, Formerly Gunner in the Royal Artillery, and late Lay-Agent of the British Sailors Institute, Boulogne; With a Sketch of the Indian Mutiny of 1857-8, up to the Final Capture of Lucknow.* London: J. Nisbet, 1873. xi & 228pp.
Cooke arrived in Calcutta September 15, 1857. He proceeded to Lucknow, back to Cawnpore, and then back to Lucknow. This is an interesting work as told by Cooke to Rev. Wright. Its accuracy can not be vouched for although only 15 years had passed since the events occurred.

1152
Bod/
BL
9056.bbb.26(5)

Wylie, Macleod. *THE ENGLISH CAPTIVES IN OUDH. An Episode in the History of the Mutiny of 1857-58.* London: W. H. Dalton. Also Calcutta: G. C. Hay. 1858 Calcutta: vi & 57pp. Paper.
    This is a manuscript from Captain A. P. Orr regarding the fate of his brother Patrick and his wife.

1153
Ames

Wylly, Colonel Harold Carmichael. *NEILL'S BLUE CAPS.* Aldershot: Gale & Polden, (For Private Circulation Only) 1925. 3 vols. Vol I Frontis of Neill. 17 illus. 6 maps [6] + 330pp. Index. Vol. II Frontis & 31 illus. 2 maps, xii & 228pp. Index. Vol III Frontis & 48 illus. & 8 maps. xii & 247pp. Index. Vol. I 1639-1826; Vol. II 1826-1914; Vol. III 1914-1922.
    Four chapters on the Mutiny covering the 1st & 2nd reliefs of Lucknow, the Alam Bagh and the re-capture of Lucknow. Second edition 1996. 3 vols. 13 maps in separate case. Schull Books. Limited to 200 copies.

1154
Bod

Wynter, Philip. *ON THE QUEENS ERRANDS.* London: Sir Isaac Pitman, 1906. 329pp. Frontis & 5 photos.
    Wynter arrived in Calcutta in mid 1857, a boy of 17. He served with the Bengal Yeomanry Cavalry. Approximately 35 pages on the Mutiny.

1155
IO

Yadav, K. C. *RAO TULARAM-HERO OF 1857. UNDOING THE BONDAGE. A STUDY OF THE LIFE OF RAO TULA RAM HERO OF 1857.* Delhi: Jullundur, S. Pamrod, 1965, 1975. Frontis and x & 94pp. 5 illus. 1 map. Index and bibliography.
    Tula Ram was a leader of the revolt in Haryana. This is a scholarly study of his life.

1156
RS

Yadav, K. C. ; *THE REVOLT OF 1857 IN HARYANA.* New Delhi: Manohar Book Service, 1977. viii & 192pp. Two maps. Bibliography and index.
    Yadav suggests there was a plot among the mutineers in Haryana prior to Meerut. "Dr. Yadav disagrees with many eminent scholars of the Uprising, such as Dr. S. N. Sen, Dr. R. C. Majumdar and others. Their methodology, and inadequate sources, he believes, have tended to perpetuate many inaccurate interpretations concerning the origins, nature, scope, and at times even actual happenings of the Uprising."

1157
RS

Yadav, K.C. ed. *DELHI IN 1857. The Trial of Bahadur Shah. Vol. I.* Gurgaon, India: Academic Press 1980, 1981 xxvi & 446pp. One map and 4 illustrations.
This work is based on the 1859 London edition of the trial. The book was noted as being the first volume of a proposed three volume work. The publisher has reported that the second and third volumes have been shelved.

1158
RS

Yalland, Zoe. *KACHERI CEMETERY KANPUR.* London: British Association for Cemeteries in South Asia, 1985. 137pp. Card covers
A complete list of inscriptions with notes on those buried there. With very few exceptions the tombs are all pre-Mutiny.

1159
RS

Yalland, Zoe. *TRADERS AND NABOBS: The British in Cawnpore 1765-1857.* Salisbury, Great Britain. Michael Russell, 1987. 376pp. Index. Illus.
This is the definitive history of Cawnpore. The last chapter deals with the Mutiny but the work is important for those who would understand the city and surrounding territory prior to the Mutiny. Contains about a four page copy of Mrs. Angelo's Diary, 1857. Her and Lieutenant Angelo were posted to Cawnpore and arrived on May 14th.
Extensive notes, glossary, and appendices. The author was born in Cawnpore and the family had an extensive history there.

1160

Yeoward, George. *AN EPISODE OF THE REBELLION AND MUTINY IN OUDH OF 1857 AND 1858.* Lucknow: American Methodist Mission Press, 1876. 63pp.
Cited by Ladendorf and Jain.

1161
Sut

Young, William Richard. *A FEW WORDS ON THE INDIAN QUESTION.* NC. NP. ND. 47pp.

Index

Bold type indicates an author.

ITALICS IN CAPS indicates a main title entry.

Italics in lower case indicates a title mentioned within an entry.

Plain type indicates a subject heading.

Military personal are indexed at their highest rank.

1

1857. 969. 624
1857 A FRIEND IN NEED. 344
1857 A PICTORIAL PRESENTATION. 443
1857 CENTENARY EXHIBITION OF PRINTED BOOKS. 36
1857 CENTENARY SOUVENIR. 171
1857 IN ASSSAM. 183
1857 IN BIHAR. 921. 888. 275
1857 IN FOLK SONGS. 582
1857 in India: Mutiny or War of Independence?. 380
1857 IN JABALPUR DISTRICT. 973
1857 SOME UNTOLD STORIES. 260
1857 THE INDIAN MUTINY. A Short Price Guide to Mutiny Titles. 983
1857, THE GREAT REBELLION. 747

2

2nd KING EDWARD VII's OWN GOORKHA RIFLES (THE SIRMOOR RIFLES). 898

9

95TH (THE DERBYSHIRE) REGIMENT IN CENTRAL INDIA. 880

A

A MEMORIAL OF THE LIFE AND SERVICE OF MAJOR GENERAL W.W.H. GREATHED. 414
A BIRDS EYE VIEW OF INDIA SHOWING OUR PRESENT POSITION, ITS DANGER AND REMEDY. 606
A BRAVE GIRL. 557
A BRIEF SUMMARY OF THE FACTS CONNECTED WITH MY REMOVAL FROM THE COMMISSIONERSHIP OF PATNA. 1021
A CHAPLAIN AT THE INDIAN MUTINY. 618
A CLASH OF CULTURES. 394
A COMPANION TO THE INDIAN MUTINY. 1048
A CONTINUATION OF THE HISTORICAL RECORDS OF THE VI DRAGOONS CARABINIERS. 987
A DEBATE ON INDIA IN THE ENGLISH PARLIAMENT. 768
A DIARY KEPT BY MRS. R.C. GERMON AT LUCKNOW. 428
A FATAL FRIENDSHIP. 653
A FEELING OF QUIET POWER. 1044
A FEW REMARKS EARNESTLY ADDRESSED TO THE. 37
A FEW REMARKS ON THE BENGAL ARMY. 561. 213
A FEW WORDS ABOUT INDIA, AND THE MUTINIES. 18
A FEW WORDS ANENT THE RED PAMPHLET. 23
A FEW WORDS ON GENERAL JACOB'S SCHEME FOR THE REORGANIZATION OF THE INDIAN ARMIES. 724
A FEW WORDS ON THE INDIAN QUESTION. 1161
A FEW WORDS RELATIVE TO THE LATE MUTINY. 510
A FLY ON THE WHEEL. 645

A FORGOTTEN CHAPTER OF INDIAN HISTORY AS DESCRIBED IN THE MEMOIRS OF SETH NAOMAL HOTCHAND C.S.I. OF KARACHI, 1804-1878. 176

A FORM OF PRAYER AND THANKSGIVING TO. 38

A FULL AND CORRECTED REPORT OF PROCEEDINGS OF THE PUBLIC MEETING IN HONOR OF LORD CANNING. 39

A FUNERAL SERMON ON THE DEATH OF THE REVEREND HENRY STEDMAN POLEHAMPTON. 612

A GLANCE AT THE EAST. 40

A GLANCE AT THE PAST AND THE FUTURE IN CONNECTION WITH THE INDIAN REVOLT. 1082

A GOOD SOLDIER. A SERMON ON THE OCCASION OF THE DEATH OF MAJOR- GENERAL SIR H. HAVELOCK. 893

A GUIDE TO INDIAN MANUSCRIPTS. MATERIALS FROM EUROPE AND NORTH AMERICA. 905

A Hindu. 772

A HISTORY OF THE INDIAN MEDICAL SERVICE. 306

A HISTORY OF THE INDIAN MUTINY. 526. 406

A HISTORY OF THE SEPOY WAR IN INDIA 1857-1858. 594. 592

A LADY'S DIARY BEFORE AND DURING THE INDIAN MUTINY. 824

A LADY'S DIARY OF THE SIEGE OF LUCKNOW. 119

A LADY'S ESCAPE FROM GWALIOR. 296

A Leader of Light Horse. 255

A LEADER OF LIGHT HORSE. 1074

A LECTURE ON THE RELIEF OF LUCKNOW. 809

A LETTER ADDRESSED TO THE RIGHT HONORABLE LORD STANLEY, SECRETARY OF STATE FOR INDIA. 192

A LETTER FROM A LAYMAN IN INDIA. 41

A LETTER ON THE INDIAN ARMY. 191

A LETTER TO AN OFFICIAL CONCERNED IN THE EDUCATION OF INDIA. 1080

A LETTER TO CAPTAIN EASTWICK. 1005

A LETTER TO R.D. MANGLES. 290

A LETTER TO RT. HON. THE EARL OF ELLENBOROUGH. 749

A LETTER TO THE RT. HON. LORD STANLEY, MP, SECRETARY OF STATE FOR INDIA. 1081

A Man of York. 1073

A MATTER OF HONOUR. 728

A MEMOIR AND RETROSPECT. 507

A MEMOIR OF GENERAL SIR HENRY DRURY HARNESS. 284

A MEMOIR OF GENERAL SIR HENRY DRURY HARNESS. 283

A MEMOIR OF LT GENERAL SIR GARNET J. WOLSELEY. 659

A MEMOIR OF MEERUT. 838

A MEMOIR OF THE KHANDESH BHIL CORPS 1825-1891. COMPILED FROM ORIGINAL RECORDS. 965

A MEMORIAL OF THE FUTTEHGURH MISSION. 1108

A METHODIST SOLDIER IN THE INDIAN ARMY. 630

A MIDDY'S RECOLLECTIONS 1853-1860. 767

A MISSING CHAPTER OF THE INDIAN MUTINY. 962

A NARRATIVE OF EVENTS CONNECTED WITH MY REMOVAL FROM THE PATNA COMMISSIONERSHIP IN 1857. 1022

A NARRATIVE OF THE CAMPAIGN OF THE DELHI ARMY. 810

A NARRATIVE OF THE SIEGE OF DELHI. 469

A PERSONAL JOURNAL OF THE SIEGE OF LUCKNOW. 29

A PERSONAL NARRATIVE OF THE OUTBREAK AND MASSACRE AT CAWNPORE. 956

A PERSONAL NARRATIVE OF THE SIEGE OF LUCKNOW. 894. 121. 42

A PICTORIAL RECORD OF THE CAWNPORE MASSACRE. 313

A PLAN FOR THE MILITARY SEIZURE AND OCCUPATION. 681

A POSTSCRIPT TO THE RECORDS OF THE INDIAN MUTINY. 435

A PRIVATE SOLDIER IN CENTRAL INDIA. 815

A RECORD OF THE LIFE AND TIMES OF CAPTAIN BERNARD McCABE. 949

A REPLY TO MR. F.W. BUCKLER'S. 341

A RETIRED BENGAL CIVILIAN. 40

A REVIEW OF COL. ADYE'S DEFENSE OF GENERAL WINDHAM. 218

A SEASON IN HELL. 366

A SERMON UPON THE INDIAN OUTBREAK. 914

A SERVANT OF JOHN COMPANY. 596

A SHORT ACCOUNT OF EVENTS DURING THE SEPOY MUTINY OF 1857-8 IN THE DISTRICT OF BELGAUM AND JESSORE. 947

A SHORT ACCOUNT OF THE LIFE AND FAMILY OF RAI JEEWAN LAL BAHADUR. 620

A SHORT ACCOUNT OF THE SERVICES OF THE GENERAL SIR CHARLES CURETON. 316

A SHORT ACCOUNT OF THE SIEGE OF DELHI. 484

A SHORT AND USEFUL COMPILATION FROM THE CALCUTTA GOVERNMENT GAZETTE ABOUT THE FALL OF DELHI. 948

A SHORT HISTORY OF LUCKNOW. 34

A SHORT REVIEW OF THE PRESENT CRISIS IN INDIA. 226

A SOLDIER'S EXPERIENCE. 454

A STAR SHALL FALL. 1045

A STATEMENT RELATIVE TO THE SUFFERERS BY THE MUTINY IN INDIA. 505

A STORY OF JUGDESPORE. 841

A SUBALTERN IN THE INDIAN MUTINY. 1053

A SUBALTERN'S DIARY. 546

A TURNING POINT IN THE INDIAN MUTINY. 964

A VARIED LIFE. 438

A VIEW OF THE DEFENCE OF ARRAH HOUSE. 1020

A VINDICATION OF MARQUIS OF DALHOUSIE'S INDIAN ADMINISTRATION. 558

A VOLUNTEER: MY JOURNAL OR WHAT I DID. 43

A WEEK IN THE MOFUSSIL IN 1857. 740. 44

A WIDOWS REMINISCENCES OF THE SIEGE OF LUCKNOW. 153

A YEARS CAMPAIGNING IN INDIA. 745

Aberigh-Mackay, James. *See 3*

ACCOUNT OF MY ESCAPE FROM BAREILLY. 453

ACCOUNT OF THE LOYAL MAHOMEDANS OF INDIA. 12

Adam, H.L. *4*

Addams, Rev. Francis Holland. *5*

ADDENDA TO CORRESPONDENCE REGARDING CLAIMS TO THE INDIAN MEDALS, FOR SERVICE IN WESTERN INDIA. 45

ADDENDA TO THE CORRESPONDENCE. 1030

Adjutant General's Office. *6*

Adye, General Sir John Miller. 7
Adye, Lt Col John. 8
AFTERMATH OF REVOLT IN INDIA. 750
Agra. 951. 928. 892. 891. 890. 854. 782. 781. 684. 668. 572. 570. 448. 430. 296
AGRA CORRESPONDENCE DURING THE MUTINY. 781
AGRA IN THE MUTINY AND THE FAMILY LIFE OF W & E MUIR IN THE FORT. 782
Ahmad Khan, Sayyid, Sir. 14. 13. 12. 11. 10. 9
Ahmad, Dr. Quyamuddin. 15
Ahmad, Safi. 16
Aikman, Lt. W.R. 17
Ainslie, Rev. A L. 18
Aitchison, Sir Charles. 19
Alavi, Seema. 20
Aldwell, James Skinner. 21
Alexander, Thomas. 22
Allahabad. 746. 740. 684. 470. 448. 4
Action at. 992. 991. 190
Allen, Charles. 23
Alli, Darogha Ubbas. 24
Allygurh. 448
Alter, James Payne. 25
Alumbagh. 1153. 928. 911. 822. 754. 663. 506. 501. 406. 327. 190. 145
Alves, Colonel Nathaniel. 26
AMBUSHES AND SURPRISES. 714
AN ACCOUNT OF THE MUTINEES IN OUDH AND OF THE SIEGE OF THE LUCKNOW RESIDENCY. 471
AN ADDRESS TO THE RECONSTRUCTORS OF OUR INDIAN EMPIRE. 667
AN ECHO OF THE INDIAN MUTINY, THE PROPOSED BANISHMENT OF BAHADUR SHAH II TO THE CAPE COLONY, 1857. 1125
AN ENGLISHWOMAN IN INDIA. 929
AN EPISODE OF THE INDIAN REVOLT. 946

AN EPISODE OF THE REBELLION AND MUTINY IN OUDH OF 1857 AND 1858. 1160
AN ESSAY ON THE CAUSES OF THE INDIAN REVOLT. 13
An Eyewitness Account of the Great Indian Mutiny. 355
An Indian Officer. 109
An Old Quarter-master of the Bengal Army. 27
An Old Resident. 28
AN OLD SOLDIER'S MEMORIES. 840
AN UNRECORDED CHAPTER OF THE INDIAN MUTINY. 1122
ANALYTICAL INDEX TO SIR JOHN W. KAYE'S HISTORY OF THE SEPOY WAR AND COLONEL G.B. MALLESON'S HISTORY OF THE INDIAN MUTINY. 857
Anderson, Captain R(obert) P(atrick). 29
Anderson, Captain T. Carnegy. 30
Anderson, Colonel W. 31
Anderson, George. 32
Anderson, H.S. 33
Anderson, Maj. A.T. 34
Andrews, C.F. 35
ANECDOTES AND REMINISCENCES OF SERVICE IN BENGAL. 853
Angelo, Major. 845
ANGELS OF ALBION. WOMEN OF THE INDIAN MUTINY. 915
ANGLO-INDIAN RULE HISTORICALLY CONSIDERED. 826
ANNALS OF THE INDIAN REBELLION (THE). 271. 270
ANNALS OF THE KINGS ROYAL RIFLE CORPS. 209
Annand. 1015
ANNEXATION OF THE KINGDOM OF OUDE (THE). 87
ANNUAL REGISTER (THE). 89. 88
Anson, Harcourt S. 132
ANSWERS TO LETTER 235. 560. 413

ARCHDALE WILSON'S LETTERS DURING THE MUTINY. 1133

Archer, J.L. *133*

ARCHITECTS OF INDIAN FREEDOM STRUGGLE. 174

ARMIES OF THE RAJ; FROM THE MUTINY TO INDEPENDENCE, 1858-1947. 389

ARMY PURCHASE QUESTION (THE). 90

Arrah. *714. 471*

Arrah House. *1139. 1071. 1062. 1031. 1020. 964. 597. 406. 216*

ARRAH IN 1857. 637

Arthur, Reverend William. *127*

Ashraf, K.M. *134*

Ashraf, Mujeeb. *135*

ASSAULT OF DELHI (THE). 158

AT HOME AND IN INDIA. 960

AT THE FRONT. 130

Atkinson, Captain George Francklin. *136*

AUTOBIOGRAPHY AND REMINISCENCES OF SIR DOUGLAS FORSYTH. 410

AUTOBIOGRAPHY OF AN OLD SOLDIER (THE). 887

AUTOBIOGRAPHY OF LUTFULLAH. 361

AWADH IN REVOLT 1857-58. 788

Aylen, Rev. W. H. *137*

Azamgarh. *714*

AZIMULLAH KHAN YUSUFZAI: THE MAN BEHIND THE WAR OF INDEPENDENCE. 676

B

Badger, Rev. George Percey. *138*

Bagh-i-Hindustan. 602

BAHADUR SHAH: THE LAST MOGHUL EMPEROR OF INDIA. 202

Bahadur Shah. *1157. 883. 871. 839*

BAHADUR SHAH II AND THE WAR OF 1857 IN DELHI. 539

Baillie, Rev. John. *139*

Baird, J.G. *140*

Baldwin, Reverend J.R. *141*

Ball, Charles. *142*

Banda. *448*

BANDA AND KIRWEE BOOTY. 675. 674

Banerjee, Brojendra Nath. *143*

Bannu. *479*

Barat, Amiya. *144*

Bareilly. *453. 448*

Barker, General George Digby. *145*

Barnes, George Carnac. *146*

Barrackpore. *843. 308*

BARRACKS AND BATTLEFIELDS IN INDIA. 707. 230

Barrier, N Gerald. *147*

Bartarya, Dr. S.C. *148*

Barter, Richard. *149*

Barthorp, Michael and Douglas Anderson. *150*

Bartlett, D.W. *151*

Bartrum, Mrs. Katherine Mary. *153. 152*

Basu, Baman Das. *154*

BATTLES OF THE INDIAN MUTINY. 367

Battye, Evelyn Desiree. *155*

Battye, Quentin
Related to George Malleson. *594*

BAYARD OF INDIA (THE). 1075

Bayley, Major John Arthur. *158. 157. 156*

Bayly, C.A. and D.H.A. Kolff. *159*

Beato, Felice. *160*

BEATO'S DELHI 1857, 1997. 730

Becher, Augusta. *161*

Beck, Theodore of Aligarh. *162*

Beg, M.A. *163*

BEGINNING OF THE INDIAN MUTINY. 157

Bell, Thomas Evans. *166. 165. 164*

Benares. *448*

BENGAL NATIVE INFANTRY (THE). 144

BENGAL HORSE ARTILLERY 1800-1861 (THE). 534

BENGAL MUTINY. 326

BENGAL MUTINY (THE). 17

BENGAL UNDER THE
LIEUTENANT GOVERNORS. *200*
Benson, A. C. *167*
Bernays, Leopold John. *168*
Berncastle, Julius MD. *169*
Betts, Esther Anne. *110*
Bhalla, Alok & Sudhir Chandra. *170*
Bhalla, Piyarelal. *171*
Bhargava, K D and S N Prasad. *172*
Bhargava, Moti Lal. *174. 173*
Bhatnagar, O.P. *175*
Bhojwani, Rao Bahadur. *176*
Bihar. *340. 331. 330. 329. 275*
Bijnor Rebellion. *9*
Bijnour. *448*
BIOGRAPHICAL MEMOIRS WITH
HIS PRIVATE JOURNAL. *416*
BIOGRAPHICAL SKETCH OF SIR H.
HAVELOCK. *193*
BIOGRAPHY OF KUNWAR SINGH
AND AMAR SINGH. *330*
Bird, James. *177. 97*
Bird, Robert Wilberforce. *178*
Blake, Mrs. *179*
BLOODY PROVOST. *1087*
BLUE PAMPHLET (THE). *31*
Blunt, E.A.H. *180*
BOBS. *485*
Boileau, Colonel A Henry E. *181*
BONDAGE AND FREEDOM 1707 TO
1947. *864*
Bonham, Colonel John. *182*
Bora, Mahendra. *183*
Bost, Isabella. *184*
Bourchier, Colonel George. *185*
Boyle, Major C.A. *186*
Boyle, Richard Vicars. *216*
Brackenbury, General Sir H. *187*
Bradley-Birt, F.B. *188*
Brantlinger, Patrick. *189*
Brasyer, Jeremiah. *190*
Brendish, George. *994*
Brief Account of the Outbreak at
Cawnpore. 956

BRIEF NARRATIVE CALLED
FOR BY SIR JAMES OUTRAM
SHOWING HOW THE 73RD
NATIVE INFANTRY WAS SAVED.
957
BRIEF NARRATIVE OF EVENTS
CONNECTED WITH THE
REMOVAL OF W. TAYLER FROM
PATNA. 131
BRIEF NARRATIVE OF THE
DEFENCE OF. 216
BRIEF OBSERVATIONS
ADDRESSED TO THE GENERAL
READER ON THE. 28
BRIEF SURVEY OF RAGHOGARH
STATES SERVICES DURING THE
INDIAN MUTINY. 1858-1859. 967
Briggs, Lt Gen John. *192. 191*
BRITAIN CAUGHT IN THE SNARE.
900
BRITAIN'S GUILT & DUTY WITH
REFERENCE TO HER INDIAN
EMPIRE. 801
British Administration During the Revolt
of 1857. 595
BRITISH AGGRESSION IN AVADH.
16
BRITISH INDIA, ITS RACES AND
ITS HISTORY CONSIDERED
WITH REFERENCES TO THE
MUTINIES OF 1857. 670
BRITISH POWER IN THE PUNJAB
1839-1859. 603
BRITISH RAJ (THE). 411
BRITISH ROUTE TO INDIA. 531
BRITISH SOLDIER IN INDIA (THE).
777
BRITISH TROOPS (THE). 150
Brock, Reverend William. 193
Broehl, Wayne G. Jr. *195. 194*
Brougham, J.P. *94*
Broughton, H. *1071*
Browne, General Sir Sam. *196*
Browne, John. *198. 197*
Brydon, Dr. William. *773*
Buchanan, C. *199*
Buckland, C. E. *200*
Buckler, F. W. *201*

Budaon. *448*

Bukht Khan. *999*

Bundelkhand. *922. 907. 448*

Burke, S.M. & Salim al-Din Quraishi. *202*

Burne, Major General Sir Owen Tudor. *205. 204. 203*

Burnes, James. *206*

Burton, James. *207*

Burton, Maj. R.G. *451. 208*

BUTCHER OF CAWNPORE (THE). *459*

Butler, Lewis William George and Stewart Hare. *209*

Butler, Rev. William D.D. *210*

Butler, Spencer Harcourt. *211*

Buxton, Charles. *212*

By a Barrister. *217*

By A Bombay Officer. *213*

By a Civilian. *218*

By a Former Editor of the Delhi Gazette. *221. 220. 219*

By a General Officer. *96*

By a Hindu. *785. 222. 69*

By a Lady Who Was One of the Survivors. *113*

By a Military Officer. *223*

By a Plain Speaker. *224*

By a Retired Bengal Civilian. *225*

BY A RETIRED OFFICER. 26

By a Roving Irishman. *226*

By a Scotchman. *63*

By a Staff Officer. *227*

By A Wounded Officer. *214*

By A.D. *64*

By an Indian Nationalist. *129*

By an Officer. *71*

BY AN OFFICER ONCE IN THE BENGAL ARTILLERY. 31

By an Old Bengalee. *114*

By and Eye Witness. *228*

By and Old Indian. *229*

By One of the Besieged Party. *216*

By One Who Served in the Campaigns. *111*

By One Who was Present. *215*

By One Who Was There in 1857-58. *112*

BY THE QUEEN: A PROCLAMATION FOR A DAY OF SOLEMN FAST, HUMILIATION, AND PRAYER. 381

By Y. *80*

C

Caine, Rev. Caesar. *230*

Cairns, Rev. John. *231*

CALCUTTA OLD AND NEW. 300

CALL OF THE BLOOD OR ANGLO-INDIANS AND THE SEPOY MUTINY (THE). *994*

CAMBRIDGE SOUTH ASIAN ARCHIVE: RECORDS OF THE BRITISH PERIOD IN SOUTH ASIA HELD IN THE CENTRE OF SOUTH ASIAN STUDIES, UNIVERSITY OF CAMBRIDGE. 1056

CAMP AND CANTONMENT. 830

CAMPAIGN IN INDIA 1857-58 (THE). 136

CAMPAIGNING EXPERIENCES IN RAJPOOTANA. 352

CAMPAIGNING IN OUDE. 817

Campbell, Col. Walter. *232*

Campbell, George Douglas, 8th Duke of Argyll. *234. 233*

Campbell, Robert James Roy. *236. 235*

Campbell, Sir Colin. *952. 855. 658. 610. 506. 397. 204. 130. 115. 7*

Campbell, Sir George. *237*

Canning, Charles John. *952. 743. 696. 634. 315. 234. 233. 58*

Cardew, Francis Gordon. *239. 238*

Cardwell, Pamela. *240*

Carey, W.H. *242. 241*

Carmichael-Smyth, Major General G. *244. 243*

Carnegy, C.W. *245*

Carthill, Al. *246*

Carus-Wilson, Rev. W. *247*

CASE OF ISSREEPERSAUD. 849

Case, Mrs. Adelaide. *248*

CASTE IN INDIA. CASTE EVERYWHERE. HOW TO KEEP OR LOSE AN EMPIRE. 851

CASUAL LETTERS. 152

CASUALTY ROLE FOR THE INDIAN MUTINY. 1019

CATALOG OF HOME MISCELLANEOUS SERIES OF THE INDIA OFFICES RECORDS. 512

CATASTROPHE (THE). 309

CAUSE AND EFFECT: THE REBELLION IN INDIA. 46

CAUSE OF THE INDIAN MUTINY (THE). 22

CAUSES OF THE CRISIS 1857-1858. 566

CAUSES OF THE INDIAN REVOLT. 646

CAUSES OF THE INDIAN REVOLT (THE). 11

CAVALRY EXPERIENCES AND LEAVES FROM MY JOURNAL. 823

CAVALRY SURGEON. THE RECOLLECTIONS OF DEPUTY SURGEON-GENERAL JOHN HENRY SYLVESTER, F.G.S. 1015

Cave-Browne, John. *249. 250. 251*

Cavenagh, General Sir Orfeur. *252*

Cavendish, Alfred Edward John. *253*

Cawnpore. *1159. 1151. 1144. 1109. 1059. 908. 849. 823. 799. 789. 778. 684. 679. 664. 640. 628. 614. 474. 455. 450. 449. 448. 406. 398. 393. 167. 145. 108. 68. See 3*

Photo of well. *382*

Siege of, 41. *956. 586. 508. 497. 491. 430. 405. 313. 283. 257. 190. 189. 91*

Windham at. *1141. 844. 645. 440. 284. 218. 215. 8*

CAWNPORE. 1072

CAWNPORE AFFAIR (THE). 215

CAWNPORE AND THE NANA OF BITHOOR. 197

CAWNPORE OUTBREAK AND MASSACRE (THE). 91

Cawnpore Well Memorial. *758*

CENTENARY SOUVENIR. 622

Central India. *448*

Central India Campaign. *1009*

CENTRAL INDIA DURING THE REBELLION OF 1857 AND 1858. 665

Central India Field Force. *1100. 1089. 1015. 997. 977. 916. 880. 815. 795. 733. 665. 645. 451. 406. 352. 204. 203*

CENTRAL INDIA IN 1857. 356

Chachar. *276*

Chalmers, Colonel John. *254*

Chamberlain, Crawford Trotter. *255*

Chamier, Lieut. Edward. *256*

Chand, Nanak. *258. 257*

Chand, Tara. *259*

Chanda, S.N. *260*

Chandra, Nirmal Kanti. *261*

CHAPLAIN'S NARRATIVE OF THE SIEGE OF DELHI (THE). 919

CHAPTER OF THE BENGAL MUTINY. 112

CHARLES ASHE WINDHAM. 716

Charter Act of 1858. *865*

Chatterjee, H.P. *262*

Chattopadhyaya, Haraprasad. *263*

Chaturbhuj. *264*

Chaturvedi, Jayati. *265*

Chaudhry, Nazir Ahmad. *266*

Chaudhuri, S. B. *267*

Chaudhuri, Sashi. *269. 268*

Cheek, Ensign Arthur. *992. 321*

Chick, Noah Alfred. *271. 270*

CHIEF COMMISSIONERS ADMINISTRATION, PUNJAB, FROM 10TH FEBRUARY 1853 TO 31ST DECEMBER 1858: POLITICAL DEPARTMENT (XIII). 875

CHILDREN OF THE MUTINY. 1111

CHINA JIM. 495

Cholmeley, Johnstone Montague. *272*

Cholmeley, R. E. *273*

Chopra, P.N. *274*

Chota Nagpore. *764. 324*

CHOTA NAGPORE: A LITTLE. 188

Choudhury, P.C.R. *275*

Choudhury, Sujit. *276*

CHRISTIAN RESEARCHES IN INDIA. 199

CHRISTIAN SOLDIER (THE). 456

CHRISTIANITY IN INDIA. 47

CHRISTIANS OF ENGLAND (THE). 92

CHRONICLE OF PRIVATE HENRY METCALFE (THE). 1083

CHRONICLES OF THE MUTINY & OTHER HISTORICAL SKETCHES. 1046

Church Missionary Society. *277*

Churcher, E J. *84*

Churcher, E. J. *278*

Civicus. *279*

CIVIL REBELLION IN THE INDIAN MUTINIES. 268

CLEMENCY CANNING. 696

Clive, William. *280*

Clyde Memorial Fund Executive Committee. *115*

COLIN CAMPBELL, LORD CLYDE. 397

Collier, Richard. *282. 281*

Collinson, Major General T.B. *284. 283*

Collister, Peter. *285*

Colvin, Auckland. *286*

Combe, Charles. *287*

COMMUNICATIONS AND TESTIMONIALS SHOWING THE LOYAL CONDUCT OF THE LATE MUNSHI RAJA RAN, KOTWAL AND RAIS OF AGRA, DURING THE MUTINY OF 1857. 854

COMPANY'S RAJ (THE). 1073

COMPETITION WALLAH (THE). 1071

COMPLETE HISTORY OF THE INDIAN MUTINY. 1117

COMPLETE LIST OF DEATH CASUALTIES. 543

COMPLETE NARRATIVE OF THE MUTINY. 415

Congreve, Richard. *289. 288*

CONNAUGHT RANGERS (THE). 584

Connon, John. *290*

Conran, H.M. Major. *291*

CONTEMPORARY NEWSPAPER ACCOUNTS OF EVENTS DURING THE MUTINY IN CENTRAL INDIA 1857-59. 666

CONTENT ANALYSIS IN PSYCHOHISTORY. 194

Conybeare, H.C. and Atkinson, Edwin. *292*

Cooper, Frederic Henry. *117*

Cooper, Frederick. *294. 293*

Cooper, L. *295*

Coopland, Ruth M. *296*

Cope, William. *297*

COPIES OF SUNDRY DISPATCHES. 301

COPY OF A MEMORIAL. 1023

COPY OF LETTER WRITTEN DURING THE SIEGE OF LUCKNOW, 1857. 501

Cork, Barry Joynson. *298*

CORRESPONDENCE CONNECTED WITH MY FIRST MEMORIAL. 1024

CORRESPONDENCE CONNECTED WITH THE REMOVAL OF MR. WILLIAM TAYLER FROM THE COMMISSIONERSHIP OF PATNA. 1025

CORRESPONDENCE REGARDING AN OMISSION IN A PARLIAMENTARY RETURN. 567

Corrigan and Family. *448*

Cosens, Francis R. and C.L. Wallace. *299*

Cotton, Harry Evan August. *300*

Cotton, Sydney. *302. 301*

Couper, Sir George. *140. 93*

Court, M. H. *303*

Court, M.H. *304*

Cox. P. *305*

Cracklow, George. *195*

Crawford, Lt.-Colonel D.G. *306*

Crawshay, George. *309. 308. 307*

Crawshay, George. *426*
Crimea and Indian Mutiny. *310*
CRIMEA AND INDIAN MUTINY. 310
*CRIMEAN DIARY AND LETTERS
OF LIEUTENANT GENERAL
SIR CHARLES ASH WINDHAM
(THE). 844*
CRISIS IN INDIA (THE). 223
*CRISIS IN THE PUNJAB (THE). 293.
117*
*CRISIS OF THE RAJ: The Revolt of
1857 through British Lieutenants'
Eyes. 195*
Cromb, James. *311*
Crommelin, Captain William Arden.
312
Crommelin, Major. *796. 548*
*CRUISE OF THE PEARL ROUND
THE WORLD (THE). 1126*
Crump, Charles Wade. *313*
Culrose, James. *314*
Cummins, Nicholas Marshall. *688*
Cunningham, Henry Stewart. *315*
Cureton, C. *316*
*CURSORY VIEW OF THE PRESENT
CRISIS IN INDIA. 420*
Cuthell, Edith. *318. 317*

D

D. M. *321*
Da Costa, Samuel. *See* 2
DACOITEE IN EXCELSIS. 48
*Daily Life During the Indian Mutiny.
959*
*DAILY LIFE DURING THE INDIAN
MUTINY. 958*
Dalhousie, Marquess of. *1078. 877. 710.
643. 558. 553. 481. 233. 140. 23*
Dall, Reverend C.H.A. *322*
Dallas, A.R. *323*
Dalton, Colonel E.T. *324*
Daly, Major H. *325*
DAMN TIGHT PLACE. 688
DANDO ON DELHI RIDGE. 280
Dangerfield, George. *326*
Danvers, Robert William. *327*

*DARING DEEDS OF THE INDIAN
MUTINY. 433*
*DASTANBUY: A DIARY OF THE
REVOLT OF 1857. 429*
Datta, Kalikinkar K. *331. 330. 329. 328*
David, Saul. *332*
Davidson, Hugh. *333*
Dawson, Capt. Lionel. *334*
DAY BY DAY AT LUCKNOW. 248
Day, Maurice Fitzgerald. *335*
DAYS IN NORTH INDIA. 684
De Fonblanque, Edward Barrington.
336
DEEDS OF VALOUR. 541
*DEFECTS, CIVIL AND MILITARY
OF THE INDIAN GOVERNMENT.
797*
*DEFENCE OF CAWNPORE THE:
BY THE TROOPS UNDER THE
ORDERS OF. 8*
*DEFENSE OF ARAH HOUSE
AGAINST THREE MUTINOUS
REGIMENTS AND A LARGE
BODY OF INSURGENTS UNDER
KOER SINGH. 1031*
*DEFENSE OF LUCKNOW (THE).
227*
DeKantzow, C.A. *337*
Delhi. *684. 167. 35*
Siege of, 85. *1133. 1116. 1105. 1103.
1102. 1101. 1098. 1098. 1087.
1086. 1085. 1084. 1067. 1054.
1053. 1038. 981. 948. 937. 929.
919. 913. 909. 898. 896. 856. 848.
846. 845. 823. 810. 807. 794. 793.
751. 748. 745. 741. 735. 730. 686.
652. 642. 635. 626. 625. 614. 556.
539. 537. 508. 503. 492. 490. 486.
484. 480. 469. 464. 455. 452. 442.
429. 414. 405. 387. 379. 371. 325.
294. 281. 254. 221. 220. 185. 156.
149. 146. 136. 132. 94. 54*
*DELHI 1857: THE SIEGE, ASSAULT
AND CAPTURE. 807*
DELHI IN 1857. 1157. 802
DELHI MASSACRE (THE). 113
*DELHI RESIDENCY AND AGENCY.
1806-1857. 869*

DELHI, PAST AND PRESENT. 387

DEPOSITIONS TAKEN AT MEERUT.
    447

DEPUTY SURGEON-GENERAL
    CHARLES THOMAS PASKE
    1830-1920. 899

Desai, Sanjiv P. *339*

DESCRIPTION OF THE MEASURES
    TAKEN AT AGRA DURING THE
    INDIAN MUTINY. 890

DESPATCH OF BRIGADIER INGLIS
    (THE). 93

DeValbezen, E. *338*

DEVELOPMENT OF AN INDIAN
    POLICY (THE). 32

Devi, Ritambhari. *340*

DEVIL'S WIND (THE). 1097. 708

Dewar, Douglas. *341*

Dharaiya, Dr. R.K. *342*

DIARY. 982

DIARY AND LETTERS OF LT. A M.
    LANG. 625

DIARY OF A MEDICAL OFFICER
    DURING THE GREAT INDIAN
    MUTINY. 1144

DIARY OF THE DOCTOR'S LADY.
    773

DIARY OF THE MUTINY AT
    CAWNPUR. 799. 258

DIARY OF THE MUTINY AT
    CAWNPUR. WRITTEN BY
    NANAK CHAND. 586

Dickinson, John. *343*

Digby, William. *344*

Dinapore. *230*

DISAFFECTION IN THE NATIVE
    ARMY 1857. *790*

DISTRICT DUTIES DURING THE
    REVOLT IN THE NORTH WEST
    PROVINCES OF INDIA IN 1857.
    912

Diver, Katherine Helen Maud. *345*

Dixon, James. *346*

Doab. *937*

Dobrolyubov, Nikolai. *347*

Dodd. *417*

Dodd, George. *348*

Dodgson, David Scott. *349*

Domin, Dolores. *350*

Dormer, J. *351. 318*

D'Oyly, Major General Sir Charles
    Walters. *320. 319*

Duberly, Mrs. Henry. *353. 352*

Duff, A. *354*

Duff, Rev. A.
    The Indian Rebellion. *639*

Dunlop, Robert Henry Wallace. *355*

Durand, Sir Henry Mortimer. *358.*
    357. 356

E

EARL CANNING. 315

EARLY DAYS OF MARLBOROUGH
    COLLEGE (THE). 656

EARLY WRITINGS ON INDIA. 587

EAST INDIA. 460

EAST INDIA (NATIVE CAVALRY).
    461

East India Company. *359*

EAST INDIES PRIZE MONEY. 463

Eastwick, Edward Backhouse. *361*

Eastwick, William Joseph. *360*

Eckford, Lieut. J.J. *362*

Eden, Charles. *363*

Edwardes, Emma. *364*

Edwardes, Major General Sir Herbert
    Benjamin and Herman Merivale.
    365

Edwardes, Michael. *370. 369. 368. 367.*
    366

Edwards, Captain R.F. *371*

Edwards, William. *375. 374. 373. 372*

EIGHT MONTHS CAMPAIGN
    AGAINST THE BENGAL SEPOY
    ARMY DURING THE MUTINY
    OF 1857. 185

EIGHT MONTHS EXPERIENCE OF
    THE REVOLT IN 1857. 320

EIGHTEEN FIFTY-SEVEN. 943

Elliot, Charles Alfred. *376*

Elliot, Joseph A. *377*

Elliott, Major W.J. & Lieut-Colonel
    Knollys. *378*

Elsmie, G.R. *379*

Embree, Ainslie T. *380*

ENGAGING SCOUNDRELS: TRUE TALES OF OLD LUCKNOW. 654

England. Proclamations 11

Chronological Series, Victoria. *381*

ENGLAND'S INFIRMITY. 5

ENGLAND'S TROUBLES IN INDIA. 49

ENGLISH AND INDIA (THE). 1092. 338

ENGLISH CAPTIVES IN OUDH (THE). 1152. 819

ENGLISH GOVERNMENT OF INDIA. 559

ENGLISH HISTORICAL WRITING ON THE INDIAN MUTINY 1857-1859. 269

ENGLISH IN INDIA (THE). 166

ENGLISH TENURE OF INDIA. 935

Entract, J(ohn) P(atrick). *382*

Erskine, W.C. *112*

ESCAPE FROM MEERUT. 978

ESSAYS AND LECTURES ON INDIAN HISTORICAL SUBJECTS. 712

ESSAYS ON THE INDIAN ARMY IN OUDH. 632

ESSAYS ON THE INDIAN MUTINY. 524

ESSAYS, MILITARY AND POLITICAL WRITTEN IN INDIA. 633

Etah. *448*

EVACUATION OF INDORE (THE). 1069

Evans, Thomas. *383*

Evans, W. Downing. *384*

EVENTS AT MEERUT. 362

Ewart, J.A. *385*

EX ORIENTE: SONNETS ON THE INDIAN REBELLION. 50

EXETER HALL VERSUS BRITISH INDIA. 51

EXPERIENCES OF LIFE IN INDIA IN 1857-1858. 748

EXTRACTS FROM INDIAN JOURNALS. 122

EXTRACTS FROM LETTERS. NOTES WRITTEN DURING THE SIEGE OF DELHI IN 1857. 896

EXTRACTS FROM LETTERS FROM CAPTAIN FENWICK TO HIS FRIENDS IN ENGLAND. 391

EXTRACTS FROM THE DIARY OF A BENGAL CIVILIAN 1857-59. 904

EXTRACTS FROM THE DIARY OF LT. F.W. STUBBS, BENGAL ARTILLERY, IN 1857-58. 1010

EXTRACTS FROM THREE SPEECHES DELIVERED BY THE LATE JOHN POYNDER. 863

EYEWITNESSES TO THE INDIAN MUTINY. 508

Eyre, Sir Vincent. *715. 386*

F

FACT v. FALSEHOOD. Being a Brief Summary of Mr. W. Tayler's Refutation. Presented March 15, 1880, in Reply to the Memorandum to The House of Commons (24th June, 1879) by Sir Frederick Halliday. 1026

FACTS AND REFLECTIONS CONNECTED WITH THE INDIAN REBELLION. 372

FACTS FOR A CHRISTIAN PUBLIC. 776

Fagan, Major General C.S. *1132*

Faizabad. *644*

FALLEN HEROES OF THE INDIAN WAR. 1132

FAMILIAR EPISTLES OF MR JOHN COMPANY TO MR. JOHN BULL. 576

Fanshawe, H.C. *387*

Farquhar, Lieut. John. *388*

Farwell, Byron. *389*

FAST DAY SERMONS (THE). 687

Fatehgarh. *580. 299*

FATEHGARH AND THE MUTINY. 299

FATEHGARH CAMP, 1777-1857. 1106

Fayrer, Surgeon General Sir Joseph. *390*

Fenwick, Captain. *391*

Ferozepore. *469*

Fforde, Major C(harles) del. W. *392*

FICTIONS CONNECTED WITH THE INDIAN OUTBREAK OF 1857 EXPOSED. 639

FIELD MARSHAL LORD NAPIER OF MAGDALA. 795

FIELD MARSHAL SIR DONALD STEWART. 379

FIFTY TWO STORIES OF THE INDIAN MUTINY AND THE MEN WHO SAVED INDIA. 752

FIFTY YEARS WITH JOHN COMPANY. 662

FIGHTING TEN (THE). 155

FIRST BENGAL EUROPEAN FUSILIERS (THE). 94

FIRST INDIAN WAR OF INDEPENDENCE (THE). 727

FIRST SHOT IN 1857 (THE). 731

Fisher, James. *393*

Fisher, Michael H. *394*

Fitchett, W. H. *395*

FIVE LETTERS ON INDIAN REORGANIZATION. 52

FIVE STORMY YEARS: SAVARKAR IN LONDON. 989

Fletcher, Reverend W.K. *396*

Forbes, Archibald. *399. 398. 397*

Forbes, Mrs. Hamilton. *400*

Forbes-Mitchell. *951*

Forbes-Mitchell, Sgt. W(illiam). *402. 401*

Forjett, Charles. *404. 403*

Forrest, George William. *409. 408. 407. 406. 405*

Forrest, Lieut. George VC. *405*

Forsyth, Ethel. *410*

FORTY ONE YEARS IN INDIA. 909

FOUR FAMOUS SOLDIERS. 527

FOUR HEROES OF INDIA: CLIVE, WARREN HASTINGS, HENRY HAVELOCK, JOHN LORD LAWRENCE. 525

Framji, Dosabhai. *411*

Fraser, Captain Hastings. *412*

FREEDOM STRUGGLE IN UTTAR PRADESH. 907

Frere, Sir Bartle. *715. 413*

Friend and Brother Officer. (Henry Yule). *414*

FROM CADET TO COLONEL. 937

FROM EIGHT TO EIGHTY. 573

FROM ENGLAND TO THE ANTIPODES AND INDIA-1846 TO 1902. 1089

FROM LONDON TO LUCKNOW. See 3

FROM MIDSHIPMAN TO FIELD MARSHAL. 1149

FROM MINNIE, WITH LOVE. 1093

FROM NEW YORK TO DELHI. 755

FROM SEPOY TO SUBADAR. 806. 673

Frost, Thomas. *415*

Fulton, Captain G.W.W. *416*

Furruckabad. *448*

FURTHER PAPERS. 462

Futtehghur. *1108. 1106. 572. 449. 445. 374. 125*

Futtehgurh. *See 3*

Futtehpoor. *448*

FUTURE GOVERNMENT OF INDIA (THE). 304

Fyzabad. *992*

  Maulvi of. *472*

G

G.D. *417*

GALLANT SEPOYS AND SOWARS. 378

Gambier-Parry, Ernest. *418*

Ganguly, Dr. Anil Baran. *419*

GARDEN OF FIDELITY (THE). 995

Gardiner, General Sir Robert William. *421. 420*

Gardner, Frank M. *423. 422*

Garrett, Herbert Leonard Offley. *425. 424. 341*

Gateshead, The Mayor of. *426*

GAZETTEER AND GAZETTEER MAP OF THE SEAT OF REBELLION IN INDIA. 27

GENERAL FREDERICK YOUNG. 570

GENERAL HAVELOCK AND CHRISTIAN SOLDIERSHIP. 1127

GENERAL ORDERS AND DISPATCHES RELATING TO THE RELIEF OF THE GARRISON OF LUCKNOW, THE DEFENSE OF THE ALLUMBAGH. 822

GENERAL SIR ALEXANDER TAYLOR. 1038

GENERAL SIR RICHARD MEADE. 1063

GENERAL VIEWS AND SPECIAL POINTS OF INTEREST IN THE CITY OF LUCKNOW. 349

Germon, Maria Vincent. *428. 427*

Ghalib, Asadullah Mirza. *429*

Ghazeepore. *See 3*

Ghose, Indira. *430*

Gibbon, Frederick P. *431*

Gibney, Robert D. *214*

Gilbert, Henry. *432*

Gillean. *683*

Gilliat, Edward. *434. 433*

Gimlette, Lieutenant-Colonel G(eorge) H(art) D(esmond). *435*

GLIMPSES THROUGH THE CANNON SMOKE. 398

GOD'S AVENGER. 139

GODS PROLONGED CONTROVERSY WITH BRITAIN. 988

GOLDEN COMMEMORATION OF THE INDIAN MUTINY. 53

Goldsmid, Frederic John. *436*

GOOD OLD DAYS OF JOHN COMPANY (THE). 241

GOOD SOLDIER, A MEMOIR OF MAJOR GENERAL SIR HENRY HAVELOCK (THE). 828

Gordon, Andrew. *437*

Gordon, General Sir Thomas Edward. *438*

Gordon, Surgeon General, Sir C.A. *439*

Gordon-Alexander, Lieut. Col. W. *440*

Gorman, James T. *441*

Goruckpoor. *448*

Gough, General Sir Hugh Henry, VC. *442*

GOVERNMENT IN ITS RELATIONS WITH EDUCATION AND CHRISTIANITY IN INDIA. 138

Government of India. *452. 451. 450. 449. 448. 447. 446. 445. 444. 443*

GOVERNMENT OF INDIA (THE). 95

GOVERNMENT OF THE EAST INDIAN CO (THE). 648

Gowan, I.G. *453*

Gowing, Sergeant Major T. *454*

GRAHAM MUTINY PAPERS. 496

Grant, General Sir James Hope. *455*

Grant, James P. *456*

Grant, Sir James Hope. *190*

Gray, Ernest. *457*

Gray, Robert. *458*

Graydon, William Murray. *459*

Great Britain. *463. 462. 461. 460*

GREAT INDIAN CRISIS (THE). 96

GREAT INDIAN MUTINY (THE). 1112. 281

GREAT MUTINY OF 1857, ITS CAUSES, FEATURES AND RESULTS. 600

GREAT MUTINY: INDIA 1857. 509

GREAT REBELLION (THE). 607

GREAT REVOLUTION OF 1857. 487

GREAT WARRIOR. 975

GREAT WHITE HAND OR THE TIGER OF CAWNPORE (THE). 778

Greathed

Three brothers. *414*

Greathed, H(ervey) H(arris). *464*

Greaves, General Sir George Richard. *465*

Green, Henry. *466*

Greene, Dominick Sarsfield. *467*

Greenway, J. *91*

Grey, Leopold John Herbert. *468*

Griffiths, Capt. Charles John. *469*

Groom, Lt. William Tate. *470*

GROWTH OF NATIONALISM IN INDIA 1857-1905 (THE). 787

Gubbins, Martin Richard. *471*
GUERILLA FIGHTER OF THE FIRST FREEDOM MOVEMENT. 419
Guha, Ranajit and Gayatri Spivak. *472*
GUILTY MEN OF 1857. 177. 97
GUILTY OR NOT GUILTY. 589
Gujarat. *342*
GUJARAT IN 1857. 342
GUNNER JINGO'S JUBILEE. 1008
Gupta, Pratul Chandra. *474. 473*
Gupta, Rajni Kant. *475*
Gupta, S. *476*
Gurney, Rev. John Hampden. *477*
Gwalior. *689. 665*

H

Hafeez Malik. 14
Hafeez Malik. *9*
Haigh, R.H. and P.W. Turner. *480. 479. 478*
Haldane, Julia. *1103. 118*
Hale, Williams. *481*
Hall, Major-General R.H. *62*
Halliday, Frederick James. *482*
Halls, John James. *483*
HANDBOOK FOR DELHI (THE). 294
Handcock, Col. A(rthur) G(ore). *484*
Hannah, W.H. *485*
Haq, S. Moinul. *487. 486*
Harcourt, A.F.P. *488*
Hare, Augustus and John Cuthbert. *489*
Hare, E. C. *490*
Hare, Lt. Col. R.T. *491*
Harrington, C.S. *493*
Harrington, Capt. Hastings Edward, V.C. *492*
Harris, John. *494*
Harris, Major General James T. *495*
Harris, Mrs. G(eorgina) (Maria). *119*
Harrison, A.T. *496*
Harrison, General Sir Richard. *497*
Harrison, John Bennett. *498*
Harvey, G.F. *499*

HAS OUDE BEEN WORSE GOVERNED BY ITS NATIVE PRINCES THAN OUR INDIAN TERRITORIES BY LEADENHALL STREET. 647
HAVELOCK. 399. 295
Havelock, Lieut. Harry. *610*
Havelock, Lieut.-Gen. Sir Henry Marshman. *471*
Havelock, Sir H.M. *500*
Havelock, Sir Henry. *1142. 1127. 1104. 1042. 1013. 893. 861. 855. 828. 825. 820. 811. 742. 719. 712. 658. 634. 529. 502. 488. 470. 456. 399. 384. 334. 333. 295. 285. 193. 168. 137. 66. 43*
HAVELOCK, THE GOOD SOLDIER. 168
HAVELOCK: THE BROAD STONE OF HONOUR. 529
HAVELOCK'S MARCH ON CAWNPORE 1857. 959
Hay, David. *501*
Hazrat Mahal of Lucknow. *260*
Headley, J. *502*
HEALED & SAVED: A STORY OF THE LUCKNOW MEDICAL MISSION. 720
Hearn, Gordon Risley. *503*
Hearsey, General John. *843*
Hearsey, John B. *504*
HEARSEYS, FIVE GENERATIONS OF AN ANGLO INDIAN FAMILY (THE). 843
HELLFIRE JACK,. 285
Henderson, Henry Barkley. *505*
Herford, Capt. I.S.A. *506*
HERO OF DELHI (THE). 845
HEROES OF THE INDIAN MUTINY. 434
HEROES OF THE INDIAN REBELLION (THE). 151
Hervey, Lt. Gen. Charles. *507*
Hewitt, James. *508*
Hibbert, Christopher. *509*
Hidayat Ali, Shaikh. *510*
HIGHLAND BRIGADE (THE). 311
Hill, J.R. *511*

Hill, S.C. *512*

Hilton, Edward H. *516. 515. 514. 513*

Hilton, Major General Richard. *517*

HINTS ON THE REORGANIZATION OF THE INDIAN ARMY. 1107

HINTS REGARDING THE REORGANIZATION OF THE BENGAL ARMY. 532

HISTORICAL RECORDS OF THE 34ᵀᴴ (THE). 763

HISTORICAL RECORDS OF THE 53RD SHROPSHIRE REGIMENT. 917

HISTORICAL WRITINGS ON THE PEOPLES OF ASIA. 852

HISTORIOGRAPHY OF THE INDIAN REVOLT OF 1857 (THE). 942

HISTORY AND CULTURE OF THE INDIAN PEOPLE. 704

HISTORY AND SERVICES OF THE 78TH HIGHLANDERS. 333

HISTORY AND THE PRESS. 1032

HISTORY OF THE BEHAR INDIGO FACTORIES. 1139

HISTORY OF THE BENGAL EUROPEAN REGIMENT. 555

HISTORY OF THE BRITISH EMPIRE IN INDIA (THE). 804

HISTORY OF THE BRITISH SETTLEMENTS (THE). 98

HISTORY OF THE DELHI MASSACRE. 846

HISTORY OF THE ENGLISH PRESS IN BENGAL. 261

HISTORY OF THE FREEDOM MOVEMENT IN INDIA. 702

HISTORY OF THE FREEDOM MOVEMENT IN BIHAR. 331

HISTORY OF THE FREEDOM MOVEMENT IN INDIA. 259

HISTORY OF THE INDIAN MUTINY. 713. 621

HISTORY OF THE INDIAN MUTINY (THE). 142

HISTORY OF THE INDIAN MUTINY OF 1857-1858. 591

HISTORY OF THE INDIAN NAVY 1613-1863. 661

HISTORY OF THE INDIAN REVOLT (THE). 417. 348

HISTORY OF THE RIFLE BRIGADE. 297

HISTORY OF THE ROYAL AND INDIAN ARTILLERY IN THE MUTINY OF 1857. 575

HISTORY OF THE SIEGE OF DELHI. 556. 54

History of the War in India. 706

HISTORY OF THE WAR IN INDIA. 705

Hoare, Edward. *518*

Hodgson, Col. John Studholme. *519*

Hodson, Rev. George H. *520*

Hodson, W.S.R. 1144. 1074. 636. 520. 442. 418. 298. 116

Hodson, W.S.R. *1055. 937*

HODSONS HORSE. 239

Hoey, W. *521*

Hoffman, Dr. V. *16*

Hogarth, George, Vicar of Burton-upon-Humber. *522*

Holcomb, James Foote. *523*

HOLKAR'S APPEAL: THE OFFICE OF THE EMPIRE. 165

Holloway, John. *524*

Holmes, Frederick Morell. *525*

Holmes, T(homas) R(ice) E(dward). *527. 526*

Home, Surgeon General Sir Anthony Dickson. *528*

HONORIA LAWRENCE. 345

HONORING GOD AND ITS REWARD. A LESSON FROM THE LIFE OF THE LATE GENERAL SIR HENRY HAVELOCK. 1142

Hood, Edwin Paxton. *529*

Hoseason, Commander John Cochrane, R.N. *530*

Hoskins, Lt. Col. *531*

Hough, W. Lieut-Colonel. *532*

How Does England Make and Break Treaties. 16

HOW I WON THE INDIAN MUTINY MEDAL: AND HOW THINGS WENT AFTERWARDS. 951

HOW I WON THE VICTORIAN CROSS. 590

HOW ONE OF THE MCGOVERN CLAN WON THE VICTORIA CROSS. 741

HOW WE ESCAPED FROM DELHI. 635

Hughes, Derrick. *533*

Hughes, Major General B.P. *534*

Humeerpoor. *448*

HUMILIATION IN NATIONAL TROUBLES. 1134

Humphrey, Rev. J.L. M.D. *535*

Hungerford, Townsend. *536*

Hunter, Colonel Charles. *537*

Hunter, Lt. Col. William. *538*

Husain, Mahdi. *539*

Hutchinson, Capt. G. *540*

Hutchinson, Lieut. G. *548*

Huxham. *42*

Huxham, Mrs. *121*

Hyderabad. *1039*

Hypher, P.P. *541*

I

ILLUSTRATED HISTORY OF THE BRITISH EMPIRE (THE). 805

IMMEDIATE CAUSE OF THE INDIAN MUTINY (THE). 307

IMPERIAL RULE IN PUNJAB 1818-1881. 918

IN 1857. 837

IN PIAM MEMORIAM. 1088

IN THE COMPANY'S SERVICE. 1011

IN THE DOAB AND ROHILKHAND: NORTH INDIAN CHRISTIANITY. 25

IN THE MUTINY DAYS. 317

INAM COMMSSION UNMASKED (THE). *613*

INCIDENTS IN INDIA AND MEMORIES OF THE MUTINY. 859

INCIDENTS IN THE LIFE OF. 184

INCIDENTS IN THE SEPOY WAR. 455

INCIDENTS OF INDIAN LIFE. 249

INDIA. 288

INDIA MUTINY SERMONS. 56

INDIA AND ITS FUTURE. 225

INDIA AND ITS PEOPLE. 889

INDIA AND THE INDIAN MUTINY. 706

INDIA BEFORE AND AFTER THE MUTINY. 55

INDIA HISTORICAL AND DESCRIPTIVE. 363

INDIA IN 1857-59. 350

INDIA IN 1858. 753

INDIA UNDER DALHOUSIE AND CANNING. 233

INDIA, ITS GOVERNMENT, MISGOVERNMENT. 235

India. Imperial Record Department. *542*

INDIA. THE REVOLT AND THE HOME GOVERNMENT. 58

INDIA: APPEAL TO THE CHARITY OF THE CATHOLICS. 850

INDIA: GEOGRAPHICAL, STATISTICAL, AND HISTORICAL. 59

INDIA: ITS DANGER CONSIDERED IN 1856. 25

INDIA: ITS HISTORY. 1003

INDIAN ARMY (THE). 762

INDIAN CHURCH DURING THE GREAT REBELLION (THE). 961

INDIAN CRIMINAL (THE). 4

INDIAN CRISIS (THE). 231. 99

INDIAN CRISIS. A MEMORIAL TO THE QUEEN (THE). 277

INDIAN EMPIRE WITH A FULL ACCOUNT OF THE MUTINY OF THE NATIVE TROOPS. (THE). 722

INDIAN GUP. 141

INDIAN HISTORY AND COLONEL G.B.MALLESON (THE). 963

INDIAN LITERATURE OF THE GREAT REBELLION (THE). 932

INDIAN MILITARY REVOLT VIEWED IN ITS RELIGIOUS ASPECTS (THE). 1138

INDIAN MISSIONS; VIEWED IN CONNEXION WITH THE MUTINY. 760

INDIAN MUTINIES ACCOUNTED FOR (THE). 133

INDIAN MUTINY. 498. 494

INDIAN MUTINY (THE). 1124. 936. 678. 628. 422. 332. 240. 178. 100

INDIAN MUTINY 1857 (THE). 991

INDIAN MUTINY 1857-58 (THE). A Guide to Source Material in the India Office. 945

INDIAN MUTINY A CENTENARY HISTORY (THE). 517

INDIAN MUTINY IN PERSPECTIVE (THE). 685

INDIAN MUTINY OF 1857. 711

INDIAN MUTINY OF 1857 (THE). 938. 903

INDIAN MUTINY OF 1857 AND THE SIKHS (THE). 968

INDIAN MUTINY OF 1857: AN ANNOTATED AND ILLUSTRATED BIBLIOGRAPHY. 569

INDIAN MUTINY OR INDIA'S IDOLATRY AND ENGLAND'S RESPONSIBILITY. A SERMON PREACHED ON THE FAST DAY, OCTOBER 7, 1857 (THE). 766

INDIAN MUTINY SERMON. 60

INDIAN MUTINY TO THE EVACUATION OF LUCKNOW (THE). 219

INDIAN MUTINY TO THE FALL OF DELHI (THE). 220

INDIAN MUTINY UP TO THE RELIEF OF LUCKNOW (THE). 641

INDIAN MUTINY, ITS CAUSES AND REMEDIES (THE). 236

INDIAN MUTINY, TO THE RECAPTURE OF LUCKNOW. TO WHICH IS ADDED, A NARRATIVE OF THE DEFENCE OF THE RESIDENCY, AND A MEMOIR OF GENERAL HAVELOCK (THE). 221

INDIAN MUTINY: 1857 IN BIHAR. 340

INDIAN MUTINY: A NARRATIVE OF THE EVENTS AT CAWNPORE (THE). 640

INDIAN NATIONAL MOVEMENT. 616. 265

INDIAN NATIONAL UPRISING OF 1857 (THE). 347

INDIAN NATIONALIST MOVEMENT (THE). 148

Indian News (The). *543*

INDIAN PLACARD. 289

INDIAN POLICY. 61

INDIAN REBELLION (THE). 354

INDIAN REFORM BILLS; OR, LEGISLATION FOR INDIA, FROM 1766 TO 1858. 1002

INDIAN REMINISCENCES. 1119

INDIAN RESPONSES TO COLONIALISM. 170

INDIAN REVOLUTION 1857. 878

INDIAN REVOLUTION, VIEWS AND PERSPECTIVES (THE). 941

INDIAN SKETCHES 1816-1866. 835

INDIAN SPEECHES AND DOCUMENTS ON BRITISH RULE 1821-1918. 701

INDIAN VIEWS DURING THE MUTINY. 734

INDIAN WAR OF INDEPENDENCE (THE). 931

INDIAN WAR OF INDEPENDENCE OF 1857 (THE). 129

INDIA'S MUTINY AND ENGLANDS MOURNING. 57

INDIA'S PAST AND FUTURE AND ENGLAND'S DUTY. 771

INDIA'S TROUBLE: IS THERE NOT A CAUSE. 695

Indophilus. *1070. 544*

Indumati, Sheorey. *545*
Inge, Dennison, M. Lt.Col. *546*
Inglis, John E.W. *549. 548*
Inglis, Lady (Julia Selina). *550. 547*
Inglis, Sir John. *549. 548. 93*
Innes, Lt. General John James
    McLeod V.C. *554. 553. 552. 551*
Innes, Percival Robert. *555*
*INSTRUCTIONS ON BEHALF OF
    SIR G.C. WHITLOCK, K.C.B.,
    AND THE TROOPS ENGAGED
    UNDER HIS COMMAND AT
    BANDA AND KIRWEE. 609*
INVERSION OF TIMES. 839
Ireland, William Wotherspoon. *556. 54*
Irwin, Mrs. *126*

J

Jabalpur. *973*
Jackson, Alice F. *557*
Jackson, Sir Charles. *558*
Jacob, Brig. Gen. John. *564. 563. 562.
    561. 560. 213*
Jacob, Major General Sir George Le
    Grand. *568. 567. 566. 565. 559*
Jain, Vipin. *569*
Jaloun. *448*
JAMES OUTRAM. 436
Jenkins, L. Hadow. *570*
Jenkins, Rev. John. *571*
Jennings-Bramly, William. *572*
Jervis-Waldy, W.T. *573*
Jhansee. *1118. 1046. 1017. 1016. 980.
    974. 858. 683. 638. 627. 523. 448.
    339. 305. 112*
*JHANSI HISTORY AND THE RANI
    OF JHANSI. 523*
Jivanalala, Rai Bahadur. *574*
Jocelyn, Col. Julian R. J. *575*
*JOHN NICHOLSON: THE LION OF
    THE PUNJAB. 273*
*JOHN CHALMERS, LETTERS
    FROM THE INDIAN MUTINY
    1857-1859. 1052*
John Company. *1014. 662. 651. 576. 58*

*JOHN NICHOLSON, THE BATTLE
    OF NAJAFGARH AND THE
    SIEGE OF DELHI. 480*
JOHN RUSSELL COLVIN. 286
*JOHN SHAKESPEAR OF SHADWELL
    AND HIS DESCENDANTS. 953*
Johnson, Major W(illiam) T(homas).
    577
Jones, Captain Oliver John RN. *578*
Jones, Earnest Charles. *579*
Jones, Gavin Sibbald. *580*
Jopling, L.M. *581*
Joshi, P.C. *583*
Joshi, P.C. (Compiled). *582*
Jourdain, Lieut. Colonel Henry F.N.
    and Edward Fraser. *584*
*JOURNAL OF A SOLDIER DURING
    THE CAMPAIGNS OF 1857-1858
    (THE). 950*
*JOURNAL OF AN ENGLISH
    OFFICER IN INDIA. 811*
*JOURNAL OF THE LATE GENERAL
    SIR SAM BROWNE. 196*
*JOURNAL OF THE SIEGE OF
    LUCKNOW. 427*
*Journal of the Siege Operations Against the
    Mutineers at Delhi in 1857. 371*
JOURNAL. INDIA. 1113
Joyce, Michael. *585*
Jubulpore. *112*
*JUDY O'GRADY & THE COLONEL'S
    LADY. 1129*
Jugdespore. *841*
*JULIUNDUR MUTINEERS (THE).
    272*
JUSTICE FOR INDIA. 224
*JUSTICE IN THE NINETEENTH
    CENTURY, AN APPEAL TO
    BRITISH HONOR. 1033*

K

*KACHERI CEMETERY KANPUR.
    1158*
Kaiser Bagh. *610*
Kashinath. *586. 258*
KASHMIR GATE (THE). 848
Kaul, H.K. *587*

Kavanagh, T. Henry. *141*

Kavanagh, Thomas Henry. *590. 589. 588*

Kaye and Malleson. *591*

Kaye, John William. *593. 592*

Kaye, John Williams and Col. George Bruce Malleson. *594*

KAZAN SINGH. 1114

Keene, Henry George. *596. 595*

Kelly, Charles. *597*

Kelly, Sophia. *598*

Kennedy, James. *600. 599*

Khadgawat, Nathu Ram. *601*

Khairabadi, Fazl Haq. *602*

Khan, Azimullah. *174. 106*

Khan, Salabut
Murder of the Burtons. *207*

Khilnani, Niranjan. *603*

Khobrekar, V.G. *604*

Kincaid, Charles Augustus. *605*

King, Lt. Edward. *606*

King, Theodore. *607*

Kinloch, Charles W. *608*

Kinlock, Rev. A. *609*

Kinsley, D.A. *610*

Kishori Chand Mitra. *222*

Kitchen, J.F. *122*

Kittermaster, Rev. Fred. Wilson. *612. 611*

Knight, Robert. *613*

Knollys, Capt. Henry. *614*

Knollys, Lt. Col. William Wallingford. *615*

Kuar Singh. *329*

Kumaon. *448*

Kumar, Nagendra. *616*

Kumar, Purushottam. *617*

Kunwar Singh. *714*

Kyne, J. *618*

L

LABORIOUS DAYS. 376

LACHMI BAI, RANI OF JHANSI. 1118

Ladendorf, Janice M. *619*

LAHORE TO LUCKNOW. 626

LAKSHMI BAI, RANI OF JHANSI AND OTHER ESSAYS. 605

Lal, Jivan. *620*

Lal, Kanhaya. *621*

Lall, Peary. *622*

LAND OF THE VEDA (THE). 210

Landon, Perceval. *624. 623*

Lang, Arthur. *195*

Lang, Arthur Moffatt. *626. 625*

Lang, John. *627*

Langdon-Davies, John. *628*

LAST COUNSELS OF AN UNKNOWN COUNSELLOR. 343

LAST DAY'S OF NANA SAHIB (THE). 143

LAST OF THE PALADINS (THE). 1120

LAST PESHWA AND THE ENGLISH COMMISSIONER (THE). 473

LATE CAPTAIN H. E. HARRINGTON, VC OF HM BENGAL ARTILLERY (THE). 493

LATE CAPTAIN H.E. HARINGTON, V.C (THE). 492

LATE REBELLION IN INDIA (THE). 1057

Laurence, Thomas Benson. *629*

Laverack, Alfred. *630*

LAWRENCE OF LUCKNOW. 1806-1857. 774

Lawrence, Lord John Laird Mair. *1077. 1049. 979. 808. 715. 553. 431. 369*

Lawrence, Lt. General George. *631*

Lawrence, Sir George St. Patrick. *431*

Lawrence, Sir Henry Montgomery. *1043. 992. 971. 774. 634. 633. 632. 632. 593. 554. 471. 431. 369. 365. 345. 80*

LAWRENCES OF THE PUNJAB (THE). 431

LAY THOUGHTS ON THE INDIAN MUTINY. 217

Leasor, James. *636*

Leather, G.F.T. *637*

LeBas, C. *635*

Lebra-Chapman, Joyce. *638*

Leckey, Edward. *639*

Lee, J(oseph) F. 640
Lee, J(oseph)F. And Captain F.W.
   Radcliffe. 641
Lee-Warner, Sir William. *643. 642*
Lennox, Chas. Wm. *644*
LETTER 235. 359
*LETTER CONTAINING EXTRACTS
   FROM A JOURNAL KEPT
   DURING THE SIEGE OF
   LUCKNOW. 547*
*LETTER FROM LUCKNOW AND
   CAWNPORE. 664*
*LETTER TO H. M. DURAND
   ESQ. C.S.I. COMMENTING ON
   CERTAIN STATEMENTS IN HIS
   WORKS. 164*
*LETTER TO THE MEMBERS OF
   THE EAST INDIA UNITED
   SERVICE CLUB. 565*
LETTERS AND DISPATCHES. 386
*LETTERS BRIEFLY DESCRIBING
   THE PROBABLE CAUSES OF
   THE INDIAN OUTBREAK. 109*
LETTERS FROM DELHI, 1857. 146
*LETTERS FROM FUTTEHGURH.
   125*
*LETTERS FROM INDIA AND
   CHINA. 327*
*LETTERS FROM INDIA AND
   PERSIA. 287*
*LETTERS FROM LIEUTENANT
   EDWARD CHAMIER. 256*
*LETTERS FROM MEADOWS
   TAYLOR. 1040*
*LETTERS FROM PERSIA AND
   INDIA 1857-1859. 145*
*LETTERS FROM THE FIELD
   DURING THE INDIAN
   REBELLION. 1086*
*LETTERS OF ALEXANDER SCOTT
   MONCRIEFF. 764*
*LETTERS OF EDWIN UTTERTON
   FROM THE CRIMEA AND THE
   INDIAN MUTINY. 1110*
*LETTERS OF INDOPHILUS TO THE
   TIMES (THE). 1070*
*LETTERS OF QUEEN VICTORIA
   1837-1861 (THE). 167*
*LETTERS OF SIR HENRY
   MONTGOMERY LAWRENCE.
   971. 634*
*LETTERS OF THE LATE
   MAJOR-GENERAL R.H. HALL. 62*
*LETTERS WRITTEN DURING THE
   INDIAN MUTINY. 910*
*LETTERS WRITTEN DURING THE
   SIEGE OF DELHI. 1085. 464*
*LETTERS WRITTEN FROM INDIA
   DURING THE MUTINY. 254*
*Letters Written from India During the
   Mutiny and Waziri Campaigns. 1052*
Lewin, Lt. Col. Thomas H. *645*
Lewin, Malcolm. *650. 649. 648. 647*
Lewin, Malcolm. (ed.). *646*
Lewis, Sir George. *651*
*LIEUT.-GENERAL SIR JAMES
   OUTRAM'S CAMPAIGN IN INDIA
   1857-58. 820*
*LIEUTENANT COLONEL GOULD
   HUNTER-WESTON OF
   HUNTERSTON. 663*
*LIFE AND OPINIONS OF MAJOR
   GENERAL C.M. MACGREGOR
   QUARTERMASTER- GENERAL
   IN INDIA. 680*
*LIFE AND TRAVELS OF JAMES
   FISHER. 393*
*LIFE AND WORK IN BENARES AND
   KUMAON. 599*
*LIFE OF COLIN CAMPBELL, LORD
   CLYDE (THE). 952*
*LIFE OF FIELD MARSHAL SIR
   NEVILLE CHAMBERLAIN. 407*
*LIFE OF FIELD-MARSHAL SIR
   FREDERICK PAUL HAINES
   (THE). 881*
*LIFE OF GENERAL H. HAVELOCK
   K.C.B. 502*
*LIFE OF GENERAL SIR HARRY N.
   D. PRENDERGAST, THE HAPPY
   WARRIOR. 1100*
*LIFE OF GENERAL SIR JAMES
   HOPE GRANT. 614*
*LIFE OF JOHN NICHOLSON (THE).
   1076*
LIFE OF LORD LAWRENCE. 979

LIFE OF LORD ROBERTS (THE).
409
LIFE OF LORD WOLSELEY (THE).
736
LIFE OF MAJOR GENERAL SIR
HENRY MARION DURAND
(THE). 357
LIFE OF MARQUISE OF
DALHOUSIE (THE). 643
LIFE OF MRS. SHERWOOD. 598
LIFE OF SIR HENRY LAWRENCE.
365
LIFE OF THE MARQUIS OF
DALHOUSIE. 1078
LIFE OF THE RIGHT HONORABLE
SIR ALFRED COMYN LYALL. 358
LIST OF INSCRIPTIONS ON
CHRISTIAN TOMBS. 180
LIST OF OFFICERS. 444
LIVES OF INDIAN OFFICERS. 593
Llewellyn, Alexander. *652*
Llewellyn-Jones, Rosie. *654. 653*
Lloyd, Julius. *655*
Lockwood, E. *656*
Login, Lady. *657*
Looker, Edith C. *658*
Lord Canning. *39. 7*
LORD CANNING, THE INDIAN
MUTINIES AND THE
GOVERNMENT POLICY. 63
LORD DALHOUSIE'S
ADMINISTRATION OF THE
CONQUERED AND ANNEXED
STATES. 877
LORD ELLENBROUGHS BLUNDER.
64
LORD LAWRENCE. 1049. 19
LORD LAWRENCE AND THE
MUTINY. 808
LORD LAWRENCE: A SKETCH OF
HIS PUBLIC CAREER. 1077
LOST DOMINION (THE). 246
Low, Charles Rathbone. *661. 660. 659*
Low, Ursula. *662*
Low, W.D. *663*
Lowe, E.D. *664*
Lowe, Thomas. *665*

Lowrie, John C. *123*
LOYAL RAJPUTANA(THE). 927
Luard, Major C.E. *666*
Luaro, Robert Davies. *667*
Lucas, J.J. *668*
Lucknow. *1144. 816. 803. 791. 684. 669.*
664. 654. 653. 614. 581. 577. 398.
349. 318. 167. 145. 34
Siege of, *132. 1153. 1151. 1145.*
1097. 1096. 1083. 1055. 1054.
1053. 1044. 1018. 1013. 977. 971.
949. 925. 917. 911. 909. 908. 894.
860. 840. 835. 825. 822. 820. 810.
809. 796. 795. 775. 773. 745. 744.
742. 700. 691. 663. 626. 612. 585.
578. 552. 551. 550. 549. 528. 524.
514. 513. 508. 507. 501. 493. 492.
488. 471. 470. 442. 441. 440. 439.
428. 428. 416. 406. 405. 402. 401.
400. 393. 392. 390. 388. 385. 366.
334. 333. 327. 325. 283. 281. 248.
227. 221. 219. 198. 190. 182. 132.
121. 119. 94. 93. 79. 42. 29
LUCKNOW 1857:. 1018
LUCKNOW ALBUM (THE). 24
LUCKNOW AND ITS MEMORIALS
OF THE MUTINY. 198
LUCKNOW AND OUDE IN THE
MUTINY. A NARRATIVE AND A
STUDY. 552
LUCKNOW GUIDE. 65
LUCKNOW SIEGE DIARY OF MRS.
C.M. BRYDON (THE). 392
Lucknow State Library. *669*
Ludlow, John Malcolm. *671. 670*
Lumsden, General Sir Peter S(tark)
and George R. Elsmie. *672*
Lunt, J. (ed.). *673*
Lushington, Right Honourable
Stephen. *675. 674*
Lutfullah, Syed. *676*

M

M.W. (Macleod Wylie). *677*
Macbean, Major N.I. *691*
MacCarty, J. *678*
MacCrea, R. *679*

MacGregor, Charles Metcalf. *680*

MacIntyre, James J. *681*

Mackee, Reverend James. *692*

Mackenzie, Alexander R.D. *693*

Mackenzie, James Thompson. *694*

MacKenzie, Mrs. C. *682*

Mackenzie, W. B. *695*

Maclagan, Michael. *696*

MacLean, J. *683*

Macleod, Major Gen. A. *697*

MacLeod, Norman D.D. *684*

MacMunn, Sir George. *686. 685*

MacNeele. *687*

MacNeile, Hugh. *687*

MacPherson, Lorne C. *688*

MacPherson, Maj. Samuel Charters. *689*

MacQueen, Kenneth. *690*

Madras Military Male Orphan Asylum. *698*

MAGNA EST VERITAS. 1027

MAHARASHTRA ARCHIVES, BULLETIN OF THE DEPARTMENT OF ARCHIVES NOS. 9 AND 10. THE LEGEND OF NANA SAHEB. 604

MAHOMEDAN REBELLION (THE). 242

Majendie, Lt. V(ivian) D(ering). *700*

Majumdar, J.K. ed. *701*

Majumdar, Ramesh Chandra. *704. 703. 702*

MAKING OF COLONIAL LUCKNOW 1856-1877 (THE). 816

MAKING OF INDIAN POLICY 1853-65. 865

Malcolm, Henry Frederick. *706. 705*

Malcolm, Thomas (See Caine, Rev. Caesar). *707*

Malgonkar, Manohar. *708*

Malik, Salah-uddin. *709*

Malleson, Col. George Bruce. *715. 714. 713. 712. 711. 710. 124*

Malleson, George Bruce. *594*

Malwa. *990*

Manchester Man. *See* 1

Mansfield, H.O. *716*

Maradabad. *448*

MARGARET OUTRAM 1778-1873. 821

Margolioth. *717*

Mariwalla, C.L. *718*

Marshman, John Clark. *719*

Marston, Louise. *720*

Martin, Major W. *721*

Martin, Robert Montgomery. *723. 722*

Martin, W. *724*

Martin, William. *726. 725. 130*

MARTINIERE BOYS IN THE BAILEY GUARD (THE). 513

MARTINIERE BOYS IN THE RESIDENCY (THE). 515

Martyr of Allahabad. 992

MARTYR OF ALLAHABAD (THE). 746

MARTYRS OF THE INDIAN REBELLION (THE). 829

MARTYRS OF THE MUTINY. 571

Marx, Karl and Frederick Engels. *727*

Mason, Philip Woodruff. *729. 728*

Masselos, Jim and Narayani Gupta. *730*

Matthews, Charles Richard. *731*

Maude, Captain Francis Cornwallis, V.C. and John Walter Sherer. *732*

Maude, Col. Edwin. *733*

Maude, Col. Francis Cornwallis, V.C. *734*

MAULVI ZAKA ULLAH OF DELHI. 35

Maulvi of Fyzabad. *260*

Maunsell, General Sir Frederick Richard K.C.B. *735*

Maurice, Maj. Gen Sir F. and G. Arthur. *736*

MAURITIUS TO INDIA, 1857-8-9. 754

Mawe, Mrs. *737*

Mayne, F.O. *738*

McAree, James Gregory. *739*

McCallan, Andrew. *740. 44*

McGovern, Joseph Henry. *741*

McKenzie, Captain Thomas. *742*

Mead, Henry. *743*

Sepoy Revolt. *639*

Mecham, C. H. *744*

Medley, Capt. J. G. *745*

Meek, Rev. R. *746*

Meerut. *1144. 1130. 1128. 1121. 1067. 1053. 1010. 977. 838. 836. 814. 794. 793. 453. 448. 442. 362. 320. 257. 244. 243*

Mehta, Asoka. *747*

Melville, S. S. *748*

MEMOIR OF COLONEL WHELER. 291

MEMOIR OF JOHN LOVERING COOKE. 1151

MEMOIR OF MAJOR GENERAL SIR HENRY TOMBS. 1067

MEMOIR OF MAJOR GENERAL WILLIAM GEORGE LENNOX. 644

MEMOIR OF REV. ROBERT STEWARD FULLERTON. 668

MEMOIR OF THE LATE MAJOR GENERAL SIR HENRY HAVELOCK. 66

MEMOIR, LETTERS AND A DIARY OF THE REV. HENRY S. POLEHAMPTON M.A. CHAPLAIN OF LUCKNOW. 860

MEMOIRS. 465

MEMOIRS AND LETTERS OF THE LIFE OF SIR HERBERT B. EDWARDES. 364

MEMOIRS OF DELHI AND FAIZABAD. 521

MEMOIRS OF EDWARD HARE. 490

MEMOIRS OF FIELD MARSHAL SIR HENRY WYLIE NORMAN. 642

MEMOIRS OF GENERAL SIR HENRY DERMOT DALY G.C.B. 325

MEMOIRS OF HAKIM AHSANULLAH KHAN. 486

MEMOIRS OF JEREMIAH BRASYER (THE). 190

MEMOIRS OF MAJOR GENERAL SIR HENRY HAVELOCK. 719

MEMOIRS OF MY INDIAN CAREER. 237

MEMOIRS OF THE GEMINI GENERALS. 1123

MEMOIRS OF WILLIAM TAYLER. 264

MEMORANDUM FOR REORGANISING THE INDIAN. 181

MEMORANDUM ON THE MUTINY AND OUTBREAK AT MEERUT. 1128

MEMORANDUM ON THE RECONSTRUCTION OF THE BENGAL ARMY. 725. 67

MEMORANDUM ON THE THREE PASSAGES OF THE RIVER GANGES. 312

MEMORANDUM, OR A FEW WORDS ON THE MUTINY. 243

MEMORIAL CHURCH AT CAWNPORE. 68

MEMORIAL TO LORD CLYDE. 115

MEMORIALS OF CHRISTIAN MARTYRS AND OTHER SUFFERERS FOR THE TRUTH IN THE INDIAN REBELLION. 827

MEMORIALS OF GENERAL SIR EDWARD HARRIS GREATHED. 913

MEMORIALS OF SERVICE. 689

MEMORIES 1857-1872. 205

MEMORIES OF SEVEN CAMPAIGNS. 1062

Memories of the Mutiny. 958

MEMORIES OF THE MUTINY. 732

MEN AND EVENTS OF MY TIME IN INDIA. 1050

MEN WHO RULED INDIA (THE). 729

Mercer, Edward Smyth. *749*

Metcalf, Thomas R. *750*

Metcalfe, Charles Theophilus. *751*

Miles, A. H. and A. J. Pattle. *752*

MILITARY ANALYSIS OF THE REMOTE AND PROXIMATE CAUSES OF THE INDIAN REBELLION. 421

MILITARY LIFE OF H.R.H. GEORGE, DUKE OF CAMBRIDGE (THE). 1095

MILITARY MUTINY IN INDIA ITS ORIGIN AND ITS RESULTS (THE). 818

MILITARY TRAITS OF TATYA TOPE. 475

Mills, A. *753*

Milman, Lieut-General G. Bryan. *754*

Minturn, R. B. *755*

MINUTE BY THE LT. GOVERNOR OF BENGAL. 482

Misr, Koonwar Gunga Pershad. *756*

Misr, Rajah Byjenath. *757*

Misra, Anand Swarup. *758*

MISSIONARY MARTYR OF DELHI (THE). 314

Mistry, Homi D. *759*

Mitchell, Rev. J. Murray. *760*

MOHAMMED MASIH UDDIN KHAN BAHADUR. 16

Mohan, Krishan. *761*

Mollo, Boris. *762*

Molloy, Maj. G. M. *763*

Monckton, Rose. *125*

Moncrieff, Alexander Scott. *764*

Moncrieff, Ascott Robert Hope. *765*

MONEY OR MERIT. 336

Money, Reverend C.F.S. *766*

Montagu, Rear-Admiral Victor Alexander. *767*

Montalembert, M. Le Comte De. *768*

Montgomery, Brian. *769*

Montgomery, Robert. *770*

Montgomery, Sir Robert. *769*

MONTY'S GRANDFATHER. 769

Moody, Rev. N.J. *771*

Mookerjee, Sambhu Chandra. *222*

Mookerjee, Sambhu Chandra (also known as Mukharji). *772*

Moore, Geoffrey. *773*

MORAL OF A SAD STORY. FOUR SERMONS ON THE INDIAN MUTINY (THE). 477

MORAL OF THE INDIA DEBATE (THE). 101

Morison, J.L. *774*

Morradabad. *257*

Morrison, Rev. C. *775*

Morrison, Rev. W. Robert. *776*

Mouat, Fred J. *777*

Moulvi Liaicat Ali. *4*

Mozuffernugger. *448*

MRS. DUBERLY'S CAMPAIGNS. 1066

Muddock, Joyce Emerson. *779. 778*

Muin, Al-Din Hasan Khan. *780*

Muir, Sir William. *783. 782. 781*

Mujeeb, Muhammad. *784*

Mukerjee, Sambhu Chandra. *785. 120*

Mukharya, P.S. *786*

Mukherjee, Haridas and Uma Mukherjee. *787*

Mukherjee, Rudrangshu. *789. 788*

Mukhopadhyaya. *772*

Mukhopadhyaya, S.C. *69*

Mukhopadhyaya, Sambuchandra. *222*

Munro, Sir Thomas. *790*

Munro, Surgeon General William. *792. 791*

Musings on Military Matters. 519

MUSLIM AND THE HINDOO. A POEM ON THE SEPOY REVOLT. 611

MUSLIM ATTITUDE TOWARDS BRITISH RULE. 135

MUSLIM REVIVALISTS AND THE REVOLT OF 1857. 134

Muslims and the Mutiny. *266*

Muslims in the Mutiny. *1057. 771. 709. 701. 681. 487. 242. 226. 135. 13. 12. 9*

Muter, Mrs. Dunbar Douglas (Elizabeth McMullin). *794. 793*

MUTINIES AND REBELLIONS IN CHOTANAGPUR. 617

MUTINIES AND THE PEOPLE OR STATEMENTS OF NATIVE FIDELITY. 785. 772. 120. 69

MUTINIES IN INDIA. 70

MUTINIES IN RAJPOOTANA (THE). 867

MUTINIES IN THE BENGAL ARMY (THE). 608

MUTINIES, THE GOVERNMENT AND THE PEOPLE (THE). 222

Mutiny

    Causes, 139. *1082. 1070. 1004. 968. 966. 955. 946. 942. 936. 935. 909. 889. 876. 866. 851. 818. 813. 802. 797. 761. 750. 749. 743. 726. 697. 695. 692. 690. 682. 677. 670. 617. 600. 578. 519. 517. 496. 487. 479. 421. 420. 403. 375. 372. 361. 354. 340. 308. 289. 288. 262. 243. 242. 236. 229. 226. 225. 223. 222. 212. 192. 191. 178. 173. 159. 144. 133. 127. 123. 109. 104. 87. 72. 64. 52. 46. 40. 22. 17. 13. 11*

    Historiography. *852*

    Social origins. *1000*

MUTINY. 1143

MUTINY AND THE BRITISH LAND POLICY IN NORTH INDIA 1856-1868 (THE). 882

MUTINY AND THE CONGRESS (THE). 114

MUTINY AT MEERUT, 1857-58. 1121

MUTINY CHAPLAINS (THE). 533

MUTINY IN INDIA. 518. 448

MUTINY IN INDIA, A SERMON. 522

MUTINY IN SIALKOT (THE). 902

MUTINY IN THE BENGAL ARMY (THE). 102

MUTINY MEMOIRS. 693

MUTINY OF THE BENGAL ARMY. 710. 124

MUTINY OF THE BENGAL ARMY (THE). 308

MUTINY OF THE BENGAL ARMY. A SERMON(THE). 655

MUTINY OUTBREAK AT MEERUT IN 1857 (THE). 836

MUTINY PERIOD IN CHACHAR (THE). 276

MUTINY RECORDS: OUDH AND LUCKNOW 1856-57. 514

MUTINY TELEGRAMS. 972

MUTINY: REVOLUTION OR MUSLIM REBELLION. 709

Muttra. *448*

Muttra (Mathura). *1061*

MY DIARY IN INDIA IN THE YEAR 1858-59. 926

MY ESCAPE FROM THE MUTINEERS IN OUDH. 214

MY GARDEN IN THE CITY OF GARDENS. 351. 318

MY INDIAN JOURNAL. 232

MY JOURNAL OR WHAT I DID AND SAW BETWEEN THE 9TH JUNE AND 25TH NOVEMBER 1857 WITH AND ACCOUNT OF GENERAL HAVELOCK'S MARCH FROM ALLAHABAD TO LUCKNOW BY A VOLUNTEER. 1013

MY LIFE AS A SOLDIER. 742

MY RECOLLECTIONS OF THE SEPOY REVOLT 1857-58. 793

MY SERVICES IN THE INDIAN ARMY AND AFTER. 1094

Mynpoory. *448*

N

Nagpore. *112*

Nana Sahib. *834. 758. 708. 676. 627. 623. 604. 474. 473. 197. 143*

NANA SAHIB. 955

NANA SAHIB AND THE RISING AT CAWNPORE. 474

NANA SAHIB PESHWA AND THE FIGHT FOR FREEDOM. 758

Napier, Lt. Colonel Henry Dundas. 795

Napier, Robert Cornelis. 796

Napier, Sir Charles James, Lt.-Gen. 797

NARRATIVE OF AN ESCAPE FROM GWALIOR. 179

Narrative of Events at Cawnpore. 956

NARRATIVE OF EVENTS ATTENDING THE OUTBREAK OF DISTURBANCES AND THE RESTORATION OF AUTHORITY IN THE AGRA DIVISION 1857-1858. 499

NARRATIVE OF EVENTS ATTENDING THE OUTBREAK OF DISTURBANCES AND THE RESTORATION OF AUTHORITY IN THE DISTRICT OF BANDA IN 1857-58. 738

NARRATIVE OF EVENTS ATTENDING THE OUTBREAK OF DISTURBANCES AND THE RESTORATION OF AUTHORITY IN THE DISTRICT OF MEERUT IN 1857-58. 1130

NARRATIVE OF EVENTS ATTENDING THE OUTBREAK OF DISTURBANCES AND THE RESTORATION OF AUTHORITY IN THE DISTRICT OF MORADABAD IN 1857-58. 1137

NARRATIVE OF EVENTS ATTENDING THE OUTBREAK OF DISTURBANCES AND THE RESTORATION OF AUTHORITY IN THE DIVISION OF JHANSI IN 1857-58. 858

NARRATIVE OF EVENTS ATTENDING THE OUTBREAK OF DISTURBANCES AND THE RESTORATION OF AUTHORITY IN THE FURRUCKABAD. 868. 445

Narrative of Rajah Misr's Sufferings During the Rebellion. *375*

NARRATIVE OF THE ESCAPE OF W.E. FROM BUDAUN TO CAWNPORE. 373

NARRATIVE OF THE INDIAN MUTINIES. 698

NARRATIVE OF THE MUTINIES IN OUDE. 540

NARRATIVE OF THE MUTINY OF THE 12TH N.I. AT NAWGONG. 737

NARRATIVE OF THE MUTINY OF THE 29TH N.I. AT MORRADABAD. 446

NARRATIVE OF THE OUTBREAK AT SEETAPORE. 504

NARRATIVES OF RAJAH BYJENATH MISR'S SUFFERINGS DURING THE REBELLION. 757

Nash, John Tullock. *798*

Nath, Kashi. *258*

Nath, Kashi (Translator). *799*

NATIONAL ARCHIVES OF INDIA. 172

NATIONAL CHRISTIANITY FOR INDIA. 862

NATIVE FIDELITY. 833

NAVAL BRIGADES IN THE INDIAN MUTINY 1857-1858 (THE). 920

NECESSARY HELL (THE). 369

Neill, Brig. Gen. James. *1153. 1132. 634. 628. 593. 401. 334*

NEILL'S BLUE CAPS. 1153

Nicholl, Lt. General T. *800*

Nicholson, General John. *1132. 1122. 1076. 964. 845. 842. 593. 480. 479. 478. 457. 273. 157. 110*

Nicholson, Rev. Maxwell. *801*

Nigam, N.K. *802*

NIKKAL SEYN. 457

Nilsson, Sten and Narayani Gupta. *803*

NINE YEARS ON THE NORTH WEST FRONTIER. 302

NINETIETH LIGHT INFANTRY (THE). 103

Nolan, Edward H. *805. 804*

Norgate, Lt. Col D.C. *806*

Norgate, Lt. Col. D.C. *884*

Norman, General Sir Henry Wylie. *810. 809. 808*

Norman, General Sir Henry Wylie and Mrs. K. Young Ed. *807*

North, Major (Charles Napier). *811*

Norton, John. *866*

Norton, John Bruce. *813. 812*

NOT TO REVENGE BUT TO PROTECT. 1150

NOTE OF THE MUTINY FIGHTING AT LUCKNOW. 581

NOTES ON THE REVOLT IN THE NORTH WESTERN PROVINCES OF INDIA. 879

NOTES ON THE WOUNDED FROM THE MUTINY. 1131

NOVELS OF THE INDIAN MUTINY. 970

O

Oatts, L.B. *815*

OBSERVATIONS ON A SCHEME FOR THE RE-ORGANIZATION OF THE INDIAN ARMY. 563

OBSERVATIONS ON THE CIVIL, CRIMINAL. 303

OBSERVATIONS ON THE LATE EVENTS IN THE BENGAL PRESIDENCY. 71

OBSERVATIONS ON THE PROPOSED COUNCIL OF INDIA. 72

OBSERVATIONS SUPPORTED BY DOCUMENTS BEING A SUPPLEMENT TO COL. ADYE'S DEFENSE OF CAWNPORE. 1141

OBSTACLES TO THE PROGRESS FOR CHRISTIANITY IN INDIA. 692

O'Callaghan, Daniel. *814*

OCCASIONAL PAPERS OF THE ROYAL ARTILLERY INSTITUTION. 924

ODE ON THE DEATH OF GENERAL SIR HENRY HAVELOCK. 384

OLD MEMORIES. 442

Oldenburg, Veena Talwar. *816*

Oliver, John Ryder. *817*

ON INDIA. 697

ON THE FACE OF THE WATERS. 996

ON THE QUEENS ERRANDS. 1154

OPINIONS ON THE INDIAN ARMY. 519

ORCHID HOUSE (THE). 370

ORDEAL 1857. 784

ORDEAL AT LUCKNOW. 585

ORIENTAL CAMPAIGNS AND EUROPEAN FURLOUGHS. 733

Orlich, Leopold Von. *818*

Orr, A. P. See Wylie, Macleod. *819*

OTHER SIDE OF THE MEDAL. 1058

OUDE IN 1857, SOME MEMORIES OF THE INDIAN MUTINY. 182

OUDE QUESTION STATED AND CONSIDERED (THE). 481

OUDE: ITS PAST AND ITS FUTURE. 895

Oudh. *1160. 847. 819. 817. 791. 788. 671. 647. 643. 632. 540. 514. 497. 481. 471. 455. 406. 401. 394. 379. 374. 370. 316. 245. 233. 214. 211. 204. 182. 166. 140. 87. 16*

OUDH POLICY CONSIDERED HISTORICALLY. 211

OUR BONES ARE SCATTERED. THE CAWNPORE MASSACRES AND THE INDIAN MUTINY OF 1857. 1109

OUR CONDUCT, AFTER THE DISAFFECTION AND MUTINY OF THE NATIVE REGIMENTS HAD BROKEN OUT. 73

Our Crisis or Three Months in Patna. 1034

OUR ESCAPE FROM DELHI. 1102

OUR ESCAPE IN JUNE, 1857. 126

OUR FAITHFUL ALLY, THE NIZAM. 412

OUR INDIAN MISSION. 437

OUR REAL DANGER IN INDIA. 403

Outram, Lieut.-General Sir James. *820*

Outram, Mary Frances. *821*

Outram, Sir James. *1075. 822. 548. 506. 436. 333. 285*

Ouvry, Col. Henry A. *823*

Ouvry, Mrs. Matilda H. *824*

Owen, Arthur. *825*

Owen, Rev William. *829. 828. 827*

Owen, Sidney. *826*

P

PADRE ELLIOT OF FYZABAD. 377
Paget, Mrs. Leopold. *830*
PAINTER'S EYE (THE). 803
Pal, Dharm. *832. 831*
Pal, Kristo Das. *833*
Palande, M.R. Executive Secretary. *834*
Palmer, General Henry. *835*
Palmer, J.A.B. *836*
Pande, Mangal. *731. 291*
Panikkar, Kavalam Modhava. *837*
PAPERS REGARDING THE INDIAN MUTINY. 244
Parker, Neville Thornton. *838*
Parkinson, Yehza-en-Nasr. *839*
Parry, Captain Sidney Henry Jones. *840*
Parsons, Richard. *841*
PARTICULARS OF THE MUTINY OF 1857 IN BAREILLY AND BUDAEON. 756
Paske, Major A.G. *842*
PASSAGE OF THE GOVERNMENT OF INDIA BILL OF 1858 (THE). 739
PASSAGES FROM THE LIFE OF A HERO, W.S.R. HODSON. 116
Patna. *656*
Patna Crisis. *1079. 1070. 1037. 1036. 1035. 1033. 1032. 1030. 1029. 1028. 1027. 1026. 1025. 1024. 1023. 1022. 131. 15*
PATNA CRISIS (THE). 1034
PATRIOTISM IN BENGAL. 322
Pearse, Colonel Hugh. *844. 843*
Pearson, Hesketh. *845*
PEASANT AND THE RAJ (THE). 1001
PEASANT ARMED (THE). 1000
Peile, Fanny. *846. 113*
Pemble, John. *847*
PERIL OF THE SWORD; CONCERNING HAVELOCK'S RELIEF OF LUCKNOW. 488
Perkins, Roger. *848*

Pershad, Issoree. *849*
Persico, Right Rev. Dr. *850*
PERSONAL ADVENTURES AND ANECDOTES OF AN OLD OFFICER. 911
PERSONAL ADVENTURES AND EXPERIENCES OF A MAGISTRATE DURING THE RISE, PROGRESS AND SUPPRESSION OF THE INDIAN MUTINY (THE). 1061
PERSONAL ADVENTURES DURING THE INDIAN REBELLION IN ROHILCUND, FUTTEHGHUR AND OUDE. 374
PERSONAL NARRATIVE OF THE ESCAPE FROM NOWYONG TO BANDA. 934
PERSONAL REMINISCENCES IN INDIA 1830-1888. 161
PERSONAL REMINISCENCES OF AN INDIAN MUTINY VETERAN. 537
PERSONAL REMINISCENCES OF THE INDIAN MUTINY. 985
Peshawur. *302. 301*
Peter the Pearker. *851*
Philips, Cyril Henry ed. *852*
Phillipps, Alfred. *853*
Phillips, A.L.M. *854*
Phillips, E.C. *855*
PHOTOGRAPHY. 160
PHOTOS OF LUCKNOW FROM 1858. 669
Picton-Turberville, Edith. *856*
Pincott, Frederick. *857*
Pinkney, F.W. *858*
PIONEER SERIES. DUTY AND DANGER IN INDIA (THE). 1007
Pitt, F.W. ed. *859*
PLATOON EXERCISE, AND DIFFERENT FIRINGS FOR THE ORDINARY OR RIFLE MUSKET (THE). 6
Polehampton, Rev. Henry. *612*
Polehampton, Reverend Henry Stedman. *860*

POLITICAL PROFILE OF SIR
SAYYID AHMAD KHAN. 9
Political Theory of the Cause of the
Mutiny. 380
POLITICAL THEORY OF THE
INDIAN MUTINY (THE). 201
POLITICS OF A POPULAR
UPRISING: BUNDELKHAND IN
1857. 923
Pollack, J.C. 861
Poorbeah Mutiny. 251
POORBEAH MUTINY (THE). 250
POORBEAH SOLDIER. THE
HERO OF INDIA'S WAR OF
INDEPENDENCE 1857(THE).
832
POPULAR UPRISING AND THE
INTELLIGENTSIA (THE). 940
Porter, John Leech. 862
Poynder, John. 863
PRACTICAL OBSERVATIONS. 74
Prasad, Bisheshwar. 864
Prashanto, K. Chatterji. 865
Pratt, Hodgson. 866
PRAYER FOR OUR CAUSE IN
INDIA. 75
PRAYER, THE REFUGE OF A
DISTRESSED CHURCH. 1135
PRESENT CRISIS IN INDIA (THE).
104
PRESS LIST OF MUTINY PAPERS.
542. 452
Prichard, Iltudus Thomas. 867
PRIVATE COPY OF LETTERS
RECEIVED THURSDAY 28TH
OF JANUARY FROM LIEUT.
JOHN FARQUHAR 7TH B.L.
CAVALRY. 388
PRIVATE CORRESPONDENCE OF
J.W. SHERER,. 175
PRIVATE JOURNAL OF BREVET
MAJOR ALEXANDER ROBERT
DALLAS (THE). 323
PRIVATE LETTERS OF THE
MARQUESS OF DALHOUSIE. 140

PRIVATE MEMORANDA OF THE
SECOND PUNJAB WAR OF 1848
AND OF THE MUTINY IN INDIA,
1857. 1115
PRIZE MONEY; OR, THE RIGHT OF
MAJOR-GENERAL WHITLOCK.
76
Probyn, W.G. 868
PROFESSIONAL PAPERS OF THE
CORPS OF ROYAL ENGINEERS.
371
PUBLIC FEELING IN REGARD
TO THE REMOVAL OF MR. W.
TAYLER. 77
Punjab. 875. 872. 871. 870. 869. 478
PUNJAB AND DELHI IN 1857 (THE).
251
PUNJAB HISTORY IN PRINTED
BRITISH DOCUMENTS. 147
PUNJAB IN PEACE AND WAR
(THE). 1060
PUNJAB MOVEABLE COLUMN
(THE). 478
Punjab Record Office. 874. 873
PUNJAB RECORD OFFICE, PRESS
LIST OF MUTINY PAPERS OF
1857-1858. 424

Q

QUARREL OF GODS COVENANT, A
FASTDAY SERMON (THE). 717
QUEEN IN INDIA (THE). 396
QUESTIONS RAISED BY THE
MUTINY (THE). 212
Qui Hi. 876

R

Raghogarh State. 967
Rahim, M.A. 877
Rahman, B. Abdur. 878
Raikes, C. 879
Raines, General Sir Julius. 880
Rait, Robert Sangster. 881
Raj, Jagdish. 882
RAJ, THE INDIAN MUTINY, AND
THE KINGDOM OF OUDH
1801-1859 (THE). 847

RAJASTHAN'S ROLE IN THE STRUGGLE OF 1857. 601

Rajpootana. *448*

Ram, Moti. *883*

Ram, Sita. *884*

RAMBLES IN NORTHERN INDIA. 1136

Ramsay, Lieut-Colonel Balcarres Dalrymple Wardlaw. *885*

RANE: A LEGEND OF THE INDIAN MUTINY (THE). 683

RANEE OF JHANSI (THE). 1017

RANI LAKSHMI BAI OF JHANSI. 974

Rani of Jhansi. *605*

RANI OF JHANSI. 638

RANI OF JHANSI (THE). 305

RAO TULARAM. 1155

Rawding, F. W. *886*

Rawlins, Major-General J.S. *887*

Raychawdhury, P. C. *888*

Read, Rev. Hollis. *889*

Reade, Edward A. *892. 891. 890*

REBELLION 1857. 583

Rebellion in India. 866

REBELLION IN INDIA (THE). 812

REBELLION IN INDIA. 1857 (THE). 886

REBELLION OF 1857 VIS-A-VIS ASSAM (THE). 954

REBELLION OF INDIA (THE). 1090

REBELLIOUS RANI (THE). 980

REBELS OF DESTINY. 759

RECENT WRITINGS ON THE REVOLT OF 1857. 944

RECOLLECTIONS OF A HIGHLAND SUBALTERN. 440

RECOLLECTIONS OF A LIFE. 497

RECOLLECTIONS OF A LUCKNOW VETERAN 1845-1876. 925

RECOLLECTIONS OF A MILITARY LIFE. 7

RECOLLECTIONS OF A VETERAN OF THE DAYS OF THE GREAT INDIAN MUTINY. 825

RECOLLECTIONS OF A WINTER CAMPAIGN IN INDIA IN 1857-1858. 578

RECOLLECTIONS OF MY LIFE. 390

RECOLLECTIONS OF THE CAMPAIGN IN MALWA AND CENTRAL INDIA UNDER MAJOR GENERAL SIR HUGH ROSE, G.C.B. 1016

Recollections of the Mutiny. 328

Recollections of the Siege of Delhi. 1055

RECOLLECTIONS OF THIRTY NINE YEARS IN THE ARMY. 439

RECORD OF SERVICE OF FIELD MARSHAL LORD STRATHNAIRN. 203

RECORD OF SERVICES IN INDIA. 337

RECORD OF SERVICES IN THE FIELD. 897

RECORD OF THE SEVENTY-THIRD REGIMENT NATIVE INFANTRY AT JULPIGOREE. 128

RECORDS OF SERVICE AND CAMPAIGNING. 791

RECORDS OF THE DELHI RESIDENCY AND AGENCY. 870

RECORDS OF THE INTELLIGENCE DEPARTMENT OF THE GOVERNMENT OF THE NORTH-WEST PROVINCES OF INDIA DURING THE MUTINY OF 1857. 783

RECREATIONS OF AN INDIAN OFFICIAL. 715

RED FORT (THE). 636

Red Pamphlet. *710. 124*

RED YEAR. 1068

RED YEAR; THE INDIAN REBELLION OF 1857. 368

RED, WHITE AND BLUE SKETCHES OF MILITARY LIFE. 78

Redan Windham. *844*

Reed, Andrew. The Younger. *893*

Rees, L.E. Ruutz. *895. 894*

REFLECTIONS ON THE MUTINY. 328

Reid, General Sir Charles. *898. 897. 896*

Reilly, Patrick. *899*

RELATIONS OF THE RANI OF JHANSI. 339

RELIEF OF ARRAH. 597

RELIEF OF LUCKNOW. 402

Religious Tracts. 1145. 1142. 1138. 1135. 1134. 1127. 1081. 1073. 1070. 1012. 1005. 961. 914. 900. 893. 863. 862. 851. 850. 829. 827. 801. 776. 771. 766. 717. 687. 655. 559. 522. 518. 477. 396. 346. 335. 277. 247. 231. 217. 168. 139. 138. 127. 100. 99. 97. 92. 86. 75. 66. 60. 56. 47. 41. 38. 22. 5. 1

REMARKS ON CAPTAIN TROTTERS BIOGRAPHY OF MAJOR W.S.R. HODSON. 255

REMARKS ON THE RAPID TRANSMISSION OF TROOPS TO INDIA. 530

REMINISCENCES. 986

REMINISCENCES DURING FORTY-FIVE YEARS SERVICE IN INDIA. 33

REMINISCENCES OF (THE). 998

REMINISCENCES OF 1857. 79

Reminiscences of a Bengal Civilian. 372

REMINISCENCES OF A BENGAL CIVILIAN. 375

REMINISCENCES OF A MUTINY VETERAN. 491

REMINISCENCES OF A SOLDIER. 1009

REMINISCENCES OF A VETERAN. 908

REMINISCENCES OF AN INDIAN OFFICIAL. 252

REMINISCENCES OF FORTY THREE YEARS IN INDIA. 631

REMINISCENCES OF INDIA. 458

REMINISCENCES OF MILITARY SERVICE WITH THE 93RD SUTHERLAND HIGHLANDERS. 792

REMINISCENCES OF SCHOOL AND ARMY LIFE. 156

REMINISCENCES OF THE GREAT AND GOOD SIR HENRY LAWRENCE AND ALSO OF THE INDIAN MUTINY OF 1857. 80

REMINISCENCES OF THE GREAT INDIAN MUTINY. 245

Reminiscences of the Great Mutiny. 402

REMINISCENCES OF THE GREAT MUTINY. 401

REMINISCENCES OF THE INDIAN MUTINY. 1055. 572. 110

REMINISCENCES OF THE INDIAN REBELLION. 1064

REMINISCENCES OF THE INDIAN REBELLION, 1857-58. BY A STAFF OFFICER (E.A. THURBURN). 992

REMINISCENCES OF THE SEPOY REBELLION OF 1857. 1101

Renaud, Brevet Major S.G.C. 190

Renaud, George. 900

REPLY TO GENERAL JACOBS PAMPHLET. 404

REPORT OF OCCURRENCES AT MHOW. 536

REPORT OF THE AFFAIRS OF KHELAT FROM 1857 TO 1860. 466

REPORT ON ENGINEERING OPERATIONS AT THE SIEGE OF LUCKNOW. 796

REPORT ON THE MUTINY IN CHOTA NAGPORE. 324

REPORTS ON THE ENGINEERING OPERATIONS DURING THE DEFENCE OF LUCKNOW. 549. 548

REST IN THE LORD. 1012

RETROSPECT OF 1857. 81

REVIEW OF THE EVIDENCE TAKEN AT CAWNPORE. 450

REVIEWS ON SYED AHMED KHAN'S LIFE AND WORKS. 162

REVOLT IN 1857. 976

REVOLT IN CENTRAL INDIA (THE). 208

REVOLT IN CENTRAL INDIA 1857-1859 (THE). 451

REVOLT IN HINDUSTAN 1857-59 (THE). 1147

REVOLT IN INDIA 1857-58 (THE). 619

REVOLT OF 1857 AND THE INDIAN FREEDOM MOVEMENT. 761

REVOLT OF 1857 IN CENTRAL INDIA-MALWA (THE). 990

REVOLT OF 1857 IN HARYANA (THE). 1156

REVOLT OF 1857: SAUGOR (THE). 786

REVOLT OF HINDOSTAN, OR THE NEW WORLD. 579

REVOLT OF THE BENGAL SEPOYS (THE). 169

REVOLT OF THE SEPOY. 123

REYNELL TAYLOR CB CSI. 418

Reynolds, Reginald. *901*

Rich, Capt Gregory. *902*

RICHARD BAIRD SMITH. 1098

Richardson. *903*

Ricketts, George H. M. *904*

Riddick, John F. *905*

RIDER ON A GREY HORSE. 298

RISE AND PROGRESS OF THE INDIAN MUTINY. 723

RISE OF CHRISTIAN POWER IN INDIA. 154

Ritchie, John Gerald. *906*

RITCHIES IN INDIA (THE). 906

Rizvi, S.A. and M.L. Bhargava. *907*

Robb, Alexander. *908*

ROBERT LUMSDEN OF THE GUIDES. 672

Roberts, Field Marshal Frederick. *1150. 939. 485. 409. 195. 53*

Roberts, Field Marshal Sir Frederick. *910. 909*

Robertson, Colonel James P. *911*

Robertson, Henry Dundas. *912*

Robertson, Lieut-General Alexander Cunningham. *913*

Robertson, Reverend A. *914*

Robinson, Jane. *915*

Robson, Brian. *916*

Rogerson, Colonel William. *917*

Rohilcande. *1105. 1054. 937. 907. 791. 693. 492. 440. 406. 401. 379. 374. 316. 145*

Roorkee. *448*

Rose, Field Marshal Sir Hugh. *1120. 916. 712. 665. 204. 203*

Roseberry, J Royal III. *918*

Rotton, John Edward Wharton. *919*

ROUGH JUSTICE. 479

ROUGH NARRATIVE OF THE SIEGE OF LUCKNOW. 551

ROUGH RECOLLECTIONS OF MILITARY SERVICE AND SOCIETY. 885

Rowbotham, Commander W(illiam) B(evill) R.N. *920*

Roy, Choudhury. *921*

Roy, Tapti. *923. 922*

Royal Artillery. *924*

Ruggles, Major General J. *925*

RULE OF DARKNESS. 189

RULERS OF INDIA. 204

Russell, William Howard. *926*

S

SAGA OF 1857: SUCCESS AND FAILURES. 173

Sahai, Jawala, Nazim of Bharatpur. *927*

Saharunpoor. *448*

SAHIB AND SEPOY OR, SAVING AN EMPIRE. 1041

Sahib, Nana. *174*

SALMOND OF WATERFOOT. 928

Salmond, Albert Louis. *928*

Saran.
    District of. *616*

Sattin, Anthony. *929*

Sauboz. *82*

Saugor. *786. 112*

Saugor and Nerbudda. *448*

Saugor District. *83*

SAUGOR: A STORY OF 1857. 800

Savakar, V.D. *989*

Savarkar, Vinayak Damodar. *931. 930. 129*

SCATTERED CHAPTERS. 814

SCENES FROM THE LATE INDIAN MUTINIES. 321

Scholberg, Henry. 932

Schorn, J. Arnold. 933

Scot, Patrick G. 934

SCRAPS FROM MY SABRETASCHE. 997

Scrutator. 936. 935

Seaton, Major-General Sir Thomas. 937

Secunder Bagh. 610

Sedgwick, F(rancis) R. 938

Seetaram. 806

SEIGE OF LUCKNOW (THE). 441

SELECTED SUBALTERN STUDIES. 472

SELECTION OF ARTICLES AND LETTERS ON VARIOUS INDIAN QUESTIONS. 866

SELECTION OF LETTERS. 1028

SELECTION OF PAPERS FROM THE OFFICE OF COMMISSIONER OF FINANCE. 891

SELECTION OF PAPERS ON VARIOUS SUBJECTS. AGRA 1857, 1858. 892

SELECTIONS FROM LETTERS. 1029

SELECTIONS FROM OFFICIAL RECORDS OF THE CRIMINAL DEPARTMENT. 207

SELECTIONS FROM THE LETTERS. 405

SELECTIONS FROM THE PUBLIC CORRESPONDENCE OF THE ADMINISTRATION FOR THE AFFAIRS OF THE PUNJAB. 770

SELECTIONS FROM THE RECORDS OF THE GOVERNMENT OF THE PUNJAB AND ITS DEPENDENCIES. NEW SERIES. 871

SELECTIONS FROM THE RECORDS. VOL. VIII. PART I and PART II. 873

SELECTIONS FROM THE RECORDS. VOLUME VII, PART I AND PART II. 874

Sellar, Edmond Francis. 939

Sen, Ashoka Kumar. 940

Sen, Mohit. 941

Sen, Snigdha. 942

Sen, Surendranath. 943

Sengupta, Kalyan Kumar. 944

SEPOY GENERALS. 408

SEPOY MUTINIES (THE). 966. 105

SEPOY MUTINY. 703

SEPOY MUTINY (THE). 1099. 262

SEPOY MUTINY AND THE UPRISING OF 1857 IN BUNDELKHAND. 922

SEPOY REBELLION (THE). 127

SEPOY REVOLT (THE). 743

SEPOY REVOLT IN 1857 (THE). 319

SEPOY REVOLT; A CRITICAL NARRATIVE. 553

SEPOYS AND THE COMPANY (THE). 20

SEPOYS DAUGHTER (THE). 228

Sermon on the Death of Havelock. 66

SERVICE AND ADVENTURE WITH THE KHAKEE RESSALAH. 355

SERVICE JOURNAL OF CHARLES WILLIAM USHERWOOD, 19TH FOOT & 8TH FOOT, 1852-1864. 1091

SERVICE MEMORIES. 528

SERVICES OF THE 31ST NLI...IN THE SAUBOZ DIST. 82

SERVICES OF THE LATE 31ST NOW 2ND N.I. 83

Seton, Rosemary. 945

Seton-Karr, George Berkeley. 946

Seton-Karr, Walter Scott. 947

SEVEN CITIES OF DELHI. 503

SEVENTH RAJPUT REGIMENT IN THE INDIAN MUTINY OF 1857 (THE). 1065

Sevestre, Allan Alexander. 948

Sewell, Colonel J.W. 949

Sewell, J.C. 950

Seymour, Charles Crossley. 951

Shadwell, Lt. Gen. *952*
Shah, Mubarak
   Narrative of. *368*
Shahjanpoor. *448. 210*
Shakespear, Lt.Col. J. *953*
Shannon Brigade. *1113*
*SHANNON'S BRIGADE IN INDIA
   (THE). 1096*
Sharma, Benudhar. *954*
Shastitko, Pyotr. *955*
Shepherd, J.W. *956*
Sherer, G.M. *957*
Sherer, John Walter. *960. 959. 958*
Sherring, Mathew Atmore. *961*
*SHORT ACCOUNT OF THE LIFE
   AND FAMILY OF RAI JEEWAN
   LAL BAHADUR. 574*
Showers, Lt. General Charles Lionel.
   962, 963
Sialkot. *902*
SIEGE OF DELHI. 652
SIEGE OF DELHI (THE). 735. 149
SIEGE OF LUCKNOW: A DIARY. 550
*SIEGE OF LUCKNOW: BRIGADE
   ORDERS ISSUED BETWEEN
   OCTOBER 2ND AND
   NOVEMBER 18TH, 1857. 775*
*SIEGE, DEFENCE AND VICTORY
   OF THE ILLUSTRIOUS
   GARRISON OF ARRAH ZILLAH
   SHAHABAD IN JULY 1857-58 AD.
   2*
Sieveking, I.G. *964*
Simcox, Arthur Henry Addenbrooke.
   965
Sinclair, William. *105*
Sinclair, William. Rector of
   Pulborough. *966*
Singh, Amar. *330. 329*
Singh, Balbhadra. *967*
Singh, Ganda. *968*
Singh, Govind. *969*
Singh, Shailendra Dhari. *970*
Singh, Sheo Bahadur. *971*
Sinha, Dr. S.N. (ed). *972*
Sinha, R.M. *973*
Sinha, S. N. *976. 974*

Sinha, S.K. *975*
*SIR HENRY HAVELOCK AND
   COLIN CAMPBELL, LORD
   CLYDE. 855. 658*
*SIR HENRY LAWRENCE THE
   PACIFICATOR. 554*
*SIR HUGH ROSE AND THE
   CENTRAL INDIA CAMPAIGN.
   916*
*SIR JOHN LOGIN AND DULEEP
   SINGH. 657*
*SIR SAYYID AHMAD KHAN'S
   HISTORY OF THE BIJNOR
   REBELLION. 14. 10*
Sirmoor Rifles. *897*
Sita Ram. *673*
Sitaram. *806*
SIX YEARS IN INDIA. 682
*SIX YEARS IN THE NORTH-WEST.
   629*
SIXTY YEARS AGO. 842
SKETCH OF THE SERVICES. 238
*SKETCHES AND INCIDENTS OF
   THE SIEGE OF LUCKNOW. 744*
*SKETCHES OF DELHI TAKEN
   DURING THE SIEGE. 1084*
Small, E. Milton. *977*
Smith, Juliet. *978*
Smith, R. B. *979*
Smyth, Sir John. *980*
*SOLDIER AND THE SAINT (THE).
   137*
*SOLDIER'S CRY FROM INDIA
   (THE). 247*
*SOLDIERS OF THE VICTORIAN
   AGE. 660*
*SOME ACCOUNT OF THE
   ADMINISTRATION OF INDIAN
   DISTRICTS DURING THE
   REVOLT OF THE BENGAL
   ARMY. 595*
*SOME ACCOUNT OF THE
   PART TAKEN BY THE 79TH
   REGIMENT OR CAMERON
   HIGHLANDERS IN THE INDIAN
   MUTINY CAMPAIGN. 1140*
*SOME MEMORIES OF MY SPARE
   TIME. 187*

SOME OF THE WORDS, DEEDS, AND SUCCESS OF HAVELOCK IN THE CAUSE OF TEMPERANCE IN INDIA. 1104

SOME RECOLLECTIONS OF THE SIEGE OF LUCKNOW. 400

SOME REMINISCENCES OF THREE QUARTERS OF A CENTURY IN INDIA. 278. 84

SOME REMINISCENES OF THE DEFENSE OF HOUSE NO. 5. 21

Somerville, E. and Martin Ross. *981*

Soppitt, Elizabeth. *982*

Sorsky, R. *983*

SORTIE FROM FORT ST. GEORGE. 111

SOUND OF FURY (THE). 282

SOURCE MATERIAL FOR A HISTORY OF THE FREEDOM MOVEMENT IN INDIA. COLLECTED FROM BOMBAY GOVERNMENT RECORDS. 834

Spear, Percival. *984*

SPECTRE OF VIOLENCE. THE 1857 KANPUR MASSACRES. 789

SPEECH IN THE HOUSE OF COMMONS ON THE FINANCIAL RESOURCES OF INDIA. 993

SPEECH OF CAPTAIN EASTWICK. 360

SPEECH OF COLONEL SYKES. 1014

SPEECH OF SIR GEORGE LEWIS. 651

SPEECH OF THE DUKE OF ARGYLL. 234

SPEECH ON THE INDIA QUESTION. 206

Spencer, Margaret. *985*

Spottiswoode, Col. Robert Collinson D'esterre. *986*

Sprot, Captain A. *987*

Squire, E. B. *988*

SQUIRES AND SEPOYS. 334

Srivastava, Harindra. *989*

Srivastava, K.L. *990*

Srivastava, M.P. *991*

Staff Officer. *1064. 992*

Stanley, Right Honorable Lord. *993*

STAR OF FORTUNE (THE). 779

Stark, Herbert Alick. *994*

STATEMENTS OF REGIMENTS OF CAVALRY. 85

STATISTICAL, DESCRIPTIVE, AND HISTORICAL ACCOUNT OF THE NORTH-WESTERN PROVINCES OF INDIA. 292

Steel, Mrs. Flora Annie. *996. 995*

Stent, George Carter. *997*

Steuart, Lt. Colonel Thomas Ruddiman. *998*

Stewart, Charles Edward. *999*

STIRRING TIMES UNDER CANVAS. 506

Stokes, Eric. *1001. 1000*

Stokes, William. *1002*

Stoqueler, J.H. *1004. 1003*

STORIES OF THE INDIAN MUTINY. 1006

STORY OF A SOLDIERS LIFE (THE). 1146

STORY OF A SOLDIERS LIFE OR PEACE, WAR, AND MUTINY. 385

STORY OF ALGAR TEMPLE AND THE INDIAN MUTINY (THE). 856

STORY OF CAWNPORE (THE). 1059

STORY OF LORD ROBERTS (THE). 939

STORY OF MY ESCAPE FROM FATEHGARH. 580

STORY OF MY LIFE. 1039

STORY OF MY LIFE (THE). 1051

STORY OF OUR ESCAPE FROM DELHI IN 1857(THE). 118

STORY OF OUR ESCAPE FROM DELHI IN MAY 1857(THE). FROM PERSONAL NARRATIONS BY THE LATE GEORGE WAGENTREIBER AND MISS HALDANE. 1103

STORY OF SIR HENRY HAVELOCK, THE HERO OF LUCKNOW (THE). 1042

STORY OF SIR HENRY LAWRENCE (THE). 1043

*STORY OF THE CAWNPORE
   MISSION. 511*
*STORY OF THE CAWNPORE
   MISSION (THE). 106*
*STORY OF THE INDIAN MUTINY
   (THE). 765. 432. 423*
STORY OF TWO NOBLE LIVES. 489
Strachan, J.M. *1005*
Strang, Herbert. *1007. 1006*
Strange, General Thomas Bland. *1008*
Stuart, W.K. Col. *1009*
Stubbs, Major-General Francis
   William. *1010*
Sturges, Octavious. *1011*
Subadar, Manilal Bhagrandas. *32*
*SUGGESTIONS FOR THE
   RECONSTRUCTION OF THE
   GOVERNMENT OF INDIA. 694*
*SUGGESTIONS RELATIVE TO THE
   REORGANISATION OF THE
   BENGAL ARMY. 538*
Sulivan, Reverend Henry. *1012*
Suppression of Mutiny. 352
*SUPPRESSION OF THE MUTINY.
   353*
Swanston. 43
Swanston, Major-General William
   Oliver. *1013*
*SWORD OF THE LORD IN THE
   INDIAN CRISIS (THE). 346*
Sykes, Colonel W.H. *1014*
Sylvester, Deputy Surgeon General
   John Henry. A. McKenzie Annand
   (ed.). *1015*
Sylvester, John Henry. Assistant
   Surgeon. *1016*
*SYNOPSIS OF THE EVIDENCE OF
   THE CAWNPORE MUTINY. 449*

T

*TABLETS IN THE MEMORIAL
   CHURCH, CAWNPORE. 679*
Tahmankar, D.V. *1017*
TALE OF OUR GRANDFATHER. 468
*TALE OF THE GREAT MUTINY
   (THE). 395*
TALES OF THE EAST. 933

Taqui, Roshan. *1018*
TATYA TOPE. 545
*TATYA TOPE, THE HERO OF
   INDIA'S FIRST WAR OF
   INDEPENDENCE 1857-1859. 831*
Tavender, I. T. *1019*
Tayler, William. *1037. 1036. 1035.
   1034. 1033. 1032. 1031. 1030. 1029.
   1028. 1027. 1026. 1025. 1024. 1023.
   1022. 1021. 1020. 131*
Tayler, William of Patna. *264. 200. 77*
Taylor, A(licia) Camero. *1038*
Taylor, Colonel Philip Meadows. *1040.
   1039*
Taylor, General Sir Alexander. *1038.
   735*
Taylor, Lucy. *1043. 1042. 1041*
Taylor, P.J.O. *1048. 1047. 1046. 1045.
   1044*
Temple, Algar. *856*
Temple, Sir Richard. *1051. 1050. 1049*
Terrell, Richard. *1052*
Tewarree, Nujoor. *91*
Thackeray, Brevet Colonel C.B. *1053*
Thackeray, Col. Edward Talbot. *1055.
   1054*
*THANKSGIVING THOUGHTS ON
   THE INDIAN MUTINY. 86*
Thatcher, M. and L. Carter. *1056*
*THE 93RD SUTHERLAND
   HIGHLANDERS. 253*
THE DEVIL'S WIND. 382
THE GREAT RISING OF 1857. 266
THE GUIDE TO LUCKNOW. 163
*THE HISTORY OF PROBYN'S
   HORSE. 186*
The Indian War of Independence. 989
The Mutiny Correspondence. 424
*The Political Theory of the Indian Mutiny.
   341*
THE SEPOY MUTINY, 1857. 263
THEORIES OF THE INDIAN
   MUTINY. *704*
*THEORIES OF THE INDIAN
   MUTINY 1857-59. 267*
THEY FIGHT LIKE DEVILS. 610

THIRTY EIGHT YEARS IN INDIA.
1037
Thomas, Henry Harington. *1057*
Thompson, Edward John. *1058*
Thomson, Captain Mowbray. *1059*
Thorburn, Septimus S. *1060*
Thornhill, Mark. *1061*
Thornton, Dep. Surgeon General
James Howard. *1062*
Thornton, Thomas Henry. *1063*
*THOUGHTS OF A NATIVE OF
NORTHERN INDIA ON THE
REBELLION, ITS CAUSES AND
REMEDIES (THE). 677*
*THOUGHTS ON THE INDIAN
CRISIS. 279*
*THOUGHTS ON THE MUTINY IN
INDIA. 335*
*THREE LECTURES ON THE
REVOLT OF THE BENGAL ARMY
IN 1857. 383*
*THREE MAIN MILITARY
QUESTIONS OF THE DAY. 500*
*THROUGH PERSIA IN DISGUISE
WITH REMINISCENCES OF THE
INDIAN MUTINY. 999*
THROUGH THE MUTINY. 1105
Thurburn, E.A. *1064*
Thurburn, E.A. *992*
Tickell, Captain James E. *128*
Tindall, Captain John William
Brooke. *1065*
Tisdall, Evelyn Ernest Percy. *1066*
TOLD FROM THE RANKS. 977
Tombs, Henry V.C. *1067*
Tope, Tatya. *1063. 1046. 1016. 962. 831.
830. 627. 545. 474. 419. 406. 352.
174*
*TOPICS FOR INDIAN STATESMEN.
813*
*TOURISTS GUIDE TO LUCKNOW
(THE) \t, 111*
*TRACTS ON THE NATIVE ARMY OF
INDIA. 562*
Tracy, Louis. *1068*
TRADERS AND NABOBS. 1159
*TRANSLATION OF A NARRATIVE
OF EVENTS AT CAWNPORE. 257*

*TRAVELS AND ADVENTURES OF
AN OFFICER'S WIFE IN INDIA,
CHINA AND NEW ZEALAND. 794*
Travers, Lieut. Gen. Jas. *1069*
Trench, Dr. Richard. *66*
Trevelyan, Charles Edward. *1070*
Trevelyan, Sir Charles. *90*
Trevelyan, Sir George Otto. *1072.
1071*
Trevor, George. *1073*
*TRIAL OF MUHAMMAD BAHADUR
SHAH, TITULAR KING OF
DELHI. 872*
*TRIAL OF MUHAMMED BAHADUR
SHAH (THE). 425*
Trotter, Captain Lionel James. *1079.
1078. 1077. 1076. 1075. 1074*
*TRUE CAUSES OF THE REVOLT OF
THE BENGAL ARMY (THE). 1004*
Tucker, Henry Carre. *1081. 1080*
Tucker, Major General H.T. *1082*
Tuker, Lt. General Sir F. ed. *1083*
Turnbull, Lt. Colonel John Robertson.
1085. 1084
Tweeddale, Lord ed. *1086*
Tweedie, Ensign William. *610*
*TWELVE YEARS OF A SOLDIERS
LIFE. 577*
*TWELVE YEARS OF A SOLDIER'S
LIFE IN INDIA. 520*
TWENTY ONE YEARS IN INDIA. 535
TWILIGHT OF THE MUGHULS. 984
TWO COLONIAL EMPIRES. 159
*TWO HISTORIC TRIALS IN THE
RED FORT. 883*
*TWO INDIAN CAMPAIGNS IN
1857-58. 1054*
*TWO MONTHS IN ARRAH IN 1857.
483*
Two Native Narratives. *780*
*TWO NATIVE NARRATIVES OF
THE MUTINY IN DELHI. 780.
751*
Tyler, R.A.J. *1087*
Tyrrell, F. H. Lieut. General. *1088*
Tyrrell, Isaac. *1089*
Tytler, Harriet. *929*

U

UBIQUE: WAR SERVICES OF ALL OF THE. 30
UNDER THE SUN. 623
UNREST AGAINST BRITISH RULE IN BIHAR 1831-1859. 329
UP AMONG THE PANDIES. 700
Urquhart, David. *1090*
Usherwood, Charles William. *1091*
Utterton, Edwin. *1110*

V

Valbezen, Eugene de. *1092*
Vansittart, Jane. Ed. *1093*
Vaughan, John Luther. *1094*
VERDICT T.H.K. 588
VERITAS VICTRIX. 1035
Verner, Col. W. *1095*
Verney, Lieut. Edmund Hope. *1096*
Verney, Major General G.L. *1097*
Vibart, Col. H.M. *371*
Vibart, Colonel Edward. *1099*
Vibart, Colonel Henry M. *1100. 1098*
VICTORIAN CROSS IN INDIA (THE). 615
VIEWS AND OPINIONS OF BRIGADIER GENERAL JOHN JACOB. 564
VIEWS IN INDIA FROM DRAWINGS TAKEN DURING THE SEPOY MUTINY. 467
VIEWS IN LUCKNOW; FROM SKETCHES TAKEN DURING THE SIEGE. 691
VIGNETTES FROM THE INDIAN WARS. 686
Villars, Philip. *214*
VOLCANO, OR, THE FIRST WAR OF INDEPENDENCE (THE). 930
VOLUNTEERING IN INDIA. 798

W

Wagentreiber, Florence. *1101. 113*
Wagentreiber, George. *1102. 118*
Wagentreiber, Miss. (Florence). *1103*

Wahabi Movement. *329*
WAHABI MOVEMENT IN INDIA. 15
Wakefield, Lieut-Col Henry Funj. *1104*
Walker, Col. T. N. *1105*
Wallace, Charles Lindsay. *1106*
Walmsley, Joshua. *1107*
Walsh, Rev. J. Johnston. *1108*
WANDERINGS IN INDIA. 627
WAR IN OUDH (THE). 671
WAR OF INDEPENDENCE, CENTENARY VOLUME. 476
Ward, Andrew. *1109*
Ward, Beatrice (ed.). *1110*
Waterfield, Arthur J. *1111*
Watson, Bruce. *1112*
Watson, Edward Spencer. *1113*
Watson, Thomas. *195*
WAY TO GLORY. THE LIFE OF HAVELOCK OF LUCKNOW. 861
WAY TO LOSE INDIA WITH ILLUSTRATION FROM LEADENHALL STREET (THE). 649
WAY TO REGAIN INDIA (THE). 650
WESTERN INDIA BEFORE AND DURING THE MUTINIES. 568
Weston, Major C.S. *1115. 1114*
WHAT IS HISTORY AND WHAT IS FACT?. 108
WHAT IS TO BE DONE WITH THE BENGAL ARMY. 876
WHAT IS TRUTH?. 1036
WHAT REALLY HAPPENED DURING THE MUTINY. 1047
WHAT SHALL WE DO AT DELHI?. 1116
WHEEL TRACKS. 981
Wheeler, Edmund H. *1116*
Wheler, Brevet-Col. S.G. *308. 291*
WHEN THE STORM CAME 1857. 718
WHITE CROSS AT DELHI (THE). 107
WHITE SAHIBS IN INDIA (THE). 901
White, Col. Samuel Dewe. *1119. 1117*

White, Michael. *1118*

Whitlock, Major General Sir George. *323. 111*

Whitton, Lieut-Colonel F.E. *1120*

WHO IS TO BLAME FOR THE INDIAN MUTINIES. 690

WHO SHALL REGENERATE INDIA. 721

WHO'S WHO OF INDIAN MARTYRS. 274

WHY IS THE ENGLISH RULE ODIUS TO THE NATIVES OF INDIA?. 726

WHY IS THE NATIVE ARMY DISAFFECTED. 229

Wigram, Francis Spencer. *1121*

Wilberforce, Reginald Garton. *1122*

Wilkinson, Osborn and Johnson Wilkinson. *1123*

Wilkinson-Latham, Christopher. *1124*

WILLIAM TAYLOR OF PATNA. 1079

Williams, Donovan. *1125*

Williams, Edward Adams Rev. *1126*

Williams, Frederick Smeeton. *1127*

Williams, George Walter. *1128*

Williams, Major G.W. *447*

Williams, Noel St. John. *1129*

Williams. F. *1130*

Williamson, George M.D. *1131*

Williamson, John Vaughan. *1132*

Wilson, Archdale. *1133. 1133*

Wilson, Daniel. Bishop of Calcutta. *1135. 1134*

Wilson, Francesca Henrietta. *1136*

Wilson, John. *1138*

Wilson, John Cracroft. *1137*

Wilson, Minden. *1139*

Wilson, Thomas Fourness. *227*

Wimberley, Douglas. *1140*

Windham. *7*

Windham, Lieut. General Charles Ash. K.C.B. *1141*

WINNOWED MEMORIES. 1148

Winslow, Octavius. *1142*

Wintringham, Thomas. *1143*

Wise, James M.D. *1144*

WITH H.M. 9TH LANCERS DURING THE INDIAN MUTINY. 132

WITH HAVELOCK FROM ALLAHABAD TO LUCKNOW. 470

Witts, The Rev. B.L. *1145*

Wolseley, Field Marshal Viscount. *1146*

WOMEN TRAVELLERS IN COLONIAL INDIA: THE POWER OF THE FEMALE. 430

Wood, Field Marshal Sir Henry Evelyn V.C. *1149. 1148. 1147*

WORDS SHE WROTE (THE). 1145

Wrench, Lieut. Colonel Edward Mason. *1150*

Wright, Rev. Charles H(enry) H(amilton). *1151*

Wylie, Macleod. *1152*

Wylly, Colonel Harold Carmichael. *1153*

Wynter, Philip. *1154*

Y

Yadav, K.C. *1156. 1155*

Yadav, K.C. ed. *1157*

Yalland, Zoe. *1159. 1158*

Yeoward, George. *1160*

Young, William Richard. *1161*